THE CAMBRIDGE COMPANION TO
DEMOCRACY IN AMERICA

This collection of chapters is an invaluable companion for understanding the composition, reception, and contemporary legacy of Alexis de Tocqueville's classic work *Democracy in America*. Chapters by political theorists, intellectual historians, economists, political scientists, and community organizers explore the major intellectual influences on Tocqueville's thought, the book's reception in its own day and by subsequent political thinkers, and its enduring relevance for some of today's most pressing issues. Chapters tackle Tocqueville's insights into liberal democracy, civil society and civic engagement, social reform, religion and politics, free markets, constitutional interpretation, the history of slavery and race relations, gender, literature, and foreign policy. The many ways in which Tocqueville's ideas have been taken up – sometimes at cross-purposes – by subsequent thinkers and political actors around the world are also examined. This volume demonstrates the enduring global significance of one of the most perceptive accounts ever written about American democracy and the future prospects for self-government.

RICHARD BOYD is Associate Professor in the Department of Government at Georgetown University.

OTHER VOLUMES IN THE SERIES OF CAMBRIDGE
COMPANIONS

Continued at the back of the book

The Cambridge Companion to

DEMOCRACY
IN AMERICA

Edited by

Richard Boyd

Georgetown University

 CAMBRIDGE
UNIVERSITY PRESS

CAMBRIDGE
UNIVERSITY PRESS

University Printing House, Cambridge CB2 8BS, United Kingdom

One Liberty Plaza, 20th Floor, New York, NY 10006, USA

477 Williamstown Road, Port Melbourne, VIC 3207, Australia

314–321, 3rd Floor, Plot 3, Splendor Forum, Jasola District Centre, New Delhi – 110025, India

103 Penang Road, #05–06/07, Visioncrest Commercial, Singapore 238467

Cambridge University Press is part of the University of Cambridge.

It furthers the University's mission by disseminating knowledge in the pursuit of education, learning, and research at the highest international levels of excellence.

www.cambridge.org
Information on this title: www.cambridge.org/9781107189812
DOI: 10.1017/9781316995761

First published 2022

A catalogue record for this publication is available from the British Library.

ISBN 978-1-107-18981-2 Hardback
ISBN 978-1-316-63943-6 Paperback

Contents

Contributors

José Antonio Aguilar Rivera is Professor of Political Science at the División de Estudios Políticos, CIDE (Mexico City). His books include *El sonido y la furia: La persuasión multicultural en México y Estados Unidos* (2004); *En pos de la quimera: Reflexiones sobre el experimento constitucional atlántico* (2000); *La geometría y el mito: Un ensayo sobre la libertad y el liberalismo en México, 1821–1970* (2010); and *Ausentes del Universo: Reflexiones sobre el pensamiento político hispanoamericano en la era de la construcción nacional, 1821–1850* (2012). He is the editor of *Liberty in Mexico: Writings on Liberalism from the Early Republican Period to the Second Half of the Twentieth Century* (2012).

Richard Avramenko is Professor of Political Science at the University of Wisconsin–Madison, where he is also Director of the Center for the Study of Liberal Democracy and Editor-in-Chief of the *Political Science Reviewer*. He is the author of *Courage: The Politics of Life and Limb* (2011) as well as the coeditor of *Friendship and Politics: Essays in Political Thought* (2008), *Dostoevsky's Political Philosophy* (2013), and *Aristocratic Souls in Democratic Times* (2018). He has recently published articles in the *Review of Politics, American Journal of Political Science, Perspectives on Political Science, Perspectives on Politics, Polis, Political Science Reviewer*, and *Political Theory*.

Jeremy D. Bailey holds the Sanders Chair in Law and Liberty in the Department of Classics and Letters at the University of Oklahoma. His books include *The Idea of Presidential Representation: An Intellectual and Political History* (2019), *James Madison and Constitutional Imperfection* (2015), *The Contested Removal*

Power, 1789–2010 (2013, coauthored with David Alvis and Flagg Taylor), and *Thomas Jefferson and Executive Power* (2007). He has also published articles on the political thought of Alexander Hamilton in *American Political Science Review* and *History of Political Thought*. With Susan McWilliams Barndt, he is the editor of *American Political Thought: A Journal of Ideas, Institutions, and Culture* as well as the American Political Thought book series published by the University Press of Kansas.

Lawrie Balfour is James Hart Professor of Politics and a core faculty member in American Studies at the University of Virginia. The author of *Democracy's Reconstruction: Thinking Politically with W. E. B. Du Bois* (2011) and *The Evidence of Things Not Said: James Baldwin and the Promise of American Democracy* (2001), she has written widely on African American political thought and literature, feminist theory, and theories of democracy. Much of her recent writing has focused on the politics of reparations, and her current book project is *Imagining Freedom: Toni Morrison and the Work of Words*.

Rachael K. Behr is a PhD student of economics at George Mason University, a graduate teaching fellow with the Department of Economics at George Mason University, a PhD fellow with the Mercatus Center at George Mason University, and a graduate fellow with the F. A. Hayek Program in Philosophy, Politics and Economics, at the Mercatus Center. Her work and research are in the fields of economic sociology, political economy, and Austrian economics. She researches moral questions regarding friendships and marketplaces and is currently studying the effects of COVID-19 on market and social relationships.

Eileen Hunt Botting is a political theorist whose scholarly interests cover modern political thought, feminism, the family, rights, ethics of technology, and philosophy and literature. She has taught at the University of Notre Dame since 2001. Her books are *Family Feuds:*

Wollstonecraft, Burke, and Rousseau on the Transformation of the Family (2006); *Wollstonecraft, Mill, and Women's Human Rights* (2016); *Mary Shelley and the Rights of the Child: Political Philosophy in Frankenstein* (2017); and *Artificial Life after Frankenstein* (2020). She is also an editor of several academic volumes and scholarly editions, including *Feminist Interpretations of Alexis de Tocqueville* (coedited with Jill Locke for Penn State University Press's Feminist Interpretations series, 2009).

Richard Boyd is Associate Professor of Government at Georgetown University where he teaches social and political theory and is Director of the Tocqueville Forum for Political Understanding. He is the author of *Uncivil Society: The Perils of Pluralism and the Making of Modern Liberalism* (2004); coeditor of *Tocqueville and the Frontiers of Democracy* (2013); and has written more than forty journal articles and book chapters on the intellectual history of liberalism.

Aurelian Craiutu is Professor of Political Science at Indiana University Bloomington. An expert on French political thought and the co-translator and coeditor (with Jeremy Jennings) of *Tocqueville on America after 1840: Letters and Other Writings* (2009), he is the author, most recently, of *A Virtue for Courageous Minds: Moderation in French Political Thought, 1748–1830* (2012) and *Faces of Moderation: The Art of Balance in an Age of Extremes* (2017).

Robert T. Gannett, Jr. is an independent scholar and veteran community organizer in Chicago where he serves as Director of the Institute for Community Empowerment. A graduate of the Committee on Social Thought at the University of Chicago in 1998, he is the author of *Tocqueville Unveiled: The Historian and His Sources for "The Old Regime and the Revolution"* (2003), as well as articles and reviews in *The Tocqueville Review/La Revue Tocqueville, American Political Science Review, The Review of*

Politics, and *Twenty-First Century Bimonthly* (Hong Kong). He is currently writing a book on the field of community organizing in the United States, with a special focus on Tocqueville's influence as muse to several of its most prominent activists.

Ryan Patrick Hanley is Professor of Political Science at Boston College. Prior to joining the faculty at Boston College, he was the Mellon Distinguished Professor of Political Science at Marquette University and held visiting appointments or fellowships at Yale, Harvard, and the University of Chicago. A specialist on the political philosophy of the Enlightenment period, he is the author of *Adam Smith and the Character of Virtue* (2009), *Love's Enlightenment: Rethinking Charity in Modernity* (2017), and *Our Great Purpose: Adam Smith on Living a Better Life* (2019). His most recent books are *The Political Philosophy of Fénelon* (2020) and a companion translation volume, *Fénelon: Moral and Political Writings* (2020).

Christine Dunn Henderson is Associate Professor of Political Science at Singapore Management University. She holds a BA in French studies and government from Smith College and a PhD in political science from Boston College. She is the contributing editor of *Seers and Judges: American Literature As Political Philosophy* (2001), coeditor (with Mark Yellin) of *Joseph Addison's "Cato" and Selected Essays* (2004), editor of *Tocqueville's Voyages* (2015), translator and editor of Tocqueville's *Memoirs on Pauperism and Other Writings* (2021), and co-translator (with Henry Clark) of *Encyclopedic Liberty: Political Articles from the "Dictionary" of Diderot and D'Alembert* (2016). She has published extensively on Tocqueville, Beaumont, French liberalism, and politics and literature.

Carson Holloway is Ralph Wardle Diamond Professor of Arts and Sciences and Professor of Political Science at the University of Nebraska-Omaha and a Washington Fellow in the Claremont Institute's Center for the American Way of Life. He is the coeditor, with Bradford P. Wilson, of the two-volume work *The Political Writings of Alexander Hamilton* (2017). He is also the author of *Hamilton versus Jefferson in the Washington Administration: Completing the Founding or Betraying the Founding?* (2015). He has been a visiting fellow in Princeton University's James Madison Program in American Ideals and Institutions and a visiting fellow and visiting scholar at the Heritage Foundation.

Alan Levine is Associate Professor of Government and Director of the Political Theory Institute at American University. His publications include *Sensual Philosophy: Toleration, Skepticism, and Montaigne's Politics of the Self* (2001), *Early Modern Skepticism and the Origins of Toleration* (editor, 1999), and *A Political Companion to Ralph Waldo Emerson* (coeditor, 2011) as well as articles on Montaigne, Machiavelli, Nietzsche, Chinua Achebe, Judith Shklar, European views of America, the Enlightenment idea of commerce, and the origins of toleration. He has held fellowships at Princeton's James Madison Program; the Hoover Institution at Stanford; and the Institute of US Studies, School of Advanced Study, University of London.

Joshua Mitchell is currently Professor of Political Theory at Georgetown University. His research interest lies in the relationship between political thought and theology in the West. His books include *Not by Reason Alone: Religion, History, and Identity in Early Modern Political Thought* (1993); *The Fragility of Freedom: Tocqueville on Religion, Democracy, and the American Future* (1995); *Plato's Fable: On the Mortal Condition in Shadowy Times* (2006); *Tocqueville in Arabia: Dilemmas in the Democratic Age* (2013); and, most recently, *American Awakening: Identity Politics and Other Afflictions of Our Time* (2020).

James T. Schleifer is Professor Emeritus of History and former Dean of Gill Library, College of New Rochelle. He received his PhD in history from Yale University. From 1986 to 2017, he served as a member of the French National Commission for the Publication of the Complete Works of Alexis de Tocqueville. He received, among other honors and prizes, the prestigious Merle Curti Award in American Intellectual History (1981) from the Organization of American Historians. In addition to numerous articles and essays, his major publications include *The Making of Tocqueville's "Democracy in America"* (1980; Spanish translation, 1984; 2nd rev. ed., 2000); *Tocqueville* (2018; Chinese translation, 2020); and *The Chicago Companion to Tocqueville's "Democracy in America"* (2012). He is also coeditor of the Pléiade critical edition of *De la démocratie en Amérique* (1992) and translator of the complete critical edition of *Democracy in America*, edited by Eduardo Nolla, 4 vols. (2010).

Rogers M. Smith has been the Christopher H. Browne Distinguished Professor of Political Science at the University of Pennsylvania since 2001. He was previously the Alfred Cowles Professor of Government at Yale University, where he taught from 1980 to 2001. He is the author or coauthor of many articles and eight books, including *That Is Not Who We Are!* (2020), *Political Peoplehood* (2015), and *Civic Ideals* (1997). *Civic Ideals* received six best book prizes and was a finalist for the 1998 Pulitzer Prize in History. Smith was elected Fellow of the American Academy of Arts and Sciences in 2004, the American Academy of Political and Social Science in 2011, and the American Philosophical Society in 2016. He served as Associate Dean for Social Sciences at the University of Pennsylvania from 2014 to 2018 and as President of the American Political Science Association in 2018–2019.

Virgil Henry Storr is Vice President of Academic and Student Programs at the Mercatus Center, Associate Professor of Economics in the Department of Economics, George Mason University and Don C. Lavoie Senior Fellow in the F. A. Hayek Program in Philosophy, Politics and Economics, Mercatus Center, George Mason University. His books include *Understanding the*

Culture of Markets (2012); *Community Revival in the Wake of Disaster: Lessons in Local Entrepreneurship* (2015, with Stefanie Haeffele-Balch and Laura E. Grube); and *Do Markets Corrupt Our Morals?* (2019, with Ginny Seung Choi).

Acknowledgments

Collaborative projects rely on the generosity of many people, and this is an imperfect reckoning of all those who so kindly lent their assistance along the way. Thanks especially to fellow contributors for their professionalism and patience as the book came together. Insofar as this volume inspires future generations of scholars, students, and citizens, it is a tribute to their outstanding scholarship.

I am grateful to Robert Dreesen of Cambridge University Press, who first conceived the idea for a series Companion on Tocqueville's *Democracy in America*. His confidence made the book possible. Linsey Hague, Mathivathini Mareesan, Claire Sissen, and Erika Walsh at Cambridge University Press were all a pleasure to work with during copyediting and production. It was both an invaluable resource and at moments a daunting challenge to have as a model Cheryl Welch's superb *Cambridge Companion to Tocqueville*. While the present volume differs greatly in scope and organization, that predecessor guided its composition in many ways.

Early versions of several chapters were first presented at Georgetown University under the auspices of the Tocqueville Forum for Political Understanding, and I would like to thank panelists, attendees, Associate Director Thomas Kerch, and the Lynde and Harry Bradley Foundation for organizing those events and stimulating conversations about Tocqueville's relevance. More generally, I am appreciative of colleagues, current and former PhD students, and undergraduates who have made the Government Department at Georgetown such a congenial place for teaching and studying political theory.

Ewa Atanassow, Richard Avramenko, Joshua Cherniss, Aurelian Craiutu, Gianna Englert, Steven Grosby, Christine Dunn

Henderson, and Joshua Mitchell all kindly commented on drafts in progress or discussed topics of general concern. My own contributions – not to mention the book as a whole – are immeasurably better for their incisive feedback and suggestions.

The project benefited from the able research assistance of Nicholas Barden, who caught a myriad of typos, standardized all the translations and references, and compiled the References list. All remaining errors and oversights are mine alone, of course.

Many close friends and loved ones offered personal encouragement throughout this process, and for their friendship I am eternally grateful. To my children, Liliane and Louis, I dedicate this volume with love.

Chronology

1805

July 29, 1805 Alexis Charles-Henri Clérel de Tocqueville is born in Paris, the third son of Hervé and Louise-Madeleine de Tocqueville. Elder siblings Hippolyte and Édouard were born in 1797 and 1800, respectively. Several immediate members of this old and distinguished Norman family were killed during the Reign of Terror, with Tocqueville's mother and father imprisoned and barely escaping the guillotine.

1820–1821

During his childhood Tocqueville is tutored by Abbé Christian Lesueur, a conservative Jansenist priest, until being summoned by his father to Metz in the French Lorraine in 1820. There he reads the *philosophes* of the Enlightenment, reportedly loses his religious faith, and enrolls in the *lycée* in 1821.

1824–1827

Tocqueville studies law at the University of Paris, receives his degree in 1826, and in 1827 is appointed *juge auditeur* (apprentice judge) in Versailles.

1828

Tocqueville meets his wife-to-be, Mary ("Marie") Mottley, an Englishwoman of middle-class background and six years his elder of whom his Catholic aristocratic family disapproves.

1829–1830

Attends lectures at the Sorbonne by François Guizot on the history of civilization in France and Europe. Later during his visit to the United

States Tocqueville writes to a friend asking that volumes of Guizot be sent to help him understand and analyze American society.

1830

In July the Restoration monarchy of Charles X collapses in the face of popular protests against his illiberal ordinances. This marks the end of the reign of the Bourbon kings whose rule had been reestablished as a constitutional monarchy by the Charter of 1814 and gives rise to the July or "bourgeois" Monarchy led by Louis-Phillipe, Duke of Orléans. At least in part because of their political discomfort serving under this new regime, Tocqueville and his friend Gustave de Beaumont contrive a visit to America, ostensibly to study the US penitentiary system.

1831–1832

Tocqueville and Beaumont set sail from Le Havre, France on April 2, 1831 bound for Newport, Rhode Island, arriving in the United States on May 9. This launches their nine-month journey throughout the United States. Starting in New York City they head west through upstate New York, Ohio, Michigan, and north into Canada before returning to Boston in September. After touring various cities on the East Coast and mid-Atlantic, in November the two head southwest from Philadelphia by stagecoach and steamboat down to New Orleans. They arrive in January and spend just a few days in the city before turning back northeastward to Philadelphia and New York, by way of Washington, DC. While in the US capital the two have a brief interview with President Andrew Jackson in late January. They depart New York City for Le Havre on February 20, 1832 and are back in Paris by at least early April.

1832

Publication of Frances Trollope, *Domestic Manners of the Americans* (London, 1832).

1833

Publication of Gustave de Beaumont and Alexis de Tocqueville, *Du Système pénitentiaire aux États-Unis et de son application en France, suivi d'un appendice sur les colonies pénales et de notes statistique* (Paris, 1833).

1835

First volume of *De la démocratie en Amérique* published by Charles Gosselin in Paris on January 23, 1835. First print run of 500 copies instantly sells out, and numerous printings follow over the next few years.

Publication of Gustave de Beaumont, *Marie, ou l'esclavage aux États-Unis: Tableau de moeurs américaines* (Paris, 1835).

Henry Reeve undertakes the first English-language translation of the 1835 *Démocratie*, which is published in England later in 1835 with a revised version following shortly thereafter in 1836.

Marriage to Marie Mottley on October 26 during a trip to England, where he also visits the industrial cities of Birmingham, Liverpool, and Manchester.

John Stuart Mill reviews the first *Democracy* in the October 1835 *London Review*.

Publication of Tocqueville's essay *Mémoire sur le paupérisme*.

1836

Publication of Michel Chevalier, *Lettres sur l'Amérique du Nord* (Paris, 1836).

At the request of John Stuart Mill, Tocqueville publishes *L'État social et politique de la France avant et après 1789* in the *London and Westminster Review*.

1837

Publication of Édouard Alletz, *De la démocratie nouvelle, ou Des moeurs et de la pouissance des classes moyenne en France* (Paris, 1837).

Tocqueville narrowly loses his first campaign for election to the Chamber of Deputies.

1838

Tocqueville is elected to the *Académie des sciences morales et politiques* on January 6.

First American edition of Henry Reeve's English translation of *Democracy in America* is published in the United States.

1839

After his first failed effort Tocqueville is successful in his second campaign to win a seat in the Chamber of Deputies representing the commune of Valognes in the Manche region of Normandy.

1840

Second volume of *Démocratie* is published in 1840 by Gosselin on April 20, but this time with a disappointing reception.

John Stuart Mill reviews both volumes as well as the Reeve translation in the October 1840 issue of the *Edinburgh Review*.

1841

Tocqueville travels with Beaumont and his brother Hippolyte to Algeria where he investigates the prospects for colonization, contracts dysentery, and writes a lengthy essay *Travail sur l'Algérie* that remains unpublished until 1962.

Tocqueville is elected to the *Académie Française* in December.

1843

Tocqueville increasingly opposes the actions of François Guizot, Adolphe Thiers, and other leaders of the July Monarchy as scheming and "unprincipled."

1844

Tocqueville is one of several investors in the journal *Le Commerce*, which he envisions as a vehicle for centrist liberal opposition. The journal shortly fails and he loses his entire investment.

1847

In the face of rising popular discontent Tocqueville cautiously supports modest electoral reforms against steadfast resistance by Guizot and Louis-Phillipe.

1848

The February Revolution overturns the July Monarchy of Louis-Phillipe and gives rise to the elected government of the Second Republic.

Tocqueville and Beaumont are part of a committee tasked with drafting a new constitution.

In June the provisional government closes down the public workshops established in March to support the working classes. During the "June Days" of the 23–26, mobs of angry workers engage in a violent insurrection throughout Paris with thousands killed. Tocqueville is in the midst of these events, supports their suppression by force, and his firsthand account of this tumultuous period and retrospective of the July Monarchy form the basis of his *Souvenirs*.

In December Louis-Napoleon Bonaparte is elected President of the Second Republic.

1849

Tocqueville appointed Minister of Foreign Affairs under Louis-Napoleon but serves only five months before the entire cabinet is dismissed and replaced by Bonaparte.

1850

Tocqueville begins writing the *Souvenirs*, which was first published posthumously in 1893.

He begins to conceive of a book on the French Revolution that will eventually become the *Ancien Régime*.

1851

Coup d'état staged by Louis-Napoleon, who shortly thereafter becomes Napoleon III under the Second Empire, which he declares in December 1852.

1852

Tocqueville resigns from political life to avoid swearing an oath of loyalty to the new regime.

1853

After moving to the Loire Valley for health reasons Tocqueville begins archival research that will form the basis for the *Ancien Régime.*

1856

Publication of the *L'Ancien Régime et la Révolution* on June 16 in Paris by Michel Lévy. The book is widely heralded as another masterpiece.

The Old Regime and the Revolution translated by Henry Reeve is simultaneously published in London.

1859

Publication of John Stuart Mill, *On Liberty* (London, 1859).

After several years of declining health, Tocqueville passes away from tuberculosis on April 16, 1859 in Cannes, where he had moved with Marie in the hope that the climate would cure his terminal illness.

He is buried in the ancestral church cemetery in the village of Tocqueville.

Organizational scheme and certain basic historical information loosely adapted from the more detailed chronologies of Cheryl Welch (*Cambridge Companion to Tocqueville*, ed. Cheryl Welch [Cambridge: Cambridge University Press, 2006], xix–xxvii) and Olivier Zunz (*Democracy in America*, translated by Arthur Goldhammer [New York: Modern Library of America, 2004], 878–906); as well as biographical details from André Jardin, *Tocqueville: A Biography* (New York: Farrar, Straus, and Giroux, 1988); Lucien Jaume, *Tocqueville: Aristocratic Sources of Liberty* (Princeton: Princeton University Press, 2013); Hugh Brogan, *Alexis de*

Tocqueville: A Life (New Haven, CT: Yale University Press, 2006). Publication information of contemporaneous travelogues derives from René Rémond's comprehensive catalogue of annual publications of French works on the United States (Rémond, *Les États-Unis devant l'opinion française, 1815–1852*, 2 vols. [Paris: Colin, 1962], 873–97).

Abbreviations of Tocqueville's Major Works

English Editions

AR. *The Ancien Régime and the French Revolution.* Translated by Arthur Goldhammer. Cambridge University Press, 2011. Citations are by book, chapter, and page numbers: e.g., AR I.2, 17–18.

DIA (G). *Democracy in America.* Translated by Arthur Goldhammer. New York: Library of America, 2004. Cited by volume, part, chapter, and page numbers: e.g., DIA (G) I.2.vii, 290.

DIA (L). *Democracy in America.* Translated by George Lawrence. Edited by J. P. Mayer. New York: Harper, 1961. Cited by volume, part, chapter, and page numbers: e.g., DIA (L) I.1.iv, 97.

DIA (MW). *Democracy in America.* Translated and edited by Harvey Mansfield and Delba Winthrop. Chicago: University of Chicago Press, 2000. Cited by volume, part, chapter, and page numbers: e.g., DIA (MW) I.2.iii, 174–175.

DIA (N). *Democracy in America.* Critical bilingual edition. Translated by James T. Schleifer, 4 vols. Edited by Eduardo Nolla. Indianapolis: Liberty Fund, 2009. The pagination is identical to the English edition published in 2 volumes by Indianapolis: Liberty Fund, 2012. Citations are by page number: e.g., DIA (N) 1265.

OR.   *The Old Regime and the Revolution.* Vol. 1: *The Complete Text.* Vol. 2: *Notes on the French Revolution and Napoleon.* Translated by Alan S. Kahan. Edited by François Furet and Françoise Mélonio. Chicago: University of Chicago Press, 1998 and 2001. Citations are by page number.

R (M).   *The Recollections of Alexis de Tocqueville.* Translated by A. Teixeira de Mattos. New York: Meridian, 1959. Citations are by page number.

SLPS.   *Selected Letters on Politics and Society.* Translated by Roger Boesche and James Toupin. Berkeley: University of California Press, 1985. Citations are by page number.

TR.   *The Tocqueville Reader.* Edited by Olivier Zunz and Alan Kahan. Oxford: Blackwell, 2002. Citations are by page number.

WES.   *Writings on Empire and Slavery.* Translated and edited by Jennifer Pitts. Baltimore: Johns Hopkins University Press, 2001. Citations are by page number.

French Editions

OC.   *Œuvres Complètes.* Definitive edition prepared at the behest of the *Commission nationale pour la publication des Œuvres d'Alexis de Tocqueville,* under the direction of J. P. Mayer. 18 vols., 32 tomes in total. Paris: Gallimard, 1951–2021. Cited by volume, tome (where present), and page numbers: e.g., OC 15:1, 68.

OC (B). *Œuvres Complètes de Alexis de Tocqueville.* Edited by Gustave de Beaumont, 9 vols. Paris: Michel Lévy, 1861–1866. Cited by volume and page number: e.g., OC (B) II, 315.

DEA (F). *De la démocratie en Amérique.* Edited by François Furet. Paris: Garnier-Flammarion, 1981.

Introduction

Revisiting *Democracy in America* in the Twenty-First Century

Richard Boyd

Originally published in two volumes in 1835 and 1840, and translated into English in multiple recent editions, Alexis de Tocqueville's classic *Democracy in America* is among the most widely cited accounts of the distinctiveness of American democracy. US presidents as different as Ronald Reagan, Bill Clinton, George W. Bush, and Barack Obama have all invoked the authority of Tocqueville's *Democracy* in support of divergent visions of the American regime. The work is selectively quoted – often at cross-purposes – by politicians, pundits, and intellectuals on both the Left and the Right. Hardly a week passes by without a snippet from *Democracy* appearing in a newspaper of record or some major popular journal of opinion. It is no exaggeration to say that Americans have come to know themselves, at least in part, through the pages of Tocqueville's book.

Democracy is not only ubiquitously referred to as an authoritative account of American politics and culture. It has also exerted a remarkable influence on the academic disciplines of political theory, sociology, American studies, American political development, intellectual history, and even literature. Some of the most noteworthy currents in postwar sociology took as their starting point Tocqueville's criticisms of democratic culture and mass society, the vagaries of public opinion, the pathologies of individualism, and the alleged breakdown of civic life in the United States.[1] Recent fascinations with civil society – both in the United States and abroad – can be traced back to the author's insights into the role that intermediary associations play in the well-functioning of democratic institutions.[2] Major debates in history and political sociology over "American exceptionalism," or indeed whether America's political development should be understood as primarily "liberal" or "illiberal," originate in observations drawn from *Democracy*.[3] In sum, the book's views of the global tendencies of democracy and the peculiarities of America live on in some of today's liveliest academic debates.

Like many great works, *Democracy* also has a compelling back-story. As reconstructed by George Wilson Pierson, James T. Schleifer, and other more recent biographers, the story of the book's composition is by now legendary.[4] The young aristocrat Tocqueville – accompanied by his boon companion Gustave de Beaumont – contrives a visit to the United States in 1831, ostensibly to study the American penitentiary system.[5] While doing so, the two take a quick measure of polite society on the East Coast before decamping for the American West in pursuit of the wilderness, not to mention a better understanding of the peculiar institution of slavery. Their nine-month tour of North America – retraced by C-Span in 1997 – carries them across a wide swath of the United States and Canada. Upon returning to France in 1832, Tocqueville sits down to his notes and over the next few years produces a work that is both panoramic in its vision of the universal tide of democratic equality and scrupulous in its grasp of the minutiae of American culture, manners, and mores. The book he composed – to great acclaim both at home and abroad – became an instant classic.

Some of *Democracy*'s allure in the United States has always stemmed from the mistaken notion that the book is all about *America*. How flattering that a brilliant young nobleman should come all the way across the Atlantic and deem the Americans' political institutions, habits, and everyday life to be of world historical significance! Yet despite the book's gratifying pretense that Americans are the sole people on the earth in the 1830s who have managed to make democracy work, it is important to keep in mind that the book was intended to be a broader meditation on the genus of democracy as a "social condition," especially in Tocqueville's native France. America may be remarkable as the regime that has most successfully balanced democracy and political liberty, but it is also worth studying as a harbinger of that "providential" equality unfolding around the world. The riddle, whose partial solution he finds in the United States, is how, in the face of this inexorable democratic revolution, can the novel equality of conditions be reconciled with a respect for political liberty? Given the book's profound insights into this dilemma, it is no surprise that *Democracy* has been hailed as a resource for democratic revolutions in successive centuries from Latin America to Eastern Europe and the Middle East.

Much has changed in the nearly two centuries since Tocqueville's visit. The French have managed to achieve what Tocqueville despaired of during his own lifetime, namely a stable balance between democracy and individual liberty. As he predicted, the Americans have proven to be both a superpower and the vanguard for the dissemination of democratic equality across the globe. Even so, many perils he spied on the horizon have also come to pass. By many accounts, Americans have become less civically engaged than Tocqueville found them in the first half of the nineteenth century. If neo-Tocquevillean critics of the strange decline of social capital in the United States are to be believed, latter-day Americans are more akin to nineteenth-century Frenchmen than the sturdy New England citizens Tocqueville lionized. Pathologies of "individualism," "tyrannical majoritarianism," "materialism," and even "soft despotism" have arguably reared their ugly heads in the intervening century and a half, as he feared;[6] and some of the anomalous illiberal institutions Tocqueville glimpsed beneath the pleasing facade of "democratic paint" – the nagging problem of race relations, the banality of bourgeois culture, the vagaries of public opinion, the vestiges of old privileges, and the growth of a new industrial aristocracy – seem only to have compounded in the following centuries.[7]

This present volume is not meant to serve as hagiography in service of the notion that the visionary Tocqueville once and for all "got America right." Nor is it intended to suggest, as have critics in the intervening decades, that Tocqueville was wildly off target.[8]

Rather, the aim is to show that, for all of his limitations, Tocqueville nonetheless managed to identify in *Democracy* the quintessential tendencies, contradictions, and dynamics inherent in the global process of democratization and that his book remains just as relevant in the twenty-first century as the day its first two tomes of volume 1 appeared in 1835.

In what follows, I sketch out some of the major questions raised by the text – and explored in more depth by the contributions that follow. These are organized around several key themes. First, there are matters surrounding the composition and reception of the book. How did it come about, from what sources, and how has it been read by subsequent generations in France, the United States, and elsewhere in the world? Second, we must take note of substantive issues Tocqueville identified and the extent to which his insights still hold sway in light of democracy's transformations over the past 190 years since his visit. Finally, how do his ideas point us ahead and guide attempts to reckon with some of the greatest challenges – many old, others novel – that democracy faces in the twenty-first century?

DEMOCRACY IN CONTEXT

Democracy may strike readers as *sui generis*. Or at least it is hard to fathom what kind of book Tocqueville meant it to be. Although normative in its lessons and philosophical in its conceits, *Democracy* is not an abstract rumination on the origins of government in the manner of Hobbes, Locke, or Rousseau. While it surveys history and makes surmises based on a distinctive schema of historical development reminiscent of G. W. F. Hegel or Karl Marx, neither is it a work of history in any straightforward sense. It purports to be a work of nonfiction, at least insofar as Tocqueville denies interjecting his own opinions beyond where firsthand evidence would lead him, but its themes and manner of argumentation are distinctively literary in character.[9] It may bring to mind earlier and roughly contemporaneous travelogues on America by the likes of François-René de Chateaubriand, Michel Chevalier, Captain Basil Hall, and

Mrs. Frances Trollope, but many of *Democracy*'s most profound insights are not so much artifacts of foreign discovery as confirmation of ideas Tocqueville held well before he set sail for the United States.[10]

One common way of understanding any book is to read it in light of conspicuous influences. In the case of *Democracy*, however, we confront a twofold dilemma of obscurity and even misdirection. Tocqueville is notoriously opaque about sources.[11] When commenting on general features of the United States he occasionally refers to an authoritative author or book – say, Thomas Jefferson or *The Federalist*. Yet he also takes pains to hide his immediate interlocutors, lest he be accused of betraying their confidence or implicating them in his controversies. With the benefit of his working notes and correspondence we can identify traces of his American associates, but even in hindsight their insights seem to have been deliberately cast in the shadows.[12] With respect to broader philosophical sources, the task is more complicated still. Earlier philosophical inspirations can be intuited in Tocqueville's writings, but these usually rest on similarities rather than specifiable matters of cause and effect. Thus, on the one hand, we have a reticent author who takes pains to disguise the provenance of his ideas.

On the other hand, though, *Democracy*'s author may have complicated the task of assessing the book by his own testimony. Readers of *Democracy* have long been preoccupied by Tocqueville's famous quip to his lifelong friend Louis de Kergorlay about communing daily with the intellectual triumvirate of "Montesquieu, Pascal, and Rousseau."[13] As confirmation, many read *Democracy* as developing the political sociology and study of regimes found in Montesquieu's *Spirit of the Laws*.[14] Surely there is much to support the centrality of Montesquieu to Tocqueville's thinking, and his most astute contemporary readers were quick to apprehend similarities between these two works. Many including the likes of Pierre Paul Royer-Collard and John Stuart Mill heralded Tocqueville as the Montesquieu of his age.[15] High praise, indeed.

Like his distinguished eighteenth-century predecessor, Tocqueville is concerned with regime types. Collapsing Montesquieu's tripartite forms of tyranny, monarchy, and republics into two, Tocqueville ends up with a typology of "aristocracy" and "democracy." Each of these is oriented toward a sort of Montesquieuean virtue, "honor" and "well-being," respectively. Rather than confining his attention to formal institutions, though, Tocqueville focuses like Montesquieu on the animating spirit or underlying cultural mores that breathe life to each regime. In terms of the independent variables that account for political liberty in the United States, Tocqueville again follows Montesquieu in trying to disentangle the relative influence of circumstances, mores, and laws. More broadly, in terms of methodology, Tocqueville emulates *Spirit of the Laws* in moving back and forth between abstract generalizations and specific empirical examples.

Less obvious was the influence of Pascal, although here too the fingerprints are discernible. As many interpreters have suggested, Tocqueville's theological notions of historical development, his sense of moral freedom, his emphasis on the naturalness of the religious experience, and his understanding of human agency and finitude are steeped in Pascalian language. Whether it is his view of the restlessness of the modern condition or his reckoning of freedom as a spiritual dilemma, it is hard to read *Democracy* without being deeply impressed by the significance of Christianity in Tocqueville's Jansenist worldview.[16]

Tocqueville's self-professed debt to Jean-Jacques Rousseau is more puzzling, for, as Allan Bloom has noted, it is hardly intuitive what the relationship could be between the Genevan apostle of republicanism and the young French aristocrat's ambivalent rendition of American democracy.[17] At the institutional level one could point to Tocqueville's celebration of the New England township as a cradle for American democracy. Rousseau's romanticized Swiss cantons appear on the other side of the Atlantic disguised as Puritan municipalities. At a deeper level, however, Rousseau leaves his imprint on Tocqueville's moral psychology of equality. Both thinkers conceive of democracy in terms of the passing of aristocracy's invidious conventions. Their affirmation of the naturalness of democracy and the ways in which it elevates feelings of compassion and a common sense of humanity seems one of the most appreciable sources of agreement, if not outright influence, between the two thinkers.[18]

Whereas each of these three enumerated figures has already proven the subject of voluminous scholarly discussion, which need not be replicated here, Tocqueville's other sources for *Democracy* are less obvious. Despite the wide range of classical and contemporary philosophical sources we know he consulted during the period of composition of volume 2, there are scant references to particular thinkers.[19] Suggestive reconstructions of Tocqueville's immediate political context have established the young Frenchman's indebtedness to the scheme of historical development espoused by François Guizot and other liberal Doctrinaire thinkers such as Royer-Collard and Charles de Rémusat.[20] We know that Tocqueville attended François Guizot's lectures on European civilization at the Sorbonne in 1829–1830 and that he went so far as to write from America asking that copies of Guizot's lectures be sent to him to aid in his project.[21] Both thinkers identify a dawning tide of equality spreading throughout the globe, express concerns for how a liberal regime can be established in the wake of a democratic revolution, eschew centralization in favor of local liberties, and seek to understand democracy primarily in terms of a novel "social condition."[22]

Lucien Jaume has further sketched out the aristocratic intellectual milieu of Restoration France from which Tocqueville may have derived some of his most renowned ideas. While *Democracy* strikes contemporary readers as novel, many of its central themes were widely debated in Legitimist circles of the day.[23] If Jaume is right, some of *Democracy*'s most distinctive ideas may be much less original than we have come to believe. Concepts such as "the social," "generative principles," and the critique of "individualism," materialism, and "administrative despotism" for which Tocqueville is renowned were already found in writings of reactionary figures such as Félicité Robert de Lamennais, Joseph de Maistre, and Guillaume-Chrétien de Lamoignon de Malesherbes, not to mention Tocqueville's own kinsman Chateaubriand.

Beyond direct comparisons with an already familiar cast of characters, this volume seeks to reframe Tocqueville's ideas against the broader context of the seventeenth, eighteenth and nineteenth centuries. Should Tocqueville be considered an Enlightenment or anti-Enlightenment thinker? How much ground does he ultimately break from his innumerable seventeenth- and eighteenth-century sources? What ideas and concepts does he share with other leading thinkers of his own generation, and to what extent does his aristocratic vantage inform his concern to preserve some remnants of an aristocratic age?

For his part, Ryan Patrick Hanley in Chapter 1 observes that Tocqueville's political thought has often been cast in terms of whether he sides with or against the Enlightenment philosophies of the seventeenth and eighteenth centuries. Yet, as Hanley notes, this oversimplifies to the point of meaninglessness. Rather than a binary choice, we may more profitably ask what *kind* of Enlightenment figure is Tocqueville? Of the various strands of Enlightenment thinking, which ones does he endorse or denounce as pernicious? Locating Tocqueville's thought squarely in the path of the so-called Moderate Enlightenment, Hanley suggests that one of the most illuminating comparisons is to the Scottish economist and moral philosopher Adam Smith, whose relationship to Tocqueville has been lamentably unexplored.

In Chapter 2, Aurelian Craiutu surveys Tocqueville in light of the concerns of his immediate generation and identifies traces of this milieu in some of the key themes of *Democracy*. What is often referred to as the Generation of 1820 came of age during the Bourbon Restoration. Its notable members such as Théodore Jouffroy, Charles de Rémusat, François-René de Chateaubriand, and Félicité de Lamennais all shared with Tocqueville a distrust of revolution, a sense of the providential march of equality, and unease about the novel social conditions of skepticism and individualism. With respect to Chateaubriand's influence in particular, Craiutu offers a clue as to why Tocqueville may have first turned to America – rather than Montesquieu's England, like so many peers – as a model for France to emulate in its own pursuit of liberty.

One perennial question about Tocqueville's formative environment is his relationship to aristocracy. Most readers take Tocqueville at his word when he says at the opening of *Democracy* that the passing of an aristocratic age is by now a *fait accompli*. Yet even if democracy is the wave of the future, as he says, this may be all the more reason to hold on to vestiges of an aristocratic past. Should this prove impossible, maybe new forms of aristocracy can be cultivated to leaven democracy's most deleterious features? Some have gone so far as to make nostalgia for the passing of the *Ancien Régime* the centerpiece of Tocqueville's thought.[24] Yet, as Richard Avramenko argues in Chapter 3, the key to appreciating Tocqueville's fondness for aristocracy may not be vague nostalgia, family pedigree, or the ostensible influence of French royalist thinkers, as others have assumed. Rather, we can best understand his affinities for aristocracy by consulting the most unlikely of sources, namely *Democracy* and his quest to create a new political science for a new age.

While many ideas and concepts found in *Democracy* were hardly original to Tocqueville, as we will see, it is almost surely not the case, as Lucien Jaume has gone so far as to allege, that there is little new in Tocqueville's analysis of democracy.[25] Despite the difficulty of pinpointing Tocqueville's ultimate inspirations, situating *Democracy* against these backdrops helps readers to appreciate better the book's originality and the author's undeniable genius.

CONTEMPORANEOUS RECEPTIONS

Besides likely sources and intellectual influences, we learn important things about any classic text by considering how it has been received and deployed by others. Indeed, the measure of a great work is its ability to speak to a wide range of audiences, fulfill different contemporary needs, and inspire divergent interpretations. If longevity and global relevance are hallmarks of classic texts, then *Democracy* is surely a book of the foremost caliber. *Democracy* not only served contradictory aims in the France, Britain, and United States of its own day but has subsequently been adopted for a wide range of political causes, whether liberal, conservative, or revolutionary.

French Celebrity

It may seem obvious in hindsight that *Democracy* would cause a stir, but the book's wary publisher Charles Gosselin committed to an initial print run of only 500 copies. His surprise upon the book's success ("Now then! It seems you've written a masterpiece!") sums up the instant celebrity the author achieved in his native France with the publication of the first part of the work in 1835.[26] Tocqueville professed to be just as taken aback not only by the magnitude of attention the book garnered but also by the degree to which this favorable assessment was shared across the political spectrum.[27] Three print runs totaling 2,000 copies rapidly followed in 1835, and within a few years of subsequent editions the total copies in circulation numbered approximately 6,000.[28]

Other European commentaries on the United States were of interest in direct proportion to their political tendentiousness, but Tocqueville's book succeeded at least in part because his analysis impressed readers as dispassionate. As detailed by many historians, the book struck timely chords in its French readership: a perennial French fascination with understanding America, all the more so during a period in the 1830s of great diplomatic stress between the two nations; concerns about the future trajectory of democratic equality in French politics; matters of constitutionalism and legislation; and the vexing question of the relationship between religion and politics.[29]

Democracy's notoriety began with the first published review by Léon Faucher appearing before the book was in print in the

December 24, 1834 number of *Le Courrier français*.[30] Approximately thirty others followed in the French press with generally favorable estimation.[31] The work was endorsed by Legitimists, who glimpsed in Tocqueville not only the kindred reckonings of a fellow aristocrat but also a critic of the perils of democratic equality, leveling, secularism, rationalism, and the rule of numerical majorities.[32] As Ernest de Blosseville approvingly notes in *L'Echo français*, Tocqueville's great accomplishment was to apprehend democracy not as a secular innovation sprung from the pen of Jefferson's "Declaration of Independence," or dating back no farther than the convocation of the last Estates General in 1789. Rather, the growth of democracy is a providential process underwritten by law and God and consistent with Christian equality.[33] Despite their favorable predilections, many Legitimists nonetheless took issue with Tocqueville's acceptance of some form of popular government and his abandonment of the cause of absolute monarchy.[34]

The book found a warmer reception still among republicans, socialists, and others on the Left, who intuited in Tocqueville a voice sympathetic to the inevitability and virtues of democratization. Francisque de Corcelle's appreciation in *Revue des deux mondes* provides a thoughtful overview of many of the book's key themes.[35] For all of Tocqueville's apprehensions, however, Corcelle doubts whether envy is really any more pronounced in democracy than in other regimes and wonders what the financial system of the United States and its laws of taxation might tell us about the relationship among social classes.[36] While he does not deny that Tocqueville correctly assays some of democracy's present shortcomings, there is no reason to judge the future prospects of democracy based on the defects of a single nation.[37] Louis Blanc similarly affirms the usefulness of Tocqueville's dissection of American institutions, even if he questions their practical or theoretical efficacy in securing true republican government.[38] America is, if anything, not republican enough.

Paradoxically, the group most critical of *Democracy* were liberal Doctrinaires who, much like Tocqueville, found themselves in search of a "*juste milieu*" in French politics.[39] Its chilly reception by the centrist faction in whom one might have expected Tocqueville to find natural allies parallels his lifelong ambivalence toward Guizot, Adolphe Thiers, and other bourgeois liberal supporters of the July Monarchy.[40] Édouard Alletz offers what came to be the orthodox criticism by liberals and Doctrinaires. In his *De la démocratie nouvelle*, a thinly veiled response to *Democracy* that appeared in April 1837, Alletz mocks providential notions of democratic equality as akin to some "mysterious current" pulling the French kicking and screaming toward "a vortex ready to engulf them."[41] *Democracy* cannot be reduced to antiquated categories such as majoritarianism, absolute leveling, or the rule of the "poor and ignorant."[42] *Democracy* is guilty of confusing the past with the future, mistaking the "old democracy" of numerical majorities for the "new democracy" of the middle classes. It posits a false choice between a glorious aristocratic past, on the one hand, and a desultory democratic future, on the other. Its greatest shortcoming lies in giving short shrift to the middle classes, the new bourgeois standard-bearers of liberty, who combine the excellence of the aristocracy with the inclusiveness and social mobility of democracy. As if by way of reproach Alletz appends lengthy excerpts from Michel Chevalier's 1836 *Letters on North America*, whose sense of the energy and commercial dynamism of the middle classes presumably offers the right lessons to be drawn from America.

Not all concurred with Tocqueville's 1835 assessment, but all sides took notice. The second volume of *Democracy*, however, was met with less enthusiasm when it finally appeared nearly five years later in 1840. The book was partially the victim of Tocqueville's poor health. More or less continuous illnesses plagued him and his wife Marie Mottley in the years between 1835 and 1840 when he struggled to produce the follow-up volume. Perhaps out of a desire to surpass the first volume's success, Tocqueville wrote and rewrote obsessively, suffering periods of excruciating self-doubt.[43] While today regarded as in many ways more profound than the first volume, the

1840 *Democracy* nonetheless fell flat among French readers. As Françoise Mélonio summarizes, the belated second volume aligned poorly with the concerns of the era.[44]

Tocqueville's influence in France has been explored elsewhere and to great illumination in important scholarly works by Mélonio, Serge Audier, and others, and we need not retrace here in detail.[45] Yet in broad terms the trajectory of *Democracy* in France follows an arc: meteoric success in 1835, puzzlement or apathy toward the 1840 follow-up, relative neglect if not "dusty oblivion" in the latter part of the nineteenth and early twentieth centuries, and a full-blown renaissance in the second half of the twentieth and first decades of the twenty-first century.[46] By all accounts, one key point in the rehabilitation of Tocqueville's ideas came via sociologist Raymond Aron's 1965 *Main Currents in Sociological Thought* and shortly thereafter by way of the historian François Furet's commendation of Tocqueville's other masterpiece the *Ancien Régime* as basis for a non-Marxist historiography of the French Revolution.[47]

In subsequent decades, Tocqueville's *Democracy* has become a lodestar for French intellectuals across the political spectrum in fields such as political science, philosophy, sociology, and anthropology. Rather than just a retrospective of the American regime, the book continues to inspire novel French reflection on the nature of democratic modernity, the fate of France and European politics, liberalism, the anthropology of modern individualism, and the status of religion by the likes of Pierre Manent, Marcel Gauchet, Louis Dumont, Claude Lefort, Dominique Schnapper, Pierre Rosanvallon, and countless others.[48] Indeed, a disproportionate amount of so-called New French Thought has been inspired, whether directly or indirectly, by a renewed sense of the relevance of Tocqueville's ideas.[49]

Divergent English Appropriations

Word of *Democracy* quickly spread across the English Channel, where the book caught the attention of Henry Reeve, Tocqueville's young friend, soon-to-be translator, and later editor of the *Edinburgh Review*. Reeve's translation became, for better or worse, the standard English-language version of the book for decades. Then twenty-one years old, Reeve's commitment to undertaking a translation was complicated by his own Tory politics, which he struggled to reconcile with his reading of the book as radical in thrust. Reeve's personal ambivalence about Tocqueville's ideas was a microcosm of contemporaneous British attempts to square Tocqueville's dispassionate analysis of American democracy with contentious debates in the 1830s over liberal reforms.[50]

As in France, *Democracy* enjoyed an eager reception by partisans on both the Left and the Right. The book's dispassionate rendition, its notable lack of "prejudice and party spirit," is the feature most remarked upon by the 1836 reviewer for the *Quarterly Review*, presumed to be Sir Basil Hall.[51] The *British and Foreign Review* echoed this appreciation of Tocqueville's "even-handed justice" and "dispassionate philosophy."[52] Yet, rather than being inspired by Tocqueville's objectivity, some English readers took advantage by superimposing their own partisan spirit onto the book. In the shadow of the Reform Act of 1832, Sir Robert Peel and other Conservative politicians touted *Democracy* as a book all thinking persons should read to appreciate the debilities of the tyranny of the majority and democratic despotism.[53] Peel invokes Tocqueville's vision of democratic America as an apocalyptic tale that all Britons should heed – a view many Tory leaders shared and for which Tocqueville was warmly received in conservative circles of English society.[54] John Stuart Mill complained indignantly in 1840 that Peel's conservative misappropriation demonstrates how, improperly understood, "some of [Tocqueville's] phrases are susceptible of a Tory application."[55]

Peel was hardly the only Conservative to embrace Tocqueville, and, Mill's demurrer notwithstanding, their justifications for doing so go far deeper than a few twisted turns of phrase. *Blackwoods' Edinburgh Magazine* ran an early review of the work in 1835 that extolls Tocqueville's Burkean rejection of abstract theory, his appreciation of the role of growth and contingency in political life, and his sense of the uniqueness of national institutions.[56] According to the reviewer, America's strengths are English in origins, most notably dissenting Protestantism and municipal liberties, whereas its weaknesses stem from the innovation of an unstable federal union of states held together by mere opinion.[57] Universal suffrage inevitably "sacrifices intelligence to ignorance," the reviewer affirms.[58] Then of course there is the dire repetition of Tocqueville's warnings about the tyranny of the majority, whereby the minority are not only outvoted but faced with "moral annihilation," their intelligence quashed and voices stifled by ignorant mobs.[59]

While Conservatives trumpeted Tocqueville's ostensible criticisms of democracy, his main English interlocutors were at the opposite end of the political spectrum. Tocqueville found himself most at home intellectually among a circle of liberal-minded Benthamite Radicals, which included the likes of John Stuart Mill; the banker and historian George Grote and his wife Harriet; and, most notably, the distinguished economist Nassau William Senior, a figure decisive to Tocqueville's English reception and lifelong intellectual formation.[60] Then unknown, a young Tocqueville had boldly introduced himself to Senior during a visit to England in 1833, making an instant impression of intellectual gravity, and the two struck up a lifelong friendship and correspondence.[61] Letters between them reveal that Tocqueville was particularly concerned about *Democracy* being well received in England, which he described as "in an intellectual sense, my second country."[62] At Senior's suggestion, and with his apparent intercession, Tocqueville sent copies of *Democracy* to the leading reviews where they generated largely favorable notices.[63]

The first mention of Tocqueville in the *Edinburgh Review* in 1837 pertains to Tocqueville's earlier publication with Beaumont on penitentiary reform, although the author alludes to "M. de Tocqueville's profound and admirable essay on American Democracy, which we cannot mention without expressing our regret at having so long delayed to examine it."[64] The pages of subsequent issues of the journal were dotted with references to *Democracy*, clear evidence of its acclaim, but it was not until 1840 that a full review was printed. This extensive essay covered the second 1840 French volume as well as the Reeve translation into English, which had appeared in 1835 with a second and substantially corrected edition in 1836.[65] The review's uncredited author was no less illustrious a figure than John Stuart Mill.

Reeve's translation was an important vehicle for *Democracy*'s passage to England and eventually to the English-speaking Americas, but arguably no British thinker did more to disseminate its ideas than John Stuart Mill. Any sense of the relationship between Tocqueville and Mill needs to begin with the latter's October 1835 review of *Democracy* in the *London Review*, partially reproduced by Mill in his collection of *Early Essays* of 1869.[66] What strikes Mill as decisive about *Democracy* – and illustrative for British debates – is that Tocqueville accepts as given something still perversely being debated in England, that is, the question of whether democracy is here to stay.[67] For Tocqueville, and other European thinkers, this has already been resolved in the affirmative. For Mill, then, the only legitimate question is how to prepare for the advent of democracy and make best use of its native tendencies. Tocqueville's work allows for consideration of democracy and aristocracy not "in the mass," as undifferentiated wholes to be cheered or jeered by partisans, but with an objective sense of their distinctive strengths and weaknesses.[68]

Mill commends *Democracy*'s attention to municipal government in New England and the practice of local liberties as the only effective mode of political education.[69] The contention that democracy can only be learned by actually doing it becomes an important theme in his own work on representative government.[70] Mill doubts, however, whether *Democracy*'s worries about representative government are well founded in practice and, conversely, accuses Tocqueville of overstating the virtues of aristocracy.[71] We find similar differences in the 1840 *Edinburgh Review* essay. Mill allows that worries about tyrannical majoritarianism, democratic leveling, and mediocrity may be legitimate but insists that these defects are incidental rather than constitutive features of modern democratic society. Moreover, insofar as they are valid observations, they may be pathologies of commercial civilization rather than of democratic equality, per se.[72] That is to say that even if Tocqueville is correct in his diagnosis of the symptoms, he may have misattributed the underlying causes of the disease. Civilization is not democracy.[73]

Beyond these two appreciative review essays, Mill's formative engagement with *Democracy* remains among his most enduring influences.[74] In fact, Tocqueville's ambivalence about the side effects of democratic equality and the "tyranny of the majority" underwrites much of Mill's 1859 classic *On Liberty*.[75] As the "social eminences" of an aristocratic age are "levelled," democracy's tendency toward "general similarity" and "collective mediocrity" threatens to impede historical progress and civilizational development. Echoing Tocqueville, Mill laments that "individuals are lost in the crowd."[76] Among the various sorts of tyranny to which the modern world gives rise, "tyranny of the majority" by means of public opinion appears "more formidable than many kinds of political oppression," "penetrating much more deeply into the details of life, and enslaving the soul itself."[77] This is nothing if not Tocqueville's "spiritualized despotism," which strikes not at the body but at the soul, leading those whose views diverge from the majority to question their own individual conscience lest they be mocked or scorned.

These two great liberal thinkers of the nineteenth century eventually grew apart over matters of nationalism and foreign policy – with Mill castigating Tocqueville in 1842 for jingoistic saber-rattling.[78] Their personal rift was healed only much later in life, but in the intervening years Mill's corpus remained suffused by his encounter with *Democracy*.[79] Mill's *Autobiography* credits Tocqueville for appreciating the modern state's drift toward centralization.[80] In his 1862 essay on "Centralization," as well as in *Principles of Political Economy*, Mill fears that centralization of administrative power in the hands of the state will lead not only to sundry bureaucratic inefficiencies but, most crucially, to the moral enervation of the population.[81] In language reminiscent of the last few chapters of volume 2 of *Democracy*, the preeminent danger of centralization is that it saps all energy, spontaneous initiative, and moral dignity from a people, leaving them dependent and herd-like. Administrative centralization is potentially debilitating; voluntary association is the cure.[82] As Seymour Drescher perceptively notes, the socialist Mill repurposed Tocqueville's fascination with political associations into a panacea for improving the social and economic conditions of the working classes by means of voluntary and cooperative associations.[83]

Gratifying the Americans

After several brief notices appeared in 1835, the first two substantial American reviews of *Democracy* were published in the summer of 1836. The first, at least by publication date, was in the March/June number of the *American Quarterly Review*. Still smarting from "flippant satirists" such as Sir Basil Hall, Mrs. Frances Trollope, and other Europeans travelers whose caricatures betrayed the hospitality of their hosts, the reviewer is moved to literary ecstasies by M. de Tocqueville's ability to suspend his prejudices and give Americans a fair shake.[84] "It is doubtless the fate of all countries to be misrepresented," but the appearance of *Democracy* gives the reviewer hope that the days of "small tourists" and "supercilious visitants" are over.[85]

One major theme underscored by reviewers was America's debts to the New England Puritans. Americans derived from their Puritan forebears their love of liberty and hatred of tyranny; their embrace of universal education; and, contrary to Tocqueville's attribution to the Virginians, the de facto abolition of primogeniture and entail.[86] With respect to America's celebrated equality of conditions, the reviewer concurs as to its existence but suggests that

Tocqueville's misunderstanding of its sources is one of his "most serious errors."[87] Tocqueville hardly overstates the drawbacks of an "equality of conditions," whose mediocrity and leveling the reviewer largely concedes. Still, Tocqueville has not understood the Americans to be egalitarian enough, failing to perceive the extent to which popular sovereignty and equal political rights undergird the entire political and social edifice. Even the presence of black chattel slavery, the reviewer notes, serves to forge a common equality between whites of different socioeconomic stations.[88] "To us, aristocracy is a legend, nothing more," an anachronism of medieval knights in shining armor, whereas "no germ of feudality was ever imported hither."[89]

While affirming Tocqueville's paeans to township government and the federal constitution, the strongest criticisms are reserved for *Democracy*'s famous observations about the tyranny of the majority. As Olivier Zunz has noted in his comprehensive review of American receptions, this first reviewer's reaction held true for many subsequent American readers: sheer incredulousness.[90] Not only is Tocqueville mistaken about the very existence of the tyranny of the majority; he is doubly wrong to suggest, by comparison, that there is less real freedom of thought in the United States than in overtly repressive regimes. "We question much if he could save his head if he undertook to publish the 'Democratie' in Warsaw," the *American Quarterly Review* peevishly objects.[91] An 1837 reviewer likewise rejects this characterization of the American government not only as empirically wrong but, worse still, as fodder for Tory British critics who on the basis of Tocqueville's characterization sought to indict the American regime.[92]

Another common objection is to the "Three Races" chapter, which reviewers of the age correctly read as a scathing indictment of the tragic injustices of settler colonialism and black chattel slavery. Of the former dispossession of Native Americans, the *American Quarterly Review* hides behind the familiar trope of Americans as agents of civilization against native savagery and raises the British colonization of India by way of moral equivalency. With respect to black chattel slavery, the reviewer professes that "we ask no advice from Europeans, thrusting upon us from the distance of three thousand miles, casuistical observations, in utter ignorance of our real situation."[93] Citing the history of European imperialism and bloodshed, the author's reaction boils down to "glass houses."

The second review of *Democracy*, authored by famed Massachusetts educator and politician Edward Everett, appeared in July 1836 in the *North American Review*. Everett echoes many points of concurrence: the centrality of equality and doctrines of popular sovereignty; the providential view of history with the United States understood as its vanguard; and the significance of decentralized municipal institutions, particularly the township. Here again the New England Puritans are decisive in forming the American character, but Everett drops a fascinating hint about why contemporaneous readers in the United States seized so eagerly on Tocqueville's Puritan rendition of America's "point of departure." As Everett explains, the notion that the United States was founded by high-minded and idealistic Puritans serves as a gratifying counterpoint to British slurs of the day alleging America's barbarous character could be explained by the fact that its "Adam and Eve came out of Newgate," which is to say, the nation was settled by convicts and vagrants.[94] What Tocqueville called the "point of departure" mattered to Americans themselves – symbolically as much as institutionally.

Early reactions to *Democracy* in the United States were largely dictated by whether the book supported or deflected criticisms by previous European – in particular, British – visitors. For example, Tocqueville's appreciation of the salutary role of the separation of church and state in the United States gets cited as a rejoinder to complaints by Europeans about American indifference to religion, which according to Everett visitors had mistakenly inferred from its lack of an established church.[95] So too for their ridicule of the "prudery" of American women, which is presumably refuted by Tocqueville's praise of how religion strengthens the bonds and augments the pleasures of the conjugal union.[96] From an American vantage, *Democracy*'s reception can only be fully understood in the conjunction between earlier and largely critical European travelogues and what Tocqueville was to call the "irritable patriotism of the Americans."[97]

A trickle of notices followed in the years between its original appearance and the publication of the first American edition in 1838, a loosely reprinted version of the Reeve translation with a new introduction by John Canfield Spencer.[98] Thereafter the floodgates opened and appreciative commentary proliferated. While enjoying popularity in the decades after Tocqueville's visit, many have claimed that *Democracy*'s status declined precipitously from the Civil War onward to the point of complete neglect, only to be rediscovered in the 1940s and 1950s.[99] As Matthew Mancini has helpfully documented, however, *Democracy* was never entirely forgotten or even, for that matter, out of print in the United States throughout the late nineteenth and early twentieth centuries.[100] Its American legacy is better understood as a story of continuous evolution than of loss and rediscovery.

The present volume surveys a number of different ways in which *Democracy* has shaped subsequent American political thought. Richard Boyd (Chapter 4) takes up the story of *Democracy*'s legacy in the nineteenth and twentieth centuries and how the liberal Tocqueville came to be a resource for American conservatives. As Boyd notes, while *Democracy* never wholly disappeared from the American intellectual scene, its resurgence in the twentieth century took place against the background of Cold War politics and the critique of the welfare state. Tocqueville became a resource for conservatives such as Robert Nisbet, Russell Kirk, and others who amplified conservative themes in *Democracy*. They did so, however, in ways that were sometimes at cross-purposes to Tocqueville's original arguments as well as other strands of American conservatism.

Conservative or neoconservative appropriations of Tocqueville have been so pervasive that at least in the United States readers tend to think of Tocqueville as a figure of the political Right.[101] Yet, as Robert T. Gannett, Jr. demonstrates in Chapter 5, *Democracy* cast a long shadow across the political Left as well, both in the United States and in other parts of the world. Gannett highlights the many ways in which Tocqueville's ideas of civic engagement and political action proved central influences on progressive intellectuals and social activists such as Albert Salomon, Max Lerner, Louis Hartz, Hannah Arendt, Saul D. Alinsky, and contemporary "communitarians." This affinity, Gannett reminds us, is no mere intellectual abstraction. It reflects genuine activism Tocqueville evinced in his own lifetime on behalf of the causes of abolition and social reform.

Democracy's appeal on both the Right and the Left has been at least partially motivated by his nagging dissatisfaction with the bourgeois capitalist modernity whose emergence he and so many other commentators have identified with the United States. As Alan Levine (Chapter 6) argues in his contrast between Tocqueville and latter-day European "Anti-Americans," there is in fact much to separate Tocqueville's keen assessment of America's weaknesses from the polemics of Anti-Americans. By sharply distinguishing Tocqueville from subsequent Anti-American intellectuals such as Max Horkheimer, T. W. Adorno, and Herbert Marcuse, many of whom claim Tocqueville as inspiration, Levine reveals how, and exactly why, Tocqueville's friendly criticism is both more empirically defensible and politically responsible than the Anti-Americanism it might seem to resemble if not to have actually inspired.

Global Legacies

Beyond Western Europe and the United States, we also have to take note of *Democracy*'s global footprint. As José Antonio Aguilar Rivera describes in Chapter 7 on Latin American receptions of *Democracy*, Tocqueville's work was widely discussed in other nascent democracies of the Western hemisphere. Confirming a familiar pattern of selective appropriation, Aguilar Rivera meticulously shows how a wide range of nineteenth-century Latin American thinkers used Tocqueville for their own purposes and in strikingly divergent ways. Different parts of Tocqueville's analysis stood out as salient to the political circumstances of nations such as Mexico, Colombia, Chile, and Argentina or were ignored when inconvenient. Not only does this chapter offer a fascinating historical case study in intellectual receptions, but it also highlights the contemporary relevance of *Democracy* by showing how nations less favored by circumstances than the North Americans have concretely drawn upon Tocqueville's ideas.

James T. Schleifer's study of the cases of Japan and China (Chapter 8) likewise serves a dual purpose. As Schleifer notes, Japanese interest in Tocqueville's ideas dates all the way back to the late nineteenth century when parts of *Democracy* were translated into Japanese during a transitional period away from aristocracy and toward more egalitarian reforms. This marked the beginning of a more or less continuous interest by Japanese intellectuals in Tocqueville for his insights into the role of administrative decentralization and democratic mores in facilitating political liberty. By way of contrast, Chinese interest in Tocqueville is more recent. Chinese scholars have reckoned with Tocqueville's prediction of a sweeping tide of democratic equality moving throughout the globe. How the future of China might be assimilated to this narrative, whether the advent of Western liberal democracy is a good thing, and what role various Tocquevillean institutions might play in that transition are all key themes explored by Chinese intellectuals. In addition to raising timely questions about cross-cultural understanding and concept travel between Western and non-Western traditions, Schleifer's case study illustrates how intellectuals in nondemocratic regimes might draw on different arguments in *Democracy* – whether affirmatively or critically – to clarify their own situation.

With the rise and fall of communist authoritarianism in the Soviet Union and Eastern Europe we find yet another context where intellectuals, political dissidents, and policymakers turned to *Democracy* for guidance. From the vantage of the West,

Tocqueville's ideas reinforced the conviction that liberal democracy was the culmination of history, a political condition to which all peoples inevitably aspire.[102] Likewise, many in both the East and the West were drawn to Tocqueville's emphasis on civic engagement and civil society. Civil society proved to be a vector for democracy in nations such as Poland, where trades unions and other associations functioned as seedbeds for oppositional movements that would come to topple authoritarian governments, not to mention being prerequisites for stable democracies in post-communist nations such as East Germany and Russia.[103] Political scientists and sociologists of various inspirations – Marxists and post-Marxists, critical theorists, and deliberative democrats – were drawn to versions of democratic theory deeply suffused by Tocquevillean concepts and themes.[104] Democracy promised abundant resources for answering the dilemma of what cultural, institutional, and intellectual resources are necessary to produce a stable balance between equality and liberty.[105]

The vogue of civil society is arguably Tocqueville's single greatest contribution to contemporary political science, sociology, and democratic theory. Latter-day Tocquevilleans such as Robert Putnam have demonstrated the significance of civil society, social capital, and associational life in established liberal democracies such as the United States or Western Europe.[106] The spirit of voluntary association and civic engagement, the salutary exercise of local liberties, explains in large part why democracy "works."[107] Conversely, dissidents and opposition leaders such as Adam Michnik, Vaclav Havel, Andrei Sakharov, and others turned to civil society for support in challenging authoritarian regimes and fostering democracy in Eastern Europe, the former Soviet Union, and around the globe.[108] Among academics, this vision of civil society as radically participatory and imminently democratic was captured well by democratic theorists such as Mark Warren, Ernest Gellner, Jean Cohen, Andrew Arato, and many others.[109]

Yet, despite Democracy's preeminent influence and ubiquitous mentions, its characterization of civil society remains poorly understood. There is of course the "bumper-sticker" Tocqueville who hails the associational spirit of Americans and laments its absence in nations such as France. "Americans of all ages, all stations in life, and all types of disposition are forever forming associations," he famously declares. Whether "commercial and industrial" or "religious, moral, serious, futile, very general and very limited, immensely large and very minute," at the heart of any undertaking in the United States "you are sure to find an association."[110] The democratic "knowledge of how to combine is the mother of all other forms of knowledge," and "better use" has been made of this technique of association in America than anywhere else in the world.[111]

Amplified by neo-Tocquevilleans such as Putnam, these resounding declarations have not only shaped the American self-understanding; they have also given rise to a romanticized vision of civil society among social scientists, political theorists, and policy-makers. Under the sway of this idealization, many exponents assume that civil society is benign and includes only democratic forms of association.[112] Others take for granted the background context of settled Western liberal democracies in which civil society bolsters existing regimes without acknowledging its oppositional or even tyrannical capacity.[113] It seems fair to say that most readers of *Democracy* have failed to acknowledge, let alone heed, Tocqueville's warnings about the dangers of "uncivil society."[114]

This is surprising insofar as Tocqueville makes no secret of his apprehension about certain kinds of associations. There is, first, a clear distinction between civil and political associations. Civil associations are mostly beneficial in bringing neighbors together to make money, clear roads, repair churches, or build hospitals. Their purposes are as salutary as they are infinite. By way of contrast, Tocqueville is wary of the potentially illiberal and destabilizing effects of political associations. "One must not shut one's eyes to the fact that unlimited freedom of association for political ends is, of all forms of liberty, the last that a nation can sustain," he warns. Freedom of association may not actually lead a nation to anarchy, but it "does constantly bring it to the verge thereof."[115] Absent the unique circumstances of the Americans, political associations in Europe are akin to "armies" or "weapons of war," whose intransigence transforms a "fount of life into a cause of destruction."[116] Americans are lucky to have a long history of making good use of political associations, and their system lacks the "great parties" that bedevil European politics.[117] As such, they mostly avoid political association's worst dangers. Yet the American exception ought not to overshadow Tocqueville's more general rule: political associations tend toward incivility in direct proportion to their absolute freedom.

If civil associations are generally benign and political associations often dangerous, then why not just cultivate the former and discourage the latter? The matter, Tocqueville clarifies when he returns to the subject in 1840, is more complicated. The difficulty is that political associations often serve as training grounds for other forms of civil associations. Tocqueville calls political associations "great free schools to which all citizens come to be taught the general theory of association."[118] Discouraging or even outlawing political associations not only robs citizens of the chance to cultivate a taste and aptitude for benign forms of civil associations; it would raise doubts in their minds, for "when some types of association are forbidden and others allowed," people tend to steer clear of all associations as something illicit.[119] That is to say, there is no easy way to draw a bright line between good and bad, civil and political forms of association.

Michael Foley and Bob Edwards express the practical conundrum well, namely "if civil society is a beachhead secure enough to be of use in thwarting tyrannical regimes, what prevents it from being used to undermine democratic governments?"[120] Recognizing the importance – as per Tocqueville – of genuinely civil society in fostering trust, social capital, tolerance, and democratic equality has a darker obverse that is apparent when one looks outside the largely democratic culture of the United States and Western Europe. Witness the cases of Far Right nationalist parties, ethnic militias, fundamentalist movements, or other forms of tribalism and separatism in parts of Eastern Europe, the former Soviet Union, the Middle East, and North Africa. To be clear, this is hardly a problem unique to the non-Western world. Even in Tocqueville's nineteenth-century America, lawless lynch mobs, hate groups, vigilantism, and other instances of citizen activism undermine the goodwill, trust, inclusion, and spirit of cooperation fostered by genuinely civil associations.[121] Wherever in the world, and for whatever ends one invokes *Democracy*'s vision of civil society, it is important to recall the sociological reality of political associations as potentially uncivil, anti-democratic, and illiberal.

DEMOCRACY'S FORM AND GENRE?

Among the most common questions about *Democracy* is the alleged inconsistency between the 1835 and 1840 volumes.[122] The latter's disappointing follow-up, nearly five years after the 1835 *Democracy*'s immediate sensation, not to mention what many readers have described as a shift in tone between the two works, hints at a change of heart. Indeed, much had changed in the world – and Tocqueville's own life – between 1835 and 1840. This all lends credence to the impression that the second *Democracy* is more pessimistic in its assessment of the democratic future. Yet even more basic than whether *Democracy* is two books or one is the question, what kind of book is it, after all? By way of response, this volume features three insightful attempts to decenter *Democracy*'s reputation as primarily, if not exclusively, a work of political philosophy or sociology.

As Christine Dunn Henderson reveals in Chapter 9, while it may go too far to characterize *Democracy* as a work of literature, Tocqueville's manner of writing does have a distinctively literary quality. When depicting the interactions of the three races of America, the depredation of the Native Americans, or the stoicism of pioneer women, the literary vignettes that populate the book are meant to strike an emotional register. This literary quality – on display in both volumes of the work – is arguably what allows

Democracy's normative lessons to be conveyed with such power, subtlety, and sympathy. Henderson further suggests that Tocqueville's literary pursuit of his readers' imaginative identification is a quality that links *Democracy* to the writings of Adam Smith.

Careful readers have often taken note of *Democracy*'s humanistic dimensions, but its relationship to other disciplines such as economics and constitutional law has not always been clearly appreciated. Whereas some have accused Tocqueville of ignoring economics altogether, Richard Swedberg, Jon Elster, and others have identified formal aspects of Tocqueville's method that establish his relevance in matters of political economy.[123] Even so, it remains unclear whether Tocqueville is ultimately a friend or foe of market economies and modern capitalism. Critics cite his ambivalence about materialism in America, his worries about "individualism," or his complaints about a new industrial aristocracy. Yet as Rachael K. Behr and Virgil Henry Storr argue persuasively in Chapter 10, Tocqueville's understanding of economics is predicated on the social role of markets. Rather than dissolving civil society and discouraging community, as critics such as Marx have alleged, commercial society facilitates association and technological progress and fosters an important set of commercial virtues. Their careful reading of *Democracy* reveals that the very same habits of sociability, mutual self-interest, and cooperation are essential both for markets and for associations.

Although discussions of American political culture often mention *Democracy*, its comments on the technical workings of the US Constitution have attracted less attention. There may be good reason for this oversight. By his reckoning, America's real Founding was accomplished by the Puritans of 1620 rather than the statesmen of 1776 or 1787–1788. Even so, Tocqueville analyzes the US Constitution at great length in *Democracy*, and we might wonder what his analysis of the various provisions of the US Constitution tells us about the trajectory of American political development, the status of the American Constitution, and the role of the Founding

Fathers. Is *Democracy* still as useful a starting point as, say, *The Federalist*, for studying American political development, or did something change with the advent of the Civil War, the New Deal, the Great Society, and the contemporary welfare state?

As Jeremy D. Bailey demonstrates in Chapter 11, what stands out is how much Tocqueville's interpretation of the US Constitution diverges from *The Federalist*. By showing how Tocqueville understood institutions such as the presidency or federalism, we can better understand the actual workings of the American system. Of particular interest in Bailey's discussion is Tocqueville's view of the presidency. Contrary to Alexander Hamilton's canonical rendition of the US presidency as a counter-majoritarian institution, Tocqueville regards the presidency as popular or majoritarian in theory and practice. In this and other interpretive moves, he follows the Jeffersonian understanding of the Constitution and anticipates contemporary dilemmas of populism, where elections are akin to referenda and the president acts in ways that closely mirror public opinion, for better or worse.

DILEMMAS OF RELIGION AND POLITICAL LIBERTY

Another major theme of *Democracy* is the salutary role of religion in a liberal democracy. As Carson Holloway explains in Chapter 12, Tocqueville's assessment of American Christianity highlights how the forces of religion and politics not only coexist but lend mutual support. As Holloway notes, some of the ways in which Christianity further advances the cause of political liberty in the United States are obvious and rely on a straightforward reading of *Democracy*. Yet Holloway encourages us to look at more subtle dynamics by which the spirit of religion supports political liberty.[124] Religion is perhaps the greatest bulwark against both the mediocrity and the injustice of tyrannical majorities, in Tocqueville's view. It also acts to discourage the pathologies of excessive materialism and individualism. In these and many other cases, Tocqueville falls back on religion as an antidote to numerous ails he glimpses on the horizon of a democratic age.

For all of Tocqueville's optimism about the salutary function of Christianity in America, critics have identified potentially darker aspects as well. Some worry that, while religion once played a healthy role in the United States, with religion and state existing in separate but mutually supportive spheres, this harmony may have been undermined in the intervening centuries.[125] What if neither the state nor religion respects the boundaries Tocqueville elucidated? Worse still, others have warned that religion itself might contribute to the tyranny of the majority, insofar as religious beliefs impose a stifling moral conformity on the whole society.[126]

Joshua Mitchell in Chapter 13 identifies another potentially troubling contemporary tendency to which *Democracy* helps call attention.[127] Holloway and Mitchell concur that Christianity has contributed much that is inspiring to American politics and culture. Puritan New England's intellectual descendants led nineteenth-century abolitionist movements; the civil rights and anti-war movements of the 1950s and 1960s drew inspiration from Christianity, especially the black churches. Constantly challenging injustices and appealing to a higher law, American Christianity has contributed to causes of individual liberty, equality, and social justice. Still, America's Puritan legacy is Janus-faced, Mitchell contends, occasionally giving rise to Manichean intolerance and even persecution. Mitchell worries that, in the current moment, America's Puritanical obsession with sin might assume illiberal forms under the guise of secular progressivism and identity politics.

ENDURING CHALLENGES: DEMOCRATIC EQUALITY RECONSIDERED

Was Tocqueville right about democracy's constitutive features and the challenges it would face in the twenty-first century and beyond? We might be excused for thinking that our contemporary world bears only a passing resemblance to the democratic landscape of Tocqueville's nineteenth century. Much has changed, to be sure. Not even a visionary like Tocqueville could have foreseen the myriad ways that technology has transformed culture and political economy. Contemporary society is not just global in scale but increasingly virtual in format. Much of today's civic life takes place online, anonymously, rather than face-to-face among neighbors in townships and local communities. Nor does Tocqueville seem to have anticipated how the moral, political, and cultural dynamics of democracy would transcend the boundaries of the nation-state. European Union and Brexit, open borders and right-wing populism, mass migrations and sectarian violence, identity politics and insurrections – which, if any, among these late developments are consistent with tendencies identified in *Democracy*? The final three chapters of this volume reckon with how *Democracy* sheds light on central dilemmas of the current age – race, gender, diversity, and inequality – that might seem at first glance foreign to the author. Properly understood, however, *Democracy* offers powerful lessons.

With respect to concerns about diversity and social justice that have come to the foreground in the last decade or so, Tocqueville's ideas are by no means self-evidently helpful. In fact, Tocqueville's views of race, gender, empire, and settler colonialism have been targeted by critics over the past several decades for being illiberal and exclusionary.[128] As Eileen Hunt Botting notes in Chapter 14, however, Tocqueville's views on gender are complex and evolve over the course of his life, even between volumes 1 and 2 of *Democracy*. Botting notes that *Democracy* starts with a somewhat dismissive view of the frivolity of American girls, in whom Tocqueville might even seem to indicate a prurient interest. Yet in the intervening years between the two volumes Tocqueville appears to develop a more appreciative sense of the courage and sacrifices that the institution of marriage requires of American women. What emerges from Botting's portrayal is a Tocqueville who – while perhaps not fully a proto-feminist – nonetheless shares certain sympathies with latter-day feminist criticism about the ways in which American women are captive to the domestic sphere and the unique virtues they may bring to political life.

Race has proven another controversial aspect of Tocqueville's vision of American democracy.[129] *Democracy*'s chapter on the "Three Races" is an extended meditation on the tragic dilemmas of racial exclusion in the United States experienced in different ways by African Americans and Native Americans. Tocqueville might be credited for appreciating, first, that racial exclusion is not monolithic and that the circumstances of African Americans (free and slave) and Native Americans are different. He also deserves credit for his foresight into the seemingly intractable conflicts over race that would continue to vex American society even after the abolition of black chattel slavery; and yet one frustrating feature of *Democracy* is how these meditations on race seem to exist outside of – and in contradiction to – much of what he says elsewhere about the unprecedented "equality of conditions" prevailing throughout the rest of American society.

As Lawrie Balfour suggests in her illuminating comparison between Tocqueville's writings and the novels of Toni Morrison (Chapter 15), Tocqueville's discussion of race may have succeeded in capturing some of the sources of enduring exclusion and injustice in America. Parallels between the literary vignettes of *Democracy* and Morrison's 2008 novel *A Mercy* are striking. Balfour argues, however, that, unlike Morrison, who models a narrative perspective that apprehends racialized injustice from multiple vantages of the people who suffered through these crimes, Tocqueville's literary pretensions offer little in the way of philosophical solutions or concrete political remedies. By accepting racial injustices as given, and indulging in narratives that deny their victims any voice or accessible history, Tocqueville's portrayal of these events serves to enshrine their inevitability. Even with the best of intentions, *Democracy* works better to identify problems than to offer tangible solutions for deeply embedded structural injustices.

As Rogers M. Smith notes in Chapter 16, central to Tocqueville's thesis is his conviction that equality represents the wave of the future. Nothing in America struck Tocqueville so vividly as its equality of conditions.[130] Yet as the struggle for equality has pressed onward it has become clear that our best efforts to secure substantive equality for all may actually require treating different groups differently. How do we deal with the question of equality, Smith wonders, in a world where treating everyone equally – as democracy demands – has proven consistent with significant substantive inequalities? Conversely, how can the growing tendency in American law and public life toward special accommodation of groups by virtue of their differences be squared with Tocqueville's vision of a democratic future? In a world where ensuring formal equality and uniform treatment for all in the eyes of the law has reached its limits, Smith proposes that certain kinds of differential treatment might be justified if – and only if – this unequal treatment is consistent with the Tocquevillean imperative of securing greater equality.

In conclusion, and as these chapters so ably demonstrate, *Democracy* has proven to be an enduring source of philosophical reflection, political inspiration, and cultural criticism in the nearly two centuries since it first appeared. That it continues to resonate with readers around the globe in contexts that are democratic and authoritarian, Western and non-Western, celebratory as well as critical, is a testament to the panoramic scope of the questions it raises and the sheer brilliance of its analysis. Not everything in *Democracy* has passed the test of time; but even where the contemporary world has evolved and new dilemmas have emerged, the book remains an invaluable resource for scholars, engaged citizens, and policymakers in the unfinished work of democracy to which we are collectively dedicated.[131]

NOTES

1. See, most notably, David Riesman, Nathan Glazer, and Reuel Denney, *The Lonely Crowd: A Study of the Changing American Character* (New Haven, CT: Yale University Press, 1950) and Robert Nisbet, *The Quest for Community: A Study in the Ethics of Order and Freedom* (New York: Oxford University Press, 1953).

2. Jean Cohen and Andrew Arato, *Civil Society and Political Theory* (Cambridge, MA: MIT Press, 1994); Joshua Cohen and Joel Rogers, *Associations and Democracy* (London: Verso, 1995); Robert Putnam, *Bowling Alone: The Collapse and Revival of American Community* (New York: Simon & Schuster, 2000); Mark E. Warren, *Democracy and Association* (Princeton: Princeton University Press, 2001).

3. Seymour Martin Lipset, *The First New Nation: The United States in Historical and Comparative Perspective* (New York: Basic Books, 1963); Louis Hartz, *The Liberal Tradition in America* (New York: Harcourt, Brace, 1955); Rogers M. Smith, "Beyond Tocqueville, Myrdal, and Hartz: The Multiple Traditions in America," *American Political Science Review* 87, no. 3 (1993): 549–566; James T. Kloppenberg, *The Virtues of Liberalism* (Oxford: Oxford University Press, 1998), chap. 5.

4. For detailed accounts of Tocqueville's life and the work's composition, see especially George Wilson Pierson, *Tocqueville and Beaumont in America* (New York: Oxford University Press, 1938); James T. Schleifer, *The Making of Tocqueville's Democracy in America* (Chapel Hill: University of North Carolina Press, 1980); André Jardin, *Tocqueville: A Biography*, trans. Lydia Davis and Robert Hemenway (New York: Farrar, Straus and Giroux, 1988); Hugh Brogan, *Alexis de Tocqueville: A Life* (New Haven, CT: Yale University Press, 2007); Leo Damrosch, *Tocqueville's Discovery of America* (New York: Farrar, Straus and Giroux, 2011); Tocqueville, *Alexis de Tocqueville and Gustave de Beaumont in America: Their Friendship and Their Travels*, ed. Olivier Zunz (Charlottesville: University of Virginia Press, 2010).

5. The fruit of this project was published as *On the Penitentiary System in the United States and Its Application to France* (1833).

6. DIA (L) II.2.iii, 506–508; DIA (L) I.2.vii, 246–260; DIA (L) II.4.vi, 690–700.

7. DIA (L) I.1.ii, 49.

8. For a dissenting opinion, see especially Gary Wills, "Did Tocqueville 'Get' America?," *New York Review* 51 (2004), 52–56.

9. DIA (L) "Author's Introduction," 19–20.

10. Noteworthy examples include François-René de Chateaubriand, *Atala, ou Les Amours de deux sauvages dans le désert* (Paris, 1801); Basil Hall, *Travels in North America in the Years 1827 and 1828* (Edinburgh: Cadell & Co., 1829); Frances Trollope, *Domestic Manners of the Americans* (London: Whittaker, Treacher & Co., 1832); Michel Chevalier, *Society,*

Manners, and Politics in the United States (Boston: Weeks, Jordan & Co., 1839). For more in-depth examinations of these and other European encounters with America from a broadly Tocquevillean vantage, see Aurelian Craiutu and Jeffrey Isaacs, eds., *America through European Eyes: British and French Reflections on the New World from the Eighteenth Century to the Present* (University Park: Penn State University Press, 2009).

11. Robert T. Gannett, Jr. has characterized this hermeneutic difficulty with respect to another of Tocqueville's classic works. See Gannett, *Tocqueville Unveiled: The Historian and His Sources for the Old Regime and the Revolution* (Chicago: University of Chicago Press, 2003).

12. For a sense of these reflections and sources, see especially Schleifer, *Making of Democracy in America*; Tocqueville, *Alexis de Tocqueville and Gustave de Beaumont in America*. On Tocqueville's evolving view of the United States and correspondence with associates, see especially Aurelian Craiutu and Jeremy Jennings, eds., *Tocqueville on America after 1840* (Cambridge: Cambridge University Press, 2009).

13. "Letter to Kergorlay, November 10, 1836," in OC 13:1, 418.

14. See especially Melvin Richter, "Comparative Political Analysis in Montesquieu and Tocqueville," *Comparative Politics* 1 (1969): 129–60; Richter, "The Uses of Theory: Tocqueville's Adaptation of Montesquieu," in Melvin Richter, ed., *Essays in Theory and History: An Approach to the Social Sciences* (Cambridge, MA: Harvard University Press, 1970), 74–102; Raymond Aron, *Main Currents in Sociological Thought, Vol. 1: Montesquieu, Auguste Comte, Karl Marx, Alexis de Tocqueville, The Sociologists and the Revolution of 1848* (New York: Basic Books, 1965).

15. On this widely shared comparison, see especially Pierson, *Tocqueville in America*, 4–5.

16. This Pascalian dimension has been explored thoroughly by Peter Augustine Lawler, *The Restless Mind: Alexis de Tocqueville on the Origin and Perpetuation of Human Liberty* (Lanham, MD: Rowman & Littlefield, 1993). Others who have called attention to these religious dimensions of Tocqueville's theory are Joshua Mitchell, *The Fragility of Freedom: Tocqueville on Religion, Democracy, and the American Future* (Chicago: University of Chicago Press, 1999); David Selby, "Tocqueville's Politics of Providence: Pascal, Jansenism, and the Author's Introduction

to *Democracy in America*," *The Tocqueville Review/La revue Tocqueville* 33 (2012), 167–190; Lucien Jaume, *Tocqueville: The Aristocratic Sources of Liberty*, trans. Arthur Goldhammer (Princeton: Princeton University Press, 2013), 158–191.

17. Allan Bloom, *Giants and Dwarfs* (New York: Simon & Schuster, 1990), 312–314. See also Harvey Mitchell, "The Changing Conditions of Freedom: Tocqueville in the Light of Rousseau," *History of Political Thought* 9 (Winter 1988), 431–453; John C. Koritansky, *Alexis de Tocqueville and the New Science of Politics* (Durham, NC: Carolina Academic Publishers, 2009); Mathew Maguire, *The Conversion of Imagination: From Pascal through Rousseau to Tocqueville* (Cambridge, MA: Harvard University Press, 2006); Michael Locke McLendon, *The Psychology of Inequality: Rousseau's "Amour Propre"* (Philadelphia: University of Pennsylvania Press, 2019), chap. 4.

18. DIA (L) II.2.ii, 506–507.

19. For a sense of the enormous range of philosophical figures from antiquity to the seventeenth, eighteenth, and nineteenth centuries that Tocqueville consulted during this period of composition, see Schleifer, *Making of Democracy in America*, 26–27. For an attempt to unveil the sources behind Tocqueville's other masterwork, the *Ancien Régime*, see Gannett, *Tocqueville Unveiled*. François Furet has likewise sought to downplay the influence of particular thinkers and to consider Tocqueville's life, letters, notes, and broader intellectual milieu in light of core questions and dilemmas. See especially François Furet, "The Intellectual Origins of Tocqueville's Thought," *The Tocqueville Review/La revue Tocqueville* 7 (1985), 117–129.

20. Aurelian Craiutu, "Tocqueville and the Political Thought of the French Doctrinaires (Guizot, Royer-Collard, Rémusat)," *History of Political Thought* 20, no. 3 (1999), 456–493. For a sense of differences between Tocqueville and the Doctrinaires, see Françoise Mélonio, *Tocqueville and the French*, trans. Beth G. Raps (Charlottesville: University of Virginia Press, 1998), 7–24, 34–38.

21. Craiutu, "Tocqueville and the French Doctrinaires," 474–475.

22. Craiutu, "Tocqueville and the French Doctrinaires," 479–491.

23. Jaume, *Aristocratic Sources of Liberty*.

24. For a sense of Tocqueville's political theory as deeply inflected with aristocratic sensibilities, see especially Alan Kahan, *Aristocratic*

Liberalism: The Social and Political Thought of Jacob Burckhardt, John Stuart Mill, and Alexis de Tocqueville (New York: Oxford University Press, 1992); Roger Boesche, *The Strange Liberalism of Alexis de Tocqueville* (Ithaca, NY: Cornell University Press, 1987); Sheldon Wolin, *Tocqueville between Two Worlds: The Making of a Political and Theoretical Life* (Princeton: Princeton University Press, 2003); Jaume, *Aristocratic Sources of Liberty*.

25. Jaume, *Aristocratic Sources of Liberty*, 9, 17.

26. "Letter to Beaumont, April 1, 1835," OC 8:1, 151.

27. For comprehensive assessments of the French reception of *Democracy*, see especially Pierson, *Tocqueville in America*, 3–6; Jardin, *Tocqueville*, 224–228; Mélonio, *Tocqueville and the French*; Serge Audier, *Tocqueville retrouvé: Genèse et enjeux du renouveau Tocquevillien français* (Paris: VRIN, 2004).

28. Mélonio, *Tocqueville and the French*, 28.

29. Mélonio, *Tocqueville and the French*; Pierson, *Tocqueville in America*, 3–10, 789–793; Jaume, *Aristocratic Sources of Liberty*; René Rémond, *Les Etats-Unis devant l'opinion française, 1815–1852*, 2 vols. (Paris: Librarie Colin, 1962), 376–389.

30. Léon Faucher, "De la démocratie aux Etats-Unis," *Le Courrier français* (December 24, 1834).

31. Mélonio, *Tocqueville and the French*, 29–30.

32. See, Jardin, *Tocqueville*, 224–227; Mélonio, *Tocqueville and the French*, 33–36; Jaume, *Aristocratic Sources of Liberty*, 36–64.

33. Ernest de Blosseville, "De la démocratie en Amérique," *L'Echo français* (February 11, 1835), 1–3.

34. Mélonio, *Tocqueville and the French*, 33.

35. Francisque de Corcelle, "De La Démocratie Américaine," *Revue des deux mondes* (June 14, 1835), 739–761.

36. Corcelle, "De la Démocratie Américaine," 754.

37. Corcelle, "De la Démocratie Américaine," 757.

38. Louis Blanc, "De la Démocratie en Amérique," *Revue républicaine* (May 1835), 129–163.

39. See, for example, Aurelian Craiutu, *Liberalism under Siege: The Political Thought of the French Doctrinaires* (Lanham, MD: Lexington Books, 2003).

40. Mélonio, *Tocqueville and the French*, 34–35.

41. Édouard Alletz, *De la démocratie nouvelle* (Paris: Lequien, 1837), xi.

42. Alletz, *De la démocratie nouvelle*, viii.

43. Schleifer, *Making of Democracy in America*, 18–34; Brogan, *Alexis de Tocqueville*, 340–372.

44. Mélonio, *Tocqueville and the French*, 55, 66–83.

45. Mélonio, *Tocqueville and the French*; Audier, *Tocqueville retrouvé*.

46. For this characterization of the arc of Tocqueville's influence, see Cheryl Welch, *De Tocqueville* (Oxford: Oxford University Press, 2001), 221–223.

47. Aron, *Main Currents*; François Furet, *Interpreting the French Revolution* (Cambridge: Cambridge University Press, 1981).

48. Among many such works, see Pierre Manent, *Tocqueville et la nature de la démocratie* (Paris: Fayard, 1993); Dominique Schnapper, *Community of Citizens: On the Modern Idea of Nationality* (New Brunswick, NJ: Transaction Publishers, 1998); Louis Dumont, *Essais sur l'individualisme* (Paris: Seuil, 1983); Marcel Gauchet, "Tocqueville, America, and Us: On the Genesis of Democratic Societies," *The Tocqueville Review/La revue Tocqueville* 37 (2016), 163–231; Claude Lefort, *Democracy and Political Theory* (Minneapolis: University of Minnesota Press, 1988); Pierre Rosanvallon, *Democracy Past and Future* (New York: Columbia University Press, 2006).

49. See, for example, Mark Lilla, ed. *New French Thought: Political Philosophy* (Princeton: Princeton University Press, 1994).

50. On Reeves' meeting with Tocqueville and his pained decision to undertake the translation, see Matthew Mancini, *Alexis de Tocqueville and American Intellectuals: From His Times to Ours* (Lanham, MD: Rowman & Littlefield, 2006), 64–67.

51. [Basil Hall], "Tocqueville on the State of America," *Quarterly Review* 57 (1836), 133–134.

52. *British and Foreign Review* 2 (January–April 1836), 304–327.

53. Sir Robert Peel, *A Correct Report of the Speeches Delivered by The Right Honourable Sir Robert Peel, BART., MP., at Glasgow, January 1837* (London: John Murray, 1837), 82–86; Ada Zemach, "Alexis de Tocqueville on England," *Review of Politics* 13 (1951), 331.

54. Jardin, *Tocqueville*, 234; Zemach, "Tocqueville on England," 330–332.

55. John Stuart Mill, "Review of *Democracy in America*," *Edinburgh Review* 72 (1840), 2–3. See also Brogan, *Alexis de Tocqueville: A Life*, 290–291.

56. "*Democracy in America*. By Mons. de Tocqueville," *Blackwoods' Edinburgh Magazine* 37 (1835), 758–766.

57. "*Democracy in America*. By Mons. de Tocqueville," 763–764.

58. "*Democracy in America*. By Mons. de Tocqueville," 765.

59. "*Democracy in America*. By Mons. de Tocqueville," 766.

60. Jardin, *Tocqueville*, 234; Zemach, "Tocqueville on England," 331.

61. Jardin, *Tocqueville*, 233; M. C. M. Simpson, "Preface" to M. C. M. Simpson, ed., *Correspondence and Conversations of Alexis de Tocqueville with Nassau William Senior, 1834–1859* (London: Henry King, 1872), iii–iv. See also Zemach, "Tocqueville on England," 329–343 and Seymour Drescher, *Tocqueville and England* (Cambridge, MA: Harvard University Press, 1964).

62. "Tocqueville to Nassau Senior, February 21, 1835," in Simpson, *Correspondence and Conversations*, 5.

63. "Tocqueville to Nassau Senior, February 21, 1835," 2–6.

64. "Prison Discipline," *Edinburgh Review* 64 (1837), 318–319.

65. "Review of *Democracy in America*," *Edinburgh Review* 72 (1840), 1–47.

66. John Stuart Mill, "Tocqueville on Democracy in America [I] 1835," in *The Collected Works of John Stuart Mill, Vol. XVIII: Essays on Politics and Society*, ed. John M. Robson (Toronto: University of Toronto Press, 1977), 49–91.

67. Mill, "De Tocqueville on Democracy in America [I]," 50–51.

68. Mill, "De Tocqueville on Democracy in America [I]," 57.

69. Mill, "De Tocqueville on Democracy in America [I]," 63.

70. Mill, "Considerations on Representative Government," in *On Liberty and Other Essays*, ed. John Gray (Oxford: Oxford Classics, 1991), chap. VIII.

71. Mill, "De Tocqueville on Democracy in America [I]," 74–80.

72. John Stuart Mill, "Tocqueville on Democracy in America [II] 1840," in *The Collected Works of John Stuart Mill, Vol. XVIII: Essays on Politics and Society*, ed. John M. Robson (Toronto: University of Toronto Press, 1977), 190–200.

73. Compare Mélonio, *Tocqueville and the French*, 70–1.

74. The long and fraught relationship between Tocqueville and Mill is immensely complicated. For a sense of their affinities and disagreements, see especially H. O. Pappe, "Mill and Tocqueville," *Journal of the History of Ideas* 25 (1964), 217–234; James T. Schleifer, *Tocqueville* (Cambridge: Polity, 2018), 131–133.

75. John Stuart Mill, "On Liberty," in *On Liberty and Other Essays*, ed. John Gray (Oxford: Oxford World Classics, 1991), 8.

76. Mill, "On Liberty," 73, 81–82.

77. Mill, "On Liberty," 8–9.

78. "Mill to Tocqueville, August 9, 1842," OC 6:1, 334–338.

79. As Pappe has observed, Tocqueville apparently "disappeared" from Mill's corpus between the review article of 1840 and explicit references to him by name in later works of the 1850s and 1860s. Nonetheless, it is not hard to identify traces of Tocqueville's influence in Mill's major works of the 1840s such as the *Logic* (1843) and *Principles of Political Economy* (1848). Compare Pappe, "Mill and Tocqueville," 218–220.

80. Mill, *Autobiography* (London: Penguin, 1989), chap. 6.

81. Mill, "Centralization," in *The Collected Works of John Stuart Mill, Vol XIX: Essays on Politics and Society*, ed. John M. Robson (Toronto: University of Toronto Press, 1977), 580–614.

82. Mill, *Principles of Political Economy* (New York: Harper & Brothers, 1885), book V, chap. xi.

83. Drescher, *Tocqueville and England*, 149.

84. For an overview of this genre and some of the standard stereotypes of American "barbarism" by European visitors, see especially Robert H. Wiebe, *Self-Rule: A Cultural History of American Democracy* (Chicago: University of Chicago Press, 1995), chap. 2.

85. "Review of Democracy in America, by Alexis de Tocqueville," *American Quarterly Review* 19 (1836), 124–128. We find the same complaints about European visitors, and appreciation of Tocqueville's relative objectivity, in Edward Everett's review: "De Tocqueville's Democracy," *North American Review* (July 1836), 179–182.

86. "Review of Democracy in America," 135–140.

87. "Review of Democracy in America," 142.

88. "Review of Democracy in America," 142.

89. "Review of Democracy in America," 165.

90. Olivier Zunz, "Tocqueville and the Americans," in Cheryl B. Welch, ed., *The Cambridge Companion to Tocqueville* (Cambridge: Cambridge University Press, 2006), 367–369.

91. "Review of Democracy in America," 152.

92. "European Views of American Democracy, Part I," *The United States Magazine, and Democratic Review* 1 (1837), 102–104.

93. "Review of Democracy in America," 158.

94. Everett, "De Tocqueville's Democracy," 193. On the trope of American "barbarism," see Wiebe, *Self-Rule*, chap. 2.

95. Everett, "De Tocqueville's Democracy," 203.

96. Everett, "De Tocqueville's Democracy," 203–204.

97. DIA (L) I.2.vi, 237.

98. Alexis de Tocqueville, *Democracy in America*, trans. Henry Reeve (New York: Adlard & Saunders, 1838), with a preface by John Canfield Spencer.

99. See, for one influential example, Robert Nisbet, "Many Tocquevilles," *American Scholar* 46, no. 1 (Winter 1977), 59–75.

100. Mancini, *Tocqueville and American Intellectuals*. For a contrary view of the work's twentieth-century genealogy that differs considerably from Mancini's characterization of the book's continuous availability and unbroken influence, see Filipe Carreira da Silva and Monica Brito Vieira, "Books that Matter: The Case of Tocqueville's *Democracy in America*," *The Sociological Quarterly* 61, no. 4 (2020), 703–726.

101. The historian Michael Kammen famously declared Tocqueville to be the favorite philosopher of American conservatism. See Kammen, *Alexis de Tocqueville and Democracy in America* (Washington, DC: Library of Congress, 1998), 34–38. For more on intellectual appropriations of Tocqueville by the American Right, see Welch, *De Tocqueville*, 245–248 and Mancini, *Tocqueville and American Intellectuals*, 202–212.

102. Notably, Francis Fukuyama, *End of History and the Last Man* (New York: Free Press, 1992).

103. Jan Kubik, *Power of Symbols against the Symbols of Power: The Rise of Solidarity and the Fall of State Socialism in Poland* (University Park: Penn State University Press, 1994); Marc Morjé Howard, *The Weakness of Civil Society in Post-Communist Europe* (Cambridge: Cambridge University Press, 2003).

104. For a fuller account of this engagement with Tocqueville by Eastern and Western European intellectuals, see for example Françoise Mélonio, "Tocqueville à l'Est" *The Tocqueville Review/La revue Tocqueville* 15 (1994), 193–205 and Aurelian Craiutu, "Tocqueville and Eastern Europe," in Christine Dunn Henderson, ed., *Tocqueville's Voyages: The Evolution of His Ideas and Their Journey Beyond His Time* (Indianapolis: Liberty Fund, 2014), 390–424.

105. For example, Aurelian Craiutu and Sheldon Gellar, eds., *Conversations with Tocqueville: The Global Democratic Revolution in the Twenty-First Century* (Lanham, MD: Rowman & Littlefield, 2009).

106. Putnam, *Bowling Alone*.

107. Robert Putnam, Robert Leonardi, and Raffaella Nanetti, *Making Democracy Work: Civic Traditions in Modern Italy* (Princeton: Princeton University Press, 1993).

108. On this "return of civil society" on the part of Eastern European intellectuals and its relationship to Tocqueville, see Aurelian Craiutu, "From the Social Contract to the Art of Association: A Tocquevillian Perspective," *Social Philosophy & Policy* 25, no. 2 (2008), 263–265; Vladimir Tismaneanu, *Reinventing Politics: Eastern Europe from Stalin to Havel* (New York: Free Press, 1992); and Krishan Kumar, *1989: Revolutionary Ideas and Ideals* (Minneapolis: University of Minnesota Press, 2001).

109. Warren, *Democracy and Association*; Cohen and Arato, *Civil Society and Political Theory*; Ernest Gellner, *Conditions of Liberty: Civil Society and Its Rivals* (London: Penguin, 1994); Michael Foley and Bob Edwards, "The Paradox of Civil Society," *Journal of Democracy* 7, no. 3 (1996), 38–52; Archon Fung, "Associations and Democracy: Between Theories, Hopes, and Realities," *Annual Review of Sociology* 29, no. 1 (2003), 515–539.

110. DIA (L) II.2.v, 513.

111. DIA (L) II.2.v, 517; DIA (L) I.2.iv, 189. On this aspect of Tocqueville as an anticipation of the neo-Tocquevillean arguments of Robert Putnam and others, see especially Robert T. Gannett, Jr., "Bowling Ninepins in Tocqueville's Township," *American Political Science Review* 97, no. 1 (2003), 1–16.

112. Notable exceptions in the civil society literature include Michael Walzer, "The Idea of Civil Society: A Path to Social Reconstruction," *Dissent* 39 (Spring 1991), 292–304; Nancy Rosenblum, *Membership and Morals: The Personal Uses of Pluralism in America*. (Princeton: Princeton University Press, 1998); Simone Chambers, "A Critical Theory of Civil Society," in Simone Chambers, ed., *Alternative Conceptions of Civil Society* (Princeton: Princeton University Press, 2002), 90–110; and Simone Chambers and Jeffrey Kopstein, "Bad Civil Society," *Political Theory* 29, no. 6 (2001), 837–865; Jennet Kirkpatrick, *Uncivil*

Disobedience: Studies in Violence and Democratic Politics (Princeton: Princeton University Press, 2008).

113. This point is nicely developed by Foley and Edwards, "Paradox of Civil Society."

114. For a more extensive account of the ambivalence of civil society – more generally as well as specifically in Tocqueville – see Richard Boyd, *Uncivil Society: The Perils of Pluralism and the Making of Modern Liberalism* (Lanham, MD: Lexington Books, 2004), especially chap. 6; Craiutu, "From the Social Contract to the Art of Association," 263–287; Jeffrey C. Alexander, "Tocqueville's Two Forms of Association," *The Tocqueville Review/La revue Tocqueville* 27, no. 2 (2006), 175–190; Dana Villa, "Tocqueville and Civil Society," in Cheryl B. Welch, ed., *The Cambridge Companion to Tocqueville* (Cambridge: Cambridge University Press, 2006), 216–244.

115. DIA (L) I.2.iv, 193.

116. DIA (L) I.2.iv, 193.

117. DIA (L) I.2.i, 174–9; I.2.iv, 192–195.

118. DIA (L) II.2.vii, 521–522.

119. DIA (L) II.2.vii, 522–523.

120. Foley and Edwards, "Paradox of Civil Society," 46.

121. Tocqueville documents two contemporaneous instances of mob violence (actual and implicit) that he regards as evidence of the tyranny of the majority. See DIA (L) I.2.vii, 252–253n4. For historical context, see especially Keith Whittington, "Revisiting Tocqueville's America: Society, Politics, and Association in the Nineteenth Century," *American Behavioral Scientist* 42, no. 1 (1998), 21–32.

122. On the question of whether *Democracy* is best understood as one or two different works, see especially Seymour Drescher, "Tocqueville's Two Democracies," *Journal of the History of Ideas* 25, no. 2 (1964), 201–216; Jean-Claude Lamberti, *Tocqueville and the Two Democracies* (Cambridge, MA: Harvard University Press, 1989); and James T. Schleifer, "How Many Democracies?" in Eduardo Nolla, ed., *Liberty, Equality, Democracy* (New York: New York University Press, 1992), 193–206.

123. August Nimtz, *Marx, Tocqueville and Race in America: The "Absolute Democracy" or "Defiled Republic"* (Lanham, MD: Lexington Books, 2003). By contrast, see Richard Swedberg, *Tocqueville's Political*

Economy (Princeton: Princeton University Press, 2009) and Jon Elster, *Alexis de Tocqueville: The First Social Scientist* (Cambridge: Cambridge University Press, 2009).

124. For other nuanced views of the indirect but essential effects of religion for democracy, see Catherine Zuckert, "Not by Preaching: Tocqueville on the Role of Religion in American Democracy," *Review of Politics* 43, no. 2 (1981), 259–280 and Alan Kahan, *Tocqueville, Democracy and Religion: Checks and Balances for Democratic Souls* (Oxford: Oxford University Press, 2015).

125. William Galston, "Tocqueville on Liberalism and Religion" *Social Research* 54, no. 3 (1987), 499–518.

126. Dana Villa, *Teachers of the People: Political Education in Rousseau, Hegel, Tocqueville and Mill* (Chicago: University of Chicago Press, 2017).

127. For a more optimistic rendition, see Mitchell, *Fragility of Freedom*.

128. Cheryl Welch, "Colonial Violence and the Rhetoric of Evasion: Tocqueville on Algeria," *Political Theory* 31, no. 2 (2003), 235–264; Jennifer Pitts, *A Turn to Empire: The Rise of Imperial Liberalism in Britain and France* (Princeton: Princeton University Press, 2005); Laura Janara, *Democracy Growing Up: Authority, Autonomy, and Passion in Tocqueville's Democracy in America* (Albany: State University of New York Press, 2002). For a more appreciative reading of Tocqueville on gender, see the classic essay by Delba Winthrop, "Tocqueville's American Woman and the 'True Conception of Democratic Progress'," *Political Theory* 14, no. 2 (1986), 239–261.

129. Jack Turner, "American Individualism and Structural Injustice: Tocqueville, Gender, and Race," *Polity* 40, no. 2 (2008), 197–215; Jenny Ikuta and Trevor Latimer, "Aristocracy in America: Tocqueville on White Supremacy," *Journal of Politics* 83, no. 2 (2021), 547–559. For a more sympathetic reading, see Alvin B. Tillery, Jr., "Tocqueville As Critical Race Theorist: Whiteness As Property, Interest Convergence, and the Limits of Jacksonian Democracy," *Political Research Quarterly* 62, no. 4 (2009), 639–652.

130. DIA (L) "Author's Introduction," 9.

131. While we would typically use gender-neutral language, this volume does not. All the quotes from Tocqueville and his contemporaries use he/him/his pronouns, and thus we follow suit for the sake of consistency.

PART I   **Sources and Contexts**

I Tocqueville and the Philosophy of the Enlightenment

Ryan Patrick Hanley

Tocqueville finds few phenomena entirely good or entirely bad. Despotism he of course thinks an evil without an upside. Yet when it comes to the principal categories and concepts of *Democracy in America* (*DIA*) – equality, commerce, individualism, indeed democracy itself – Tocqueville tends to present these as having both benefits and costs. This tendency is especially evident in his extended engagement with seventeenth- and eighteenth-century philosophy, the philosophy of the Enlightenment.

On the one hand, Tocqueville is manifestly critical of Enlightenment philosophy and at several points presents it as highly pernicious – most notably in his critiques of its legacy with regard to materialism and secularization. Beneath this obvious and vociferous critique of the Enlightenment, though, lies another and very different sort of engagement with the philosophy of the seventeenth and eighteenth centuries in *DIA*. On this front, Tocqueville often engages in robust if unacknowledged ways with central doctrines of key Enlightenment philosophers, borrowing and building on them in ways that suggest not hostility but affinity.

The aim of this chapter is to document these two sides of Tocqueville's engagement with the philosophy of the Enlightenment in *DIA* and suggest one way in which they might be seen as working together. The limits of space available here of course make it impossible to provide any comprehensive review of Tocqueville's engagement with his early modern philosophical sources.[1] My aim is much more modest, namely to call attention to certain details of what has been called Tocqueville's "hidden dialogue with the writers of the seventeenth and eighteenth centuries," and thereby to bring to the

47

forefront a specific guiding thread that might help us better understand how exactly the two sides of Tocqueville's treatment of the Enlightenment might be seen as two sides of the same coin.[2] By so doing, I especially hope to show that Tocqueville's view of the Enlightenment – which on its face indeed seems "occasionally ambivalent"[3] – is in fact guided by a set of consistent principles and specifically his preference for moderation over radicalism.

Put simply, this chapter's central argument is that Tocqueville cannot be reduced to being somehow either "for" or "against" Enlightenment. Charles Taylor famously divided the warring camps over modernity's legacy into "boosters" and "knockers."[4] Yet Tocqueville is neither a mere booster nor a mere knocker; his assessment of Enlightenment philosophy is more nuanced and closer to his essential position on democracy. One especially insightful formulation of that position puts it this way: "from the perspective of justice, Tocqueville preferred modern democracy, though from the perspective of freedom and grandeur he preferred pre-modern aristocracy."[5] Much the same might be said of his position on the philosophy of the Enlightenment: from the perspective of faith, Tocqueville was critical of the philosophy of the Enlightenment, yet from the perspective of justice and human well-being, Tocqueville clearly preferred the Enlightenment to its alternatives.

To this end, what follows begins by profiling Tocqueville's critique of Enlightenment philosophy. This critique focuses on the Enlightenment's role in encouraging the spread of several phenomena that Tocqueville regards as deeply pernicious to morality and political order, including materialism and secularization and a particular form of rationalism. The chapter then turns to the more positive engagement with the Enlightenment that can also be found in *DIA*, albeit less explicitly. In its pages, Tocqueville frequently invokes key Enlightenment concepts, often without acknowledgment and indeed often in the service of demonstrating that modernization has brought many gains in addition to its many clear costs. Taken together, I hope to show, these two sides of his engagement can be seen as two sides of the same coin, namely a hostility to the hyperrationalism of the Radical Enlightenment and an embrace of the more nuanced understandings of both human nature and a political order characteristic of the Moderate Enlightenment.[6]

THE FIRST FACE OF ENLIGHTENMENT: RADICALISM AND RATIONALISM

In both *DIA* and *The Old Regime*, Tocqueville's most prominent engagement with the Enlightenment is with its most radical side. Indeed, in both works he explicitly criticizes Enlightenment philosophy for formulating and propagating doctrines of materialism, secularism, and hyperrationalism. This critique is especially evident in the later book, which devotes two full chapters to the eighteenth-century philosophers' war on revealed religion, a war waged with "a kind of fury," in which ostensibly charitable minds "worked constantly and ardently to sever souls from the faith that had filled them."[7] Here, Tocqueville even goes so far as to identify the whole of Enlightenment political philosophy with this single-minded aim, thus his claim that "what may properly be called the political philosophy of the eighteenth century consisted of this single idea," namely "that it would be good to substitute basic and simple principles, derived from reason and natural law, for the complicated and traditional customs which ruled the society of their times." Animated by "a disgust for old things and for tradition," the *philosophes* are thus portrayed as seeking "to rebuild contemporary society according to an entirely new plan, that each of them drew from the inspiration of his reason alone."[8]

What Tocqueville thinks of all of this is clear enough; referring directly to Diderot and Helvétius, he tells us that the political experience of the decades since the Revolution "has been enough to disgust us with this dangerous literature."[9] Yet this animus was not limited to the older man who wrote the *Old Regime*. Two decades earlier, he had already reached these same conclusions, and indeed Tocqueville writes into *DIA* precisely this same critique of the Enlightenment's anti-theological campaign on behalf of secularization and reason. Thus, in the most explicit account of the Enlightenment that we are offered in *DIA*, Tocqueville emphasizes that "the philosophers of the eighteenth century" were chiefly concerned to hasten "the gradual weakening of beliefs" – "religious zeal, they say, will be extinguished as freedom and enlightenment increase."[10]

As a political sociologist, Tocqueville is skeptical of this claim, which he regards as altogether too "simple." The example of America, in which enlightenment and faith have grown together, he takes as clear evidence that "the facts do not accord with this theory."[11] In general, however, Tocqueville treats the Enlightenment and its philosophy less from the perspective of the impartial scientific observer than from the perspective of one deeply concerned by its normative implications. Interestingly, just as he portrays the *philosophes* as hostile to faith, Tocqueville often portrays himself as seeking to unite those concerned with the future of society to combat the Enlightenment legacies of materialism and pantheism. At several points in *DIA*, we thus find conspicuous calls to arms meant to rouse friends of greatness and genuine individualism to band together to resist this side of the Enlightenment. On this front Spinoza, the hero of Radical Enlightenment, is presented as the figurehead of the enemy movement.[12] Spinoza's pantheism is thus described as a system that not only has "made great progress in our day" but "destroys human individuality"; and to this, we are told, there can be only one response: "all who remain enamored of the genuine greatness of man should unite and do combat against it."[13] Here and elsewhere, when Tocqueville calls on the good and the great to come together to resist materialism and pantheism, it is this Spinozistic or Radical Enlightenment that he has squarely in his sights.[14]

Spinoza, however, is of course only one among several of the seventeenth-century champions of Enlightenment rationalism to figure in *DIA*. Even more central than Spinoza to Tocqueville's core concerns in the text is Descartes. The second volume of *DIA* famously begins with the striking claim that America is "the one country in the world where the precepts of Descartes are least studied and best followed."[15] Tocqueville's arresting formulation here of what he calls Americans' "philosophical method" cannot help but capture our attention, yet it is crucial to see what Tocqueville is and is not claiming here. His claim is that Americans are Cartesians insofar as "in most of the operations of the mind, each American calls only on the individual effort of his reason."[16] Tocqueville clearly finds much to admire in this commitment to intellectual self-reliance: in the hands of genius, intellectual self-reliance is what makes any genuine intellectual progress possible – as Tocqueville's own example arguably shows. Yet Tocqueville also finds much of concern in the Americans' efforts to translate enlightenment into mass or popular enlightenment. First, the general propensity of the Americans to go it alone in matters of the mind severs their minds from the minds of yesterday; disdaining the authority of their intellectual predecessors, they deprive themselves of a useful foundation on which they might build. So too they sever themselves from any genius that may exist in their midst; always committed to equality and "not perceiving in anyone among themselves incontestable signs of greatness and superiority," each "withdraws narrowly into himself and claims to judge the world from there."[17] In committing himself to going it alone, however, the American only goes as far as his individual reason will take him. As a result, all that lies beyond the narrow limits of his direct empirical experience becomes anathema; Americans thus "willingly deny what they cannot comprehend" and have "little faith in the extraordinary and an almost invincible distaste for the supernatural."[18]

The democratization of enlightenment that Descartes represents is thus at once the safeguard of freedom of thought as well as the impediment to genuine freedom of thought. The Americans' love of intellectual independence leads them to resist any attempt by the powers-that-be to limit their freedoms at the same time that it truncates the horizons of their intellects by leading them to resent all that lies beyond their narrow comprehension. The promise of rational individualism thus gives way to intellectual conformity, intellectual mediocrity, and "the loss of genuine intellectual liberty."[19] Enlightenment thusly conceived is less an expansion of thought than a self-imposed limitation on the breadth and the depth and the height of the range of ideas available to the enlightened; and it is a movement that has been making its way to this point for some time, hence Tocqueville's understanding of the progress of early modern philosophy:

> In the sixteenth century, the reformers submit to individual reason some of the dogmas of the ancient faith, but they continue to exclude all others from discussion. In the seventeenth, Bacon, in the natural sciences, and Descartes, in philosophy properly so-called, abolish the received formulas, destroy the empire of traditions, and overturn the authority of the master. The philosophers of the eighteenth century, finally generalizing the same principle, undertake to submit the objects of all beliefs to the individual examination of each man. Who does not see that Luther, Descartes, and Voltaire made use of the same method, and that they differ only in the greater or lesser use that they claimed one might make of it?[20]

Theirs was, in the end, a "philosophic method with whose aid one could readily attack all ancient things and open the way to all new ones."[21] However dazzling this may seem (and however useful this may in fact be in the right hands), though, enlightenment of this sort strikes Tocqueville as deeply inimical to social and political stability, hence his insistence on the need to establish certain firewalls capable of holding back the full effects of Radical Enlightenment. Yet in fact it was precisely in the thought of several other seventeenth- and eighteenth-century philosophers that he discovered a set of resources indispensable to his efforts to mitigate the potential implications of this side of the Enlightenment.

THE SECOND FACE OF ENLIGHTENMENT: MONTESQUIEU, PASCAL, AND ROUSSEAU

To this point, we have focused on Tocqueville's critique of Enlightenment philosophy and in particular the encouragement it gave to materialism and secularism. Yet the story of his engagement with the philosophy of the seventeenth and eighteenth centuries of course hardly ends here. In concluding *DIA*, Tocqueville memorably announces, "I see that goods and evils are split equally enough in the world."[22] The same might be said of his vision of Enlightenment philosophy itself. For all the pernicious implications he found in its radical wing, another more moderate side, he understood, offered several resources well worthy of the attention of democratic peoples concerned to resist the more pernicious tendencies of Radical Enlightenment.

To see this, we need to shift our attention from Tocqueville's engagement with such thinkers as Bacon and Descartes and Spinoza and the later *philosophes* to his engagement with another group of seventeenth- and eighteenth-century thinkers. A letter well known to Tocqueville scholars provides a convenient point of departure for this inquiry. In 1836, Tocqueville told his friend Louis de Kergorlay that "there are three men with whom I live every day."[23] He went on to name the three as Montesquieu, Pascal, and Rousseau, and on the basis of such these three thinkers have often been seen as the "most influential overall" on his thought.[24] Now, whether indeed these thinkers should be understood, individually or collectively, as decisive influences on *DIA* is not my concern here; my concern is simply to show that each author helped Tocqueville to see how certain concepts in Enlightenment philosophy could offer salutary checks on the implications of other of its concepts.

We begin with Montesquieu. Montesquieu's influence on Tocqueville has been well canvased. Among the most prominent and explicit connections that scholars have noted is the way in which Tocqueville's engagement with Montesquieu shaped his understanding of despotism.[25] Both Tocqueville and Montesquieu regard despotism as the political *summum malum*, a state of political decay healthy states must always strive to avoid. Yet of course Tocqueville's and Montesquieu's views on despotism have their differences; for Tocqueville, it is mass or democratic despotism that is to be most feared – the despotism that emerges directly from the democratic republic – whereas Montesquieu's concern was the "indefinite power" of absolute princes who succeed republics.[26] Elsewhere, Tocqueville also explicitly distances himself from his predecessor on the question of whether despotism has "a force of its own";[27] but this unto itself leads to a second point of contact between the two thinkers. As many have noted, both Tocqueville and Montesquieu evaluate various political orders by the degree of their relative adherence to the fundamental principle that defines them.[28] Montesquieu calls this the regime's "principle" while Tocqueville invokes the idea of its "social state."[29] Yet these terminological differences aside, the sociologies of both thinkers are connected by their shared commitment to evaluating regimes in terms of their internal coherence rather than in terms of comparative hierarchies.

For all this, Tocqueville's greatest debt to Montesquieu, and indeed the debt that is of most concern to us given the substantive themes of this chapter, concerns the concept of mores (moeurs). Mores famously lie at the very heart of Montesquieu's political analysis in the Spirit of the Laws, and they are no less central to the political and philosophical analysis of DIA. Tocqueville indeed could hardly be more forthright on this front, insisting that "the importance of mores is a common truth to which study and experience constantly lead back" – a truth that Tocqueville goes so far as to say he placed in his mind "as a central point": "I perceive it at the end of all my ideas."[30] Mores are thus no less central to Tocqueville than to Montesquieu. Moreover, both thinkers have roughly the same concepts and categories in mind in invoking mores. For Tocqueville, mores not only comprise what he famously called "the habits of the heart" but also extend "to the different notions that men possess, to the various opinions that are current in their midst, and to the sum of ideas of which the habits of the mind are formed."[31] Yet all of this suggests only the centrality of mores to Tocqueville's political sociology. Of particular interest to students of his normative political philosophy, however, is the role Tocqueville attributes to mores in sustaining a democratic body politic and indeed in enabling democracy to resist the more radical side of Enlightenment. Tocqueville is clear in insisting that it is mores that prevent the degeneration of democracy into despotism: "I consider mores to be one of the great general causes to which the maintenance of a democratic republic in the United States can be attributed."[32] The preservation of social stability thus depends on the preservation of mores, and indeed not only must one "attribute the maintenance of democratic institutions in the United States to circumstances, to laws, and to mores" but it is mores that prevent the loss of freedom in democracies.[33] Tocqueville himself claims that demonstrating this point is his "goal": "to show, by the example of America, that laws and above all mores can permit a democratic people to remain free."[34]

Montesquieu thus taught Tocqueville the indispensability of mores to both political understanding and political stability. Yet saying that mores are necessary invites at least two further questions. In the first place, which mores exactly are necessary? Second, why exactly are mores necessary? Answering these questions, in turn, requires us to shift attention to Tocqueville's engagement with his other two daily authors. We might begin with the second question: why mores? To this, Tocqueville argues mores are necessary in democratic ages because they preserve a social bond that would otherwise be ruptured by the pernicious tendencies of rational individualism characteristic of American Cartesianism and indeed democracy more generally. Tocqueville knows despotism thrives on the "isolation" of human beings – much as Montesquieu emphasizes in his descriptions of the seraglio in *Persian Letters*.[35] Indeed, one of the most worrisome aspects of the philosophical methods of the Americans to Tocqueville is precisely that these philosophical methods do much of despotism's work for it. Thus, as the American tends to "form all his opinions and to pursue the truth in isolation down paths cleared by him alone," it is precisely to counter the potential political effects of this isolation that Tocqueville recommends those "opinions men receive on trust" as an indispensable bulwark against pernicious individualism:

> It is easy to see that there is no society that can prosper without such beliefs, or rather that there is none that could survive this way; for without common ideas there is no common action, and without common action, men still exist, but a social body does not. Thus in order that there be society, and all the more, that this society prosper, it is necessary that all the minds of the citizens always be brought and held together by some principal ideas, and that cannot happen unless each of them sometimes comes to draw his opinions from one and the same source and unless each consents to receive a certain number of ready-made beliefs.[36]

Democracy requires a common commitment to shared beliefs – beliefs that are inherited rather than invented, received rather than reasoned out – if one hopes to prevent it from degenerating into despotism.

Yet even to put matters this way is to invite another question: inherited or received from whom? To see this, we need to turn to Tocqueville's engagement with Rousseau that was invoked in his letter to Kergorlay. Now, at first glance, that Tocqueville would have found much to sympathize with in Rousseau's political thought may strike some as odd. In both Tocqueville's day and our own, Rousseau of course has often been regarded as a chief inspiration of and influence on the Revolution that Tocqueville himself famously described and decried. Whether or not, however, Rousseau deserves to be seen as a father of the Revolution, it remains the case that Tocqueville was deeply indebted to Rousseau, a fact that may seem somewhat less incongruous once we appreciate (as scholars now do better than ever) the degree to which Rousseau drew from Montesquieu.[37] In any case, readers of Rousseau and Tocqueville cannot help but be struck by many parallels in their thought. On the most general front, Tocqueville shares Rousseau's commitment to seeing the progress of modernity as neither an unmitigated evil nor an unalloyed blessing. Indeed, while Rousseau's *Discourse*

on Inequality – the text generally thought to have been the most significant of Rousseau's for Tocqueville[38] – is often regarded and remembered
as an anti-modern screed, the truth, as more careful readers know well,
is that Rousseau is very explicit in insisting that amidst the vast number
of "bad things" that the modern march of progress has brought, there are
also a number of "good things" as well – a more sober if critical assessment that anticipates in both style and substance Tocqueville's essential position in the closing of *DIA*.[39] On a more fine-grained level, one
finds throughout *DIA* invocations of several of Rousseau's most characteristic and original ideas in the *Discourse on Inequality*. Thus, when
Tocqueville says of the human being that "one feature is peculiar to him
alone" and identifies this feature as "the indefinite faculty of perfecting
himself," he draws on one of Rousseau's most famous conceptual
innovations.[40] When he calls attention to the degree to which democratic social life is shaped by "the love of esteem, the need of real
interest, the taste for power and attention," he draws on a concept of
amour propre central to Rousseau (among others).[41] When he tells us
that patriotism "most often is only an extension of individual selfishness," he restates Rousseau's theory of patriotism.[42] Finally, when he
insists that "the great object of justice is to substitute the idea of right for
that of violence," he restates the core problem that Rousseau takes as his
point of departure in the *Social Contract*.[43]

Allusions and general parallels aside, though, for our purposes
one particular point of contact between the two thinkers is especially
significant, namely their views on the origin or source of mores. Both
Tocqueville and Rousseau indeed agree that democratic peoples cannot be left to discover mores on their own but require the guidance of
those capable of fashioning mores suited to them. In Rousseau, this
idea famously emerges in his notorious account of the legislator who
provides direction to the general will by shaping mores.[44] Tocqueville
cites Alexander Hamilton to the same effect:

> It is a just observation that the people commonly intend the public
> good. This often applies to their very errors. But their good sense

would despise the adulator who should pretend that they always reason right about the means of promoting it. They know from experience that they sometimes err. And the wonder is that they so seldom err as they do, beset as they continually are by the wiles of parasites and sycophants . . . When occasions present themselves in which the interests of the people are at variance with their inclinations, it is the duty of the persons whom they have appointed to be the guardians of those interests to withstand the temporary delusion in order to give them time and opportunity for more cool and sedate reflection.[45]

Tocqueville thus would have found in both Hamilton and Rousseau, among others, the idea that, while the will of a democratic people ought always to be regarded, this will is not itself infallible but requires direction, and specifically direction by those capable of giving it mores.

Where Montesquieu taught Tocqueville the import of mores, Rousseau then offered him guidance on the source of mores. Yet it was to Pascal rather than either Montesquieu or Rousseau that Tocqueville turned for guidance on the question of which mores are best suited to a democratic people. As scholars have often noted, Pascal was a leading influence on Tocqueville.[46] Not only does Tocqueville explicitly invoke Pascal more often than either Montesquieu or Rousseau but he also is especially explicit in his admiration of the image Pascal presents of a truth-seeker in action.[47] Here, though, I want to focus on two other sides of Tocqueville's engagement with Pascal, each of which concern his interest in mores.

First, Pascal helped to illuminate for Tocqueville the ways in which democracy can corrupt mores and specifically the encouragement it gives to "restiveness of heart."[48] In his *Pensées*, Pascal famously documented the misery of human restiveness.[49] One clearly hears these same laments echoing across *DIA* and its accounts of the

way in which pursuit of social equality and individual material comforts together serve to torment the democratic soul. Thus Tocqueville:

> Democratic institutions awaken and flatter this passion for
> equality without ever being able to satisfy it entirely. Every day
> this complete equality eludes the hands of the people at the
> moment when they believe they have seized it, and it flees, as
> Pascal said, in an eternal flight; the people become heated in the
> search for this good, all the more precisely as it is near enough to be
> known, far enough not to be tasted.[50]

Pascal clearly shaped Tocqueville's understanding of restiveness; but
Pascal also helped Tocqueville explain the ways in which restiveness
might be resisted. Most importantly, he helped Tocqueville appreciate
the ways in which religion – and specifically the longing for the infinite
that Tocqueville privileges within religion – can help to lead human
beings out of themselves in the self-transcendent quest both for greatness and for God. Now Pascal of course was hardly Tocqueville's only
source on these questions; Pascal was himself only one of a number of
participants in the leading philosophical and theological controversy
of late seventeenth-century France, that concerning the relationship of
self-love to pure love. This debate has largely escaped the attention of
English-language scholars, yet it is crucial to understanding later theories of self-love in the Enlightenment.[51] It is especially crucial for appreciation of Tocqueville and his thought. As Lucien Jaume has recently
and rightly noted, Tocqueville's famous concept of "self-interest rightly
understood" was itself in fact a "commonplace" in seventeenth-century
French moralism.[52] Yet, in addition to this idea of self-interest rightly
understood, Tocqueville also drew from Pascal and his fellow Jansenists
a commitment to and fascination with "moral grandeur."[53] Take, for
example, his summary statement of aristocratic morality:

> When the world was led by a few powerful and wealthy individuals,
> these liked to form for themselves a sublime idea of the duties of

man; they were pleased to profess that it is glorious to forget oneself and that it is fitting to do good without self-interest like God himself. This was the official doctrine at the time in the matter of morality.[54]

Moral greatness – specifically understood as the transcendence of narrow self-love via the capacity to "forget oneself" – was, for Tocqueville, not merely the vestige of a bygone age but an indispensable virtue that modern democracies needed to preserve in order to survive.

ENLIGHTENMENT BEYOND FRANCE: AMERICA, ENGLAND, AND SCOTLAND

Tocqueville's engagement with Montesquieu and Rousseau and Pascal attests to his capacity to find in certain early modern French thinkers the resources to counter strains to be found elsewhere in the French Enlightenment. Yet Montesquieu's reading was of course hardly limited by the boundaries of his homeland. In particular, his engagement with many of the leading anglophone thinkers of the Enlightenment suggests not merely the extent of his influences but also his concern to discover further afield other resources that were also capable of advancing the cause of Moderate Enlightenment.

Among the most striking of Tocqueville's references to anglophone authors are his many references to American thinkers. Across *DIA*, Tocqueville invokes the ideas and texts of several of the leading thinkers of the founding generation, including Washington, Hamilton, Madison, and Jefferson. Oftentimes his references are only factual; Jefferson's *Notes on the State of Virginia* is, for example, a frequent source for Tocqueville's understanding of physical conditions in America. More interesting and significant, however, are Tocqueville's frequent references to the greatness and the nobility of these figures. For all their contributions to the enlightened science of government, the Founders are of interest to Tocqueville insofar as they represent "the finest minds and the noblest characters that had ever appeared in the new world,"[55] moral heroes who had the courage to say what they thought because they possessed hearts animated by a "sincere and ardent love" of freedom.[56] These Americans represented to Tocqueville the possibility that the moral greatness he admired in Pascal might persist even in a democratic and enlightened age.

Tocqueville's most sustained and important engagement with anglophone authors was, however, with eighteenth-century British authors. On this front, one finds more than a few traces in *DIA* of his engagement with the leading eighteenth-century political philosophers of both England and Scotland. Among English authors, perhaps the most important for Tocqueville is Burke; as scholars have noted, Tocqueville's extensive later engagement with Burke was a crucial influence on the *Old Regime*.[57] Yet even in his earlier book Tocqueville anticipates in various places his later engagement with Burke's thought. In the context of our present study, two parallels deserve particular attention. The first is Tocqueville's key distinction between two different types of equality:

> There is in fact a manly and legitimate passion for equality that incites men to want all to be strong and esteemed. This passion tends to elevate the small to the rank of the great; but one also encounters a depraved taste for equality in the human heart that brings the weak to want to draw the strong to their level and that reduces men to preferring equality in servitude to inequality in freedom.[58]

Tocqueville's distinction between two types of equality – an admirable equality of leveling-up and a pernicious equality of leveling-down – is both reminiscent of a similar distinction in Burke and suggests another way Tocqueville sought to counter Radical Enlightenment ideas with Moderate Enlightenment ideas.[59] Second, Tocqueville also shares many of Burke's sympathies concerning the sorts of institutions democracies need to preserve in order to stave off certain of democracy's worst effects:

> I have already said enough to put the character of Anglo-American civilization in its true light. It is the product (and this point of

departure ought constantly to be present in one's thinking) of two perfectly distinct elements that elsewhere have often made war with each other, but which, in America, they have succeeded in incorporating into one another and combining marvelously. I mean to speak of the spirit of religion and the spirit of freedom.[60]

It will be difficult for some readers to read these lines without hearing Burke's notorious defense of "the spirit of religion" and the "spirit of a gentleman" as the necessary fences against populist tyranny.[61]

Alongside these and other English and American authors, Tocqueville was also very deeply indebted to certain of the leading philosophers of the Scottish Enlightenment, and to David Hume and Adam Smith in particular. Across *DIA* we indeed find a host of Humean ideas. When Tocqueville tells us "there is no philosopher in the world so great that he does not believe a million things on faith in others or does not suppose many more truths than he establishes," he restates the central and signature tenet of Hume's philosophy of common life.[62] When he tells us that public opinion is not only the "directing power" but indeed the "dominant power" in politics,[63] and indeed that "more and more it is opinion that rules the world," he develops a signature claim of Hume's political theory.[64] When he tells us "there is real sympathy only among people who are alike,"[65] and that democrats "show a general compassion for all members of the human species,"[66] he restates a central premise of Hume's treatments of the concepts of sympathy and humanity that are foundational to his moral philosophy.[67]

For all this, it is arguably in his engagement with Hume's friend and fellow Scot Smith that Tocqueville's commitment to Moderate Enlightenment and his distance from Radical Enlightenment is most clearly evident. Smith is of course today remembered as a pioneering political economist and a champion of the system of free markets that came to be known in Tocqueville's day as capitalism. Yet Tocqueville's own engagement with Smith's thought suggests a deep sensitivity to the fact that Smith was at once a champion of the benefits of market society as well as a sober critic of certain negative externalities that both thinkers also emphasize as necessary concomitants to the progress of market society. In *DIA* this emerges especially clearly in its engagement with Smith's conception of the division of labor. For while one can find parallels to Smith's ideas in many of Tocqueville's discrete claims regarding estate law,[68] the love of well-being,[69] and the prudential and methodical pursuit of long-term self-interest,[70] Tocqueville's comments on divided specialized labor most clearly suggest his direct engagement with Smith.

Smith's *Wealth of Nations* famously opens with the story of the pin factory, the aim of which is to demonstrate the superior efficiency and productivity unleashed by divided and specialized labor; but readers who persist to the end of the *Wealth of Nations* know that the book ends with a decidedly less optimistic picture of divided labor's effects. Here, Smith explains that, even as divided labor generates cheap consumer goods, these come at the cost of what he calls the "mental mutilation" of the laborer himself, and the corruption of all his "intellectual, social, and martial virtues."[71] Tocqueville restates Smith's argument in almost the same terms:

> When an artisan engages constantly and uniquely in the manufacture of a single object, in the end he performs this work with singular dexterity. But at the same time he loses the general faculty of applying his mind to the direction of the work. Each day he becomes more skillful and less industrious, and one can say that the man in him is degraded as the worker is perfected.[72]

Tocqueville's concluding rhetorical question – "what should one expect from a man who has used twenty years of his life in making pinheads?" – is a strong hint that he has Smith's argument in mind here.[73] Questions of influence aside, though, the key point is that Smith's moderate perspective on political economy, one that emphasized the costs as well as the gains of modern progress, would have naturally attracted Tocqueville in his capacity as the nineteenth century's great friend of Moderate Enlightenment.

NOTES

1. Two especially useful efforts in this vein with which I engage in more detail in what follows include Lucien Jaume, *Tocqueville: The Aristocratic Sources of Liberty*, trans. Arthur Goldhammer (Princeton: Princeton University Press, 2013); and Paul Rahe, *Soft Despotism, Democracy's Drift: Montesquieu, Rousseau, Tocqueville, and the Modern Project* (New Haven, CT: Yale University Press, 2009).

2. The quoted phrase is Jaume's; see Jaume, *Tocqueville*, 12. In this vein see also Alan S. Kahan, *Alexis de Tocqueville* (London: Bloomsbury, 2013), 27–28.

3. Nathaniel Wolloch, "Alexis de Tocqueville, John Stuart Mill, and the Modern Debate on the Enlightenment," *The European Legacy* 23, no. 4 (2018), 349–364, at 352. See also Aaron Herold's observation that Tocqueville took a "critical but friendly attitude towards the political world that the Enlightenment created" in Herold, "Tocqueville on Religion, the Enlightenment, and the Democratic Soul," *American Political Science Review* 109, no. 3 (2015), 523–534, at 524.

4. Charles Taylor, *The Ethics of Authenticity* (Cambridge, MA: Harvard University Press, 1991), 10ff.

5. Pierre Manent, "Tocqueville, Political Philosopher," in Cheryl B. Welch, ed., *The Cambridge Companion to Tocqueville* (Cambridge: Cambridge University Press, 2006), 117.

6. In both my use of these terms in this context and in taking this position, I follow Wolloch; see "Tocqueville, Mill, and the Modern Debate on the Enlightenment," especially 351–352.

7. OR, 203.

8. OR, 196–197. Cf. Gita May's claim that Tocqueville remained "all his life" a "thoughtful disciple of the *philosophes*" in "Tocqueville and the Enlightenment Legacy," in Abraham S. Eisenstadt, ed., *Reconsidering Tocqueville's Democracy in America* (New Brunswick, NJ: Rutgers University Press, 1988), 25.

9. OR, 207.

10. DIA (MW), 282.

11. Ibid. For helpful explication, see Herold, "Tocqueville on Religion," 524ff.

12. DIA (MW), 281.

13. DIA (MW), 425–426.

14. See, for example, DIA (MW), 519; as well as Harvey Mansfield, "Intimations of Philosophy in Tocqueville's *Democracy in America*," in Christine Dunn Henderson, ed., *Tocqueville's Voyages: The Evolution of His Ideas and Their Journey Beyond His Time* (Indianapolis: Liberty Fund, 2014), 241; and Peter A. Lawler, "Tocqueville on Pantheism, Materialism, and Catholicism," *Perspectives on Political Science* 30, no. 4 (2001), 218–226, especially 220–224. It should also be noted that, for all his critiques of Spinoza, Tocqueville's privileging of the moral implications of the Americans' religious beliefs as the most significant aspect of their religion (see, for example, DIA (MW), 278 and 406) suggests an implicit acceptance of one of Spinoza's signature claims (see especially Spinoza, *Theologico-Political Treatise*, chap. 14).

15. DIA (MW), 403.

16. Ibid.

17. DIA (MW), 404.

18. DIA (MW), 404.

19. See L. Joseph Hebert, "Individualism and Intellectual Liberty in Tocqueville and Descartes," *Journal of Politics* 69, no. 2 (2007), 525–537, especially 526–527.

20. DIA (MW), 404–405.

21. DIA (MW), 405.

22. DIA (MW), 674.

23. Tocqueville to Louis de Kergorlay, as quoted in, for example, Alexander Jech, "Tocqueville, Pascal, and the Transcendent Horizon," *American Political Thought* 5, no. 1 (2016), 109–131, at 109; Kahan, *Alexis de Tocqueville*, 6; Rahe, *Soft Despotism*, 154.

24. Kahan, *Alexis de Tocqueville*, 29.

25. On Tocqueville's profound debts in general to Montesquieu, see, for example, May, "Tocqueville and the Enlightenment Legacy," 41; and Rahe, *Soft Despotism*, especially 154–157. James Schleifer has observed that Montesquieu's notes also include a transcription of Diderot's definition of despotism in the *Encyclopédie*; see *The Making of Tocqueville's Democracy in America* (Chapel Hill: University of North Carolina Press, 1980), 173.

26. DIA (MW), 382. See, for example, Charles de Secondat, Baron de Montesquieu, *The Spirit of the Laws*, ed. Anne M. Cohler, Basia C. Miller, and Harold S. Stone. (Cambridge: Cambridge University Press, 1989), 2.5.

27. DIA (MW), 89.

28. On this front, see especially Jaume, *Tocqueville*, 96, 101–105; Schleifer, *The Making of Democracy in America*, 234–235; and F. Flagg Taylor IV, "Montesquieu, Tocqueville, and the Politics of Mores," in Brian Danoff and L. Joseph Hebert, eds., *Alexis de Tocqueville and the Art of Democratic Statesmanship* (Lexington: University of Kentucky Press, 2010), 94 and 97.

29. Cf. Montesquieu, *Spirit of the Laws*, 3.1.

30. DIA (MW) 295. Cf. Montesquieu, *Spirit of the Laws*, 1.4, 19.

31. DIA (MW), 275.

32. DIA (MW), 274.

33. DIA (MW), 292.

34. DIA (MW), 302.

35. DIA (MW), 485.

36. DIA (MW), 407.

37. See, for example, Rahe, *Soft Despotism*, especially 73–74, 77, 81, 168.

38. See Kahan, *Alexis de Tocqueville*, 30.

39. DIA (MW), 673–676. Rousseau, *Discourse on the Origins of Inequality*, in *The Major Political Writings of Jean-Jacques Rousseau*, ed. John T. Scott (Chicago: University of Chicago Press, 2012), 113.

40. DIA (MW), 427. Cf. Rousseau, *Discourse on the Origins of Inequality*, 72; see also Rahe, *Soft Despotism*, 179.

41. DIA (MW), 64. Cf. Rousseau, *Discourse on the Origins of Inequality*, 147.

42. DIA (MW), 352. Cf. Rousseau, *Discourse on Political Economy*, in *The Discourses and Other Early Political Writings*, ed. Victor Gourevitch (Cambridge: Cambridge University Press, 1997), 16.

43. DIA (MW), 131. Cf. Rousseau, *The Social Contract*, 1.3.

44. Cf. Rousseau, *The Social Contract*, 2.7.

45. DIA (MW), 144. Cf. Rousseau, *The Social Contract*, 2.3 (first paragraph) and 2.6 (last paragraph).

46. In addition to Kahan, *Alexis de Tocqueville*, 30ff., see especially Rahe, *Soft Despotism*, 40; Jaume, *Tocqueville*, especially 146 and 163; Peter A. Lawler, *The Restless Mind: Alexis de Tocqueville on the Origin and Perpetuation of Human Liberty* (Lanham, MD: Rowman & Littlefield, 1993).

47. See especially DIA (MW), 179 and 435; and Herold, "Tocqueville on Religion, the Enlightenment, and the Democratic Soul," 531.

48. DIA (MW), 298.

49. Blaise Pascal, *Pensées*, trans. A. J. Krailsheimer (London: Penguin Books, 1995), especially nos. 131–139.

50. DIA (MW), 189.

51. See especially Jacques Le Brun, *Le Pur Amour de Platon à Lacan* (Paris: Éditions du Seuil, 2002); in English, see, for example, Charly Coleman, *The Virtues of Abandon* (Stanford: Stanford University Press, 2014).

52. Jaume, *Tocqueville*, 150n17; see also 179. May, in the same vein, also rightly calls for more extended attention to Tocqueville's relationship to the *moralistes*; see "Tocqueville and the Enlightenment Legacy," 26.

53. Jaume, *Tocqueville*, 170; see also 10, 146, 149; as well as Jech, "Tocqueville, Pascal, and the Transcendent Horizon," especially 110 and 118; Ralph Lerner, *Revolutions Revisited: Two Faces of the Politics of Enlightenment* (Chapel Hill: University of North Carolina Press, 1994), 114; and Lawler, *The Restless Mind*, especially 78.

54. DIA (MW), 500. Among the leading "aristocratic" thinkers of seventeenth-century France to advance this claim was Fénelon; see, for example, his "On Pure Love," in *Fénelon: Moral and Political Writings*, ed. Ryan Patrick Hanley (Oxford: Oxford University Press, 2020), 224–230. I analyze his concept of self-interest and disinterestedness in *The Political Philosophy of Fénelon* (Oxford: Oxford University Press, 2020), especially chap. 6.

55. DIA (MW), 107.

56. DIA (MW), 144.

57. See, for example, Kahan, *Alexis de Tocqueville*, 27. For an extensive treatment of Edmund Burke and *The Old Regime*, see especially Robert T. Gannett, Jr., *The Historian Unveiled: Tocqueville and His Sources for The Old Regime and the Revolution* (Chicago: University of Chicago Press, 2003), especially chap. 4.

58. DIA (MW), 52.

59. See, for example, Edmund Burke, *Reflections on the Revolution in France*, ed. Conor Cruise O'Brien (London: Penguin Books, 1986), 169–171; cf. especially Montesquieu, *Spirit of the Laws*, 8.2.

60. DIA (MW), 43; see also DIA (MW), 282.

61. See Burke, *Reflections on the Revolution*, 173–174.

62. DIA (MW), 408. See, for example, David Hume, *Dialogues Concerning Natural Religion*, 1.5.

63. DIA (MW), 117.

64. DIA (MW), 409. See, for example, Hume, "Of the First Principles of Government," in *Essays, Moral, Political, and Literary*, especially para. 1; for helpful recent analysis of this side of Hume's political theory, see Paul Sagar, *The Opinion of Mankind* (Princeton: Princeton University Press, 2018).

65. DIA (MW), 536.

66. DIA (MW), 538.

67. See, for example, Hume, *Essay Concerning the Principles of Morals*, 9.5; I analyze the significance of this claim in *Love's Enlightenment* (Cambridge: Cambridge University Press, 2017), chap. 2.

68. DIA (MW), 47, 334; cf. Smith, *Wealth of Nations*, 3.2.1–7.

69. DIA (MW), 153; cf. Smith, *Wealth of Nations*, 1.8.44, 2.3.28; and Smith, *Theory of Moral Sentiments*, 1.3.2.1.

70. DIA (MW), 504–505 and 588; cf. Smith, *Theory of Moral Sentiments*, 6.1.1–13.

71. Smith, *Wealth of Nations*, 5.1.f.50 and 5.1.f.60.

72. DIA (MW), 530. These parallels have been recently noted and developed insightfully and at greater length by Jimena Hurtado; see her "Adam Smith and Alexis de Tocqueville on Division of Labour," *European Journal of the History of Economic Thought* 26, no. 6 (2019), 1187–1211 (especially 1190, 1195–1196).

73. DIA (MW), 530; cf. DIA (MW), 387.

2 Tocqueville's Dialogues

Aurelian Craiutu

> Quand j'ai un sujet quelconque à traiter, il m'est quasi impossible de lire
> aucun des livres qui ont été composés sur la même matière; le contact des
> idées des autres m'agite et me trouble au point de me rendre douloureuse
> la lecture de ces ouvrages.

Alexis de Tocqueville[1]

INTRODUCTION

The first volume of *Democracy in America* appeared in January 1835 when Tocqueville was only twenty-nine years old. The success of his book took everyone by surprise, including the editor Charles Gosselin, who had initially envisaged printing only 500 copies. Tocqueville's work was immediately praised as a masterpiece and its author was hailed as a true heir to Montesquieu.[2] Although the second volume published in 1840 met with less public success, *Democracy in America* eventually became a classic book that showed the French what they could hope and must fear from democracy's advance, its institutions, and its mores.

Tocqueville's readers have always wanted to learn more about his sources and writing style in order to understand how he was able to write such a great book at such a young age. A scion of a distinguished aristocratic family and great-grandson of Malesherbes (1721–1794), Tocqueville received a classic education that introduced him to a few favorite authors to whom he returned again and again, such as Pascal, Montesquieu, and Rousseau.[3] Those authors remained a constant source of inspiration for him over the years. Tocqueville also admired other writers – La Bruyère, Nicole, Bossuet, and Corneille, to name only a few – whose style and rhetoric he sometimes sought to imitate. Equally important for Tocqueville's early intellectual development was the mentorship of Abbé Lesueur (1751–1831), whom Tocqueville described as "the man to whom I owe the greatest gratitude and whose memory is the most precious and respectable for me."[4] In his correspondence, Tocqueville referred to Lesueur as "a father" on whose knees he and his brothers had learned to discern the good from evil and who made them "if not distinguished people, at least honest ones."[5] At the same time, Tocqueville was a child of his century who followed the political debates of his age and shared his contemporaries' anxieties. The task of his generation was to close what Tocqueville once called "the bloody book"[6] of the French Revolution after the agonizing period of the Terror, the uncertainty of the Thermidor, and the tragic defeat of the First Empire.

Reconstituting Tocqueville's intellectual dialogue with his contemporaries has never been an easy task. The topic had always been shrouded in mystery, and Tocqueville himself bore some responsibility in this regard. An ambitious and elusive personality, he was notoriously reluctant to acknowledge his sources and intellectual debts. His hesitancy has to do in part with his peculiar writing style.[7] In a letter to Duvergier de Hauranne from September 1, 1856 (from which the epigraph of this chapter was selected), Tocqueville made a rare but revealing confession about his peculiar working habits and method. He pointed out that, when writing something, he needed absolute focus and total concentration; contact with the ideas of others agitated and disturbed him and made him lose sight of his own train of thought.[8]

Nonetheless, if *Democracy in America* was conceived in solitude, it did not emerge out of nowhere. While writing the book, Tocqueville engaged in a dialogue with his contemporaries and attempted to rise above the passions of his age. In the end, he was able to see differently and farther than his contemporaries, as he put it in the introduction. Yet he remained a man of his times, and *Democracy in America* should be read and interpreted in the context in – and for which – it was written.

It is important to remember that his audience was a French one familiar with the parliamentary debates of the Bourbon Restoration (1814–1830) that addressed key issues related to the history of France, liberalism, constitutionalism, and democracy.[9] These topics were also present in Tocqueville's correspondence with family members – Hervé and Édouard de Tocqueville – and close friends such as Gustave de Beaumont, Louis de Kergorlay, Jean-Jacques Ampère, Eugène and Charles Stöffels, and Francisque de Corcelle.[10] Their epistolary exchanges are well documented in volumes 7, 13, 14, 15, 17, and 18 of Tocqueville's *Œuvres Complètes* as well as the rich notes included in Eduardo Nolla's bilingual critical edition of *Democracy in America*. Since Tocqueville had a habit of soliciting suggestions and comments on his writings, the final version of his masterpiece owes a lot to his intellectual exchanges with – and the suggestions received from – his closest friends and family members as well as from a few Americans such as Theodore Sedgwick, Edward Livingston, and Nathaniel Niles, whose collaboration Tocqueville solicited.[11]

Almost two decades ago, in *Liberalism under Siege*, I explored the intellectual dialogue between Tocqueville, François Guizot, and Pierre Royer-Collard, the leading representatives of the French Doctrinaires.[12] Although neither of them traveled to America, they exercised in varying degrees a significant influence on their younger disciple, whose understanding of the relationship between social and political order owed a lot to their writings and discourses during the Bourbon Restoration. Here, I would like to focus on a few other prominent contemporaries of Tocqueville whose ideas resonated with the author of *Democracy in America*: Charles de Rémusat, François-René de Chateaubriand, and Félicité Robert de Lamennais.[13] The only one to have visited America was Chateaubriand, who wrote an account of his voyage with which Tocqueville was familiar.

Exploring select themes from their writings may enrich our knowledge of the intellectual landscape from which Tocqueville's masterpiece emerged without diminishing its originality. It also gives us an idea of the main topics that preoccupied his generation such as individualism, greatness, authority, and order. At the same time, it allows us to better assess the novelty of Tocqueville's work and the ways in which his ideas overlapped with and differed from those of his contemporaries. While it would be an exaggeration to speak of direct influences in his case, it is possible to point out certain affinities and a common sensibility that made all these thinkers anxious participants in a journey toward an uncertain democratic future.

TOCQUEVILLE AND THE FRENCH GENERATION OF 1820

Studying the profile of the French Generation of 1820 to which Tocqueville belonged is essential for anyone seeking to understand how he managed to write his masterpiece.[14] A society is defined not only by its peaks but also by its entire intellectual landscape. In this regard, as Pierre Roland-Marcel, a perceptive interpreter of Tocqueville, remarked a century ago, "Camille Jourdan, Jouffroy, and Rémusat anticipate Tocqueville and help us understand him."[15]

Tocqueville's generation came of age during the Bourbon Restoration, a period that Tocqueville regarded as a time of great issues and parties, "which seemed to increase in greatness and prosperity as it increased in liberty."[16] The Restoration witnessed a remarkable renaissance of liberal thought when the French, tired of innovation, tried for once – and *almost* succeeded – to be British.[17] New laws were passed, old restrictions were lifted, the salons reopened, the opposition parties emerged, and new journals were published. Alas, this liberal rebirth was jeopardized when the ultra-conservatives gained the majority in the Chamber of Deputies in the early 1820s. By the middle of that decade, the prospects for liberal politics became rather dim, and the shores of the promised land looked more distant than ever.

The question that preoccupied Tocqueville's generation was how to find a new philosophical and political doctrine that could provide an effective blueprint for rebuilding French society, torn between a bygone aristocratic past and an uncertain democratic future. For many, democracy was still equated with mob rule and aroused deep feelings of mistrust in the aftermath of the Terror.[18] A topic of general concern in the aftermath of Napoleon's Empire was the growing moral decline of French culture, which was dominated by increasing cupidity, petty ambitions, and commercial interests. As religion was losing its hold on society, the spread of doubt engendered a cynical and skeptical mood that threatened the moral fabric of society. These issues loomed large in Théodore Jouffroy's influential essay "How Dogmas Come to an End?," which illustrated and gave voice to the mixture of restlessness, hope, and anxiety felt by Tocqueville's entire generation.[19]

Published as a supplement to the May 24, 1825 issue of *Le Globe*, Jouffroy's article appeared at a critical moment when old dogmas and principles became subject to relentless questioning from all sides. More so than ever before, the young felt the poverty of their parents' doctrines, which they felt called to replace with new ideas. "When a dogma approaches the end of its reign," Jouffroy wrote, "a profound indifference is first seen springing up for the received faith. This indifference is not doubt, men continue to believe . . . but it is the characteristic of a belief which has no longer any life and which subsists only by custom."[20] Faith itself slowly becomes an indifferent routine observed ritualistically, even if nobody knows exactly why; doctrines once so full of life turn into little more than "a collection of ancient, mutilated symbols."[21] Once awakened, the spirit of inquiry and examination challenges the uncritical attachment to old formulas and doctrines. "This is not an act of hostility," Jouffroy believed, "but of good sense."[22]

Nonetheless, after having accomplished the work of destruction, skepticism alone could not fill the void and quench the thirst for a new faith among the young. Left to itself, skepticism can only create indifference and moral chaos in society. Like doubt, it is unsustainable over the long run and must be replaced by a new creed. "Faith is a want of our souls," Jouffroy wrote, "because we know that there is such a thing as truth. Doubt is a state which can never be agreeable, except as the negation of a false belief. ... This satisfaction once tasted, we aspire after a new belief; error being destroyed, we wish for truth."[23] Yet what would the new belief look like, and how could truth be found amid the ruins of old beliefs?

For Jouffroy and others, the answer was eclecticism, a doctrine that sought to reconcile philosophy, religion, and politics in a novel way by combining contending ideas and principles. For his part, Tocqueville did not hold it in high esteem. He was skeptical toward abstract philosophy and struggled with religious questions. As he once confessed in a famous letter to Sophie Swetchine, Tocqueville had lost his religious belief at an early age and never recovered it after that. We know from his private correspondence that he feared the corrosive effects of doubt, which he considered as one of the three great human ails, along with illness and death. For Tocqueville, doubt was similar to an "earthquake"[24] that calls into question all the aspects of one's life, leaving in its wake a deep and sad melancholy. He believed that doubt is extremely dangerous because it makes us "incapable of all things, of great evil as well as great good."[25] Tocqueville, too, longed for a faith that would offer a fixed point that could put his restless mind at ease. Later, in *Democracy in America*, he linked faith and hope and acknowledged that "unbelief is an accident," while faith alone is the "permanent state of humanity."[26]

In this regard, Tocqueville echoed to some extent the ideas of his generation. Born "in the bosom of skepticism," the young had heard the call for a new faith and understood that their great task was to end the French Revolution. They learned to distinguish between the spirit of the revolution, which they cherished, and the revolutionary spirit, which they rejected. Some began to perceive a germ of future life fermenting in the bosom of stagnation and corruption. Others, like Jouffroy, walking in the footsteps of Victor Cousin, embraced eclecticism, committed to the interests of order and the public good. "Already these children," Jouffroy opined, "obtain a presentiment of a new and better faith, they fix their eye on this inspiring prospect with enthusiasm, with conviction, with resolution."[27] The new faith centered on equality, liberty, and democracy, the new buzzwords of the age, and relied on a providential philosophy of history as a progressive story of liberty. Few seemed to doubt anymore the irresistible progress of democracy as a social condition. Democracy was there to stay for good, and one had to adapt oneself to its novelty; but how could one live with democracy, and on what terms? This became the most pressing political question that Tocqueville's generation was called to answer.

Tocqueville was aware that the class he belonged to was destined to be defeated in the long run. Although his attachment to aristocratic values was strong, he took an oath to the July Monarchy in 1830 and was open to learning about the new democratic universe and principles that were slowly but irremediably replacing the aristocratic ones. Tocqueville intuited that, for all its obvious shortcomings, democracy could still be educated, elevated, and purified of its revolutionary elements. He understood that his generation was carried toward the port of democratic equality, yet he wondered whether he would live long enough to reach the final destination. He sometimes liked to compare himself to a wanderer engaged in an adventurous voyage at sea, lacking a good compass and direction. The feeling of drifting on a stormy sea, buffeted by powerful winds and waves, haunted Tocqueville's generation.[28] "When I watch everything around me," Tocqueville once wrote, "I see a spectacle unique in history...The ground of European civilization trembles. ... [A]ll is shaken, not only political institutions, but civil institutions, social institutions, and the old society that we know."[29] A new cosmos had to be recreated out of the existing disorder. Crammed with a heroism that hardly belonged to his bourgeois age, Tocqueville dreamt of "true and solid passions that bind up and lead life."[30] That was to be found not within the confines of an eclectic philosophy, as Jouffroy and Cousin believed,[31] but in the realm of political action. If the doctrine of eclecticism remained alien to Tocqueville's sensibility, he shared the eclectics' desire not to attach himself to any school or party.

Before Tocqueville could successfully enter the French political scene, he had to write something memorable that could make his name better known to the public in his native country. He conceived the plan of a book about America while visiting the New World in 1831–1832 and pursued it on his return to France. The idea of writing something about "the great democratic revolution"[32] that was taking place in the entire world had already been on his radar screen for a long time. In an important letter from April 21, 1830, Tocqueville took up a number of themes such as individualism, the role of government, the separation between religion and politics, and education that anticipate key ideas developed in *Democracy in America*.[33] On August 26, 1830, Tocqueville pointed out that he had wanted for some time to visit North America and confirmed he was planning on going there "to see what a great republic looks like."[34] The July Monarchy did not seem propitious to the great ambitions of the young lawyer in Versailles, and a visit to America, Tocqueville believed, could have been beneficial by distinguishing him from "the most vulgar class" of politicians.[35]

In January 1835, when the first volume of *Democracy in America* came out, Tocqueville confessed to Kergorlay: "Nearly ten years ago, I was already thinking about part of the things that I have just now set forth. I was in America only to become clear on this point. The penitentiary system was a pretext: I took it as a passport that would let me enter thoroughly into the United States."[36] In America, as he famously put it in the introduction to his masterpiece, Tocqueville saw "more than America"; he caught a glimpse of the new democracy in order "to know at least what we must hope or fear from it."[37] In other words, America was the place where Tocqueville found some answers to the main challenge faced by his generation: whether it was possible to live in freedom and order and with dignity and greatness under the laws of democracy.

TOCQUEVILLE AND RÉMUSAT: "LA DÉMOCRATIE MOUVANTE"

Not surprisingly, Tocqueville was not the first one seeking to answer this important and difficult question. A common theme in the parliamentary debates and the press during the Bourbon Restoration had been the image of democracy as a new type of society with a specific constellation of mores, laws, norms, and institutions. Tocqueville followed these debates, which had a significant influence on the development of his thought. In this regard, a special role was played by the French Doctrinaires, who were among the first to use the term *democracy* in postrevolutionary France to designate the new egalitarian society characterized by equality of conditions, social mobility, and equality before the law.[38] The full implications of this important conceptual change in the definition of democracy were fleshed out a decade later by Tocqueville in *Democracy in America*.

The intellectual dialogue between Tocqueville and the youngest member of the Doctrinaires' group, Charles de Rémusat (1797–1875), has received little attention until now. A scion of a distinguished family, Rémusat affirmed himself as a gifted writer, especially through his numerous articles published in *Les Tablettes universelles* (1822–1824), *Le Globe* (1824–1825), and *Le Courier* (later renamed *Le Courrier français* in 1820). An elected member of the French Academy in 1846, Rémusat went into exile after December 1851 and returned to France a few years later. He published many influential books and articles in the prestigious *Revue des deux mondes* on topics as diverse as the French Revolution, Protestantism, Burke, political pessimism, German philosophy, Abélard, and St. Anselm. Rémusat's most important book, *Politique libérale, ou Fragments pour servir à la defense de la Révolution française*, appeared in 1860. He also served as Minister of Foreign Affairs during the first years of the Third Republic. Rémusat's memoirs are considered among the finest testimonies on nineteenth-century French political life.[39]

In his private correspondence, Tocqueville acknowledged the importance and influence of the ideas of his slightly older colleague. He was concerned that Rémusat, who was working on similar themes, might end up writing and publishing the first definitive book on democracy before him. Tocqueville made this point in a letter to Rémusat from July 22, 1856, in which he confessed:

> Because I thought I was seeing lots of contact points between your spirit and mine, I could not bear the thought of reading you...*You were the person in this world I was fearing the most and who has precipitated the most my own work.* I had the feeling that *you were treading on the same ground as me* and I noticed that you were throwing into circulation core ideas on which I wanted to base my own work.[40]

Fortunately for Tocqueville, Rémusat never wrote his own big book on democracy. Yet, into the 1820s, he published several influential essays in *Le Courier, Le Globe,* and *Revue Française* that contained many Tocquevillean tropes addressing the rise of democracy. He also wrote a long analysis of the concept of power when the second volume of Lamennais' *Essay on Indifference* came out.[41]

A few important themes returned time and again in Rémusat's essays, leitmotifs that also loomed large in Tocqueville's *Democracy in America*: equality, social mobility, individualism, the relation between social and political order, and the unstoppable advance of democracy. Responding to those who emphasized the priority of the political sphere over society, Rémusat affirmed the primacy of the social realm and highlighted the significance of social and historical knowledge for the advance of civilization. Much like Guizot and Royer-Collard, Rémusat believed that power does not create society *ab novo* but finds it already constituted; as such, it is obliged to work with its forces and elements and guide them. On this view, what is novel and interesting must be looked for in the bosom of society where the real seeds and roots of democracy lie. If the French Revolution accelerated the advent of the new democratic social order, its roots, according to Rémusat, were much older, going back several centuries to Philippe-le-Bel. A similar argument would be made by Tocqueville in the famous introduction to *Democracy in America* a decade later or so.

To explain the new Zeitgeist and the democratic social state existing during the Bourbon Restoration, Rémusat coined a novel term: *la démocratie mouvante*, loosely translated as "shifting democracy." A concept bearing important similarities with Tocqueville's view of democracy, Rémusat's *démocratie mouvante* consecrated the triumph of equality against old class-based privileges and hierarchies. If there was one single fact universally acknowledged in France, he wrote in the mid-1820s, it was that the new society, through its composition and mores, was dominated by the irresistible progress of equality. Older hierarchies and distinctions waned, making way for new forms of authority.[42] All opinions were now equal before the law. The social fabric had become more complex and diverse, subject to a myriad of factors that could hardly be controlled any longer from a single center of power. Everything had been set in motion, and the effects of social mobility were easily visible everywhere in society. Wealth was changing hands rapidly, giving birth to a novel distribution of property reflecting the existing pluralism of interests and ideas. Social and private mores derived from equality and were permeated by its ethos. As a result, Rémusat concluded, one could easily find its influence everywhere in society, "in the division of goods, the sharing of inheritances, family relations,...the manner in which marriages are contracted, ... [and] the relationships between parents and children."[43]

In Rémusat's view, his generation faced a clear and simple choice: either acknowledge and accept the new society or wage a senseless and ultimately futile war against the democratic social state, mores, and ideas and the novel distribution of property.[44] Attacked from all sides, democratic equality proved to be invincible and irresistible. Any policy of resistance was pointless, since democracy was in full spate; no one could stop or delay the reconstitution of the social and political sphere along the new egalitarian lines.[45] As society itself was becoming more and more progressive, democracy was spreading everywhere in the fabric of society, like a torrent that could no longer be contained.

As Rémusat wrote in 1819, the new social forces were powerful enough to overcome the efforts of all those who opposed them, "similar to the fast and insensible movement that is carrying along the planet we inhabit."[46] Seven years later, in 1826, Rémusat commented on the prevailing "sentiment of equality or universal justice"[47] that gradually abolished the distance and differences between various classes and individuals. In the new democratic world, individuals count for little, while social facts become all-powerful; as civilization advances, the importance of individuals diminishes.[48] "A shifting democracy," Rémusat concluded, "escapes all efforts to contain it."[49] The only sensible path was to learn how to live under the empire of social facts and try to adjust to them as best and as quickly as possible.

The image of a powerful democracy thwarting all efforts to reverse it was not a discovery of Rémusat; it had been introduced a few years earlier by Hercule de Serre (1776–1824). An accomplished orator, he was close to the Doctrinaires' group until 1820 and occupied high ministerial positions during the first half of the Bourbon Restoration before his untimely death. "In our country," Serre said in an important parliamentary speech in 1820, "democracy is everywhere full of vitality and energy; one can find it in industry, property, laws, memories, people, and things. The flow is in full spate and the feeble dikes can hardly contain it."[50] The phrase "democracy is in full spate" – "la démocratie coule à pleins bords" – seized the imagination of Serre's contemporaries. Taking democracy as the opposite of aristocracy, Royer-Collard, too, welcomed the triumph of the new democratic order and the middle class. "We must either accept this state or destroy it," he said in response to Serre. Royer-Collard went on to add that the true work of wisdom was to use the democratic forces and principles in order to strengthen the new constitutional order and civil equality.[51]

The definitive book on democracy that spelled out the full implications of these ideas was published a decade later by Royer-Collard's disciple. Making democracy work, Tocqueville argued, meant constituting, regulating, and moderating it. While seeking to maintain his independence from the political parties of his time, he advised his contemporaries to contemplate democracy without bias or fear and taught them how to live and prosper under its laws.[52] Tocqueville insisted that, for all its shortcomings and association with mob rule, democracy was not the monster that scandalized so many in the epoch. It was still possible to educate and regulate democracy, enlighten it, and purify it of its revolutionary spirit and excesses.

TOCQUEVILLE AND CHATEAUBRIAND: THE PURSUIT OF GREATNESS IN DEMOCRATIC TIMES

In this regard, Tocqueville learned an important lesson from François-René de Chateaubriand (1768–1848). If the latter has rarely been cited in the English-speaking world as a possible source of inspiration for Tocqueville, it cannot be denied that the two thinkers shared important intellectual affinities.[53] While Montesquieu was the "formal model" followed by Tocqueville in his book, the real inspiration for him came from Chateaubriand, with whom he was united by family ties.[54] Echoes of Chateaubriand's ideas can be found everywhere in Tocqueville's writings, starting with his historical analysis of the origins of the French Revolution, continuing with his views on religion, and ending with his conception of greatness and description of the democratic mind. Chateaubriand was the great literary model whom Tocqueville secretly sought to emulate, while at the same time trying to emancipate himself from his tutelary influence.[55]

Tocqueville read several of Chateaubriand's books, most notably *Voyage en Amérique* along with *Essai sur les révolutions*, *Le Génie du christianisme*, *Études historiques*, and later *Mémoires d'outre tombe*. Chateaubriand's description of a humanity carried toward democracy by the invisible hand of an inscrutable Providence must have resonated deeply with Tocqueville's own musings on similar topics. Both thinkers felt that they were situated *entre deux rives*, as Chateaubriand used to say, or between two worlds – aristocracy and democracy – as Tocqueville liked to put it. Both saw themselves at the confluence of two centuries and rivers, swimming away with regret from the old shores where they were born, toward an unknown port whose contours were only barely visible.[56] Tocqueville and Chateaubriand had the feeling of navigating "along an unknown coast, amid shadows and tempest." They sought to offer their reader "a map for each to study in his peril, so that, like a wise pilot, he may recognize his point of departure, his present location, and his destination, and in case of shipwreck, rescue himself on some isle where the tempest cannot reach."[57]

There was also another significant affinity between Tocqueville and Chateaubriand: both were fascinated by the New World, albeit in different ways. Chateaubriand visited the United States for six months in 1791 and wrote about his voyage. Unlike Tocqueville, who visited the "civilized" part of the country, Chateaubriand traveled through the forests of America and was enthralled by them.[58] He also stopped in several cities and places, among them Baltimore, Philadelphia, New York, Albany, Niagara, and Pittsburgh, before heading south and then back up north. It is fair to say that what caught Chateaubriand's attention and attracted his interest the most in the New World were not the cities, which he found uninteresting. Inspired by Rousseau's natural man, Chateaubriand was fascinated by the image of a young, wild, and romantic America. The only old things that existed in the New World, he remarked, were virgin forests – the "children of the earth" – and liberty, which he considered the "mother" of all human societies.[59] While Chateaubriand paid little attention to America's social, cultural, or political institutions, he admired, however, the country's energy and commitment to liberty. The reader of Tocqueville's account of his voyage to Lake Oneida and his fortnight in the wilderness might detect between the lines Chateaubriand's influence and tone.[60]

Since Chateaubriand was among the first in France to suggest that America represented the political future of the old world, one might expect Tocqueville to have enthusiastically endorsed this idea. Yet he initially reacted with skepticism to an article published by

Chateaubriand in *Journal des débats* in 1825, in which the famous writer recommended the American republic as a possible political model to his countrymen. In response to Chateaubriand, Tocqueville claimed that it would have been useful and necessary to also point out the differences between the fledgling American republic and France rather than "abuse us with false resemblances."[61] It took Tocqueville some time to change his mind and the publication of Chateaubriand's *Voyage en Amérique* might have contributed to his conversion.

Nonetheless, Chateaubriand was far from being an unconditional admirer of America. He expressed reservations about the New World that remind us of Tocqueville's ambivalent attitude to America in volume 2 of *Democracy*.[62] For one thing, Chateaubriand was puzzled by the diversity of religious denominations, which, he believed, would make it difficult to create a common fatherland across the Atlantic. Equally concerning in his view were the growing inequalities of wealth, which he feared might lead to the emergence of *"une aristocratie chrysogène,"*[63] a perverted form of aristocracy, spoiled by excessive wealth. This nefarious trend was fostered by an extreme love for distinctions and an immoderate passion for titles among the American "plebeian nobles." Finally, Chateaubriand was intrigued by the Americans' excessive mobility, by their materialism and obsession with money. Among the Americans, he remarked, self-interest tends to become a national vice that gives their democracy a crude utilitarian tone, incompatible with the existence of a polite and civilized society.

Although Chateaubriand did not feel at home in America, he returned from the New World with another important intuition that he developed later in *De la Restauration et de la monarchie elective* (1831). In his inimitable style, he warned that the entire western civilization was heading in the direction of a "general revolution"[64] and universal leveling. "If the moral education of the intermediary classes is not interrupted," he wrote, "the nations will be levelled into an equal liberty; if this transformation is stopped,

[they] will level themselves into an equal despotism. This despotism will last for a short time due to the advanced level of enlightenment, but it will be rough, and it will be followed by a long period of social dissolution."[65] This was a prescient insight, but not a novel one. Chateaubriand had previously claimed that a sweeping revolution was in the offing and predicted it would have major consequences for the entire world. Chateaubriand expected the revolution of equality to level everything on its path. If it continued unabated, he warned, all nations might succumb to a "uniform despotism,"[66] with terrible consequences for liberty.

Several years later, in the April 1834 issue of the *Revue des deux mondes*, Chateaubriand revisited these ideas in an important political fragment, *"Avenir du monde,"* published at a point in time when Tocqueville himself was finishing the first volume of *Democracy in America* (the latter appeared in January 1835). Europe, Chateaubriand opined, was irresistibly heading toward democracy.[67] The signs of change were everywhere in the air. Ideas had become more powerful than individuals, monarchs, and nations together; the world needed no longer any tutors. Seen from this perspective, the French Revolution itself had been only "one moment of the general revolution"[68] advancing all over Europe. Democracy itself appeared as a "deluge" that swept everything in its wake.[69] To think that one could arrest this development would be an impiety, a futile attempt to oppose the will of God.

When Tocqueville sat down to write the first volume of *Democracy*, his ideas resonated and intersected with some of Chateaubriand's insights and concerns. Tocqueville's genius owed a lot to his double vision that allowed him to perceive both the advantages of the aristocratic past and the potential benefits of the democratic future. He shared many of Chateaubriand's aristocratic anxieties about democracy. In January 1835, two weeks before the publication of *Democracy*, Tocqueville sent Chateaubriand an advance copy of his book, accompanied by a letter that paid homage to the famous writer. "You are not only the man who offered the best image of the past," Tocqueville wrote, "but also the one who has announced the future in the most prophetic manner... Nobody has described as well as you did the progressive march of democracy in the Christian world."[70] Tocqueville's words were certainly a courteous gesture toward his famous relative, but they also demonstrate the deep affinities between the two thinkers. While both of them understood the futility of all attempts to stop the march of democracy, they were worried by the visible signs of decline of their age. They were concerned by the prevailing intellectual mediocrity, the degradation of character, the waning of honor, the predominance of money, the growing indifference toward good and evil, and the redefinition of virtue and vice. In their eyes, all these signs revealed beyond reasonable doubt "the great and universal malady" of a declining world in which aristocratic spirits no longer felt at home.[71]

For melancholy survivors such as Chateaubriand and Tocqueville, fighting against what they perceived as the mediocrity of their age became a priority. Thousands of individuals may know how to operate the new machines that bring forth material progress, Chateaubriand quipped, but they could still not equal the genius of Homer or Dante. The intellectual world was shrinking at the very moment when the physical and material world was expanding. For their part, Chateaubriand and Tocqueville remained deeply committed to nurturing oases of excellence in the new age of equality. They wondered whether preserving and maintaining greatness were possible in the new society of *abeilles laborieuses*, "industrious bees,"[72] lacking a sense of larger vistas and preoccupied exclusively with getting rich quickly. There was, however, an additional danger both thinkers foresaw: the leveling of conditions could produce new and pernicious forms of despotism. Complete equality, they warned, might lead to the harshest form of servitude ever seen on earth.[73]

These ideas were memorably developed by Tocqueville in volume 2 of *Democracy in America*. He borrowed from Chateaubriand the image of democracy as a deluge, but in the end his tone and attitude turned out to be more optimistic about the possibility of educating and moderating democracy. "In *Democracy*," Alan Kahan argued, "Tocqueville turned Chateaubriand's Romantic despair into a program for democratic action."[74] Tocqueville believed that it was still possible to build effective dikes to contain democracy and channel its energies and resources into effective institutions. He searched for a "holy ark" that could carry humankind on the shoreless ocean of democracy.[75] He looked for the concrete means that allowed his contemporaries to live peacefully with democracy, while also being able to pursue great things and retain their freedoms.

TOCQUEVILLE AND LAMENNAIS: INDIVIDUALISM AND AUTHORITY IN DEMOCRATIC SOCIETY

Was the rising tide of democratic individualism going to subvert authority and pave the way to anomie and anarchy, as Chateaubriand feared in his darkest moments? Were there any effective ways of averting this disaster? These questions preoccupied another contemporary of Tocqueville, Félicité de Lamennais (1782–1854), who reflected on the effects of individualism and the fate of authority in democratic times. A complex and controversial figure, Lamennais switched sides several times during his life. He was initially close to the agenda of ultramontanism before joining the ranks of liberal Catholics. Criticized for his liberal views by Pope Gregory XVI's encyclical *Mirari Vos* (1832), Lamennais further radicalized his ideas in *Paroles d'un croyant* (1834), which marked his official break with the Vatican.[76] A few years later, he proposed a utopian Christian-socialist vision of social progress and fraternity.

Tocqueville was familiar with the ideas of Lamennais' books, *Essai sur l'indifférence en matière de religion* (1817–1824)[77] and *De la religion considerée dans ses rapports avec l'ordre politique et civil* (1825). It is also likely he followed some of Lamennais' articles published in *L'Avenir* in 1830–1831.[78] In 1835, Tocqueville sent Lamennais a copy of volume 1 of *Democracy* accompanied by a short letter in which he wrote that no one else professed a deeper respect and warmer admiration for Lamennais than him.[79] It is safe to assume that this was much more than a polite note from a young author wishing to gain public approval for his book. One can infer that Tocqueville had, in fact, learned a great deal from Lamennais' writings in which he found a strong critique of individualism, a topic that played a central role in Tocqueville's analysis of American democracy.[80]

Lamennais' *Essay on Indifference* begins with a description of the profound transformation at work in modern society at the heart of which lies a deep and enduring division. In his view, two philosophies compete for supremacy in the modern world. One of them tends to bring people together, while the other separates and isolates them. The first protects individuals by encouraging them to uphold and follow social norms and traditions, while the second contributes to the slow destruction of society by making the legitimacy of social norms strictly conditional upon individual judgment and consent. The first principle emphasizes generality, authority, common beliefs, humility, and duties to universal and invariable laws; the second one stresses particularity, individual interests, pride, and independence. The rivalry between the two principles, according to Lamennais, threatens to undermine the stability of society in the long run. Incessant change, universal doubt, and pervasive social mobility work together to weaken established traditions, customs, social norms, ways of life, and mores.[81] On this view, modern democracy is characterized by constant mobility and uncertainty. "Everything is constantly in motion," Lamennais wrote, "everything changes with frightening rapidity, buffeted by conflicting passions and opinions. There is nothing stable in principles, institutions, or laws."[82]

In Lamennais' view, the driving forces behind this profound transformation were extreme individualism, doubt, and religious indifference. He warned that, when individuals recognize no authority other than their own will, the inevitable outcome is doubt, which calls into question the existence of "a common fund of recognized truths, proclaimed rights, and a general order which nobody imagined could be turned upside down."[83] In some respects, Lamennais offered a diagnosis similar to the one proposed by Jouffroy who emphasized the corrosive effects of skepticism and deplored the emergence of a culture of doubt. Yet Lamennais was much more critical than Jouffroy toward the philosophical foundations of modernity that, in his view, were responsible for the then existing social anarchy and political chaos.[84] In particular, Lamennais rejected the idea that individual reason and will could be the sole criterion of legitimacy and truth. Individual reason, he argued, is always inferior to public reason, that is, the mixture of traditions, customs, social knowledge, and precepts that govern social interaction. It is public reason rather than individual will that decides what legitimate authority is and helps us distinguish truth from falsehood.

Once the individual will is elevated above everything else, Lamennais warned, each individual conceives oneself as self-sufficient and autonomous. People tend to become restless and confused and espouse "terrible beliefs,"[85] which can only bring about spurious and false certitudes. All links between individuals are broken and faith in the existence (or possibility) of a common good disappears. As a result, individuals no longer know what to do or what to believe in, and this explains the growing instability in opinions and institutions.[86] That is why, Lamennais concluded, in order to survive modern society needs a new form of authority capable of keeping the emerging intellectual anarchy at bay. Religion could play a central role in this process by restraining individuals' wills and pride and providing hope.

For all the differences between the two thinkers – Tocqueville always defined himself as "a liberal of a new species,"[87] while Lamennais was hostile to liberal principles – it is easy to detect echoes of Lamennais' ideas in Tocqueville's analysis of individualism as a pathology of democracy and his interpretation of religion and public opinion as sources of authority in modern society. In a note on the philosophical method of the Americans, Tocqueville described the ultimate consequences of the rise of democracy in a tone that reminds of Lamennais' diagnosis of modern society. Referring to the "general revolt against all authority," Tocqueville ascribed it to the "attempt to appeal to individual reason in all things."[88] While this democratic phenomenon had begun in the eighteenth century, it had taken a much more radical form a century later, when conditions became increasingly equal. Paradoxically, Tocqueville warned, this development made possible new forms of servitude in the age of democracy.

Like Lamennais, Tocqueville was anxious about the political and moral implications of individuals having "only confused and changing notions" on the fundamental questions regarding their personal and social lives. As the authority of former beliefs was challenged, he worried that the world might sink into a new social, political, and intellectual disorder. Both Tocqueville and Lamennais believed that the natural state of mankind is faith rather than doubt, although they interpreted this fact in different ways.[89] They attributed the democratic tendency to selfishness, solipsism, and skepticism to the rational philosophy of the Enlightenment, although they differed in their assessment of the latter. They feared that the new democratic society might become entirely absorbed in material affairs to the point of neglecting the spiritual and transcendent aspects of life. If left unchecked, democracy would produce social disintegration, civic apathy, the coarsening of social life, and extreme forms of individualism.

Nonetheless, Tocqueville and Lamennais differed in another important respect: they disagreed on the nature (and location) of authority in modern society. Opposed to the tenets of Enlightenment and Protestantism, Lamennais remained within the framework of a traditionalist approach to authority that displayed skepticism toward liberal ideas and the power of individual reason. Tocqueville, too, understood that in democratic regimes individuals cannot form all their opinions on their own; yet he was convinced that it was possible to fit liberal ideas and the belief in individual reason into a religious frame of reference. He admitted that individuals are "always brought and held together by some principal ideas," some of which are derived from "a certain number of ready-made beliefs"[90] borrowed from public opinion. Since individuals have neither the leisure nor the necessary strength of mind to develop their own opinions on many issues, they rely on ideas received "on trust and without discussion."[91] Such ideas become dogmatic beliefs and are particularly important in democratic societies where they serve as necessary palliatives for the weakness of individual judgment.

Tocqueville came to believe that the indifference Lamennais feared was not the right word to describe the main challenge posed by the new social condition; even in democratic societies, authority does not disappear and must still be located somewhere. In Tocqueville's view, the real question then is not whether any intellectual authority might survive in democratic centuries; it is rather where this authority will be located and what its extent will be.[92] Since authority in democratic regimes is no longer derived from aristocratic persons, the danger is that the only source of influence would be a monolithic and intolerant public opinion as the prophet of the majority. *Pace* Lamennais, Tocqueville believed that the main threats to social order in democratic societies are not indifference toward religion and the disappearance of authority. The real danger is that extreme forms of individualism might create a mass of atomized individuals at the mercy of a new and powerful authority – public opinion – that promotes conformism and stifles true independence of mind.

CONCLUSION

Finding a compass to navigate the waters of the new democratic world proved to be a challenging task that required refined analytical skills, a new political science, and a novel vocabulary. Tocqueville offered all that. He invited his readers to contemplate democracy without bias in order to minimize its shortcomings and maximize its benefits. In writing *Democracy in America*, he engaged in a complex and hidden intellectual dialogue with his predecessors and contemporaries. Unlike most of them who considered England as a model for France, Tocqueville went to America to study and grasp the nature of modern democracy. His new political science outlined in

Democracy in America was a highly ambitious project that had cross-disciplinary, comparative, normative, and political dimensions.[93] Tocqueville sought to reconcile the old and the new world, showing his readers how to live moderately and humanely in both. He managed to shed fresh light on equality, liberty, the relationship between social and political order, individualism, authority, and public opinion.

Tocqueville wrote *Democracy in America* not only to propose a new political science for a novel democratic world. He also assumed the role of an educator trained in the classical tradition of the French moralists seeking to shape and change the ideas and mores of his contemporaries. As democracy's "spiritual director,"[94] Tocqueville wanted to raise the tone and scope of others' ambitions by giving them a sense of great undertakings and a strong taste for liberty. The outcome was a brilliant book that we still read today with great profit, because it continues to address and speaks so eloquently to our present concerns about the future of democracy.

NOTES

1. OC 17:3, 315. Unless noted otherwise, all translations from French are mine.
2. See Françoise Mélonio, *Tocqueville and the French*, trans. Beth G. Raps (Charlottesville: University of Virginia Press, 1998), 7–83; André Jardin, *Tocqueville: A Biography*, trans. Lydia Davis and Robert Hemenway (New York: Farrar, Straus and Giroux, 1988), 194–223; Jean-Louis Benoît, *Tocqueville: Un destin paradoxal* (Paris: Perrin, 2013), 200–365.
3. On Tocqueville's family background, see Eduardo Nolla's "Editor's Introduction" to DIA (N) I, xlviii–liv; Jardin, *Tocqueville*, 3–55; Antoine Redier, *Comme disait Monsieur de Tocqueville* (Paris: Perrin, 1925), 15–44; Benoît, *Tocqueville*, 23–109; Jean-Louis Benoît, "Malesherbes, l'abbé Lesueur et Hervé de Tocqueville, trois clés de la formation d'Alexis de Tocqueville," *Bulletin de la Société des antiquaires de Normandie*, 78 (2019), 71–94. On Tocqueville's dialogue with Pascal, see Luis Díez del Corral, *El pensamiento político de Tocqueville* (Madrid: Alianza Editorial, 1989), 227–271; Lucien Jaume, *Tocqueville: Les sources aristocratiques de la liberté* (Paris: Fayard,

2008), 218–261 (for the English translation, see *Tocqueville: The Aristocratic Sources of Liberty*, trans. Arthur Goldhammer (Princeton: Princeton University Press, 2013), 159–198); Alan Kahan, *Tocqueville, Democracy, and Religion: Checks and Balances for Democratic Souls* (Oxford: Oxford University Press, 2015), 31–67.

4. Benoît, "Malesherbes, l'abbé Lesueur et Hervé de Tocqueville," 89.

5. OC 17:1, 110.

6. OC 15:1, 68.

7. On the composition of *Democracy in America*, see Eduardo Nolla's "Editor's Introduction" in DIA (N) lxxviii–lxxxix; Jardin, *Tocqueville*, 194–276; James T. Schleifer, *The Making of Tocqueville's "Democracy in America,"* 2nd ed. (Indianapolis: Liberty Fund, 2000), especially 3–45. On the conceptual system of Tocqueville's masterpiece, see François Furet, "Le système conceptuel de la *'Démocratie en Amérique'*," in DEA (F), 7–46.

8. The letter can be found in OC 17:3, 314–317.

9. For a recent account of the Bourbon Restoration, see Francis Démier, *La France de la Restauration (1814–1830): L'impossible retour du passé* (Paris: Gallimard, 2012).

10. The influence of Hervé on Alexis is discussed in R. R. Palmer, *The Two Tocquevilles, Father and Son: Hervé and Alexis de Tocqueville on the Coming of the French Revolution* (Princeton: Princeton University Press, 1987). Benoît highlights the importance of Hervé's *Mémoires* in "Malesherbes, l'abbé Lesueur et Hervé de Tocqueville," 71–75.

11. See Nolla's "Editor's Introduction," in DIA (N) xlvii–cxlix; Mélonio, *Tocqueville and the French*, 25–28.

12. Aurelian Craiutu, *Liberalism under Siege: The Political Thought of the French Doctrinaires* (Lanham, MD: Lexington Books, 2003), 87–122. Also see Craiutu, "Tocqueville and the Political Thought of the French Doctrinaires," *History of Political Thought* 20, no. 3 (1999), 456–493. A classic study remains François Furet, "The Intellectual Origins of Tocqueville's Thought," *The Tocqueville Review/La Revue Tocqueville*, 7 (1985–1986), 117–129. It is also known that Tocqueville drew upon the writings of James Kent and Joseph Story on the US Constitution.

13. Another interesting parallel might be drawn with the writings of Stendhal who was fascinated with America without having ever visited it. On this issue, see Michel Crouzet, *Stendhal et l'Amérique* (Paris: Éditions de

Fallois, 2008). On Stendhal and Tocqueville, see Eugenia Parise, *Pasione e ordine nella trama del moderno tra Tocqueville e Stendhal* (Naples: Edizione scientifiche italiane, 1989); Francesco Spandri, "La vision de l'histoire chez Stendhal et Tocqueville," *Revue d'Histoire littéraire de la France* 106, no. 1 (2006), 47–66.

14. See Alan B. Spitzer, *The Generation of 1820* (Princeton: Princeton University Press, 1987) and Robert Warren Brown, "The Generation of 1820 during the Bourbon Restoration in France: A Biographical and Intellectual Portrait of the First Wave, 1814–1824." PhD dissertation, Duke University, 1979. On Tocqueville's intellectual and personal trajectory during the second half of the 1820s, see Benoît, *Tocqueville*, 69–109.

15. Pierre Roland-Marcel, *Essai politique sur Alexis de Tocqueville* (Paris: Félix Alcan, 1910), 53. The French liberals' ideas are analyzed in Lucien Jaume, *L'Individu effacé ou le paradoxe du libéralisme français* (Paris: Fayard, 1997); Ephraïm Harpaz, *L'École libérale sous la Restauration* (Geneva: Droz, 1968); Jean-Jacques Goblot, *La Jeune France libérale: Le Globe et son groupe littéraire 1824–1830* (Paris: Plon, 1995). The economic ideas are examined in Brown, "The Generation of 1820," 137–190. The overlap and differences between Tocqueville and Benjamin Constant's political ideas are analyzed in George Armstrong Kelly, *The Humane Comedy: Constant, Tocqueville, and French Liberalism* (Cambridge: Cambridge University Press, 1992), especially chap. 2 (39–84), and Jaume, *Tocqueville*, 178–187 (English trans., 129–138). While Constant relied on the distinction between the liberty of the moderns and the liberty of the ancients, Tocqueville worked with the contrast between aristocratic and democratic freedom.

16. R (M), 68.

17. See J. A. W. Gunn, *When the French Tried to be British: Party, Opposition, and the Quest for Civil Disagreement 1814–1848* (Montreal and Kingston: McGill-Queen's University Press, 2009).

18. Pierre Rosanvallon, "The History of the Word 'Democracy' in France," *Journal of Democracy* 6, no. 4 (1995), 140–154.

19. On Jouffroy and Tocqueville, also see Roland-Marcel, *Essai politique sur Alexis de Tocqueville*, 52–54 and Mélonio, *Tocqueville and the French*, 11–12. For an intellectual portrait of Jouffroy, see Charles Augustin Sainte-Beuve, "Jouffroy," in *Portraits littéraires*, ed.

Gérald Antoine (Paris: Robert Laffont, 1993), 204–222; Jean-Philibert Damiron, *Les philosophes français du XIXe siècle* (Paris: CNRS Éditions, 2011), 373–387; Charles de Rémusat, "Théodore Jouffroy," in *Critiques & études littéraires ou passé et présent*, Vol. 2 (Paris: Didier, 1859), 175–222; Kelly, *The Humane Comedy*, 34–35, 134–138.

20 Théodore Jouffroy, *How Dogmas Come to an End* in *Philosophical Miscellanies of Cousin, Jouffroy, and B. Constant*, Vol. 2, ed. and trans. George Ripley (Boston: Hilliard, Gray, and Company, 1838), 121.

21. Jouffroy, *How Dogmas Come to an End*, 123.

22. Jouffroy, *How Dogmas Come to an End*, 122.

23. Jouffroy, *How Dogmas Come to an End*, 128–129.

24. OC 15:2, 315. For an English translation, see TR, 334–337.

25. SLPS, 153.

26. DIA (N) 482.

27. Jouffroy, *How Dogmas Come to an End*, 135.

28. See Brown, "The Generation of 1820," 128–130.

29. Tocqueville as quoted in Roger Boesche, *The Strange Liberalism of Alexis de Tocqueville* (Ithaca, NY: Cornell University Press, 1987), 33–34.

30. SLPS, 153. The extent of Tocqueville's great political ambitions is conveyed well by his correspondence (OC 8:1; OC 17:1).

31. See Théodore Jouffroy, "De la philosophie morale de M. Droz ou de l'Éclectisme moderne," *Le Globe* 92 (April 9, 1825), 457–458. Tocqueville commented on the differences between his views on democracy and Jouffroy's in a letter sent to Francisque de Corcelle on April 12, 1835, published in Tocqueville, OC 15:1, 52–54. Tocqueville thought Jouffroy exaggerated the dangers of democracy without offering any realistic solutions for mitigating them. On Jouffroy and Cousin's eclecticism, see Paul Bénichou, *The Consecration of the Writer, 1750–1830*, trans. Mark K. Jensen (Lincoln: University of Nebraska Press, 1999), 171–182; Kelly, *The Humane Comedy*, 140–168.

32. DIA (N) 6.

33. See Tocqueville's letter to Charles Stöffels in OC 17:1, 59–62.

34. OC 17:1, 64.

35. OC 17:1, 69. The idea of a book on America was also mentioned in Tocqueville's letter to Eugène Stöffels from February 21, 1831 (OC 17:1, 73–74).

36. SLPS, 95.

37. DIA (N) 28. Also see Furet, "Le système conceptuel de la '*Démocratie en Amérique*'," in DEA (F), 7–46.

38. On the French Doctrinaires, see Luis Diez del Corral, *El liberalismo doctrinario* (Madrid: Instituto de estudios políticos, 1956); Pierre Rosanvallon, *Le Moment Guizot* (Paris: Gallimard, 1985); Craiutu, *Liberalism under Siege*. On democracy as social condition, see Jaume, *Tocqueville*, 27–32 (English trans., 15–20); Darío Roldán, *Charles de Rémusat: Certitudes et impasses du libéralisme doctrinaire* (Paris: L'Harmattan, 1999), 72–92.

39. A five-volume edition of Rémusat's *Mémoires de ma vie* was published at Éditions Plon (1958–1967) under the editorship of C.-H. Pouthas. For a recent one-volume selection, see Charles de Rémusat, *Mémoires de ma vie*, ed. Jean Lebrun (Paris: Perrin, 2017).

40. OC 17:3, 291. Emphases added.

41. This text was published posthumously in Charles de Rémusat, *La Pensée politique doctrinaire sous la Restauration: Charles de Rémusat - Textes choisis*, ed. Darío Roldán (Paris: L'Harmattan, 2003), 103–152.

42. Writes Rémusat: "S'il existe un fait universellement convenu, c'est que la société française et par sa composition comme par ses mœurs ne respire que l'égalité. Toutes les classifications hiérarchiques se sont éffacées; toutes les habitudes de subordination se sont affaiblies" (as quoted in Roldán, *Charles de Rémusat*, 84).

43. As quoted in Roldán, *Charles de Rémusat*, 91.

44. See Rémusat, *La Pensée politique doctrinaire sous la Restauration*, 90.

45. Rémusat, *La Pensée politique doctrinaire sous la Restauration*, 57.

46. Rémusat, *La Pensée politique doctrinaire sous la Restauration*, 73.

47. Rémusat, *La Pensée politique doctrinaire sous la Restauration*, 178.

48. Rémusat, *La Pensée politique doctrinaire sous la Restauration*, 54.

49. Rémusat, *La Pensée politique doctrinaire sous la Restauration*, 175.

50. As quoted in Charles de Rémusat, "L'Esprit de réaction: Royer-Collard et Tocqueville," *Revue des deux mondes* (October 15, 1861), 797. Also see Rémusat, *Mémoires de ma vie*, Vol. 2, ed. C.-H. Pouthas (Paris: Plon, 1959), 61.

51. *La Vie politique de M. Royer-Collard: Ses discours et ses écrits*, Vol. 2, ed. Prosper de Barante (Paris: Didier, 1861), 134–135. Also: "À travers beaucoup de malheurs, l'égalité des droits (c'est le vrai nom de la démocratie, et je le lui rends) a prévalu; reconnue, consacrée, garantie

par la Charte, elle est aujourd'hui la forme universelle de la société, et c'est ainsi que la démocratie est partout. Elle n'a plus de conquêtes à faire" (*La Vie politique de M. Royer-Collard*, 2137).

52. See OC 17:1, 212–214; Rémusat, "L'Esprit de réaction," 810–813; Roldán, *Charles de Rémusat*, 72–124.

53. On the intellectual dialogue between Tocqueville and Chateaubriand, see Díez del Corral, *El pensamiento político de Tocqueville*, 311–351; Marc Fumaroli, *Chateaubriand: Poésie et Terreur* (Paris: Éditions de Fallois, 2003); Lucien Jaume, *Tocqueville*, 390–424 (English trans., 291–318); Antoine Compagnon, "Tocqueville et Chateaubriand: Deux anti-modernes?," in Françoise Mélonio and José-Luis Diaz, eds., *Tocqueville et la littérature* (Paris: Presses de l'Université Paris-Sorbonne, 2005), 37–59; Kahan, *Tocqueville, Democracy, and Religion*, 44–48.

54. See Fumaroli, *Chateaubriand*, 727.

55. Kahan, *Tocqueville, Democracy, and Religion*, 44; Fumaroli, *Chateaubriand*, 738.

56. François-René de Chateaubriand, *De l'Ancien Régime au Nouveau Monde: Écrits politiques*, ed. Jean-Paul Clément (Paris: Hachette, 1987), 20.

57. These are Chateaubriand's own words from *Essai historique, politique et moral sur les révolutions anciennes et modernes* (1797), as quoted in Kelly, *The Humane Comedy*, 27.

58. Chateaubriand's American journey is described in detail in books 6–8 of his *Mémoires d'outre tombe*, 2 vols, ed. Maurice Levaillant and Georges Moulinier (Paris: Bibliothèque de la Pléiade, 1951).

59. François-René de Chateaubriand, *Voyage en Amérique*, Vol. 1, ed. Richard Switzer (Paris: Marcel Didier, 1964), 90. Also see Fumaroli, *Chateaubriand*, 323–376.

60. DIA (N) 1295–1359. Tocqueville also believed that Chateaubriand sometimes portrayed the true wilderness with false colors.

61. Tocqueville as quoted in Fumaroli, *Chateaubriand*, 721. Also see Mélonio, *Tocqueville and the French*, 15–16.

62. See also the final pages of book 8 of his *Mémoires*, especially the section "*Dangers pour les États-Unis.*"

63. Chateaubriand, *Mémoires d'outre tombe*, 1:277.

64 Chateaubriand, *De l'Ancien Régime au Nouveau Monde*, 135.

65. François-René de Chateaubriand, *Grands écrits politiques*, Vol. 2, ed. Jean-Paul Clément (Paris: Imprimerie nationale Éditions, 1993), 569. Also see Jaume, *Tocqueville*, 415 (English trans., 310–311).

66. Chateaubriand, *De l'Ancien Régime au Nouveau Monde*, 135.

67. Chateaubriand, "Avenir du monde," in *Revue des deux mondes* (April 15, 1834), 232.

68. Chateaubriand, "Avenir du monde," 234.

69. Writes Chateaubriand: "Le déluge de la démocratie les gagne: ils montent d'étage en étage, du rez-de-chaussée au comble de leurs palais, d'où ils se jetteront à la nage dans le flot qui les engloutera." Chateaubriand, *De l'Ancien Régime au Nouveau Monde*, 408–409.

70. OC 17:1, 215–216. In turn, Chateaubriand responded by confirming Tocqueville's intuitions about the irresistible advance of democracy. "Très certainement," he wrote to Tocqueville on January 11, 1835, "nous entrons dans l'ère démocratique: l'idée démocratique est partout; elle creuse sous tous les trônes, ruine toutes les aristocracies. On pourra la combattre; mais quoi qu'on fasse et quoi qu'on dise, la victoire définitive lui restera." Chateaubriand in OC 17:1, 217.

71. Chateaubriand, *De l'Ancien Régime au Nouveau Monde*, 420.

72. Chateaubriand, *De l'Ancien Régime au Nouveau Monde*, 429.

73. Chateaubriand, *De l'Ancien Régime au Nouveau Monde*, 434.

74. Kahan, *Tocqueville, Democracy, and Religion*, 48.

75. In a fascinating note, Tocqueville wrote: "Democracy! Don't you notice that these are the waters of the flood? Don't you see them advancing constantly by a slow and irresistible effort? ... You withdraw, the waves continue their march. You flee, they run behind you ... Instead of wanting to raise impotent dikes, let us seek rather to build the holy ark that must carry the human species over this ocean without shores." DIA 12, note r. Also see the important letter Tocqueville wrote to Camille d'Orglandes on November 29, 1834, in which he clarified his nuanced position on democracy and explained the goals of his book (OC 17:1, 211–214).

76. The text of *Mirari Vos* can be found at Papal Encyclicals Online: www .papalencyclicals.net/greg16/g16mirar.htm.

Lacordaire severed all ties with Lamennais in 1832 and Montalembert did the same soon thereafter. On the relationship between these thinkers, see Bernard Reardon, *Liberalism and Tradition: Aspects of Catholic Thought in Nineteenth-century France* (Cambridge: Cambridge University

Press, 1975), 107–112; Jaume, *L'Individu effacé*, 193–210. On Lamennais' thought, see Jean-René Derré, *Lamennais, ses amis, et le movement des ideés à l'époque romantique 1824–1834* (Paris: Klincksieck, 1962), 227–274, 385–459; Kelly, *The Humane Comedy*, 122–125.

77. The first volume of *Essai sur l'indifférence en matière de religion* was originally published in 1817; three more volumes followed between 1818 and 1824. For more information, see Reardon, *Liberalism and Tradition*, 66–78.

78. A selection of these articles in English can be found in Félicité Robert de Lamennais, *Lamennais: A Believer's Revolutionary Politics*, ed. Richard A. Lebrun and Sylvain Milbach (Leiden: Brill, 2018).

79. See OC 17:1, 220–221. Lamennais praised Tocqueville for his great service to political science and voiced his sympathy for the "noble sentiments" to be found on every page of the book.

80. The present section draws upon and develops some ideas originally presented in Aurelian Craiutu and Matthew N. Holbreich, "On Individualism, Authority, and Democracy as a New Form of Religion: A Few Tocquevillian Reflections," in Michael Zuckert, ed., *Combining the Spirit of Religion and the Spirit of Liberty: Tocqueville's Thesis Revisited* (Chicago: University of Chicago Press, 2017), 123–152. On individualism in the nineteenth century, see Koenraad W. Swart, "'Individualism' in the Mid-Nineteenth Century (1826–1860)," *Journal of the History of Ideas* 23, no. 1 (1962), 77–90.

81. See Félicité Robert de Lamennais, *Essai sur l'indifférence en matière de religion*, Vol. 2 (Paris: Tournachon Molin & Segun, 1830), v–viii. All subsequent references are to the second volume.

82. As quoted in Jaume, *Tocqueville*, 123, note 5 (English trans., 88n17).

83. Lamennais, *Essai sur l'indifférence en matière de religion*, x.

84. Lamennais, *Essai sur l'indifférence en matière de religion*, ii.

85. Lamennais, *Essai sur l'indifférence en matière de religion*, iv.

86. Lamennais, *Essai sur l'indifférence en matière de religion*, x–xi, xiv.

87. See OC 17:1, 296.

88. DIA (N) 708, note t.

89. See Lamennais, *Essai sur l'indifférence en matière de religion*, 192. Tocqueville explained the goal of his book (different from Lamennais' *Essai*) in two important letters to Eugène Stöffels from February 21, 1835 and July 24, 1836 (OC 17:1, 224–226; 294–297).

90. DIA (N) 713.
91. DIA (N) 712.
92. DIA (N) 717.
93. See Aurelian Craiutu, "Tocqueville's 'Sacred Ark'," *Araucaria* 21, no. 42 (2019), 351–370.
94. Kahan, *Tocqueville, Democracy, and Religion*, 17. On Tocqueville and the French moralists, see Jaume, *Tocqueville*, 201–261.

3   Fugitive Aristocracy: Tocqueville's Search for Remnants of the *Ancien Régime*

Richard Avramenko

When Alexis de Tocqueville and Gustave de Beaumont departed Le Havre in April of 1831, their stated mission was to provide a report to the French government on the new penitentiary system in the United States. While they did provide this report soon after their return,[1] Tocqueville's biographers generally consider this a "pretext" for the trip.[2] In a January 1835 letter to his cousin Louis de Kergorlay, Tocqueville himself admits that the penitentiary project was merely a pretext – a passport allowing entry everywhere in the United States.[3] Some biographers speculate that the July Revolution of 1830 left many young nobles, like Tocqueville and Beaumont, not only concerned for their careers but fearing another round of guillotining. As such, many noble families arranged for children to go abroad until the new revolutionary dust settled. *Democracy in America* was, then, a serendipitous by-product of the time away from France. Most readers of *Democracy in America*, however, suppose the purpose of Tocqueville's trip was to gather data for writing this classic study of American institutions. In same letter, though, Tocqueville denies this. He writes, "I didn't go with the idea of writing a book, but rather the idea of the book came to me there."[4]

There may be some truth in each of these suggestions about the circumstances that led to the creation of *Democracy in America*. At a deeper level, however, the title itself is deceptive. As the mountain of scholarship demonstrates, *Democracy in America* is certainly Tocqueville's effort to bring the American experience of democracy back to France, and the language he employs is unquestionably informed by his reading of a variety of eighteenth- and nineteenth-century sources.[5] Yet there is also evidence that Tocqueville was searching for something more. As Tocqueville tells us in that letter to Kergorlay, he had been harboring this idea for ten years:

> We are being drawn by our laws and mores towards an almost complete equality of conditions. When conditions are completely equal, I no longer see any middle ground between a democratic government (and by this word I don't mean the republic, but a state of society where everyone would more or less participate in governance) and the government of one man ruling without limits.[6]

If forced to choose, Tocqueville would opt for the lesser of the two evils: democratic governance. The problem, however, is that this choice – and resisting the complete tyranny of one man – requires moral resolve. In France, however, Tocqueville sees a people who are "tired, disenchanted, disappointed."[7] They are like soldiers "demoralized by fever and deprivations."[8] For Tocqueville, resisting tyranny requires a kind of "ancient energy" (*ancienne énergie*).[9]

Where, then, does one search for the moral energy necessary to resist tyranny? The central purpose of this chapter is to bring to light precisely this search. For Tocqueville, this moral resolve – this ancient energy – defined the *ancien régime* and the aristocratic age. Tocqueville's voyage to America and the masterpiece we know as *Democracy in America* are thus both bound up with what can only be considered a spiritual quest. Tocqueville was hunting down the fugitive spirit of the *ancien régime*. In language we find throughout his *oeuvre*, he was seeking what he calls "the remnant" (*le reste*) of an aristocratic spirit in the New World. This remnant, Tocqueville thought, was essential for the preservation of liberty in democratic times.

That said, Tocqueville's quest for the fugitive spirit of aristocracy is no nostalgic longing for the restoration of an idyllic aristocratic past that never existed, as Sheldon Wolin and others suggest.[10] Tocqueville harbors no illusions on this front: "There is therefore no question of reconstructing an aristocratic society, but the need is to make freedom spring from that democratic society in which God has placed us."[11] Thus, *Democracy in America* should be read as a manual instructing the new elite in France – be they a remnant of the nobility, the new bourgeoisie, or even the progeny of the 1789 revolutionaries – how to dig through the rubble of the Old World, distinguishing remnant from debris and, in so doing, to disinter (*déterrer*) the moral resolve and ancient energy necessary for resisting tyranny in the democratic age.

In what follows, I argue that this spiritual quest informed much of Tocqueville's itinerary. I also argue, however, that this quest was largely unsuccessful; rather than finding "the remnant" he sought in the New World, Tocqueville found what he calls "*débris*." The distinction between "remnant" and "debris" is not only central for understanding *Democracy in America* but also serves as a lens for seeing the world as Tocqueville saw it. In short, the space between remnant and debris is where we find Tocqueville's greatest hope for freedom in the democratic age.

I begin with a historical and etymological briefing on "remnant" and "debris." I then catalogue the various geographical and theoretical moments of Tocqueville's search. First there is the geographical quest starting in the debris on Frenchman's Island in Lake Oneida, before moving to the debris of the American Indians on the frontier, and then passing through the aristocratic debris of the American South. Next, I show Tocqueville's theoretical quest coming up empty with the industrial elite in America, espying glimmers of hope in the American military, and finally identifying his quarry in the American legal system. I conclude by suggesting that, although Tocqueville came up empty-handed in previous stops on his American journey, the remnant of aristocratic energy he seeks might be found in the legal spirit (*esprit légal*) of the American lawyer.

REMNANT AND DEBRIS

Let us begin with "the remnant." In French, it is *le reste* and is recorded in 1606 in one of the first French dictionaries.[12] There, the definition is *"qui signifie Demeurer par sus"* or "that which is left over." *Reste* is related to the Latin *reliquum* and *residuum* but derives directly from *resto. Stō* is the Latin root for "stand"; adding *re-* literally means "to stand again," but it is often understood as "to stand against" or "to resist" or "what's left standing." Thus, the origins of *le reste* are akin to modern phrases like *"un reste de cheval"* (an old racehorse that, due to some quality or another, the owner does not destroy) or *"jouer de son reste"* (a poker term – "going all in"). In other words, something honorable resides in *le reste* – it suggests a resistance to circumstances, however dire, with the hope of standing tall once more.

Conceptually, *le reste* goes back to Isaiah in the Old Testament:

> In that day the remnant [*le reste*] of Israel, the survivors of the house of Jacob, will no longer rely on him who struck them down ... A remnant [*Un reste*] will return, a remnant [*un reste*] of Jacob will return to the Mighty God. Though your people, O Israel, be like the sand by the sea, only a remnant [*qu'un reste*] will return.[13]

As the story goes, Jerusalem was sacked by the Babylonians around 590 BCE. Survivors of the sacking were deported to Babylon, where they lived in the "Babylonian Captivity." When the Persians defeated the Babylonians, Cyrus the Great allowed the exiled Jews to return to Judea. The passage in Isaiah refers to this remnant who returned to Jerusalem after the disaster of the Babylonian Captivity and began construction of the Second Temple to rebuild the nation. As we hear in Isaiah 11:1 (and 11:10), "A shoot will come up from the stump of Jesse," and "the Root of Jesse will stand as a banner for the peoples." Then, "the Lord will reach out his hand a second time to reclaim the remnant [*le reste*] from Assyria, from Lower Egypt, from Upper Egypt, from Cush, from Elam, from Babylonia, from Hamath and from the islands of the sea" (Isaiah 11:11).[14] Consulting the Tocqueville family bible in French to read Isaiah would reveal *"le reste"* and *"un reste,"* where the English has "remnant."

The earliest definition of *le débris* reads, "*Les restes d'un vais-seau qui a fait naufrage,*" or the remaining pieces of a ship that has been wrecked.[15] The fifth edition (1835) expands the definition to "*Des restes d' une chose brisée, fracassée, ou détruite en grande partie,*" or the leftovers of a thing that is broken, smashed, or in large part destroyed. The later edition also included a figurative use of *débris*: "*Ce qui reste d' une chose après sa ruine, sa destruction, son abolition; du bien qui reste à quelqu' un après un grand revers de fortune; des troupes qui restent après la défaite d' une armée.*" This is to say that, by the time Tocqueville was writing, *le débris* referred to what remains after ruination or complete destruction.

While the two terms may at first glance seem to be functionally synonymous, a return to the 1606 version of *Thresor* reveals signifi-cant differences. *Thresor* does not give a definition of *débris*, but it lists three Latin relatives: *confractio, conquassatio,* and *naufragium*. *Confractio* refers to a rupture or breach, as in Isaiah 24:19: "The earth is broken up [*confractione confringetur terra*], the earth is split asun-der, the earth is thoroughly shaken." Similarly, *conquassatio* means a shattering or a disturbance. *Naufragium* relates to the 1694 defin-ition of *débris* in that it invokes the image of a wrecked ship, as in the proverb "*istorum naufragia ex terra intueri,*" or in safety behold their ruin. All three terms emphasize the impossibility of reconciliation. Thus, while modern readers may mistakenly conflate *reste* and *débris*, there is in fact a significant difference between a notion of broken pieces that can be made to stand again and those, such as the planks of a sunken ship, that are hopelessly destroyed. A remnant is not wreckage, and this is key for understanding Tocqueville's quest.

FUGITIVE ARISTOCRATS IN AMERICA

To understand Tocqueville's search for the remnants of aristocracy, we must first grasp his vision of the aristocratic way of life. For Tocqueville, a good community is free. On this point, there is no ambiguity: "I believe that tyranny is the greatest evil, liberty the first good" and nothing "is more precious to man than his liberty."[16]

These liberties, Tocqueville argues, are not easily maintained in either aristocratic or democratic ages. In the aristocratic age, however, the nobility regarded it as their sacred duty to safeguard their own liberties and, in so doing, served the people of their local parish. This is the foundation of the aristocratic spirit in which one finds a "sublime conception of the duties of man"; it was "the age of blind sacrifice and instinctive virtue," all in the name of human liberty.[17]

My claim, then, is that Tocqueville was on a spiritual journey – a quest for the remnants of this aristocratic spirit in the seemingly democratic milieu of America. *Democracy in America*, we know, opens with the famous phrase, "No novelty in the United States struck me more vividly during my stay there than the equality of conditions."[18] As the book unfolds, however, we learn that democracy may not be as ubiquitous as originally stated. "One may put it this way," he writes early in volume 1: "The surface of American society is covered with a layer of democratic paint, but from time to time one can see the old aristocratic colors breaking through."[19] Elsewhere in the first volume he refers to the "remnants [*le reste*] of the Aristocratic Party."[20] Besides betraying a slight misunderstanding of the American political party system, Tocqueville argues that wealthy Americans form a secret class that, eschewing the public sphere and the scorn they meet there, constitutes "a private society with its own tastes and enjoyments." These American aristocrats "have a great distaste for their country's democratic institutions" and await the day when they can reestablish their superiority.[21]

More telling is a story from outside the pages of *Democracy in America*. As most readers know, after arriving in the vicinity of New York City and spending a few weeks gathering data for their penitentiary report, Tocqueville and Beaumont immediately headed west. Although they would travel as far as Green Bay, Wisconsin, their immediate western goal was Lake Oneida, New York. This seemingly obscure excursion is portrayed by many biographers as a whimsical, insignificant event, but Tocqueville's account suggests otherwise.[22] In addition to writing a lengthy letter to his sister,

Tocqueville composed a separate, unpublished text detailing the journey. In *Journey to Lake Oneida*, he describes their arrival: "No road passes by this place; in these parts one sees no great industrial establishments, and no places celebrated for their picturesque beauty. But it was not chance that led us to this solitary lake. *For it was the end and object of our journey*."[23] It is unclear whether this passage refers only to Tocqueville and Beaumont's ventures on July 8, 1831, or their journey to America more broadly. In either case, the journey to Oneida was of central importance for Tocqueville.

To appreciate the significance of this journey to a remote and largely uninhabited lake, it is important to understand Tocqueville's motives. During his childhood, Tocqueville read and revered a little novel titled *Voyage d'un Allemand au Lac Oneida* – which was an abridged, French version of *Erscheinungen am See Oneida* published by Sophie von La Roche in 1798.[24] The original manuscript by La Roche tells the story of a fugitive French couple who travel to the United States in search of asylum from the plights of revolutionary upheaval.[25] This couple settles on a small island in Lake Oneida to begin their new life. As one historian notes, to La Roche, "America offered [the couple] not the promise of freedom from feudal bonds, but, on the contrary, an asylum for those aristocratic Europeans who had been compelled to abandon temporarily their accustomed forms of civilized living."[26] It is no surprise, then, that Tocqueville was so enamored by this tale, which, he wrote, "left a deep and lasting impression on my mind."[27] When he recounts sharing this work with Beaumont, Tocqueville links the novel to their American journey:

> We often talked about it, and always ended by saying, sometimes laughing, sometimes sadly, "The only happiness in the world is on the shores of Lake Oneida." When events that could not have been foreseen took us both to America, this recollection returned to us more forcefully. We promised ourselves that we would go and see our two French people, if they were still alive, or at least visit their home.[28]

The journey to Oneida was no mere passing fancy but a long-awaited, almost spiritual quest for Tocqueville to find a couple of fugitive aristocrats in the New World.

The romantic language Tocqueville employs to describe this quest in *Journey to Lake Oneida* has led some scholars to dismiss the text as "of psychological interest only."[29] In light of his quest to discover aristocratic remnants, however, Tocqueville's romantic language takes on deeper meaning. Of his early conceptions of Oneida, Tocqueville writes: "the recollection of the two French people in Lake Oneida had always remained in my memory. How often have I envied them the tranquil joys of their solitude."[30] In the letter to his sister-in-law, he writes: "I want at least to describe our recent visit to Oneida Lake. If it doesn't make you dream for a week, by which I mean daydream, I shall no longer recognize you."[31] Tocqueville also describes the domestic life of these aristocratic exiles as "where my imagination had created a new Eden."[32] These aristocratic exiles harbored his hopes for a repository of the ancient energy he was seeking. This journey to Lake Oneida no doubt inaugurated his quest for a remnant of aristocracy.

Unfortunately for Tocqueville, the reality of Lake Oneida and Frenchman's Island did not match his hopes. Upon arrival, a local resident told Tocqueville and Beaumont that the island, once home to the French fugitives, had long been uninhabited. The wife, Tocqueville was informed, died and the husband had long since left the area. Nonetheless, Tocqueville and Beaumont paddle out to the island. What they found were not remnants but rather debris. Recognizing that "those who read these lines will not understand the feelings they record, and will treat them as exaggerated or chimerical," Tocqueville paints a moving scene of the fate of the aristocratic couple on the island.[33] With his wife gone,

> He is no longer adapted either for solitude or for the world; he does not know how to live either with men or without them; he is neither a savage nor a civilised man: he is nothing but a piece of

debris [*débris*], like those trees in the American forests which the wind has had the power to uproot, but not to blow down. He stands erect, but he lives no more.[34]

This image of the lost and helpless nobleman is a symbol for the fate of the aristocratic spirit he seeks. Like a dead, uprooted trunk that leans on surrounding new trees, it might still stand erect but it is an illusion, a veneer. It is debris that offers no ancient strength with which one can rebuild. His disappointment at Oneida, therefore, is the prelude of his remaining quest – a quest that continually comes up empty.

INDIGENOUS ARISTOCRACY IN AMERICA

Following their disappointment at Lake Oneida, Tocqueville and Beaumont made a beeline for the frontier to continue the search. As we learn from *A Fortnight in the Wilderness* and elsewhere in his works, Tocqueville arrived with the "noble savage" trope in mind – a trope made popular by Diderot, Rousseau, and Chateaubriand. Heading west, he and Beaumont sought to go spatially beyond "civilization," so as to go temporally "before" civilization. That is, they sought to catch a glimpse of fugitive aristocracy in the natives on the frontier.

There are numerous instances in which Tocqueville refers to Native Americans as aristocrats. For example, they are warriors with a rich heritage that they honor; they lead, or at least once led, "adventurous [lives] full of afflictions and dangers but also full of proud emotions."[35] They take part in aristocratic leisure activities. They talk about their land as their "heritage" transmitted to them from their "ancestors" and containing "their ashes" and bones. They are animated by honor, they hunt, and they worship their ancestors. For Tocqueville, the resemblance between indigenous people and the European nobility is striking:

> [T]he Indian in the miserable depths of his forests cherishes the same ideas and opinions as the medieval noble in his castle, and he only needs to become a conqueror to complete the resemblance. How odd it is that the ancient prejudices of Europe should reappear,

not among the European population along the coast, but in the forests of the New World.[36]

Perhaps the most aristocratic element of the Native Americans is their relation to the land. Just as Tocqueville and many other European aristocrats understand their position, duties, and heritage as bound up with a particular place, so too with the Native Americans. This spatiality and temporality are unfamiliar to the typical American democrat. In a staged dialogue between a native and Anglo-Americans, Tocqueville highlights this division with great irony:

> When the European population begins to approach the wilderness occupied by a savage nation, the United States government usually sends a solemn embassy to them; the white men assemble the Indians in a great plain, and after they have eaten and drunk with them, they say: "What have you to do in the land of your fathers? Soon you will have to dig up [déterrer] their bones in order to live. In what way is the country you dwell in better than another? Are there not forests and marshes and prairies elsewhere than where you live, and can you live nowhere but under your own sun? Beyond these mountains that you see on the horizon, and on the other side of the lake which skirts your land to the west, there are vast countries where wild beasts are still found in abundance; sell your lands to us and go and live happily in those lands." That speech finished, they spread before the Indians firearms, woolen clothes, kegs of brandy, glass necklaces, pewter bracelets, earrings and mirrors.[37]

The democrat's insensitivity to the significance of a particular plot of land, the sacred relation to ancestors, and a shared spatial heritage is ironic: the American uses the phrase "land of your fathers" but fails to understand how the natives relate to that land. This dialogue is all the more ironic insofar as Americans have, after all, abandoned the bones of their own ancestors in Europe. The very notion of digging up ancestors reveals the juxtaposition of rootless, wandering democrats and spatially and temporally grounded aristocrats. Whereas few ideas could be more repulsive to the aristocrat, for the ostensibly "civilized" democrat, land is merely a source of food and, by extension, the income one can earn from selling one's harvest. The relationship is one of extraction, or *un-earthing* (*déterrer*).

Thus, we smell irony again when the white man asks, "In what way is the country you dwell in better than another?" The answer – a livelihood that transcends the material productive capacity of the place – is irrelevant, if not unthinkable to the democrat. As if in response, Tocqueville elsewhere paraphrases the following from a Native American speech delivered to Congress: "From time immemorial, our common Father, who is in heaven, has given our ancestors the land we occupy."[38] The natives' land has been spiritually sanctioned – it is not theirs to sell and it is unsellable. To leave their land would be a disrespect to ancestors and a rejection of the divine. Such an act would be, as Jonathan Lear puts it, "culturally devastating."[39]

Recognizing this distinction reveals several political ramifications. First, the Native Americans are connected to their land not (only) through Old World faith or mystical belief in ashes and bones but by a nuanced understanding of time as static, of past and future bound up in the present. In some sense, this is but another bond that tethers the aristocratic Native Americans to their world. Likewise, it is a bond the democrat eschews. Presentism, a hallmark of the democratic mind, yields serious consequences for the soul. It offers little hesitation to propositions such as digging up ancestors, moving one's home for trivial reasons, and renouncing past agreements. Perhaps through his portrayal of the plight of the Native Americans, Tocqueville intends to help resist these democratic tendencies.

The destruction of native culture also bears some relation to why Tocqueville classified this group as debris rather than remnant. Despite these largely favorable depictions, Tocqueville's encounters with the Native Americans belie a tragedy. He argues that some tribes exhibit a "childish carelessness of the morrow characteristic of savage nature [and] wait for the danger to reach them before bothering about it."[40] They may have "ancestral fields," and "instinctive love of country holds them to the soil where they were born," but "the land is the common property of the tribe ... therefore no one has an individual interest in defending any part of it."[41] These encounters reveal that their aristocratic heritage has mostly been crushed by democratic expansion. The natives offer little hope for curbing the worst part of democracy because they have already been decimated by it.

We can contrast Tocqueville and Beaumont's ingenuous expectations with their first actual encounter with this indigenous aristocracy – the Iroquois near Buffalo. The scene from *Fortnight in the Wilderness* is heart-wrenching. Rather than unsullied aristocracy, they found a nightmarish scene – a once-proud people, dressed in mismatched European rags, lying dead drunk on the side of the road: "Yet these feeble and depraved beings belonged to one of the most celebrated tribes of the ancient American world," Tocqueville writes. "We had before us, and pity it is to say so, the last remains [*les derniers restes*] of that famous confederation of the Iroquois, which was known for its forceful intelligence no less than for its courage, and which long held the balance between the two greatest nations of Europe."[42] What is interesting, however, is that, despite this devastation at Buffalo, Tocqueville presumably still had hope, as he uses remnants (*les restes*) rather than debris.[43]

One might think that Tocqueville conflates these terms because he refers to the Native Americans as both *le débris* and *le reste*, employing either to mean something like "leftovers" or "scraps," albeit in different contexts. However, this is not the case. Specifically, when he describes the westward expansion of the American government, he says they "wished to transport the remnants [*débris*] of the native populations in the South to the part of [the] territory nearest Mexico, and at a great distance from the American settlements."[44] These tribes, already pushed from the eastern seaboard into the middle of the country, and from there to the West, have no future. Their destiny, according to Tocqueville, is to continue running westward, but "sooner or later there will be no land left for them, their only refuge will be the grave."[45] Like planks of a wrecked ship, these Native Americans are sinking into destruction; they are *débris*, not remnants.

At first glance, the treatment of Native Americans appears no less destructive than that enacted by the Spanish in the southern regions before them. As Tocqueville writes:

> The Spaniards let their dogs loose on the Indians as if they were wild beasts; they pillaged the New World like a city taken by storm, without discrimination or mercy; but one cannot destroy everything, and frenzy has a limit; the remnant [*le reste*] of the Indian population, which escaped the massacres, in the end mixed [*se mêler*] with the conquerors and adopted their religion and mores.[46]

How is it that those Native Americans pursued by Spanish dogs can be *le reste*, while those forced westward by US legislation are *débris*? The former certainly seem more subject to violent death and irreparable destruction than the latter. Yet, as Tocqueville notes, "frenzy has its limits." If we are to take seriously the etymological distinction just outlined, the Native Americans pursued by the Spanish retain some element of their identity and heritage. It may not be enough to build a new nation, but enough of their ancient energy remains to mingle [*se mêler*] with the Spanish. That is, the Native Americans mix with their conquerors to produce a new race that is an amalgamation of both cultures – they do not simply lose themselves in the Spanish.[47] Tocqueville observes that the remnant adopts Spanish religion and mores but no doubt other elements of their heritage remain. "The Spanish," he writes, "did not succeed in exterminating the Indian race and could not even prevent them from sharing their rights."[48] Although it is not clear what the end result is, something can grow forth from *le reste* of the Native Americans who mingled with their conquerors. On the other hand, those who suffered under the laws of the United States may well have been destroyed beyond hope. They are *débris*.

ARISTOCRACY IN THE SOUTH

If the remnant was neither on Frenchman's Island nor among the indigenous peoples, perhaps it was to be found amidst the very worst inequality in the United States: in the slave states of the South. Tocqueville's treatment of southern slave-owners is complicated. Although he likens American slavery to European feudalism, he condemns it both for its effects on the southern psyche and as an affront to Christian morality. However, after analyzing the economic and political perspectives of slavery, as well as evaluating several strategies for abolition, he laments, "God protect me from trying, as certain American writers do try, to justify the principle of Negro slavery; I am only saying that all those who formerly accepted this terrible principle are not now equally free to get rid of it."[49] If anything is to be gained from Tocqueville's appraisal of southerners and slavery, one must read him as an observer caught between the fugitive spirit of aristocratic values he is seeking and an evil he abhors. There is little doubt in Tocqueville's mind that the American South is aristocratic, especially concerning its approach to land and labor. However, if he intends for aristocratic society to teach us anything, it can only be a word of warning: freedom-preserving mores cannot come at the expense of actual freedom, and they must comport with the new, inevitable reality of equal social conditions.

To understand the relationship Tocqueville draws between labor and freedom, we must travel with him westward along the Ohio River, a journey he details in *Democracy in America*. On the left bank there lies Kentucky, on the right, Ohio. Tocqueville insists that the soil on either bank is full of "inexhaustible treasures" and that the people on either side are "by nature enterprising and energetic."[50] However, the relationship of the people to the land and the direction of their energies distinguish Kentucky from Ohio. For Tocqueville, the cause of this distinction is slavery: Kentucky allows it and Ohio forbids it, and the consequences are apparent. Kentucky is a "primeval forest" interrupted by "half-deserted fields" tended by slaves.[51] So quiet and unpopulated is the Kentucky riverbank that Tocqueville writes, "one might say that society has gone to sleep; it is nature that seems active and alive, whereas man is idle."[52] In Ohio, however, the "confused hum" of industry rattles over abundant fields. There, "man appears rich and contented; he works."[53] By contrast, in Kentucky, the idle man of leisure loves excitement. He hunts, duels, and is eager to go to war.[54] He owns fields, but he will not labor in them. Even when presented with an economic argument against unpaid labor, the southerner concludes that his "poverty is preferable to [slavish] industry."[55] Hence, slavery "not only prevents the [southern] white men from making their fortunes but even diverts them from wishing to do so."[56]

The southerner's disdain for labor and love of leisure is certainly redolent of aristocracy, but can it teach democratic society how to live freely? At first glance, his idleness seems barbaric. He favors hunting trips and bloody duels over material well-being and all the progress that derives therefrom. To the democratic mind, the southern aristocrat seems to hold life in contempt. However, this evaluation is not entirely fair. The workman is often willing to risk his life, too. According to Tocqueville, "he is equally equipped to turn into a sailor, pioneer, artisan, or cultivator, facing the labors or dangers of these various ways of life with even constancy."[57] The idle aristocrat chooses danger because the activity fulfills his life *qua* life, but the workman does so to earn a wage that he will spend to improve his physical well-being. Herein lies a paradox: the laboring mind is so focused on acquiring well-being that the workman is willing to do things that may limit or even completely prohibit his enjoyment of his acquisitions. In this sense, he is a slave to material possessions, especially those just beyond his grasp. Thus, Tocqueville worries that, as democratic individuals labor for the sake of an ever-lengthening list of comforts, they will blithely exchange their freedoms for despotism, as long as that despot allows them to continue "circling around in pursuit of the petty and banal pleasures with which they glut their souls."[58]

The southern aristocrat, then, might teach democrats the value of things not measured in dollars and thus free them from the oppressive allure of material well-being. Sport, adventure, and other leisurely activities can show the egalitarian, laboring mind that the good life need not be won through toil nor measured in possessions. If they can develop a taste for this way of life, democratic souls may take action to preserve it against despots that would usurp their freedom with the promise of physical comfort. Unfortunately, however, southerners cannot teach this lesson. Although they may be masterful practitioners of aristocratic leisure, this way of life is predicated on the inequality of social conditions. For Tocqueville, democratic social conditions are inevitably spreading across the globe. Nations, including the American South, will have no alternative but "to acquiesce in the [equal] social state imposed by Providence."[59] Slavery will eventually perish in the United States because it is "attacked by Christianity as unjust and by political economy as fatal."[60] Simply put, if the aristocracy in the South had a lesson to teach about the art of being free, the evil of slavery obfuscates and obviates the lesson. There's little doubt that Tocqueville regarded the American South as a vestigial aristocratic society – but not one that will (or should) last and not one that retains the most important part of aristocracy, the art of being free within a democratic social state. Aristocracy in the white South is *débris* from which there is little to salvage.

Finally, regarding the slave population in the South, Tocqueville is pessimistic. As he writes: "Then the Negroes will be no more than unlucky remnants [*malheureux débris*], a poor little wandering tribe lost amid the huge nation that is master of the land; nothing but the injustices and hardships to which they are subjected will call attention to their presence."[61] The translation here is, of course, a little inaccurate. *Débris*, unlike *le reste*, is no foundation from which new things, such as liberty, can flourish. It is not akin to the stump of Jesse from which a new shoot will grow (Isaiah 11:1). Although he describes the freed slaves as a wandering tribe, there is no indication that "the Lord will reach out … to reclaim the remnant [*le reste*]" (Isaiah 11:11). Even after emancipation, Tocqueville thinks they are doomed to lead a "wretched existence" – without land and burdened by the "memories of slavery," their souls completely degraded.[62] The language of their aristocratic past is lost and slavery has destroyed their memories and their families.

INDUSTRIAL AND BUSINESS ARISTOCRACIES

We have seen that Tocqueville's quest for the fugitive spirit of aristocracy came up empty at Lake Oneida, on the American frontier, and in the South. His quest, however, was not merely geographical. Readers of *Democracy in America* might, for example, get a sense that Tocqueville spotted a remnant of aristocracy in the wealthy elite in America. While Tocqueville did observe a privileged elite in America that he calls an industrial aristocracy (*l'aristocratie manufacturière*) or a business aristocracy (*l'aristocratie que fonde le négoce*), it is not the remnant he seeks. In fact, Tocqueville thinks that a full-blown industrial aristocracy would be "a monstrosity."[63] For Tocqueville, an industrial elite can never form a class that combines wealth and power with social and political responsibility. As Tocqueville puts it, "the territorial aristocracy (*aristocratie territoriale*) of past ages was obliged by law, or thought itself obliged by custom, to come to the help of its servants and relieve their distress. But the industrial aristocracy of our day, when it has impoverished and brutalized the men it uses, abandons them in time of crisis to public charity to feed them."[64] Put otherwise, other than callous cash payment, there are scant connections between the privileged few of the business aristocracy and the people who toil for them. In Tocqueville's words, "although there are rich men, a class of the rich does not exist at all, for these rich men have neither corporate spirit nor objects in common, neither common traditions nor hopes. There are limbs, then, but no body."[65]

For Tocqueville, a class is a relatively stable group that recognizes in themselves certain commonalities and responsibilities.[66] As he argues elsewhere, even the emergent administrative aristocracy in France was a kind of class because it had its own "traditions, virtues, honors, [and] its own pride."[67] The nobility of the *ancien régime*, he tells us, competed with one another for these honors and thereby held each other to a set of standards prompting them to public service. Because the business elite is not a class, it is nearly impossible for them to behave such that they might offer any lessons for the preservation of liberty in democratic times. The only thing that holds them together is interest, and just as interest brought them together it will pull them apart. In short, Tocqueville sees none of the aristocratic spirit he was seeking in the American industrial and business elite.

THE MILITARY

If not in the business elite, perhaps Tocqueville could find what he was looking for in the military class in America. After all, military culture displays many of the trappings of the nobility. Although the hierarchy, obedience, and honor-driven culture of the military may seem a promising remnant of an aristocracy, Tocqueville suggests that democratic armies are largely shaped by the social state they seek to defend. The veneer of aristocratic attributes in the military, in other words, is belied by the democratic conditions in which they operate. Thus, instead of looking to the American military as a potential aristocratic bulwark against democratic tendencies, Tocqueville offers largely cautionary words for the military *because* of its democratic inclinations.

Although all armies require a certain hierarchy of status and obedience, the effect of this structure is very different in aristocratic and democratic states. In an aristocracy, one's position in the military is determined by social position. Thus, the aristocratic nobleman "almost always regards his military rank as something secondary to his social position; a nobleman who joins the army as a career is less influenced by ambition than by a sense of the duties imposed by his birth."[68] Aristocratic military service, in other words, is motivated by duty stemming from one's ascribed social status. The opposite pertains in democratic armies. Democracies offer citizens little status or social differentiation and, consequently, ambitious democrats might seek status *through* their military career. As a result, "something which was only a secondary consideration in aristocratic armies has become the chief thing, the only thing, and the essence of existence" for democratic soldiers.[69] Because status cannot be gained elsewhere, democratic armies are full of "social climbers." The "desire for promotion," Tocqueville notes, "is almost universal in democratic armies; it is eager, tenacious, and continual."[70] The hierarchal structure of the military, therefore, has a distinctly democratic effect – it facilitates tenacious ambition and unbridled self-interest.

The tendency to increase one's status through military service has dangerous consequences for democratic life. Because warfare is the chief means by which promotion occurs in the military, an army full of ambitious soldiers will desire nothing but war. Tocqueville writes, "Therefore all the ambitious minds in a democratic army ardently long for war, because war makes vacancies available and allows violations of the rule of seniority, which is the one privilege natural to a democracy."[71] If Tocqueville is correct, then democratic armies are prone to subvert rather than reinforce the only marker of status in democratic life: seniority.

There is another great difference between aristocratic and democratic armies that Tocqueville brings into focus. In aristocratic states where nobles are bound to military service by duty, the best and the brightest of a society go to war for the nation. This has many salubrious effects on both warfare and society. However, when the love of wealth is the highest aim, the opposite occurs. The most talented individuals seek to elevate their position by pursuing commerce, government, or academe. Therefore,

> it is not the leading citizens, but the least important who go into the army. A man only develops military ambitions when all other doors are closed ... The elite of the nation avoid a military career because it is not held in honor, and it is not held in honor because the elite of the nation do not take it up.[72]

What happens, then, is that the army "becomes a little nation apart, with a lower standard of intelligence and rougher habits than the nation at large. But this little uncivilized nation holds the weapons and it alone knows how to use them."[73] As such, the military may pose a significant threat to liberty rather than a bulwark against tyranny. While civil-military relations in American history tend to be largely peaceful, Tocqueville's worry has proven providential in emerging democracies throughout the world.

Tocqueville's assessment of the military in *Democracy in America*, therefore, is much more cautionary than one might expect from a European aristocrat. There might, however, be an upshot to his assessment because militaries are home to two of aristocracy's greatest devotions: honor and courage. Tocqueville's take on these virtues, however, is not what one might expect. Instead of viewing the democratic army as a great reservoir preserving valor, honor codes, and traditional virtues, he redefines what honor means. The substance of honor, Tocqueville suggests, is socially contingent. "Every time men come together to form a particular society, a conception of honor is immediately established among them, that is to say, a collection of opinions peculiar to themselves about what should be praised or blamed."[74] Thus, while in aristocracies people viewed the military as a place to obtain and confirm honor, democracies open new, less violent paths. This is also true of courage. Tocqueville's rendering of American courage is telling:

> In the United States martial valor is little esteemed; the type of courage best known and best appreciated is that which makes a man brave the fury of the ocean to reach port more quickly, and face without complaint the privations of life in the wilds and that solitude which is harder to bear than any privations, the courage which makes a man almost insensible to the loss of a fortune laboriously acquired and prompts him instantly to fresh exertions to gain another. It is chiefly courage of this sort which is needed to

> maintain American community and make it prosper, and it is held
> by them in particular esteem and honor.[75]

The substance of honor and courage, therefore, have radically
changed, but these virtues must still be cultivated and maintained
to continue to benefit the American people. In the military, then,
Tocqueville see some hope – a remnant of the aristocratic spirit that
might stand firmly in the face of the worst inclinations of democratic
social conditions.

THE LEGAL PROFESSION

If Tocqueville discovered an aristocratic remnant anywhere on his
journey through America, it was in an unlikely group of teachers:
priests. These priests, however, are not Catholic. In fact, they are
not even Christian. Instead, they are "Egyptian priests" from
a strange order called the legal profession that we might find to be
a useful remnant.[76] As Tocqueville puts it, "if you ask me where the
American aristocracy is found, I have no hesitation in answering
that it is not among the rich, who have no common link uniting
them. It is at the bar or the bench that the American aristocracy is
found."[77] It is in the legal profession and the "legal spirit" (esprit
légal) that one finds the habits of mind and a language that best
approximates the aristocratic spirit he was seeking. "Men who have
made a special study of the laws," Tocqueville writes, "have derived
therefrom habits of order, something of a taste for formalities, and
an instinctive love for a regular concatenation of ideas." Such
people, he claims, "are naturally strongly opposed to the revolutionary spirit and to the ill-considered passions of democracy."[78] In
other words, Tocqueville is arguing that lawyers see the world
through an aristocratic lens.[79]

In Tocqueville's view, this spirit is not derived from the study of
just any law. Rather, it is the study of a particular kind of law: the law of
precedent. The law of precedent, or the common law, is the basis of the
legal system in both England and the United States and, as Tocqueville

puts it, the "aristocratic character which I detect in the legal mind is more pronounced still in the United States and in England than in any other land. This is not only due to English and American legal studies, but also to the very nature of the legislation and the position of lawyers as interpreters thereof in both these countries."[80] The French, Tocqueville points out, do not use such a legal system and thus France can expect no salvation from their democratic lawyers. American lawyers, however, are in the habit of seeking links between their own situation and that of others, and this pertains especially to generations past. There is, in a sense, a bond between a lawyer and his legal forefathers. Because they have kept the law of precedent, "they still derive their opinions in legal matters and the judgments they pronounce from the opinions and legal judgments of their fathers."[81] These legal habits of mind echo the aristocratic epistemology – the rules of legal interpretation were given by their legal ancestors, which in turn makes their mode of interpretation both strict and traditional.

It is thus that Tocqueville says that

> an English or American lawyer almost always combines a taste and respect for what is old with a liking for regularity and legality. This influences in yet another way the turn of lawyers' minds, and so the course of society. The first thing an English or American lawyer looks for is what has been done, whereas a French one inquires what one should wish to do; one looks for judgments and the other for reasons.[82]

When the American lawyer looks back to see what has been done, he uses judgment as to which decisions are relevant to his contemporary situation. In other words, he makes distinctions. The law of precedent requires the lawyer to make critical assessments, not unlike the connoisseur. It is no wonder that Tocqueville says that "hidden at the bottom of a lawyer's soul one finds some of the tastes and habits of an aristocracy. They share its instinctive preference for order and its natural love of formalities."[83]

Just as with literary connoisseurship, the legal profession is not for everyone. A "legal spirit" is gained only by the slow and careful consumption of the past. In France, the law is rational; it is explicit and available to all. There is nothing enchanted about the practice of law:

> Our written laws are often hard to understand, but everyone can read them, whereas nothing could he more obscure and out of reach of the common man than a law founded on precedent. Where lawyers are absolutely needed, as in England and the United States, and their professional knowledge is held in high esteem, they become increasingly separated from the people, forming a class apart. A French lawyer is just a man of learning, but an English or an American one is somewhat like the Egyptian priests, being, as they were, the only interpreter of an occult science.[84]

These priests of law, then, are fluent in a language not open to all. To the average person, the language of a lawyer is as foreign as Greek or Latin. Like books in the ancient world, it is only available to those possessing the wherewithal and temperament to pore over the occult-like texts. The instincts of the typical American democrat, Tocqueville argues, are opposed to those of the aristocrat-lawyer. Lawyers, he says, have a "superstitious respect for all that is old" but the democratic soul has a deep "love of novelty." Lawyers have "narrow views," but democrats always have "grandiose designs." The lawyers have "a taste for formalities" that contrasts to democratic "scorn of regulations."[85] In general, fluency in the judicial language is beyond the reach of the typical man.

This said, the importance of the judicial language for American society must not be overlooked. While fluency in this language may be out of reach, the spirit of the language is not. This is exactly why Tocqueville claims that "no one should imagine that in the United States a legalistic spirit is confined strictly to the precincts of the courts; it extends far beyond them."[86] The typical American, Tocqueville argues, has a proclivity for abstractions and personifications. However, when it comes to the law, this "annoying habit" seems to disappear. Tocqueville describes his experience with the American democrat thusly:

> There is hardly a political question in the United States which does not sooner or later turn into a judicial one. Consequently, the language of everyday party-political controversy has to be borrowed from legal phraseology and conceptions. As most public men are or have been lawyers, they apply their legal habits and turn of mind to the conduct of affairs. Juries make all classes familiar with this. So legal language is pretty well adopted into common speech; the spirit of the law, born within schools and courts, spreads little by little beyond them; it infiltrates through society right down to the lowest ranks, till finally the whole people have contracted some of the ways and tastes of a magistrate.[87]

In short, while not everyone speaks this judicial language fluently, it permeates the American linguistic landscape. The lawyer-priest breathes this aristocratic remnant into the language of democracy. Though not a language learned in grammatical detail, it is learned in spirit by the many; and though it does not replace aristocracy *in toto*, it nevertheless provides a minimal basis for the effective or moral adaptation of the best remnant of aristocracy.

CONCLUSION

The general argument of this chapter has been to describe Tocqueville's trip to the United States as a quest for the fugitive spirit of aristocracy. For Tocqueville, the dust of the French Revolution had not yet settled and the future of mankind was hanging in the balance. As he puts it, "The world which is arising is still half buried in the ruins (*débris*) of the world falling into decay, and in the vast confusion of all human affairs at present, no one can know which of the old institutions and former mores will continue to hold up their heads and which will in the end go under."[88] For Tocqueville, there were some mores and institutions in the aristocratic world that had, for millennia, served as a bulwark against tyranny – and these were worth saving. In this remnant, he sees an ancient energy, the love of freedom, diversity and distinction, heroic virtues, greatness and beauty, and so on. At the same time, however, the ugliest of the aristocratic institutions and mores – slavery, the most egregious institution – should be buried permanently under the debris of the old regime.

Tocqueville's great fear is that the Revolution and what he calls the "revolutionary spirit" have so demoralized citizens that few resources remain to stand firm against tyranny.[89] As he writes near the end of *Democracy in America*, "no one has yet devised a form of society or a political combination which can make a people energetic when it is composed of citizens who are flabby and feeble."[90] This is exactly why "despotism is particularly to be feared in ages of democracy."[91] What is needed, then, is a new science of politics that might sift and winnow through the debris of the old world to recover institutions and mores that might be brought to bear in the world. In Tocqueville's words, "a new political science is needed for a world itself quite new."[92] *Democracy in America* is this new science of politics.

NOTES

1. Alexis de Tocqueville and Gustave de Beaumont, *On the Penitentiary System in the United States and Its Application in France*, trans. Francis Lieber (New York: Augustus M. Kelley, 1970).
2. See, for example, André Jardin, *Tocqueville: A Biography*, trans. Lydia Davis and Robert Hemenway (New York: Farrar, Straus and Giroux, 1988), 79, 91.
3. OC 13:1, 374.
4. OC 13:1, 374.
5. On Tocqueville's influences, see Peter Augustine Lawler, "The Human Condition: Tocqueville's Debt to Rousseau and Pascal," in Eduardo Nolla, ed., *Liberty, Equality, Democracy* (New York: New York University Press, 1992), 1–20, and Aurelian Craiutu, "Tocqueville and the Political Thought of the French Doctrinaires (Guizot, Royer-Collard, Rémusat)," *History of Political Thought* 20, no. 3 (1999), 456–493.
6. OC 13:1, 373.
7. OC 2:1, 276.

8. OC 3:1, 180.

9. OC 2:1, 270, 275.

10. On Tocqueville's aristocratic influences and sensibilities, see Lucien Jaume, *Tocqueville: Les Sources aristocratiques de la liberté* (Paris: Fayard, 2008); Sheldon S. Wolin, *Tocqueville between Two Worlds: The Making of a Political and Theoretical Life* (Princeton: Princeton University Press, 2001); Alan S. Kahan, *Aristocratic Liberalism: The Social and Political Thought of Jacob Burckhardt, John Stuart Mill, and Alexis de Tocqueville* (New York: Oxford University Press, 1992). Compare also the nuanced characterization of his "vestigial nostalgia" by Cheryl Welch, *De Tocqueville* (Oxford: Oxford University Press, 2001), 25.

11. DIA (L) II.4.vii, 695.

12. Jean Nicot, *Thresor de la langue francoyse* (Paris: David Douceur, 1606).

13. Isaiah 10:20–22 (NIV).

14. The stump of Jesse is significant here, beyond invoking the image of trees. Trees, with their organic, contingent growth and countable rings, lend their symbolism to families and, at least in Tocqueville's mind, the evolution of English law. See DIA (L) 268. That this theme coincides with and provides a locus for the remnant in Isaiah 10:20–11:11 suggests *le reste* may inhere a return to a purer time. Therefore, when one speaks of the remnants of aristocracy one should keep in mind connotations of a tragically honorable resistance to decadence.

15. Académie française, *Le Dictionnaire de l'Académie française* (Paris: J. B. Coignard, 1694).

16. DIA (N) 3, 93.

17. DIA (L) II.2.viii, 525, 528. Tocqueville does recognize that the aristocratic age was also one of inequality: "At that time one found inequality and wretchedness in society, but men's souls were not degraded thereby" (DIA (L) "Author's Introduction," 14).

18. DIA (L) "Author's Introduction," 9.

19. DIA (L) I.1.ii, 49.

20. DIA (L) I.2.ii, 178–179.

21. DIA (L) I.2.ii, 179.

22. George Wilson Pierson, for example, writes of the excursion: "On a sudden [whim] they had been captured by a romantic idea." Pierson,

Tocqueville in America (Baltimore: Johns Hopkins University Press, 1996), 197.

23. Alexis de Tocqueville, "Journey to Lake Oneida," in *Journey to America*, ed. J. P. Mayer (New Haven, CT: Yale University Press), 323. Emphasis added.

24. The French translation was published by J. H. Campe. For more on the history of this work, see Victor Lange, "Visitors to Lake Oneida: An Account of the Background of Sophie von la Roche's Novel Erscheinungen Am See Oneida," *Symposium: A Quarterly Journal in Modern Literatures* 2, no. 1 (1948), 48–78.

25. This story is loosely based on the history of the Des Watines family, whose fate was relayed to La Roche by her son and daughter-in-law during their travels in America.

26. Lange, "Visitors to Lake Oneida," 63.

27. Tocqueville, "Journey to Lake Oneida," 323.

28. Tocqueville, "Journey to Lake Oneida," 323.

29. See, for example, Hugh Brogan, *Alexis de Tocqueville: A Life* (New Haven, CT: Yale University Press, 2007), 166.

30. Tocqueville, "Journey to Lake Oneida," 323.

31. In Alexis de Tocqueville and Gustave de Beaumont, *Letters from America*, trans. Frederick Brown (New Haven, CT: Yale University Press, 2010).

32. Tocqueville, "Journey to Lake Oneida," 323.

33. Tocqueville, "Journey to Lake Oneida," 326.

34. Tocqueville, "Journey to Lake Oneida," 326.

35. DIA (L) I.2.x, 328.

36. DIA (L) I.2.x, 328.

37. DIA (L) I.2.x, 324–325.

38. DIA (L) I.2.x, 338.

39. Jonathan Lear, *Radical Hope: Ethics in the Face of Cultural Devastation* (Cambridge, MA: Harvard University Press, 2006).

40. DIA (L) I.2.x, 326.

41. DIA (L) I.2.x, 323.

42. Pierson, *Tocqueville in America*, 233–234.

43. A bit later Tocqueville describes Saginaw, Michigan as the "last inhabited place till the Pacific Ocean," the edge of European civilization. There they meet Sagan-Cuisco, whom they hire as

a guide. Thus, in Michigan he catches a glimpse of what he is seeking but needs to go all the way to Green Bay to experience it fully, where he goes hunting with the natives.

44. DIA (L) I.2.x, 336.

45. DIA (L) I.2.x, 336.

46. DIA (L) I.2.x, 339.

47. Here I highlight an etymological distinction between *se mêler* (mingle) and *se confondre* (confuse) that echoes Tocqueville's distinction between *débris* and *reste*.

48. DIA (L) I.2.x, 339.

49. DIA (L) I.2.x, 360.

50. DIA (L) I.2.x, 345, 347.

51. DIA (L) I.2.x, 345.

52. DIA (L) I.2.x, 345.

53. DIA (L) I.2.x, 345–346.

54. DIA (L) I.2.x, 347.

55. DIA (L) I.2.x, 349.

56. DIA (L) I.2.x, 347–348.

57. DIA (L) I.2.x, 347.

58. DIA (L) II.4.vi, 692.

59. DIA (L) "Author's Introduction," 12.

60. DIA (L) I.2.x, 363.

61. DIA (L) I.2.x, 351.

62. DIA (L) I.2.x, 351.

63. DIA (L) II.2.xx, 560. Richard Swedberg invokes this passage to show that Tocqueville described the emergence of the business aristocracy as a small exception to his overarching thesis of the spread of equality. He implies that Tocqueville did not take the emergence of this "aristocracy," or the spread of capitalism, as a serious problem so that he could keep a coherent argument about his central thesis. Swedberg, *Tocqueville's Political Economy* (Princeton: Princeton University Press, 2009), 65–68.

64. DIA (L) II.2.xx, 557–558. For more, see Richard Avramenko and Brianne Wolf, "Disciplining the Rich: Tocqueville on Philanthropy and Privilege," *Review of Politics* 83, no. 3 (2021), 351–374.

65. DIA (L) II.2.xx, 557.

66. Seymour Drescher makes a similar argument but suggests that Tocqueville had become more pessimistic about the future of

democracy in volume 2 of *Democracy in America*, thus was not so much worried about the emergence of a new industrial elite but that their detachment from their fellows was indicative of a broader detachment that threatened liberty more generally. Drescher, "Tocqueville's Two *Démocraties*," *Journal of the History of Ideas* 25, no. 2 (1964), 208–209.

67. OR, 139.
68. DIA (L) II.3.xxii, 646.
69. DIA (L) II.3.xxii, 647.
70. DIA (L) II.3.xxii, 647.
71. DIA (L) II.3.xxii, 647.
72. DIA (L) II.3.xxii, 648.
73. DIA (L) II.3.xxii, 648–649.
74. DIA (L) II.3.xviii, 620.
75. DIA (L) II.3.xviii, 622–623.
76. DIA (L) I.2.viii, 267.
77. DIA (L) I.2.viii, 268.
78. DIA (L) I.2.viii, 264.
79. Tocqueville's view of lawyers was not unusual for the period. As Robert Ferguson argues, post-Revolution lawyers were the premier public authorities in America, a tradition that declined over time. Ferguson, *Law and Letters in American Culture* (Cambridge, MA: Harvard University Press, 1984). One is reminded of Simon Greenleaf's words upon his installation in the newly created position of Professor of Law at Harvard University in 1834: "In later days, when the integrity of that charter has been invaded, its spirit violated, and its language perverted, to whom have all eyes been imploringly directed for its preservation but to the living and honored champions and expounders of constitutional law?" Cited in Howard H. Schweber, *The Creation of American Common Law, 1850–1880: Technology, Politics, and the Construction of Citizenship* (Cambridge: Cambridge University Press, 2004), 23.
80. DIA (L) I.2.viii, 267.
81. DIA (L) I.2.viii, 267.
82. DIA (L) I.2.viii, 267.
83. DIA (L) I.2.viii, 264. For more on the aristocratic love of formalities, see Richard Avramenko and Noah Stengl, "Looking Down Tocqueville's

Nose: On the Problem of Aristocratic Etiquette in Democratic Times," in Richard Avramenko and Ethan Alexander-Davey, eds., *Aristocratic Souls in Democratic Times* (Lanham, MD: Lexington Books, 2018), 275–296.

84. DIA (L) I.2.viii, 267.
85. DIA (L) I.2.viii, 269.
86. DIA (L) I.2.viii, 269.
87. DIA (L) I.2.viii, 270.
88. DIA (L) II.4.viii, 703.
89. DIA (L) I.2.viii, 264, II.3.xxii, 645; II.4.vii, 700.
90. DIA (L) II.4.vii, 701.
91. DIA (L) II.4.vii, 695.
92. DIA (L) "Author's Introduction," 12.

PART II   **Receptions and Applications**

4 Tocqueville's Conservatism and the Conservative's Tocqueville

Richard Boyd

THE CONSERVATIVE TOCQUEVILLE?

Democracy in America (*DIA*) is a brilliant, captivating, but often perplexing book. Its mixed messages about democracy lead to a concrete interpretive difficulty, namely where do Tocqueville's ideas fall on the political spectrum? Whereas Tocqueville speaks of a great divide between aristocracy and democracy, with the author awkwardly perched "between two worlds," we today think about politics in terms of Left and Right.[1] Can the language of the former be translated into the latter? If so, what does this tell us about the political philosophy of *DIA*?

Most scholars describe Tocqueville as a peculiar kind of liberal, albeit one whose liberalism must be qualified as "aristocratic," "elitist," "conservative," or just plain "strange."[2] With respect to the political issues of his own time, we know that Tocqueville more often than not found himself on the centrist-left – sometimes alone, rarely condoning the radical positions he abhorred, but with ample daylight between his views and what we generally think of as the forces of Reaction.[3] Given abundant biographical evidence identifying Tocqueville the politician and public intellectual as a kind of political liberal, it is striking how his ideas have been embraced in the United States by the intellectual and political Right.[4] We shall see that it is no accident that so many American conservatives have been drawn to *DIA*. The shifting ways in which they have made sense of these ideas, however, is a story unto itself.

In the following chapter, I trace out two different dimensions of the "conservative" rendition of Tocqueville – highlighting both his own ideas and their concrete historical receptions. First, I flag major themes in *DIA* legitimately suggestive of conservative ideas and policies. Second, in view of these conservative affinities, I survey the divergent ways Tocqueville's ideas have been embraced over the centuries by various camps of the American Right.

THE PRIMACY OF CIRCUMSTANCES AND MORES OVER LEGISLATION

One cornerstone of conservatism is its deference to tradition and inherited institutions. They represent, in the words of Edmund Burke, "prescription," both in the literal sense of having been "written before" and in having normative force.[5] Whereas the radical seeks to remake society in the image of utopian ideals by light of pure reason alone, the conservative cautions that social institutions have an organic integrity that renders them easy to destroy but nearly impossible to recreate *de novo*.

Similarly, many of the institutions that Tocqueville credits for helping the Anglo-Americans make democracy work are not products of imaginative experimentation but may instead be traced back to America's "point of departure." Township government, public education, local liberties, and a particular brand of dissenting congregational Protestantism are all part of the baggage that Puritan settlers brought with them from the mother country. Long after the Puritans themselves have receded into the background, however, their institutions, habits, and sensibilities continue to prove determinative.[6] Not just these inherited institutions but also the practical "art," "habit," or "experience" of making good use of them are what allows the Anglo-American experiment in self-government to be so successful.

This kind of path-dependency implicitly depreciates the role of American political institutions and the novelty of the Founding Fathers, who are scarcely mentioned in *DIA*. Tocqueville surely thinks that the US Constitution works well, and he spends several

chapters in volume 1 cataloguing its details and extolling its dynamics. Yet virtually identical institutions adopted by a people lacking
the same mores are unlikely to thrive. Latin American nations
achieved their liberty through similar revolutions, Tocqueville
observes, but despite mirroring the constitution of the Anglo-
Americans, their experiments with democracy have proven less
successful.[7]

SUBSIDIARITY AND THE VIRTUES OF "CIVIL SOCIETY"

Among the most widely cited features of *DIA* is Tocqueville's paean
to voluntary association. The art of voluntary association, he boldly
proclaims, is at the very heart of political liberty in the United States.
Americans make more and better use of associations than any other
people, and these habits of association are decisive to the health and
vitality of American democracy:

> Americans of all ages, all stations in life, and all types of disposition
> are forever forming associations. There are not only commercial
> and industrial associations in which all take part, but others of
> a thousand different types – religious, moral, serious, futile, very
> general and very limited, immensely large and very minute ... In
> every case, at the head of any new undertaking, where in France you
> would find the government or in England some territorial magnate,
> in the United States you are sure to find an association.[8]

The valorization of civil society is not in and of itself conservative, of
course, and Tocqueville's praise of civic associations resonates with
the Left as well as the Right. Yet beneath the democratic veneer of
Tocqueville's famous observations about the centrality of associations to civic life in the United States lies a deeper set of conservative
assumptions. The main reason why it is so important for citizens to
freely associate in pursuit of common purposes is so that they do not
have to rely on the government. To affirm voluntary association is
ipso facto to condemn bureaucratic centralization and state power.
Unlike the French, Americans are free insofar as they are able to

organize themselves locally and informally to accomplish important public goals.

Civic associations have moral significance as well. One of the mainstays of the conservative tradition – running from Catholic notions of subsidiarity all the way through to contemporary critics of welfare dependency – is the conviction that it is better for local communities to do things themselves even if they do so less competently.[9] The intrinsic value of citizens doing things voluntarily is often harnessed to the assumption – which Tocqueville may or may not share – that decentralized initiatives are likely to do a better job of providing collective goods. Yet even if one relaxes expectations about the relative efficiency of voluntary associations in tackling thorny problems such as poverty, homelessness, crime, or education, the health of a society may be judged by the degree to which it is able to mobilize spontaneously in response to these and other social ails. Civil society is just as important for the energy and vitality it stimulates among citizens as for the efficacy of its results. Families, churches, neighborhoods, communities, cooperatives, and nonprofits are all part of a conservative vision of an organically integrated society.

THE FORMAL AND INFORMAL ROLE OF RELIGION

European conservatism of the "throne and altar" variety holds that religion's authority derives at least in part from its public establishment.[10] Tocqueville retains the traditionalist conviction about religion's public importance, but he diverges in arguing for some degree of formal independence. Separation of church and state is necessary for the spheres of religion and politics to fulfill their respective functions. As he explains, it was the comingling of religion and politics that generated so much of the anticlerical fury of the French Revolution. The animosity of liberty's friends toward the French Catholic church stemmed from the fact that it was confounded in their minds with the secular abuses of the Bourbon monarchy.[11]

Tocqueville's America, by contrast, thrives on the harmony between religious and political spheres. It is not just that the two spheres manage a delicate coexistence. They actually work hand in glove. Citizens can be politically free in the United States precisely because religion discourages them from abusing the significant formal liberties they are granted. "For my part," he explains, "I doubt whether man can support complete religious independence and entire political liberty at the same time. I am led to think that if he has no faith, he must obey, and if he is free he must believe."[12] It is not so important what Americans believe, Tocqueville famously remarks, as that they believe in something.[13] Religion is what links freedom to responsibility. Like so many latter-day conservatives who make various conceptions of an ecumenical "Judeo-Christian" morality the centerpiece of their theories and denounce contemporary secularism for having surrendered that moral sensibility, Tocqueville regards religion as an essential ingredient of a healthy public life.

First, religion affords timeless and unchanging moral standards in the face of the vagaries of public opinion and tyrannical majoritarianism. One thinks of Lincoln's invocation of a higher law over and against the notion that slavery was a morally indifferent matter to be "voted down or voted up" depending on the prevailing views of the day.[14] Exemplary moral leadership can resist the casual indecency of democratic publics.[15] Second, there is the power of religion to nudge democratic citizens out of the caustic individualism and materialism that might otherwise capture their souls. Tocqueville's worry that the democratic citizen will eventually succumb to the "misguided judgment" of individualism, and retreat into the "solitude of his own heart," is offset, at least to some degree, by a transcendent religious instinct that prompts us each to look beyond our personal well-being and toward the welfare of fellow creatures.[16] Tocqueville's vision of Christianity as a guiding moral force in public life has become a mainstay of the conservative tradition, all the more so in light of the gravitation of the contemporary Left in the direction of secularism.[17]

PATHOLOGIES OF DEMOCRATIC EQUALITY

From Aristotle's *Politics* and neo-Aristotelian theorists of natural law to various sorts of sociological, structural-functional, or social Darwinist thinkers, conservatives of almost every stripe oppose the absolute value of equality.[18] No thinker better illustrates conservatism's animus toward equality than Edmund Burke, who lamented a specious equality that reduced human dignity and excellence to a biological sentience shared even with the lowest of animals.[19]

Tocqueville's relationship to equality is obviously more complicated than that of Burke or his conservative brethren. Tocqueville regards the march of equality as providential and largely salutary. Equality facilitates social mobility, recognizes individual merit, suffuses society with generalized compassion, and relaxes stifling aristocratic conventions.[20] Even so, this is not to say that he is uncritical of the pathologies of radical egalitarianism. Equality writ large exists in at least some degree of tension with liberty. Tocqueville writes that "democratic peoples have a natural taste for liberty; left to themselves, they will seek it, cherish it, and be sad if it is taken from them. But their passion for equality is ardent, insatiable, eternal, and invincible."[21] If they have to choose between a freedom alloyed with inequality or an equality in servitude, the worry is that democratic peoples will forsake the former in favor of the latter.

Conservatives hardly need Tocqueville to identify egalitarian threats to redistribute private property, for example, nor interestingly does *DIA* spend much time discussing dangers of this sort. What seems novel are Tocqueville's insights into the subtler social and political dynamics of equality. Whether it is a matter of tyrannical majoritarianism and the omnipotence of public opinion, the caustic effects of individualism, or the growth of soft despotism – these pathologies all begin as deductions from the moral psychology of equality. A fallacious equality among persons prevents us from differentiating wisdom from ignorance, natural excellence from common mediocrity, and even virtue from vice. Equality yields individualism's "misguided judgment" that, just because we can take care of our-selves, others nominally our equals must be capable of mustering the same degree of autonomy;[22] and an otherwise well-intentioned pursuit of egalitarianism is what disposes us to place confidence in a providential state determined to secure universal well-being for all of its subjects.

MEDIOCRITY OF DEMOCRATIC CULTURE

Tocqueville's moral, cultural, and aesthetic criticisms have affinities for perennial conservative laments about the degradation of modern culture. Aristocracies are gifted with a permanent class of elites who patronize the arts and sciences, but democracies have no such leading lights. Literature and the fine arts are democratized in both senses of the term – that is to say, practiced more widely albeit less profession-ally. Americans write plenty of novels, Tocqueville concedes, but few of any real quality or distinction.[23] Many people read newspapers and books, but the tastes of this broad readership are banal. This seems to hold true for fine arts such as poetry and philosophy as well, which if they exist at all in a democracy tend to have a prosaic, indeed prag-matic flavor. Of any work of literature, art, music, architecture, higher learning, or even science, the foremost question becomes its practical use and to what profit might it be turned?

This middling quality applies not only to democracy's intellec-tual productions but also to consumer culture more generally. Mass production allows ordinary people to consume what were once luxury goods enjoyed only by a few, and yet these cheaply made reproduc-tions lack the quality of the genuine article.[24] This contempt for "bourgeois" or "mass culture" is hardly exclusive to conservatism, to be sure. The Frankfurt School and other Marxists insist that, while Tocqueville correctly identifies the defects of American culture, he mistakes their underlying causes. If American culture is shallow and materialistic, this is because artists produce mechanically to satisfy the vapid tastes of the marketplace. Capitalism, and not democracy, is responsible. Yet, as Raymond Aron appreciates, rather than attributing everything to economic causes, or vague social forces, Tocqueville affirms the centrality of "the political."[25] The shortcomings of democratic culture and the fine arts stem not from material conditions alone, as Marxists maintain, but from the political tendency in a democracy for everything to gravitate toward the uninspiring middle.

ADMINISTRATIVE CENTRALIZATION, THE PROVIDENTIAL STATE, AND SOFT DESPOTISM

Many have noted how presciently *DIA*'s polarities mapped onto a Cold War world in which the United States offered a plausible approximation of equality under liberty, on the one hand, while the Soviet Union represented the antipode of totalitarianism, on the other. Cold War conservatives, as we will see, found much confirmatory in Tocqueville's prognostications. Yet Tocqueville's stark vision of these two divergent paths of liberty and subjection overshadows another dimension of the book. Maybe Tocqueville's most enduring conceptual innovation from the vantage of conservatives is his invocation of an altogether new kind of "soft" or "administrative" despotism.[26]

The greatest threat to modern democratic regimes is not some malevolent strongman, medieval tyrant, or "authoritarian personality." Rather than "hard" tyranny in the style of a Napoleon, Stalin, or Hitler, a gentler "soft" despotism is more likely to emerge from democracy's humane sensibilities.[27] This new despotism is insidious precisely because it walks under the guise of universal beneficence and good intentions. The modern administrative state insinuates itself into every domain of life, not to tyrannize over its citizenry but rather to deliver them from sundry trials, pitfalls, and difficult decisions. Once relieved of the trouble of living freely, democratic citizens are condemned to perpetual infantilization.[28]

The agents of soft despotism are more akin to schoolmarms than slave drivers. Their goals are education and improvement, but the result Tocqueville fears is a nation of perpetual adolescents –

coddled, sheltered, inhibited in any grand undertaking, and above all else robbed of the burden of taking responsibility for their actions. His dim view of the modern providential and regulatory state has been shared by many conservatives in the early twenty-first century. Opposing policies that "nudge" citizens into eating better or saving for their own retirement, or even outright prohibitions on smoking or the sale of sugary drinks, conservatives have taken aim at the so-called nanny state and in doing so embraced arguments very much along the lines envisioned by Tocqueville.

TOCQUEVILLE'S "CONSERVATIVE" RECEPTION IN AMERICA

Thus far I have identified *DIA*'s affinities with core tenets of political conservativism. Beyond this theoretical congruence, however, are related questions such as which American conservatives have invoked *DIA* over the decades, under what circumstances, and to what concrete uses have they have put Tocqueville's ideas? A brief overview of *DIA*'s reception on the American Right gives new insights into the book itself as well as demonstrating how a single text can be appropriated differently in light of changing political circumstances.

Many commentators have noted that "conservatism" in the United States is a heterogeneous, if not conflicted tradition.[29] Spanning the centuries from the Federalist Party's opposition to the radical egalitarianism of the Jeffersonian Democratic-Republicans to antebellum sociology of the likes of George Fitzhugh and John C. Calhoun to later Social Darwinists such as William Graham Sumner to the isolationist movements of the first half of the twentieth century to the Cold War conservatism of Russell Kirk and Robert Nisbet to Barry Goldwater, the Reagan Revolution, and the "neo-conservative synthesis" – "conservatism" has meant many different things in the United States.

Untangling the skein of American conservatism is further complicated by the fact that "liberal" and "conservative" mean different things in the United States and Europe. Today's European "liberals" or "neoliberals" are often found on the same side as American "conservatives," and so it may be tempting to explain the nineteenth-century French "liberal" Tocqueville's place within American conservatism as a consequence of translating European vocabulary into an American vernacular. Taxonomical ambiguity may indeed be a complicating factor in finding Tocqueville's rightful place on the political spectrum, as noted. Nonetheless, as I have tried to indicate, it is precisely those aspects of *DIA* that are not, strictly speaking, "liberal" that have most captivated his "conservative" American admirers.

Tocqueville's influence on "conservative" America arguably begins with novelist and essayist James Fenimore Cooper. There is good reason to suspect that Cooper and Tocqueville were acquainted during the former's sojourn in France in the late 1820s and early 1830s.[30] However, even if the two men knew each other only by reputation, Cooper's *The American Democrat* (1838) is a thinly veiled rehash of many of Tocqueville's criticisms of democracy for an American public allegedly in need of instruction.[31] A self-styled American "gentleman," for no true aristocracy could be said to exist in the United States, Cooper complains about the lack of manners in America, about the dangerous pathologies of the doctrine of moral equality ("one man is as good as another"), and the infirmities of democratic government.[32] Cooper's attitudes toward democracy strike the reader as ambivalent – proudly defensive, almost jingoistic about the superiority of American institutions, and yet wary of the threat of democratic equality saturating every aspect of American society.

As the US Civil War waxed and the nineteenth century waned, so too, many allege, did Tocqueville's political capital in the United States. Some contend that Tocqueville was totally forgotten, only to be rediscovered in the 1930s and 1940s.[33] Yet as Matthew Mancini has revealed, not only was the book in print more or less continuously but many significant thinkers after the US Civil War referred to *DIA*.[34] For example, the English visitor James Bryce opens his *American Commonwealth* (1888) with a lengthy attempt to differentiate his own reportage from the monumental *DIA* with which it was inevitably compared. Henry Adams likewise professed great respect for Tocqueville's ideas.[35] Even if its novelty diminished, *DIA* never disappeared from the American scene.

Wilfred McClay's assertion about Tocqueville's "negligible influence upon American thinkers in the years between the Civil War and World War" requires qualification, but it also holds a kernel of truth, at least when it comes to prominent conservatives.[36] Mark Twain apparently never mentions him. For all of its frenetic appeal to American exceptionalism and imperial conquest as antidotes to commercial malaise – themes that scholars would belatedly discover in Tocqueville's writings on colonialism – Theodore Roosevelt's *Strenuous Life* (1899) makes no reference to Tocqueville. Despite affinities to *DIA*'s sociological emphasis on mores, the perils of democratic equality and modern individualism, and wariness of the state, neither does William Graham Sumner's *Folkways* (1906).[37] Another prominent conservative figure who seems, surprisingly in hindsight, not to have been at all influenced by Tocqueville was H. L. Mencken. Mencken's sole allusion to Tocqueville in *Notes on Democracy* (1926) is a perfunctory name-drop, and Mencken's own fulminations about the debilities of democracy – not to mention his loathing of the Puritans – take inspiration from Friedrich Nietzsche, a less friendly critic than Tocqueville of democracy and all it represents.[38] One exception to this more general rule, as well as an important bridge between the nineteenth and twentieth centuries, was the cultural critic Irving Babbitt, for whom Tocqueville stood as a formidable critic of democratic proclivities toward leveling and mediocrity. In calling for a "humane," indeed "aristocratic" vocation for higher education, Babbitt cites Tocqueville's conundrum. "The final test of a democracy," Babbitt opines, "will be its power to produce and encourage the superior individual," a sentiment he first expresses in his thoughts on the American university but which he repeats later in a more overtly political context in *Democracy and Leadership* (1924).[39]

Several developments in the 1930s and 1940s contributed to newfound American interest in Tocqueville in the United States, as Nisbet, Cheryl Welch, James Kloppenberg, and others have chronicled. There was the publication in 1938 of George Pierson's *Tocqueville and Beaumont in America*, as well as the republication by Alfred A. Knopf of a new edition of *DIA* in 1945, which stimulated greater intellectual awareness of the book.[40] There was also his central role in underwriting a liberal consensus. Tocqueville's vision of a "liberal" America arguably achieved hegemony via the so-called Hartz thesis of the 1950s. Yet Tocqueville was not always read as liberal and celebratory of America, as often alleged, but rather as critical of the modern state and democratic culture. It was this "conservative" facet of Tocqueville's thinking that was eagerly received on the American Right and did most to burnish his reputation.

Among the first postwar thinkers to accord Tocqueville weight was the conservative political theorist and intellectual historian Russell Kirk. Kirk's path-breaking 1953 work *The Conservative Mind: From Burke to Santayana* featured Tocqueville (alongside T. B. Macaulay and James Fenimore Cooper) as the centerpiece of a species of "liberal conservatism" steeped in the legacy of a Burkean marriage between Whiggish liberal sensibilities and a conservative defense of inherited institutions such as the family, the rule of law, and private property. As Bruce Frohnen explains, twentieth-century conservatives, including Kirk, were drawn to the likes of Burke and Tocqueville for their affirmation of virtue, their appeals to honor and glory, as well as their opposition to the materialism and egalitarianism of contemporary society.[41] Tocqueville's "supreme achievement," according to Kirk, was his apprehension of the dangers of "democratic despotism," the central "conundrum of modern society," which would ultimately culminate in collectivisms on the Left and Right.[42]

Robert Nisbet was another prominent postwar conservative to draw upon Tocqueville's sociological vision in characterizing the preeminent threats to freedom. Unlike Kirk, who placed Burke front and center of the conservative tradition, Nisbet's monumental *Quest for Community*, also published in 1953, is thoroughly Tocquevillean in orientation. The book opens its discussion of totalitarianism with a haunting and lengthy citation from volume 2 of *DIA*, which Nisbet commends as "one of the most astonishing prophecies to be found anywhere in political literature."[43] This vision of what came subsequently to be known as "mass society" impresses Nisbet for seeing past totalitarianism's most "transparently horrible" and "grotesque" features and getting at its underlying spiritual demoralization and destruction of humanity.[44]

In addition to criticizing totalitarian illusions and social disintegration, Nisbet is affirmatively inspired by Tocqueville's pluralism. Real community is possible only in a world where individuals are linked by a rich network of groups and intermediary associations. Nisbet is less sanguine than Tocqueville about the individual's ability to recombine into new voluntary configurations in a world where premodern bonds of family, locality, and community are eviscerated, but they share a sense of modernity's tendency to discourage community. Both the totalitarian state and capitalist markets (and this is key for the conservative appropriation) erode these bonds and give rise not only to social alienation but also to a propensity to recombine in violent and illiberal ways. As Nisbet recalls in his memoir, there is some irony of his "New Liberal" and "New Conservative" students at Berkeley in the 1950s and 1960s being drawn to precisely the same Tocquevillean criticisms of anomie and social isolation.[45]

Writing in 1953 it is hardly surprising that Nisbet would see *DIA* as prophetic of fascism, recently vanquished, and emergent Soviet-style totalitarianism; and yet there are important ways in which Nisbet's Cold War rendition misreads *DIA*. In the very passage Nisbet cites approvingly, Tocqueville is explicit that the kind of despotism democratic nations most have to fear is not the grand mal tyranny of earlier (or subsequent) ages but a newer, softer, gentler kind of despotism. In a recent work, Paul Rahe captures this exact dimension of Tocqueville as harbinger of the modern liberal welfare state.

For Rahe, Tocqueville envisions a novel "soft despotism," in which the providential state comes to be intertwined with all aspects of society and superintends over a docile and depoliticized people. The counterpoint to Tocqueville's America, in this regard, is not the Soviet Union so much as the administrative centralization of France or even the bureaucratic torpor of China.[46]

Rahe's approach to Tocqueville seems emblematic of conservatism's shifting concerns in a twenty-first-century world where Soviet-style totalitarianism has given way to endogenous threats to liberal democracy. In this vein, Straussians and other political theorists such as Allan Bloom and Harvey Mansfield have focused more on the spiritual and cultural ramifications of Tocqueville's writings. Rather than underwriting the Cold War abroad, the book is of use in guiding liberal democracy from within. From a critical vantage, Allan Bloom's bestselling *The Closing of the American Mind* (1987) makes repeated references to Tocqueville by way of illuminating what Bloom regarded as the contemporary ailments of vapid individualism, egalitarian injustice, and cultural nihilism.[47] More affirmatively, *DIA* appeals to Straussians for its endorsement of education, religion, statesmanship, traditional gender roles, and a "new political science" sufficient to counter the pathologies of democratic modernity.[48]

DIA also supplies a tailormade alternative to the infantilizing "soft despotism" of the administrative state: voluntary associations and civil society. From at least the 1980s onward, conservatives appealed to Tocqueville – not just to *DIA* but also to his "Memoir on Pauperism," which Gertrude Himmelfarb reprinted in 1997 – to supplant the welfare state. "Tocqueville's discussion of private charity as opposed to public relief takes on added significance," Himmelfarb explains, "for it confirms one of the main themes of *Democracy in America*: the importance of civil society." "If public relief is an invitation both to individual irresponsibility and to an overweening state, private charity, filtered through the institutions of civil society, may be the remedy for both," she argues.[49] Private associations, churches, local communities, and engaged citizens can do a better job of lifting people out of poverty and energizing civil society than the cumbersome and demeaning welfare state. Among numerous like-minded efforts in the 1990s to rethink the welfare state from the center-right, Daniel Coats and John Kasich's "Project for American Renewal" takes inspiration from the Tocquevillean vision of federalism, voluntary associations, philanthropy, and a rich network of civil society.[50]

Beyond its application to domestic challenges of poverty and dependency, some of the major conservative foreign policy paradigms that emerged post-1989 drew explicitly or implicitly on *DIA*. Francis Fukuyama's "End of History" (1989) makes no reference to a Tocquevillean provenance, but a subsequent Fukuyama essay titled "The March of Equality" (2000) highlights their shared providential vision of liberal democracy at the end of an inexorable process of historical development. For Tocqueville, of course, the process remained contingent, and the future of equality appeared compatible with two very different outcomes. Will history culminate in equality of all in freedom or equal subjection under despotism? For Fukuyama, writing at the close of the twentieth century, the Tocquevillean antinomy appears settled once and for all in favor of the universal triumph of liberal democracy. Yet for Fukuyama – as for Tocqueville – there is something wistful, even potentially enervating, about the triumph of capitalist liberal democracy. Fukuyama's allusion to "boredom" and subsequent amendment of the "Last Man" are, of course, reminiscent of Nietzsche's polemic against the nihilism of modernity, but the lament could just as easily be Tocquevillean.[51] What greatness can we expect from a world purged of all contradictions or struggle? Can the triumph of liberal democracy inspire anything beyond egalitarian compassion and the bourgeois comforts of materialism, what Tocqueville dismissed as mere "well-being"?

An alternative to Fukuyama's bold proclamation of liberal democratic hegemony came with the publication of Samuel Huntington's famous 1993 "Clash of Civilizations" essay;[52] and here, too, Tocqueville's vision seems to have exerted some influence. Huntington's classic work on modernization already bears traces of the Tocquevillean vision of progressive development.[53] Likewise, the significance of political culture – and the intractability of cultural differences – is a long-standing Huntingtonian theme.[54] Maybe even more so than the "Clash of Civilizations" paradigm, Huntington's controversial 2004 book *Who Are We?* leans on Tocquevillean conceits about "Anglo-Protestant" cultural origins of the United States, albeit in a manner that struck critics as unnecessarily exclusionary.[55] Putting aside Huntington's claim that "Anglo-Protestant culture" is decisive for the political and economic successes of the United States, and his controversial corollary that immigrants from other cultures cannot share these values, the broader culturalist framework seems consistent with *DIA*. Origins exert a determinative influence on political and economic development. Mores or "culture" matter as much as formal legislation; and in the case of the United States, its ability to make democracy work represents a singular achievement that is not only hard to transmit to other foreign nations, as Tocqueville himself says, but in Huntington's corollary poses a challenge to assimilation for immigrants to the United States with different mores.

Competition among American conservatives to brandish Tocqueville's authority reached an apex during the Iraq War, when neoconservatives and conservatives of a more traditionalist stripe cited Tocqueville at cross-purposes on "regime-building" in the Middle East. For some like Paul Wolfowitz, Tocqueville's providential vision of liberal democracy sweeping throughout the world justified the vocation of the United States in facilitating democratic transitions in Iraq and elsewhere.[56] Critics such as Lawrence Harrison and John Agresto, however, objected on Tocquevillean grounds that the specific cultural habits and practices necessary to make democracy work were lacking in former Middle Eastern despotisms and concluded that efforts by the United States to instill them were doomed to fail.[57] Deftly illuminating the cultural dynamics of the Middle East, Joshua Mitchell was likewise impressed by the challenges a Tocquevillean analysis reveals for the project of democratization.[58]

One point on which almost all latter-day conservatives agree is Tocqueville's affirmation of religion. Whether we regard Tocqueville as a sincere Christian or merely endorsing the civic value of religion, Tocqueville obviously thinks that religion is vital and despairs for a nation where it vanishes. In the hands of religiously inflected thinkers of all faiths such as Jean Elshtain, Richard John Neuhaus, and Peter Berger, Tocqueville's endorsement of a central role for religion in the public square serves as a cautionary warning against a secularism that threatens to deepen the materialistic tendencies endemic to democratic societies.[59] According to Jean Elshtain and her coauthors, "religion is a primary force in American life – historically, it has probably been the primary force – that transmits from one generation to another the moral understandings that are essential to liberal democratic institutions."[60] Likewise, for Mary Ann Glendon, Tocqueville affirms the moral centrality of the nuclear family for fostering virtue and educating future democratic citizens.[61] According to a variety of interpreters who are at minimum religiously conservative (if not in other respects socially liberal), civil society is coterminous with an organic network of churches and faith-based organizations that lend a religious tenor to the public sphere.

The American Right is hardly monolithic, as should be abundantly clear by now. Among issues that have tended to separate classical liberals or libertarians from genuine conservatives in the United States is the proper role of the market. Tocqueville's ambivalence about the dynamic forces of free markets, inequalities of wealth, and the "creative destruction" of capitalism has always made him difficult for pro-market thinkers to assimilate. Yet, even so, some have found aspects of Tocqueville's ideas to commend. Friedrich Hayek, who famously declared that he was never to be confused with a conservative, cites Tocqueville as one of the paradigmatic examples of a "True Individualism," that is to say, someone who champions individual liberty while avoiding the fallacy of confusing normative individualism with social atomism.[62] In Hayek's view, Tocqueville was to be commended – alongside other pluralist conservatives such as Edmund Burke and Lord Acton – for understanding that individuals are first and foremost members of families, neighborhoods, and other intermediary institutions without which society is unimaginable.

In a similar vein, Tocqueville's ideas were a source of inspiration for Elinor and Vincent Ostrom, who glimpsed not only a model of federalism but also a resource for appreciating how property rights, markets, and other complex social institutions emerge spontaneously in the absence of centralized coordination.[63] It has even been suggested that Tocqueville's description of human motivation and the dynamics of state growth could have anticipated – if not inspired – the public choice theories of James Buchanan and Gordon Tullock.[64] These figures are not exactly paradigmatic examples of American "conservatism," per se, but they do represent a significant block of thinking on the American Right that has drawn freely on Tocquevillean ideas.

In conclusion, then, we have seen that *DIA*'s arguments share fundamental affinities for various brands of political conservatism in the United States. Yet the story of Tocqueville's reception and transmission is not just a matter of how *DIA* comes to be regarded as "conservative" but also, and maybe more importantly, how its reputation evolves over the decades in response to domestic and global challenges for which conservative thinkers sought intellectual resources. The specific manner in which *DIA*'s ideas have been selectively adopted by the Right – oftentimes at cross-purposes – makes the book a fascinating case study not just in political philosophy but in the history of ideas.

NOTES

1. For this characterization of Tocqueville's political orientation, see especially Sheldon S. Wolin, *Tocqueville between Two Worlds: The Making of a Political and Theoretical Life* (Princeton: Princeton University Press, 2001).

2. See, for example, Alan Kahan, *Aristocratic Liberalism: The Social and Political Thought of Jacob Burckhardt, John Stuart Mill, and Alexis de Tocqueville* (Oxford: Oxford University Press, 1992); Aurelian Craiutu, *Liberalism under Siege: The Political Thought of the French Doctrinaires* (Lanham, MD: Lexington Books, 2003); Russell Kirk, *The Conservative Mind: From Burke to Santayana* (Chicago: Henry Regnery Co., 1953); Roger Boesche, *The Strange Liberalism of Alexis de Tocqueville* (Ithaca, NY: Cornell University Press, 1987).

3. On his shifting views on suffrage that culminated in extending the vote, see Robert T. Gannett, Jr., "Tocqueville and the Politics of Suffrage," *The Tocqueville Review/La revue Tocqueville* 27, no. 2 (2006), 208–226; on issues of social reform, see Michael Drolet, *Tocqueville, Democracy, and Social Reform* (New York: Palgrave, 2003); for his take on the "social question," see Gianna Englert, "'The Idea of Rights': Tocqueville on the Social Question," *The Review of Politics* 79, no. 4 (2017), 649–674; on Tocqueville's liberalism as a "third way" between socialism and laissez-faire, see Eric Keslassy, *Le libéralisme de Tocqueville à l'épreuve du paupérisme* (Paris: L'Harmattan, 2000); on his views of French imperialism, more generally, and the way in which his justification of imperialism diverged from the more extreme advocacy of his contemporaries, see Jennifer Pitts, *A Turn to Empire: The Rise of Imperial Liberalism in Britain and France* (Princeton: Princeton University Press, 2005) and Ewa Atanassow, "Colonization and Democracy: Tocqueville Reconsidered" *American Political Science Review* 111, no. 1 (2017), 83–96; on his opposition to corruption under the bourgeois July Monarchy, see William Selinger, "*Le grand mal de l'époque*: Tocqueville on French Political Corruption," *History of European Ideas* 42, no. 1 (2016), 73–94.

4. This "conservative" dimension of Tocqueville's political thinking is central to appreciative readings by the likes of Kirk, *The Conservative Mind*; Harvey Mansfield, *Tocqueville: A Very Short Introduction* (Oxford: Oxford University Press, 2010); Harvey Mansfield and Delba Winthrop, "Editors' Introduction" in Alexis de Tocqueville, *Democracy in America* (Chicago: University of Chicago Press, 2002); and Bruce Frohnen, *Virtue and the Promise of Conservatism: The Legacy of Burke and Tocqueville* (Lawrence: University Press of Kansas, 1993).

5. Edmund Burke, *Reflections on the Revolution in France* (Indianapolis: Liberty Fund, 1999), 255–257, 270–271; see also Russell Kirk, "Burke and

the Philosophy of Prescription," *Journal of the History of Ideas* 14, no. 3 (1953), 365–380.

6. For another sense of the institutional legacy of the Puritans, see Barbara Allen, *Tocqueville, Covenant, and the Democratic Revolution: Harmonizing Earth with Heaven* (Lanham, MD: Lexington Books, 2005).

7. DIA (L) I.2.ix, 307.

8. DIA (L) II.2.v, 513.

9. On the connection between Tocqueville and Catholic doctrines of subsidiarity, see especially David Golemboski, "Federalism and the Catholic Principle of Subsidiarity," *Publius: The Journal of Federalism* 45, no. 4 (2015), 526–551.

10. On Tocqueville's connection to this line of reactionary French thinking, see especially Lucien Jaume, *Tocqueville: The Aristocratic Sources of Liberty*, trans. Arthur Goldhammer (Princeton: Princeton University Press, 2013).

11. AR I.2, 15–16 and III.2, 136–139.

12. DIA (L) II.1.v, 444.

13. DIA (L) II.2.xv, 544.

14. Abraham Lincoln, "'A House Divided' Speech" in *Political Writings and Speeches*, ed. Terence Ball (Cambridge: Cambridge University Press, 2013), 57.

15. For a contrary set of criticisms about Tocqueville and the complicity of democratic publics, see Jack Turner, "American Individualism and Structured Injustice: Tocqueville, Gender, and Race," *Polity* 40, no. 2 (2008), 197–215.

16. DIA (L) II.1.v, 444–445; II.2.ii, 506–508.

17. For a suggestive criticism of how Tocqueville's arguments for religion may have changed in light of these new dynamics, see William Galston, "Tocqueville on Liberalism and Religion," *Social Research* 54, no. 3 (1987), 499–518.

18. On opposition to egalitarianism as the single defining characteristic of conservatism, see George Hawley, *Right-Wing Critics of American Conservatism* (Lawrence: University Press of Kansas, 2017), 267–268.

19. Burke, *Reflections*, 292–294.

20. DIA (L) II.3.i, 563–564.

21. DIA (L) II.2.i, 506.

22. DIA (L) II.2.ii, 506–507.

23. DIA (L) II.1.xiii, 470–471.

24. DIA (L) II.1.xi, 465–467.

25. Raymond Aron, *Main Currents in Sociological Thought, Vol 1: Montesquieu, Auguste Comte, Karl Marx, Alexis de Tocqueville, The Sociologists and the Revolution of 1848* (New York: Basic Books, 1965).

26. DIA (L) II.4.vi, 692–693.

27. DIA (L) II.4.vi, 691.

28. DIA (L) II.4.vi, 693–694.

29. Hawley, *Right-Wing Critics of American Conservatism*; Paul Gottfried, *Conservatism in America: Making Sense of the American Right* (London: Palgrave Macmillan, 2007); Frohnen, *Virtue and the Promise of Conservatism*.

30. On this relationship, see Thomas Clark, "'The American Democrat' Reads 'Democracy in America': Cooper and Tocqueville in the Transatlantic Hall of Mirrors," *Amerikastudien /American Studies* 52, no. 2 (2007), 187–208.

31. Alternatively, if one were to speculate about influence flowing in the opposite direction, Cooper's *Notions of the Americans: Picked up by a Travelling Bachelor* (1828) anticipates several key themes of *DIA* such as the extensive "equality of condition" prevailing in the United States; the leveling effects of this equality; the determinative nature of the New England character; and so on.

32. James Fenimore Cooper, *The American Democrat* (Washington, DC: Regnery Publishing, 2000), 416.

33. Robert Nisbet, "Many Tocquevilles," *The American Scholar* 46, no. 1 (1977), 60; James T. Kloppenberg, *The Virtues of Liberalism* (Oxford: Oxford University Press, 1998), 74; Wilfred McClay, *The Masterless: Self and Society in Modern America* (Chapel Hill: University of North Carolina Press, 1994), 235–236.

34. Matthew Mancini, "Too Many Tocquevilles: The Fable of Tocqueville's American Reception," *Journal of the History of Ideas* 69, no. 2 (2008), 245–268; Mancini, *Alexis de Tocqueville and American Intellectuals: From His Times to Ours* (Lanham, MD: Rowman & Littlefield, 2006).

35. James Bryce, *The American Commonwealth* (Indianapolis: Liberty Fund, 1995), 3–11; Lynn Marshall and Seymour Drescher, "American Historians and Tocqueville's *Democracy*," *The Journal of American*

History 55, no. 3 (1968), 514n7; Henry Adams, *The Education of Henry Adams* (Oxford: Oxford University Press, 1999), 164.

36. McClay, *The Masterless*, 235.

37. On the therapeutic appeal of empire as an alternative to bourgeois decadence, see especially Melvin Richter, "Tocqueville on Algeria," *Review of Politics* 25, no. 3 (1963), 362–398; Pitts, *A Turn to Empire*; Richard Boyd, "Tocqueville and the Napoleonic Legend," in Ewa Atanassow and Richard Boyd, eds., *Tocqueville and the Frontiers of Democracy* (Cambridge: Cambridge University Press, 2013), 264–288.

38. Mencken cites Tocqueville, alongside "the Adams brothers," on the claim that democracy is uniquely disposed to political corruption. Cf. H. L. Mencken, *Notes on Democracy* (New York: Alfred A. Knopf, 1928), 178.

39. Irving Babbitt, *Literature and the American College: Essays in Defense of the Humanities* (Boston: Houghton, Mifflin and Company, 1908), 105; *Democracy and Leadership* (Boston: Houghton, Mifflin and Company, 1924), 16.

40. See Nisbet, "Many Tocquevilles," 60; Welch, *De Tocqueville*, 224–225; Kloppenberg, *The Virtues of Liberalism*, 74–75. Matthew Mancini offers a spirited corrective to the trope that *DIA* disappeared between the US Civil War and World War II. Disputing *DIA*'s "negligible influence on American thinkers" in the first decades of the twentieth century, Mancini adduces the names of John T. Bigelow, Daniel Coit Gilman, Senator John T. Morgan of Alabama, and former Senator John J. Ingalls of Kansas. See Mancini, "Too Many Tocquevilles," 249–254. In response, Felipe Carreira da Silva and Monica Brito Vieira offer empirical metrics and anecdotal evidence that support not only a postwar renaissance but clear disciplinary and ideological shifts in the book's influence throughout the twentieth century. Carreira da Silva and Vieira, "Books that Matter: The Case of Tocqueville's *Democracy in America*," *The Sociological Quarterly* 61, no. 4 (2020), 703–726.

41. Frohnen, *Virtue and the Promise of American Conservatism*.

42. Kirk, *The Conservative Mind*, 179, 194–195.

43. Robert Nisbet, *The Quest for Community* (Wilmington, DE: ISI Books, 2010), 175.

44. Nisbet, *Quest for Community*, 175.

45. Nisbet, "Many Tocquevilles," 70. For an instance of roughly contemporaneous complaints along these lines from the Left, see David Riesman, Nathan Glazer, and Reuel Denney, *The Lonely Crowd: A Study of the Changing American Character* (New Haven, CT: Yale University Press, 1950).

46. Paul Rahe, *Soft Despotism, Democracy's Drift: Montesquieu, Rousseau, Tocqueville, and the Modern Project* (New Haven, CT: Yale University Press, 2009), 184–189.

47. Allan Bloom, *The Closing of the American Mind* (New York: Simon & Schuster, 1987), 84–86, 227–228, 252–255.

48. On the "Straussian" interest in Tocqueville, see especially Welch, *De Tocqueville*, 245–248 and Mancini, *Tocqueville and American Intellectuals*, chap. 6. For example, Mansfield, *Tocqueville*; Pierre Manent, *Tocqueville and the Nature of Democracy* (Lanham, MD: Rowman & Littlefield, 1996); James Ceaser, "Alexis de Tocqueville on Political Science, Political Culture, and the Role of the Intellectual," *American Political Science Review* 79, no. 3 (1985), 656–672; Ceaser, *Liberal Democracy and Political Science* (Baltimore: Johns Hopkins University Press, 1992).

49. Gertrude Himmelfarb, "Introduction" in Alexis de Tocqueville, *Memoir on Pauperism*, trans. Seymour Drescher (London: Civitas, 1997), 14.

50. Dan Coats and John Kasich, *Project for American Renewal* (Washington, DC: Empower America, 1995).

51. See Francis Fukuyama, "The End of History?" *National Interest* 16 (1989), 3–18; Fukuyama, "The March of Equality," *Journal of Democracy* 11, no. 1 (2000), 11–17; Fukuyama, *The End of History and the Last Man* (New York: Free Press, 1992).

52. Samuel Huntington, "The Clash of Civilizations?" *Foreign Affairs* 72, no. 3 (Summer 1993), 22–49.

53. Samuel Huntington, *Political Order in Changing Societies* (New Haven, CT: Yale University Press, 1968), 4–5.

54. Samuel Huntington, "Cultures Count," in Lawrence Harrison and Samuel Huntington, eds., *Culture Matters: How Values Shape Human Progress* (New York: Basic Books, 2000), xiii–xvi.

55. See Samuel Huntington, *Who Are We? The Challenges to America's National Identity* (New York: Simon & Schuster, 2004).

56. Paul Wolfowitz as cited in David Ignatius, "A War of Choice, and One Who Chose It," *Washington Post* (November 2, 2003), B 01. www .washingtonpost.com/archive/opinions/2003/11/02/a-war-of-choice -and-one-who-chose-it/0284d57c-b2b5-4476-89b3-72cecfa55ee8/ (accessed June 23, 2020).

57. Lawrence Harrison, "After the Arab Spring, Culture Still Matters," *The American Interest* (September 1, 2011). www.the-american-interest .com/2011/09/01/after-the-arab-spring-culture-still-matters/ (accessed June 23, 2020); see also John Agresto, "Was Promoting Democracy a Mistake?" *Commentary* 134, no. 5 (2012), 32–38.

58. Joshua Mitchell, *Tocqueville in Arabia: Dilemmas in a Democratic Age* (Chicago: University of Chicago Press, 2013).

59. Jean Bethke Elshtain, *Democracy on Trial* (New York: Basic Books, 1995); Peter Berger and Richard John Neuhaus, *To Empower People: From State to Civil Society* (Washington, DC: American Enterprise Institute, 1996).

60. Jean Elshtain, *A Call to Civil Society: Why Democracy Needs Moral Truths* (New York: Institute for American Values, 1998), 8.

61. Mary Ann Glendon, "Introduction," in Mary Ann Glendon and David Blankenhorn, eds., *Seedbeds of Virtue: Sources of Competence, Character, and Citizenship in American Society* (Lanham, MD: Madison Books, 1995), 1–4.

62. See the chapter "Why I Am Not a Conservative," in Friedrich Hayek, *The Constitution of Liberty* (Chicago: University of Chicago Press, 2011), 529; and "Individualism: True and False," in Hayek, *Individualism and Economic Order* (Chicago: University of Chicago Press, 2012), 4–5, 28–32.

63. See, especially, Vincent Ostrom, *The Meaning of Democracy and the Vulnerability of Democracies: A Response to Tocqueville's Challenge* (Ann Arbor: University of Michigan, 1997).

64. On this connection see, for example, L. L. Wade, "Tocqueville and Public Choice," *Public Choice* 47, no. 3 (1985), 491–508.

5 Tocqueville and the Political Left in America

Heeding a Call for Decisive Action

Robert T. Gannett, Jr.

Writing to his English translator and friend Henry Reeve on November 15, 1839, Alexis de Tocqueville allowed himself a rare moment of self-celebration regarding his long-gestated volume 2 of *Democracy in America*. "I arrived in Paris with my manuscript complete," he announced to Reeve: "My book is finally finished, definitively finished; hallelujah!" With the same letter, Tocqueville forwarded to Reeve his "Report on Abolition," furiously written that summer in his capacity as rapporteur for the Chamber of Deputies' Commission to address the slavery question, a position to which he had been elected by his peers after entering the Chamber himself as a freshman legislator on March 29. Thereby blending his dual roles of acclaimed author and fledgling political leader, Tocqueville proceeded to chastise Reeve for failing to capture the full extent of his "democratic" credentials when Reeve translated volume 1 of *Democracy in America*, published in 1835. To be sure, Tocqueville allowed, his first volume contained a harsh critique of democracy, as did his second volume now written "principally for France." Yet his efforts to point out democracy's flaws were designed in both volumes to prepare his readers to recognize them, counter them, and take the needed steps to make democracy work. He wrote "as friend and not as censor," consistent with his "sincere desire to see the new [democratic society] establish itself."[1]

Even as he affirmed his intentions for *Democracy in America* to help establish democracy in France – a risky proposition in an era during which France experienced two revolutions, a coup d'état, and

157

four regime changes in his short lifetime (1805–1859) – Tocqueville expressed in his next letter to Reeve six weeks later the important role he hoped his book would play in furthering his political career. Writing on New Year's Eve, he urged his translator to accelerate volume 2's publication as it would "break or make" his political success during the spring 1840 legislative session. "Until this book has appeared and produced its effect," he wrote, "I am obliged to proceed only with great circumspection in the political world."[2] Tocqueville aimed to use the authority and message of his book to make his mark in the tightly confined and claustrophobic political world of the July Monarchy, itself dominated by intellectual heavy-weights. His success as an author would support his higher ambition as a politician, well-expressed a decade earlier to his friend and American traveling companion Gustave de Beaumont: "We must make ourselves political men."[3]

Tocqueville's 1839 "Report on Abolition" attested to the dynamic results produced by this complex interweaving of his theoretical and political ambitions and skills. In it, he revisited several of the main themes he had previously addressed in his concluding chapter to his first volume of *Democracy in America*, where he had minced no words expressing his revulsion at the institution of slavery and the degradation and humiliation to which it had subjected every forced African immigrant to America. He saw no obvious path to slavery's abolition in the American South, he wrote, other than by revolution or the eradication of one race by the other. He called the conflict between blacks and whites there "a nightmare constantly haunting the American imagination" and subsequently wrote in volume 2 that "[i]f there ever are great revolutions [in the United States], they will be caused by the presence of the blacks upon American soil."[4] In the smaller and more manageable context of France's four colonies of Guadeloupe, Martinique, Bourbon, and Guiana, Tocqueville proposed in his report concrete steps consistent with this theoretical analysis as he argued for the immediate, complete, and simultaneous liberation of all 250,000 French slaves, with the state assuming responsibility in the short term for their social welfare, training, and employment.[5]

Tocqueville's report's recommendations were dramatic, even radical ones at the time, certainly not those of a timid political newcomer cautiously putting his toe into turbulent political waters. In the short term, the French consul in New Orleans responded to it by sending a special dispatch to the French government:

> It would be impossible, *Monsieur le Marechal*, to describe to you the impact produced in the United States by the mere reading of a proposal, which, if it were enacted, would cause a veritable revolution in the colonies, and would not be without effect on the future of the United States ... I believe [that] France might commit incalculable errors by [pursuing such] hasty action [as that recommended in the Tocqueville Report].[6]

In the long term, the report placed Tocqueville on record as an active supporter of slavery's abolition for the rest of his political and writing careers, culminating in his "Testimony against Slavery" published in the American abolitionist periodical *The Liberty Bell* and reprinted in *The Liberator* on April 11, 1856, four years before the outbreak of the Civil War when his "great revolution" anticipated in *Democracy in America* became a reality.[7]

If Tocqueville intended his position on the abolition of slavery in his 1839 report to be bold and controversial, he similarly set out to jolt his readers with his foreboding vision of democracy's future trials in his carefully crafted climactic political section in volume 2, part 4 of *Democracy in America*. Beginning in January 1838, Tocqueville had undertaken what I have called "a self-taught 'great books seminar'," delving into works from Muhammad and the Koran to St. Paul and the Bible, from Plato to Plutarch, and from Machiavelli to Voltaire, and then rethinking, revising, and writing from scratch key sections of volume 2, including these final eight chapters.[8] Taken together, these additions and changes shifted the focus of his work to a frightening portrait of future democracy's gravest threat: the pusillanimous surrender by citizens and nations of their rights and responsibilities, resulting in a novel kind of despotism that shifted power to a new form of despot who would encourage individualism, stifle freedom of political thought, undermine citizen action, and envelop all in a cocoon of state-sponsored benevolence and care. In Tocqueville's democratic dystopia, citizens would be neutered, men become sheep, and a despot emboldened to erect barriers to divide and isolate people, even as he "twist[ed] the natural meaning of words." To counter such threats to democracy, Tocqueville asserted that great "associations of plain citizens" must emerge to stand up, resist, and combat such insidious despotic overreach.[9]

As with his 1839 "Report on Abolition" addressing America's contemporary nightmare of slavery, his final chapters in volume 2 of *Democracy in America* predicting a future democratic psychic nightmare reverberated across the Atlantic, too. It took a century but, beginning in 1939, political activists on the American Left adopted Tocqueville as their muse to support fierce, hands-on, collective political action by citizens to bolster democracy and resist despotism, both in the United States and in regimes across the world.

To gauge the relevance of Tocqueville's *Democracy in America* for the development and trajectory of the intellectual and political Left in America, we must take into account his book's dual and complementary goals of theoretical assessment and practical action. On the one hand, he makes a reasoned case to an erudite and elite audience for democracy's substantial benefits, even while warning readers of its potential pitfalls. On the other, he validates the need for action to address such deficits. We will begin in the following section by looking at the context within which he wrote his book and the "live cinders" on which he tread as he formulated his original, counterintuitive defense of democracy in volume 1 built around freedom of the press, freedom of association, universal suffrage, and a belief that active citizen engagement must be the catalyst and essential linchpin for freedom in a democracy. In the section "Tocqueville's

Call to Action and the American Political Left's Response," we will assess how members of the intellectual and political Left in the United States have read Tocqueville's *Democracy in America* since the late 1930s, often with mixed responses. At times, theorists have ignored, dismissed, and/or disparaged the author and his work. At others, brash, self-proclaimed "radicals" and shy, media-averse university professors have drawn on his work to launch significant political movements for democracy's expansion in unexpected ways and places.

TOCQUEVILLE'S ARGUMENT FOR DEMOCRACY

Tocqueville's persona is writ large in *Democracy in America*, from the opening sentence of his "Author's Introduction" as insightful traveler to the United States to the final paragraphs of his "General Survey of the Subject" where he underscores his firm belief in the prospect for "strong and free" men and nations in the dawning democratic age. Entering the conceptual center of volume 1 in part 2, chapters 5 and 6, where he will set forth his most explicit argument for democracy, he adds a new dimension to that persona: bold participant in current French political debates. "I know that I am now treading on live cinders," he begins chapter 5, titled "Government by Democracy in America." "Every word in this chapter must in some respect offend the various parties dividing my country," he continues: "Nevertheless, I shall say all I think."[10]

Tocqueville's "live cinders" had been fanned by the conflicts and turbulence of the early years of the July Monarchy. Installed in the aftermath of the "Three Glorious Days" of the July Revolution of 1830, Louis-Philippe's constitutional monarchy had struggled to find its political footing, even as its citizens' fears were further stoked by economic crisis and the rapid spread of cholera. Opposed on the Right by legitimists seeking the return of the Bourbons and on the Left by often secret republican societies embracing fierce anticlericalism and a romantic desire to return to the barricades to uphold the legacy of '89, Louis-Philippe's government failed to solidify its legal and moral standing. "Monarchic, [the July regime] had betrayed the monarchy; revolutionary, it had betrayed the Revolution," writes François Furet in *Revolutionary France, 1770–1880*. "A risky compromise between the sovereignty of the kings and that of the people, it was despised from both sides."[11] Writing his first volume of *Democracy in America* from fall 1833 to summer 1834, Tocqueville set out to provide his readers with an original American lens through which they could reassess the regime's dual breaches of faith and reconsider their own preconceptions, enthusiasms, and/or fears about the advent of democracy in France.

Using this American lens in volume 1, part 2, Tocqueville builds a surprising case for the advantages of democracy. He begins by defining the "two main weapons" used by political parties in America to ensure their success – newspapers and associations. In France, the government was engaged at this time in "an exhausting guerrilla warfare with the press," seeking to muzzle it in ways that would culminate in the repressive censorship laws of September 1835.[12] Such a strategy was a mistake, Tocqueville argues. Encountering a press every bit as vile and vituperative as that in France, Americans had adopted an opposite course, recognizing "that the only way to neutralize the effect of newspapers is to multiply their numbers." Unlimited freedom of the press flummoxed the opposition hiding in their secret societies, put all issues out in the open for all to review, and established a common ground for debates to then take place. Ultimately, Tocqueville concludes, such freedom of the press served as "the principal and, so to say, constitutive element in freedom."[13]

Turning to political associations, Tocqueville acknowledges they pose a more complicated risk in a democracy and indeed will be "of all forms of liberty, the last that a nation can sustain." For in France, such associations have been viewed "as a weapon of war to be hastily improvised and used at once on the field of battle," turning to violence and extralegal measures whenever deemed necessary. Such politically driven organizations with their military ways and maxims required and enforced absolute obedience among their members, thus also sacrificing, in Tocqueville's eyes, "their moral strength ... [and] sacred character belonging to the struggle of the oppressed against the oppressor." In the United States, political associations took a different tack, operating within the law, eschewing violence, petitioning for change, and encouraging internal discussion and debate and thus preserving every individual's right to think, write, and act for himself – that is to say, Tocqueville's lifelong personal and political credo. Unlimited freedom of association must be nurtured, supported, and viewed as the aim of every democratic society, since only political associations can finally resist tyranny of the majority, eliminate the justification for secret societies and conspirators, and hold despots accountable.[14]

Having encountered universal white male suffrage in all of the states of the Union, and having examined it in conversations throughout his American travels, Tocqueville arrived at a conclusion about its benefits that differed sharply from those expressed by all sides in the political debates in France and tied directly to his qualified support for freedom of association. Universal suffrage, he argues in *Democracy in America*, is a moderating influence, not a revolutionary one, since it forces all types of associations seeking power to prove their majority status at the ballot box. With universal suffrage in place, political associations can no longer claim to represent a supposed but fictitious majority and then use violence to attempt to impose their political will. Power in a democracy is a new concept, unlike anything that existed in a monarchy, since it forces associations to adjust their claims and strategy to court majority support and then prove it at the polls. "Extreme freedom [of political associations] corrects the abuse of freedom, and extreme democracy [universal suffrage] forestalls the dangers of democracy," Tocqueville concludes.[15]

In the remainder of chapter 5, Tocqueville reinterprets a number of other myths about democracy to which he sees French political parties clinging. In some cases, he refutes them, in others he redefines them by deploying further counterintuitive arguments, and in others, he supports them.

Universal suffrage will result in a higher caliber of elected representative. Not so, Tocqueville argues, as he found in America that "good qualities were common among the governed but rare among the rulers." The people are solid, responsible, peaceful, and educated; but since in the main they will have to work for a living, they will lack the time or means to skillfully weigh and assess the qualities most appropriate to the country's good. "That is why," he warns, "charlatans of every sort so well understand the secret of pleasing them."[16]

Frequent elections on an annual basis will lead to perpetual feverish campaigning and result in the inconstancy and mutability of laws. Yes, that's the risk, Tocqueville agrees, but Americans have judged it to be the lesser of two evils for, when elections are infrequent, dissent is bottled up and can explode in violence and regime change.

Public officials lack the palaces, guards, and external pomp to communicate the importance of their positions. All public officials in America are paid for their services, Tocqueville explains, thus making it possible "for any man [to have] the chance as well as the right to perform them." Such access to holding office removes the ostentation, haughtiness, and advancement based on wealth and family connections of central government officials in France. While American officials are more accessible and responsive to the people who have voted to pay for them, do not assume, however, that they have less power. Because elections are regular and frequent, Tocqueville clarifies, Americans become less vigilant about abuses and often grant their officials extensive, arbitrary powers, making their government "all-powerful and omnipresent."[17]

Democratic governments lack an understanding of the science of administration and fail to keep records. True, Tocqueville agrees, commenting that American society "seems to live from day to day, like an army on active service." Such a lack of administrative art in America is mitigated by the superior skills and knowledge of its citizens and the value added by their direct engagement in the actual process of governing themselves. In the New England townships, Tocqueville had found, citizens may have "untidy budgets lacking all uniformity" but they are constructed by "an enlightened, active, and enterprising population ... a society always at work."[18]

Democratic government is cheap. Not so, Tocqueville concludes. Yes, it saves money by paying less to higher officials and doing away with the costs of a king, but it gives that back – and more – as it remunerates mid-level officials adequately and "faithful to its popular origins ... looks after the poor, distributes annually millions to schools, [and] pays for all services."[19]

Democratic government is corrupt. Yes, Tocqueville agrees. Moreover, democratic corruption is "contagious to the crowd" since it is seen by all, as opposed to aristocratic corruption that can be hidden from public view by the formalities and elegance of a court. Corruption is most corrosive in democracies when public officials use it to win election to office, fueling envy and resentment among the populace and leading to "an odious mingling of the conceptions of baseness and power, of unworthiness and success, and of profit and dishonor."[20]

Democratic government lacks the popular will and patience to sustain its great initiatives and denies the chance for its leaders to coordinate their details and keep them secret when dealing with foreign powers. True again, Tocqueville agrees. Democratic citizens may be able to respond to high-level emergencies with initial energy and resolve but they then fall back into their singular preoccupations with daily life, lose interest in long-term campaigns and in foreign affairs, and allow their popular sympathies to contradict their long-term interests.

Taken as a whole, then, government by democracy thus succeeds in creating the active, varied, and ever-agitated American political life in which its citizens read their newspapers, join their many open and deliberative political and civil associations, vote frequently, consider the chance to become a public official themselves, debate and approve budgets and taxes, see and challenge corruption with their newspapers and associations, and rise to the occasion, if only briefly, when threatened with emergency crises. On the whole, such educated, engaged, entrepreneurial citizens foster prosperity for the greatest number and combine a staunch understanding of their own self-interest with recognition of their country's common good. "Democratic freedom does not carry its undertakings through as perfectly as an intelligent despotism would," Tocqueville concludes in the heart of chapter 6, "The Advantages of Democratic Government," after highlighting other advantages including democracy's "reflective patriotism," political rights that "penetrate right down to the least of citizens," and respect for the law. "But it does that which the most skillful government often cannot do: it spreads throughout the body social a restless activity, superabundant force, and energy never found elsewhere, which, however little favored by circumstance, can do wonders. Those are its true advantages." He then ends chapter 6 with his decisive and justly famous democratic balance sheet, proof positive of his own reflective belief in democracy.[21]

Tocqueville challenges readers of *Democracy in America* to reflect for themselves on just how far such active citizen engagement should lead and what limits must be set upon it. On the one hand, too much such "populism" can produce tyranny of the majority and despotism – his democratic nightmare in volume 1. On the other hand, too little "populism" can produce apathy and a different kind of despotism – his democratic dystopia in volume 2. As with his formulations regarding political associations, religion, centralization in national government, and the proper checks and balances between national and local government, Tocqueville sought throughout his entire work to assess and settle the fragile balance required for potent citizen action to support and sustain democratic freedom, not jeopardize it.[22]

TOCQUEVILLE'S CALL TO ACTION AND THE AMERICAN POLITICAL LEFT'S RESPONSE

At important moments in his dual careers as writer and politician, Tocqueville embraced action as his personal *sine qua non*. Seeking both to win political office and to complete volume 2 of *Democracy in America*, he announced to Kergorlay in October 1837 that "I have always valued action above all else." He then qualified this commitment: when the path to *"action"* might be blocked, he could usefully pursue *"thought,"* since immaterial ideas had demonstrated successfully for 300 years their own ability to "constantly rouse the world."[23]

Tocqueville's *"thought"* in *Democracy in America* has reverberated in the United States since the book's publication in 1835 and 1840, provoking commentary and controversy while advancing at different times the trajectories of both the Right and the Left. During the 1940s, 1950s, and 1960s, such commentary was often led by Central and Eastern European scholars who either arrived themselves or whose parents had arrived in the United States as immigrant refugees, including Albert Salomon, Max Lerner, John Lukacs, Jacob Peter Mayer (situated in Great Britain but present on occasion in the United States), Louis Hartz, and Hannah Arendt. The German sociologist Salomon's path to America took him from editing a volume of Tocqueville's selected texts in Germany in the early 1930s to a position at the New School in New York City in 1935. "Salomon typified a group of Central European immigrant intellectuals, often Jewish refugees," writes Matthew Mancini in *Alexis de Tocqueville and American Intellectuals*, who were "fascinated by Tocqueville's defense of liberty and repelled by the emergence of totalitarian states with their monstrous myths of race and history ... [and] who were about to assume prominent roles in the field of Tocqueville studies." By 1959, Mancini adds, Salomon had come to see Tocqueville "as a kind of 'conservative Marxist' ... and an existentialist."[24]

Arriving herself in America in 1940, Arendt developed her own provocative views on the "banality of evil" after attending Adolf

Eichmann's trial in Jerusalem in 1961 as a reporter for *The New Yorker*. In *On Revolution*, first published the same year as *Eichmann in Jerusalem* in 1963, Arendt engaged Tocqueville directly as a dialogical presence when she sought to define the appropriate public spaces that could serve as political realms of freedom. Bracketing her discussion of the New England town with references to *Democracy in America*, she emphasized that New England's 550 towns served as just such realms of freedom where men mutually pledged and bound themselves together "for the purpose of action" and then went on to play lead roles in the American Revolution. Her analysis had many parallels to that of Tocqueville but differed in one crucial respect: while Arendt emphasized the primacy of the chosen few in creating freedom, Tocqueville had ascribed to the town a more universal educative function affecting all citizens in what he called their "primary schools" of American democracy, so much so that, when the Revolution began, "the dogma of the sovereignty of the people came out from the township and took possession of the government."[25]

Tocqueville's reputation on the intellectual Left faded during the late twentieth century, with the historian Michael Kammen noting in 1998 an "anomalous asymmetry between liberals and conservatives" regarding Tocqueville in the mid-1990s, by which he meant that conservatives had "virtually appropriated *Democracy in America* as their favorite source of cerebral ammunition" while liberals "by and large ... simply do without Tocqueville."[26] Reading Tocqueville on the Left received a further jolt in 2001 with the publication by Sheldon Wolin of *Tocqueville between Two Worlds*. Wolin briefly acknowledged in his introduction that Tocqueville "might be the last influential theorist who can be said to have truly cared about political life," only then to adopt throughout his book what one critic has called a "hermeneutic of unremitting hostility" toward Tocqueville's political career and writings. "Unmindful of the significance of his own discovery," Wolin came to argue, Tocqueville thus found in America "that [its] politics, with its mix of participatory, democratic, and religious elements, was importantly premodern," anticipating his reversion to "*ancienneté* ... [where] the common people were consigned to a kind of darkness, outside the pale of political life."[27] In a posting in an online forum of the Liberty Fund, Daniel Mahoney gave his own explanation for the decline of interest in Tocqueville on the intellectual Left: "Tocqueville is too critical of individual autonomy, of the pantheistic denial of a transcendent God, and too ambivalent about equality and human leveling for him to be truly admired by the intellectual Left." "In the end," he adds, "Tocqueville cannot appeal to those who wish to erode all the extra-democratic supports of our democratic dispensation, who wish fully to 'democratize' democracy."[28]

By contrast, on the political or activist Left, community organizers, communitarians, and promoters of nonviolent resistance to autocratic governments have found reasons to embrace Tocqueville's analysis, with three such political movements during the past eighty years using *Democracy in America* to help provide an intellectual frame for their activist work.

In 1940, Saul D. Alinsky adopted Tocqueville as muse for his version of community organizing, launched at the founding convention of the Back of the Yards Neighborhood Council on July 14, 1939. Alinsky appended a quote from Tocqueville's chapter 6 in volume 2, part 4 of *Democracy in America*, "What Sort of Despotism Democratic Nations Have to Fear," to his initial prospectus for his new organizing and training institute, the Industrial Areas Foundation (IAF): "No one will ever believe that a liberal, wise, and energetic government can spring from the suffrages of a subservient people." Likewise, in his 1946 national bestseller, *Reveille for Radicals*, he cited the entire 400-word passage leading up to this quote, beginning with Tocqueville's assertion that "[i]t must not be forgotten that it is especially dangerous to enslave men in the minor details of life."[29] Throughout his thirty-three-year career as a self-described "professional anti-fascist" in 1939 who went on to become

America's leading community organizer and "Prophet Of Power," Alinsky made repeated references to Tocqueville's warning about new forms of despotism. He also found Tocqueville to be a shrewd political observer who poked through appearances and detected the ploys of the powerful in isolating and pacifying their citizens, as well as a firm believer in civic education as action, not abstract speculation – the essence of his own new field.[30]

Alinsky trained community organizers and assigned them to marginalized communities across the United States to organize residents to demand a voice on their urgent issues. The associations he and his organizers helped residents create were "political associations" in Tocqueville's lexicon, ones that pushed to the limit the strategy and tactics residents must use to win on their issues. Alinsky saw his organizations as fighting ones and he adopted military language – of armies, enemies, battles, feints, and ruses – to describe them, even as he eschewed violence, encouraged freedom of thought and open debate among members, and kept his work within the limits of the law. After he died in 1972, Edward Chambers moved the IAF in a new direction of organizing faith-based coalitions of churches, synagogues, and mosques that today have impressive projects throughout the United States, joined by Faith in Action (formerly PICO National Network), Gamaliel National Network, and Direct Action and Research Training Center (DART). Concluding his own book, *Roots for Radicals*, in 2003, Chambers argued that twenty-first-century organizers must create "radical, nonpartisan assemblies crossing national boundaries," with such "new political instruments not based on science and technology, but rather on culture, on what de Tocqueville called 'habits of the heart' in the book he wrote on American democracy more than 150 years ago." Tocqueville thus served as bridge from the Alinsky-led "old IAF" focused on power to fight despotism to the Chambers-led "new IAF" focused on "mores" to build social knowledge, democratic organizers, and broad-based citizen organizations.[31] Writers on the Left such as Harry Boyte and Benjamin Barber traced these projects and others in the broader field of community organizing, even as they developed their own agendas of public citizenship and strong democracy.[32]

Communitarianism became the "intellectual buzzword of the 90s," defined by its own ABCs ("Aristotle," "Bowling," and "Civil Society"), announced Fareed Zakaria in *Slate Magazine* in 1996. The Communitarian Network, formed in 1993 and centered at George Washington University under the leadership of Amitai Etzioni, initially led this effort. In 1992, it unveiled and then worked to implement a "Responsive Communitarian Platform" supported by prominent academic, political, and community leaders from throughout the United States. It bolstered these efforts by publishing from 1990 to summer 2004 a quarterly journal, *The Responsive Community*, that highlighted articles and news stories explaining and promoting the importance of community as a new rallying cry for an alternate politics that explicitly contrasted itself with the "Libertarians" and "Authoritarians."[33] Robert Putnam's article in 1995, "Bowling Alone," struck a nerve of its own in academic, civic, and foundation circles. A social scientist, Putnam was committed to quantifying in his scholarly works the decline of social capital and the success of efforts to rebuild America's civic infrastructure following recommendations of his Saguaro Seminar in its 2001 report, "Better Together." In 2003, Putnam and Lewis Feinstein reported on a range of success stories initiated from different points in Tocqueville's complex associational frame, including the City of Chicago's efforts to build new styles of active and responsive branch libraries and the Texas IAF's "relational organizing" strategies to empower residents of the *colonias* to demand recognition and basic services in the lower Rio Grande valley.[34]

With such heightened interest for two decades in civil society and voluntary associations, Tocqueville's writings were "seen (not without reason) as the *locus classicus* for this subject," explains William Galston, a cofounder of the Communitarian Network, Executive Director of the National Commission on Civic Renewal, and Deputy Assistant for Domestic Policy for President Clinton from 1993 to 1995. "Although no noncontemporary writer is more frequently cited by American academics and politicians," Galston added, "Tocqueville is more often quoted than understood." Galston proceeded to redirect attention to the primacy Tocqueville attached to political associations in his first volume of *Democracy in America*, spelling out both their benefits and the dangers for democracy that we have already noted. With their abundant energy and broad participation, political associations set the tone for active engagement in society as a whole, serving as Tocqueville's "large free schools" and what Galston calls "sites of resistance against tyranny and oppression," in addition to transmitting their energy in a symbiotic and mutually reinforcing relationship with civil associations "outside the control of government."[35]

In addition to the community organizing and communitarian movements, the American academic Gene Sharp used Tocqueville to forge an intellectual frame for global movements of nonviolent resistance. In his earlier writings, especially *The Politics of Nonviolent Action, Part One: Power and Struggle* (1973) and *Social Power and Political Freedom* (1980), Sharp drew upon often overlooked passages from throughout *Democracy in America* to support his subtle examination of the social, psychological, economic, military, and media strategies used by despots past and present to intimidate their subjects and sustain their regimes. He especially noted Tocqueville's and other theorists' emphasis on the social context within which political events and decisions take place, finding that "the roots of political power reach beyond and below the formal structure of the State into the society itself." Using a brief section, "The Importance of the Foregoing in Relation to Europe," in *Democracy in America*, volume 1, part 2, chapter 9, as the starting point for his entire edifice of the essential barriers in any nation to despotic rule, he stressed the importance of strong, diffused "*loci* (or places) of power" that served to "limit the de facto political power of the theoretically omnipotent ruler." Sharp's larger and now famous argument is best expressed in his *chef d'oeuvre*, *From Dictatorship to Democracy: A Conceptual Framework for Liberation* (1993), in which he argued that "mass political defiance" must begin with precisely such independent groups in precisely such free spaces, often by working at a local level to first address simple, clear, winnable issues.[36]

Beginning in 1992, using Sharp's principles of nonviolent resistance as his curriculum, retired Army Colonel Robert Helvey began providing training to activists in countries such as Burma (Myanmar), Belarus, Venezuela, Nigeria, Iraq, Palestine, Zimbabwe, and Serbia. Activists around the globe translated *From Dictatorship to Democracy* into more than twenty-five languages by 2008. "For the world's despots," concluded *New York Times* columnist Sheryl Gay Stolberg in 2011, "[Sharp's] ideas can be fatal," as she assessed his pivotal role in providing a philosophical and practical frame for democratic revolutions, including those that toppled Slobodan Milosevic in Serbia, Zine al-Abidine Ben Ali in Tunisia, and Hosni Mubarak in Egypt.[37]

CONCLUSION

Cheryl Welch has suggested that it may be possible today to read with a fresh perspective Tocqueville's *Recollections: The French Revolution of 1848 and Its Aftermath*, given the "haunting" parallels in the political turmoil of his era and our own modern Trump era "in which Americans are experiencing the shocks of 'abnormal' democratic politics."[38] Might a similar new reading by the Left of *Democracy in America* be possible in the Trump era as well?

Democracy in America received just such a rereading outside the United States after the fall of the Berlin Wall in 1991 and the collapse of state socialism in Eastern Europe and the Soviet Union. Dana Villa has described how a Tocquevillean view of civil society took on new resonance for activists in these and other global struggles of resistance in the late twentieth century. "Outside the limited confines of the American debate, 'civil society' came to represent a newly born, newly active political and associational life," he argues:

> It referred to a diverse array of trade, women's, political and student groups, all of whom were determined to defend not just private but

also *local* and *public* liberty. It came, in a word, to stand for a decentralized and pluralistic public realm, one capable of advancing society's claims not only against the bureaucratic/authoritarian state, but also against large economic interests (such as multinational corporations).[39]

In our consideration of "Tocqueville and the Political Left in America," we have seen how American activists, especially community organizers, some communitarians, and advocates for global nonviolent resistance, have used their own readings of *Democracy in America* to define in concept and create in practice similar explosive organizations of power and resistance. The Left in the United States today can build upon and expand such readings to reconceptualize the issues, targets, majority bases, timing, and funding of their opposition to today's "abnormal" politics.

NOTES

1. "Alexis de Tocqueville to Henry Reeve, November 15, 1839," OC 6:1, 47–48.
2. "Tocqueville to Reeve, December 31, 1839," OC 6:1, 49–50.
3. "Tocqueville to Gustave de Beaumont, October 25, 1829," OC 8:1, 93.
4. DIA (L) I.2.x, 358; II.3.xxi, 639.
5. Alexis de Tocqueville, "Report on Abolition," in Seymour Drescher, ed., *Tocqueville and Beaumont on Social Reform* (New York: Harper & Row, 1968), 98–136.
6. Cited in Tocqueville, "Report on Abolition," 98n1.
7. Alexis de Tocqueville, "Tocqueville to *The Liberty Bell*, 1855," in *Tocqueville on America after 1840: Letters and Other Writings*, ed. and trans. Aurelian Craiutu and Jeremy Jennings (Cambridge: Cambridge University Press, 2009), 169.
8. Robert T. Gannett, Jr., *Tocqueville Unveiled: The Historian and His Sources for The Old Regime and the Revolution* (Chicago: University of Chicago Press, 2003), 7.
9. DIA (L) II.2.iv, 509; II.4.vii, 697.
10. DIA (L) I.2.v, 196.

11. François Furet, *Revolutionary France, 1770–1880*, trans. Antonia Nevill (Cambridge, MA: Blackwell, 1992), 351.

12. André Jardin, *Tocqueville: A Biography*, trans. Lydia Davis and Robert Hemenway (New York: Farrar, Straus and Giroux, 1988), 213.

13. DIA (L) I.2.ii, 179; I.2.iii, 184; I.2.iv, 191.

14. DIA (L) I.2. iv, 193–195.

15. DIA (L) I.2. iv, 195.

16. DIA (L) I.2.v, 197–198.

17. DIA (L) I.2.v, 204, 206.

18. DIA (L) I.2.v, 208; I.1.v, 92–93n51.

19. DIA (L) I.2.v, 219.

20. DIA (L) I.2.v, 221.

21. DIA (L) I.2.vi, 236, 239, 244.

22. For comments on each of these Tocquevillean balances, see Robert T. Gannett, Jr., "Tocqueville and Local Government: Distinguishing Democracy's Second Track," *Review of Politics* 67, no. 4 (Fall 2005), 721–736.

23. "Tocqueville to Louis de Kergorlay, October 4, 1837," OC 13:1, 479.

24. Matthew Mancini, *Alexis de Tocqueville and American Intellectuals: From His Times to Ours* (Lanham, MD: Rowman & Littlefield, 2006), 168–169.

25. Hannah Arendt, *Eichmann in Jerusalem: A Report on the Banality of Evil* (New York: Penguin Books, 1977); Hannah Arendt, *On Revolution* (New York: Penguin Books, 1990), 166 and 176n64, 175, 279; DIA (L) I.1. v, 63 and I.1.iv, 59. For additional strains of interest in Tocqueville during the 1950s and 1960s, especially those of the post–World War II consensus school of democratic pluralists such as David Truman and Robert Dahl, see Cheryl Welch, *De Tocqueville* (Oxford: Oxford University Press, 2001), 224–228.

26. Cited in Mancini, *Alexis de Tocqueville and American Intellectuals*, 202.

27. Sheldon S. Wolin, *Tocqueville between Two Worlds: The Making of a Political and Theoretical Life* (Princeton: Princeton University Press, 2001), 5, 382, 551. For Wolin's "unremitting hostility," see Melvin Richter, "The Deposition of Alexis De Tocqueville?" *The Tocqueville Review/La revue Tocqueville* 23, no. 2 (2002), 175. See also Seymour Drescher, "Who Needs *Ancienneté*: Tocqueville on Aristocracy and Modernity," *History of Political Thought* 24, no. 4 (Winter 2003), 624–646.

28. Daniel J. Mahoney, "Wisdom, Human Nature, and Political Science," a response to Aurelian Craiutu, "Tocqueville's New Science of Politics Revisited," posted May 9, 2014, *Liberty Matters: An Online Discussion Forum*, https://oll.libertyfund.org/pages/tocqueville-s-new-science-of-politics (accessed March 26, 2020).

29. DIA (L) II.4.vi, 694–695. Alinsky used an 1862 edition of *Democracy in America* for his citation, published by Barnes and Company and translated by Henry Reeve. Saul D. Alinsky, *Reveille for Radicals* (Chicago: University of Chicago Press, 1946), 68–69.

30. Sanford D. Horwitt, *Let Them Call Me Rebel: Saul Alinsky – His Life and Legacy* (New York: Alfred A. Knopf, 1989), 105; Saul D. Alinsky, *Reveille for Radicals* (New York: Vintage Books, 1969), 44–45; Marion K. Sanders, *The Professional Radical: Conversations with Saul Alinsky* (New York: Harper & Row, 1970), 31; "Radical Saul Alinsky: Prophet of Power," *Time* (March 2, 1970), 56.

31. Edward T. Chambers and Michael A. Cowan, *Roots for Radicals: Organizing for Power, Action, and Justice* (New York: Continuum, 2003), 140.

32. Harry C. Boyte, *The Backyard Revolution: Understanding the New Citizen Movement* (Philadelphia: Temple University Press, 1980); Benjamin R. Barber, *Strong Democracy: Participatory Politics for a New Age* (Berkeley: University of California Press, 1984). See also Harry Boyte and Benjamin Barber, "Civic Declaration – A Call for a New Citizenship," A Project of the American Civic Forum (An Occasional Paper of The Kettering Foundation: December 9, 1994).

33. Fareed Zakaria, "The ABCs of Communitarianism: A Devil's Dictionary," *Slate Magazine* (July 26, 1996); "The Responsive Communitarian Platform" at www.communitariannetwork.org/; *The Responsive Community: Rights and Responsibilities*, published quarterly by the Institute for Communitarian Policy Studies of The George Washington University, from 1990 to 2004.

34. Robert D. Putnam, "Bowling Alone," *Journal of Democracy* 6 (1995): 65–78; Robert D. Putnam, *Bowling Alone: The Collapse and Revival of American Community* (New York: Simon & Schuster, 2000); Robert D. Putnam, Lewis M. Feldstein, and Don Cohen, *Better Together: Restoring the American Community* (New York: Simon & Schuster, 2003).

35. William A. Galston, "Civil Society and the 'Art of Association'," *Journal of Democracy* 11, no.1 (2000), 65, 69. For further efforts to clarify the conceptual accuracy of communitarians' reading of Tocqueville, see Robert T. Gannett, Jr., "Bowling Ninepins in Tocqueville's Township," *American Political Science Review* 97, no. 1 (2003), 1–16.

36. Gene Sharp, *The Politics of Nonviolent Action, Part One: Power and Struggle* (Boston, MA: Extending Horizon Books, 1984), 10; DIA (L) I.2. ix, 311–315; Gene Sharp, *Social Power and Political Freedom* (Boston, MA: Extending Horizon Books, 1980), 27, 34; Gene Sharp, *From Dictatorship to Democracy: A Conceptual Framework for Liberation* (New York: The New Press, 2012), 2, 93–94. In *The Politics of Nonviolent Action* and *Social Power,* Sharp makes reference to forty-nine different passages drawn from fourteen different chapters of *Democracy in America.*

37. William J. Dobson, *The Dictator's Learning Curve: Inside the Global Battle for Democracy* (New York: Random House Anchor Books, 2012), 230–241; Sheryl Gay Stolberg, "Shy U.S. Intellectual Created Playbook Used in a Revolution," *New York Times* (February 17, 2011).

38. Cheryl B. Welch, "Review" of Alexis de Tocqueville, *Recollections: The French Revolution of 1848 and Its Aftermath,* ed. Olivier Zunz and trans. Arthur Goldhammer (Charlottesville: University of Virginia Press, 2016) in Welch, "Tocqueville's *Recollections* in Trump's America," *The Tocqueville Review/La revue Tocqueville* 37, no. 1 (2017), 160.

39. Welch, *De Tocqueville,* 232–234; Dana Villa, "Tocqueville and Civil Society," in Cheryl B. Welch, ed., *The Cambridge Companion to Tocqueville* (Cambridge: Cambridge University Press, 2006), 217–218.

6 Tocqueville and Anti-Americanism

Alan Levine

This chapter is on Tocqueville *and* anti-Americanism; it is not on Tocqueville's anti-Americanism because Tocqueville himself is not anti-American. By anti-American, I do not mean all critics of America, since many criticisms of it (and all countries) are legitimate and just. Rather, I mean a species of critique marked by excessive, unfounded, or selective criticisms or caricatures, akin to anti-Semitism or racism, that blames the United States alone for something that many or all countries do or exaggerates a fault beyond the realm of reality.[1] Tocqueville sees many of the same flaws as these anti-Americans, but he does not overstate them as they do. His criticisms are empirically based, complicated by attention to the complexities of American reality, linked with accounts of what he deems America's virtues, and/or contextualized to show how other countries do similar or worse things.

Anti-Americanism is not about the real America, its people and deeds; it is about what America is deemed to represent. Thus, it is a critique of the idea of America, America as symbol. In Tocqueville's time, and indeed throughout the nineteenth and twentieth centuries, America was deemed to represent "modernity," or, more precisely, modernity's liberal democratic incarnation. Anti-Americanism is thus most prevalent on the ideological Far Left and Far Right, both of which reject modern liberalism. A "friend" of the emerging modern liberal order, Tocqueville is neither simply hostile to nor a partisan of the liberal modernity of America, enabling him to see features that others ignore. Also, in describing America, many tend simply to equate America with *modernity as such*, associating it with – or even blaming it for – all the problems of the modern age. Tocqueville sees America as the fullest embodiment of modernity, but his analysis does not reduce America to it.

This chapter analyzes the views expressed by Tocqueville in *Democracy in America* in the context of European thinkers' critiques of America. It focuses on European critiques because anti-Americanism was originally a European phenomenon, found primarily among European intellectual and political elites. Europe's traditional authorities judged America harshly because liberal democratic modernity threatened their way of life and privileged positions within the established order. The radical vanguard wanted to establish the failure of liberalism as a political possibility to support the more radical communist, socialist, or anarchist alternatives to which they aspired. The ideologies and interests of both the existing authorities and the radical revolutionaries supplied them with everything they needed to know about modern liberal democratic America and enabled them to make assertions without evidence and/or in the face of contrary evidence. As these critiques emerged, they were repeated even by people with opposite ideological views. These elites' ideologies of America contrast with the views of the European masses who more typically judged America by its deeds, and thus their views of America change over time between positive and negative in accordance with their commonsense interpretation of experience.[2]

The anti-Americans' critiques are interlocking and overlapping, but I here analyze them in three main themes. First, Americans excessively love equality, leading to an unwarranted and dangerous devaluation of liberty and a fundamental sameness and drab monotonization of their world. Second, this sameness is driven by a vulgar, money-grubbing materialism. Third, this equality and money-grubbing prevent the development of greatness and refinement, leading to a spiritually void world of undesirable, petty lives.

Tocqueville shares many of the criticisms that anti-Americans articulate, but his analyses are superior to theirs. Unlike them, Tocqueville actually wrestles with the reality of America. The anti-American critics of the Far Left and Far Right are driven by their analyses of modernity and do not really care about the reality of America. Where they are content to use America to make their polemical points about the future of Europe and the world that they desire, Tocqueville tries to see America as it really is – both in its modernity and in its particularities. Tocqueville clearly understands America to be the fullest embodiment of liberal democratic modernity, but he also recognizes that America has undemocratic, illiberal, and premodern realities. Thus, for him, America and liberal democratic modernity are not simply identical or equivalent. Almost everything he claims about the phenomena of democracy is found in America, but not everything American is essential to democracy. Unlike most anti-American critics, Tocqueville clearly disentangles these threads, some of which he judges to be to America's benefit and others not. Indeed, one of the most striking features of *Democracy in America* is the way that Tocqueville can act both as a first-rate sociologist who values social science objectivity, as Raymond Aron describes him, and as a profoundly insightful normative analyst.[3] Yet Tocqueville's normative judgments are additions to his explanations of phenomena, not substitutes for them. As a result of his more serious scrutiny, Tocqueville's depth of understanding – of both America and of liberal democracy itself – is unique and unparalleled.

FIRST CRITIQUE: EXCESSIVE EQUALITY

Many anti-American thinkers in the nineteenth and twentieth centuries deem America to have an excessive equality that negates liberty, undermining individuality and leading to a profound sameness. In the nineteenth century, this critique is found predominantly on the anti-modern, anti-liberal Right; the Left tends to want more than what they see as liberalism's merely formal equality. This critique is seen in the traditional Right of Joseph de Maistre and Thomas Carlyle, who want to return to the hierarchies of the *ancien régime*, and in the radical Right of Arthur Moeller van den Bruck and Friedrich Nietzsche, who want to establish a new order of rank. In the twentieth century, this critique of sameness emerges even more powerfully on both the Left and the Right as a critique of technology and so-called Americanization. Heidegger and the Frankfurt School differ on the cause of the technological morass, a spiritual crisis or capitalism, but they agree that America represents the epitome of homogeneity. For example, Horkheimer and Adorno repeatedly characterize American society as one of uniformity and conformity, where people are "exactly the same" and "all alike" to the point of being "monads," mere cogs in the liberal capitalist machine.[4] Choice is so constrained by the "American culture industry" that people although "seemingly free" are in reality trapped in an "iron system" that fellow Frankfurt Schooler Marcuse describes as a "terroristic technocracy."[5] This, consequently, leads to "the abolition of the individual" so that "the individual is an illusion."[6] Heidegger describes America as "a boundless etcetera of indifference and always the sameness."[7] Stefan Zweig blames America for the "uniformity" and "monotonization of the world" that he equates with the "complete end of individuality."[8] Heinrich Heine condemns America because "the most repulsive of tyrants, the populace, hold vulgar sway"; "there are no princes or nobles there; all men are equal – equal dolts!"[9] Examples of this go on and on, but these quotations give the flavor of the critique.

Tocqueville agrees that America is characterized by a fundamental equality, and while he worries greatly about its consequences, his analysis is more nuanced. He is interested in actually studying America because it is the place where equality is most fully formed, and so one can best see there both its good and its bad tendencies. Insofar as equality of conditions, that is, democracy, is the future and America has achieved "an almost complete equality of conditions" and "seems nearly to have attained its natural limits," by studying America, one is glimpsing the future of Europe, and perhaps even the future of the world.[10] Note that for the Frankfurt School, Heidegger, and Tocqueville, the force at play is not unique to America – it affects the entirety of the modern world – but they all see America as its fullest manifestation, which is why America bears the brunt of the anti-modern polemics. Tocqueville acknowledges democracy's "savage instincts" but also wants to "direct" and "instruct and correct it," "to teach it to govern." He hopes "to attenuate its vices and make its natural advantages emerge."[11]

According to Tocqueville, the negatives of equality are many. Americans prefer equality to liberty, and he worries that this preference threatens to undermine liberty.[12] He is worried that people will not just try to level up, which he calls "a manly and legitimate taste for equality," but level down, which he deems "a depraved taste for equality."[13] Moreover, if everyone is deemed morally or intellectually equal ("the theory of equality applied to intellects")[14] the only legitimate principle for deciding disagreement is majority rule, which risks tyranny of the majority in both politics and thought. Tocqueville calls the "moral empire of the majority" an "irresistible force" that "crushes" dissent.[15] It enforces conformity and sameness within a limited circle of thought, such that "I do not know any country where, in general, less independence of mind and genuine freedom of discussion reign than in America."[16] Further, Tocqueville argues that, in the face of an overwhelming majority, each individual tends to feel weak and retreats into a small circle of family and friends that he calls individualism. This is not a robust individuality but an apathetic retreat from the public sphere driven by a feeling of impotence, which in turn further strengthens the dominant majority view. Moreover, since these weak individuals still have needs and wants and the only power that can fulfill them is the central government, Tocqueville fears that in time the government could emerge as a soft despotism, a kind of nanny state that fulfills citizens' desires while reducing them to passive consumers of services whose only political activity is periodic voting to maintain the all-powerful state, thus further and further eroding the populace's capacities for self-reliance. All of these problems according to Tocqueville inherently flow from the democratic attachment to equality and are thus perennially possible problems for every democracy and thus for America, too.

Yet democratic societies like the United States are premised on the equal dignity of all human beings, which Tocqueville deems a more just and more humane moral vision. Tocqueville deems unequal, aristocratic societies to be better organized, more rational, and better able to see a plan through, but they are better at these things precisely because they do not take into account the views or interests of the majority. By contrast, democratic government changes its mind with the whims of the public and is thus fickle and often incompetent. However, it allows the people both to correct mistaken government policies and to initiate action on their own, and thus "in the long term," according to Tocqueville, it is more effective. Tocqueville writes:

> Democracy does not give the most skillful government to the people, but it does what the most skillful government is often powerless to create; it spreads a restive energy through the whole social body, a superabundant force, an energy that never exists without it, and which, however little circumstances may be favorable, can bring forth marvels. Those are its true advantages.[17]

Democratic government is horribly inefficient but democratic civil society is uniquely energetic, leading ultimately to a more productive nation and – for the same reasons – equality.

Tocqueville's remedies for the problems caused by equality are also more realistic than those of anti-American critics. While the anti-Americans lament the consequences of political and social equality, their proposed alternatives verge on the utopian: returning to the *ancien régime*, fostering a revolution, or waiting for a new god. Tocqueville looks for remedies to the problems of equality from within the age of equality. He emphasizes that the same equality that leads to majority rule and its attendant problems also supports a notion of equal rights as well as freedoms of individual opinion, the press, and association, all of which strengthen individuals by uniting them and creating intermediary bodies between the individual and the state. Tocqueville also explains how the family, religion, local government, and the idea of self-interest properly understood, all ideas and institutions that thrive in America, can and do counteract modernity's negative tendencies. These remedies are available now, according to Tocqueville, and already present within America.

In sum, compared to the anti-American critics, Tocqueville's account of equality in America is more systematic, comprehensive, and complex, and Tocqueville offers more realistic remedies to its problems.

SECOND CRITIQUE: MATERIALISM, MONEY-GRUBBING, AND COARSENESS

Anti-American critics recurrently describe America as uniquely materialistic, money-grubbing, and coarse. For example, a Maxim Gorky novel on America is entitled *The City of the Yellow Devil*, where the yellow devil is gold worshipping.[18] Pierre-Joseph Proudhon writes: "The Americans are perhaps more bent on gain than any other nation." "What, in fact, is American society?," he asks: "It is composed of commoners who have suddenly acquired wealth. Now fortune, far from civilizing men, most often brings out their vulgarity."[19] The material coarseness and vulgarity of America is found everywhere in Frances Trollope's bestselling *Domestic Manners of the Americans*.[20] Stendhal in *The Charterhouse of Parma* writes that the main character would die of boredom after a few weeks in America, because they live like "beasts," and, besides, they have "no opera."[21] Volney calls the American "regime" "a true terrorism" (*un vrai terrorisme*), not for committing any specific deeds but for coarsening the souls of those living in such a materialistic country.[22] Again, one could go on, but this gives the flavor of the critique.

As with the first criticism, Tocqueville largely agrees with the critique of America as materialistic, but he analyzes it more fully and contextualizes it. Tocqueville asserts that "Materialism is a dangerous malady of the human mind in all nations; but one must dread it particularly in a democratic people because it combines marvelously with the most familiar vice of the heart in these people."[23] It dominates in America, he argues, because "The passion for material well-being is essentially a middle-class passion."[24] Tocqueville knows full well that aristocrats used to marry for wealth and so they are hardly indifferent to material well-being, but possessing great wealth enabled them not to think regularly about attaining and maintaining it. Possessing great wealth also enabled them to act in a "depraved" manner and to refine "the art of besotting themselves" by indulging in "sumptuous depravity and a brilliant corruption."[25] So in unequal societies material is also valued, but the acquisition of it does not color the tone and tenor of the whole society, other than by the indulgent depravity. By contrast, in societies defined by equality, everyone has the opportunity to make of themselves what they will, but since no one is born with a guaranteed position or status, everyone has to work to support themselves. The frontier in America presented seemingly unlimited possibilities, so everyone had both the necessity of working and the means to fulfill it, which in turn led to a kind of excited craving to do so; and when one acquires wealth by one's own means, one fears losing it.

The tone of America is thus fundamentally and widely colored by the desire to acquire material goods; but because one has to be disciplined to acquire property, it is materialism in what Tocqueville calls a "moderate and tranquil style" and compatible with an ordered society.[26] Democratic man falls into "softness rather than debauchery."[27] For Tocqueville, this softer materialism has many problems of which I here mention three. First, it loosens the soul, "loosens all their tensions," which is problematic because it undermines the desire to pursue greater and loftier things.[28] Second, it agitates but does not ultimately satisfy the deeper longings of the soul. He describes materialism as causing a "singular agitation" that gives rise to "secret restiveness," a "restiveness of the spirit," and thus leads to a "singular melancholy."[29] Finally, because its attempts to satisfy the deeper longings of the soul prove unfulfilling, Tocqueville avers that materialism, paradoxically, also gives rise to extreme religious movements that periodically erupt in excessive ways.

Like the anti-American critics, Tocqueville also links money-making to homogeneity. In an age of equality, everyone needs to work. This generalized insecurity unleashes not only incredible energy as people struggle to better themselves but also sameness as people all tend to struggle in the same way, that is, by pursuing wealth. Tocqueville writes, "the name of the actors alone is different, the play is the same. The aspect of American society is agitated because men and things change continuously; and it is monotonous because all the changes are similar."[30] Even when people strive for distinction, wealth is the only recognized way to attain it: "The prestige that attached to old things having disappeared, birth, condition, and profession no longer distinguish men or hardly distinguish them; there remains scarcely anything but money that creates very visible differences between them and that can set off some from their peers."[31] Tocqueville concludes: "Ordinarily, therefore, one finds love of wealth, as principal or accessory, at the bottom of the actions of Americans; this gives all their passions a family resemblance, and is not slow to make them a tiresome picture."[32] So, in all these ways, Tocqueville agrees with the anti-American critique of America as materialistic, money-centered, and coarse.

Even so, Tocqueville identifies something natural in the American focus on wealth and describes it as happening everywhere in the world. It is not an American phenomenon but a modern one, having to do with the rise of equality across the globe. In a beautiful passage worth quoting extensively, he writes:

> Variety is disappearing from within the human species; the same manner of acting, thinking, and feeling is found in all the corners of the world. That comes not only from the fact that all peoples deal with each other more and copy each other more faithfully, but from the fact that in each country, men diverge further and further from the particular ideas and sentiments of a caste,

a profession, or a family [i.e., from the things that determined or colored their outlooks in Europe's *ancien régime*] and simultaneously arrive at what depends more nearly on the constitution of man, which is everywhere the same. They thus become alike even though they have not imitated each other. They are like travelers dispersed in a great forest in which all paths end at the same point. If all perceive the central point at once and direct their steps in this direction, they are insensibly brought nearer to one another without seeking each other, without perceiving and without knowing each other, and they will finally be surprised to see themselves gathered in the same place. All peoples who take for the object of their studies and imitation, not such and such a man, but man himself, will in the end encounter each other in the same mores, like these travelers at the center.[33]

The American pursuit of wealth is perfectly natural and to be expected when people strip away the artifices of class, family, and profession and instead focus on the needs of "man himself." Particular virtues and vices are lost in this move toward natural sentiments, and Tocqueville to some extent regrets that loss. The pursuit of material goods is not lofty, but it is natural – natural, albeit low.

Unlike most anti-Americans, Tocqueville sees the pursuit of wealth as compatible with virtue and honor. America's virtues are not aristocratic but the bourgeois virtues that lead to self-discipline and social order. The ordinary desire to acquire wealth, even if generally excessive or feverish, forces individuals to live an orderly life: "one can say that it is the very violence of their desires that renders the Americans so methodical. It troubles their souls, but it arranges their lives."[34] The bourgeois virtues and the needs of the growing nation give rise to what Tocqueville calls a code of "American honor" that reinforces self-discipline and further orders and benefits society.[35] He describes five planks in America's honor code. First, there must be an animating motive for those who summon the energy and make sacrifices to go into the wilderness and do the hard work of clearing the forests, and this motive is the "love of" or "passion for wealth."[36] Tocqueville says this passion is thus honored because it promotes "the industrial greatness and the prosperity of the nation," provided "it does not exceed the limits that public order assigns to it."[37] The second virtue is "audacity," because material progress requires risks, not all of which will pay off. Some daring individuals will suffer, but society benefits from chance-taking, so society celebrates audacity as generally beneficial. The third is fidelity. When family life feels secure, people more easily brave risks outside the family. Fourth, and most important, is courage, not in risking life and limb in battle but in facing the wilderness or "brav[ing] the furies of the ocean to arrive sooner."[38] Finally, work is celebrated. Since "everyone works and work leads to everything," working has been turned into a "point of honor ... directed ... against idleness."[39] These are by no means lofty aristocratic virtues, but Tocqueville makes clear that they are hardly insignificant.

Indeed, unlike the anti-Americans who decry America's vulgarity and its absence of honor, Tocqueville couples his reflections on the American ethos of honor with a critique of Europe's aristocratic honor code, which he variously describes as "bizarre," "incoherent," "based on the fantasies of men," "at the expense of reason and humanity," and as against the "natural order of conscience."[40] Aristocratic codes of honor were made to lift a powerful few at the expense of everyone else, and they, like all honor codes, are culturally contingent: "what our fathers called honor par excellence was, to tell the truth, only one of its forms. They gave the generic name to what was only a species. Honor is therefore found in democratic centuries as in aristocratic times."[41]

The anti-Americans seem to mistake their own code of honor for the only code. While many anti-Americans might acknowledge that "Americans put a sort of heroism into their manner of doing commerce,"[42] for them this is simply a debasement, whereas for Tocqueville it is more complicated.

THIRD CRITIQUE: LACK OF GREATNESS

According to the anti-American critique, America lacks greatness – spiritual, cultural, and political – and through a process called "Americanization," it is alleged to be destroying greatness everywhere else in the world, too. Carlyle muses, "What great human soul, what great thought, what great noble thing that one could worship or loyally admire has yet been produced [in America]? None ... they have begotten with a rapidity beyond recorded example, Eighteen Millions of the greatest *bores* ever seen in this world before."[43] Proudhon avers, "The spiritual poverty of the Americans becomes evident in their morals"; "what is a people if it has no philosophy, no art, no rational ideas of law and morality? It seems to me that the Americans neglect these things too much and this is the reason why, in spite of their dollars and their pride, they rank last among the civilized nations." But forget "civilized." Proudhon describes Americans as living in a state of "brutality."[44] Horkheimer and Adorno describe America as having a "false society" of "non-culture" and "stylized barbarity" based on "complete quantification" that is "a parody of humanity."[45] Similarly, according to Heidegger, in America "the quantity took on a quality of its own," and for him Americanism "has become an active onslaught that destroys all rank and every world-creating impulse of the spirit."[46] Spengler predicts "a completely soulless Americanism will rule [the world] which will dissolve art, the nobility, the church, and world outlook."[47] Henry de Montherlant decries: "One nation that manages to lower intelligence, morality, human quality on nearly all the surface of the earth, such a thing has never been seen before in the existence of the planet. I accuse [*j'accuse!*] the United States of being in a permanent state of crime against humankind."[48] In sum, America is described as mere "quantity." It has no culture, no art, no rational ideas of law or morality. It is a brutish, barbaric, crime against humanity for destroying all meaning and worth, not only for its own people but across the globe. These passages suffice to give the flavor of the contempt for American culture and what "Americanism" allegedly inflicts on the world.

The idea that America lacks greatness is a vivid concern of Tocqueville, who yearns to elevate souls and promote the "genuine greatness of man."[49] Tocqueville concedes that American democracy does in fact undercut traditional ideas of greatness. Yet, while the anti-Americans find little or nothing redeeming in either American politics or culture, Tocqueville finds examples of greatness and the potential for greatness, even while warning about the factors that impede its development.

Describing the American Founding as "new in the history of societies" – a people wisely giving itself a new constitution with no blood spilled[50] – Tocqueville finds at least four embodiments of political greatness in the United States. First, he finds greatness in the United States' political Founders, describing them as "great men," "possessors of virtue or talents," "more enlightened than the rest of the world," "remarkable for their enlightenment, more remarkable for their patriotism," and possessing the "spirit of freedom."[51] They not only saw a problem in the existing political order but "saw the remedy" and "corrected" it – just as Tocqueville in *Democracy in America*'s introduction says he wants to correct the problems of democracy.[52] Second, as Tocqueville calls for a new political science for a new age, so he describes the US Constitution as a "great discovery in political science of our day" based on an "entirely new theory."[53] He praises the Constitution for creating anti-democratic, republican institutions to check the danger of tyranny of the majority by electing representatives and creating a federal republic. It astounds Tocqueville that such prudent institutions going against the tenor and trends of the democratic age were conceived, let alone instituted. He praises American federalism – "No one can appreciate more than I the advantages of a federal system"[54] – for combining the benefits of "great" (big) states, such as increasing innovation, progress, and strength, leading to self-sufficiency and self-defense, with the advantages of little republics that he describes as schools in the love of freedom and patriotism (like Burke's "little platoons").[55] "The Union," he concludes, "is free and happy like a small nation, glorious and strong like a great one."[56] Third, Tocqueville finds a kind of practical greatness in the good sense of the American people; "the good sense and the practical intelligence of the Americans" enables them to "discern with a surprising facility" how their complicated, multilevel government works.[57] America's political institutions can only work, he avers, for "a people long habituated to directing its affairs by itself, and in which political science has descended to the last ranks of society." "In a democracy, experience, mores, and instruction in the end almost always create the sort of everyday practical wisdom and science of small events in life that one names good sense";[58] and it is because this good sense and practical wisdom have penetrated to the depths of American mores and been internalized by even the lowliest citizens that Tocqueville concludes that "The Constitution of the United States resembles those beautiful creations of human industry that lavish glory and goods on those who invent them, but that remain sterile in other hands."[59] Finally, Tocqueville predicts two great political accomplishments for America. He predicts that America will be the "first maritime power on the globe ... driven to gain control of the seas, as the Romans were to conquer the world," and he predicts America to rule half the globe, ruling its half in freedom as opposed to the Russian half in servitude.[60] These, for Tocqueville, are impressive feats worthy of lavish praise.

All that being said, Tocqueville nonetheless qualifies his praise of these political achievements. The American Founding is marred by the existence of slavery, racial prejudice, and the treatment of the continent's native inhabitants. America's political institutions cannot definitively solve the problems of democracy. Tocqueville is quite clear later in *Democracy in America* that democratic political institutions are insufficient guarantees against tyranny of the majority. Insofar as every institution is run by people, and thereby typically either shaped or cowed by the majority, institutions alone are ineffectual in checking the majority's power.[61] Nor can they stop individualism and democratic despotism once apathy has set in. If the people lose their good sense or self-reliance, he worries that their institutions might only buy the country time before it slides into democratic despotism.

Tocqueville appreciates and correctly predicts particular American political achievements and failures because, unlike the more abstract critics, he cares enough to study the actually existing America instead of merely seeing it through the single prism of the (alleged) universal forces of modernity. What is so striking about *Democracy in America* is how Tocqueville combines his theories and concerns about universal modernity with a nuanced, empirically based account of the features unique to America. Few, if any, of the anti-Americans view the American Founders or the American Founding as meritorious, because they are not interested in it. For example, neither the Frankfurt School nor Heidegger analyze the American Founding, because it does not fit in their accounts of capitalism or spiritual crisis. Whereas the twentieth-century anti-Americans see America and Russia as metaphysically the same or America as the worse of the two powers,[62] Tocqueville prefers America, because he perceives its way as fundamentally better. If Tocqueville is right, it is because of his fuller, more particularistic, and complex account of the realities of America.

One might object that, while America's political greatness is a collective accomplishment by the nation, it does not necessarily imply the production of great individuals. Insofar as Tocqueville deems greatness as "a question of elevating souls,"[63] this is an important objection. In the cultural realm where individuals shine, Tocqueville's analyses of America are less sanguine – but still more careful than the anti-Americans.

Tocqueville agrees that the United States, like every democracy, will not be able to produce the lofty refinement of aristocratic culture. He asserts that democracies will not bring "loftiness to the human spirit," "contempt for material goods," "maintain profound convictions," "prepare for great devotions," or excel in "polishing mores," "elevating manners," or "making the arts shine."[64] This is not what democracies value, and to this extent Tocqueville agrees with the anti-Americans. Tocqueville laments these losses as the world moves toward equality; but the changing of values is inevitable, according to him. When conditions are equal, the majority sets society's tone and tenor. Since the majority values goods of the body, not of the soul, democratic societies are characterized not by brilliance but by the pursuit of "prosperity," the "most well-being" for each individual, and avoiding the "most misery."[65]

The first line of volume 2, part 1, chapter 1 could have been written by the most vociferous anti-Americans: "I think there is no country in the civilized world where they are less occupied with philosophy than the United States."[66] Tocqueville laments this fact even while speculating about the kinds of philosophies that might develop there. He also quickly qualifies his assertion by stating that the Americans "possess a certain philosophic method" of questioning everything so that "each American calls only on the individual effort of his reason."[67] Thus, he concludes, "America is therefore the one country in the world where the precepts of Descartes are least studied and best followed. ... Americans do not read Descartes's works because their social state turns them away from speculative studies, and they follow his maxims because this same social state naturally disposes their minds to adopt them."[68] Tocqueville spends much of volume 2, part 1 analyzing the consequences of this egalitarian way of being, some of them good and some bad, but all deriving from the equality of conditions. Tocqueville agrees with the anti-Americans about America not producing philosophers. Americans have to work and thus lack the leisure time to devote to philosophy. However, he disagrees with them in seeing America full of philosophy-in-action. Nor can we forget Tocqueville's praise of the American Founders as having created a government based on an "entirely new theory."[69] The American genius is practical; it aims at perfecting practice based on experience, reason, and enlightenment instead of at cultivating abstract or so-called high theory.

Just as the American philosophic achievements are more focused on practical results, so too is its science – and for the same reasons. Since everyone has to work, what is valued more is practical rather than theoretical science. Unlike the anti-Americans, though, Tocqueville acknowledges that the practical sciences thrive in America:

> In America the purely practical part of the sciences is cultivated admirably, and people attend carefully to the theoretical portion immediately necessary to application; in this way the Americans display a mind that is always clear, free, original, and fertile; but there is almost no one in the United States who gives himself over to the essentially theoretical and abstract portion of human knowledge.[70]

Unlike Tocqueville, the anti-Americans harp on about the absence of pure theory without acknowledging America's notable achievements.

Tocqueville expects, however, that Americans will gravitate toward the purely theoretical in the future. The main thing holding Americans back is the lack of leisure. However, as fortunes accumulate, leisure time will be created. Tocqueville thinks "the taste for pleasures of the mind is so natural" that, when they are able, "a certain number of citizens" will naturally pursue higher studies. For him, "the human mind leans at one extreme toward the bounded, material, and useful, at the other it naturally rises toward the infinite, immaterial, and beautiful" – and no less so in America. Once the cupidity of the current moment passes or is satiated, those who desire more will emerge and be well received. They will be received because "The utility of knowledge is revealed with a very particular clarity even to the eyes of the crowd. Those who do not taste its charms prize its effects and make efforts to attain it"; and in striving to excel, people will see the cultivation of the mind as a way to distinguish oneself: "From the moment when the crowd begins to be interested in works of the mind, it is discovered that a great means of acquiring glory, power, or wealth is to excel in some of them." This is obviously only an instrumental embrace of higher learning, but Tocqueville's point is that it is "not true to say that men who live in democratic centuries are naturally indifferent to the sciences, letters, and arts; one must only recognize that they cultivate them in their own manner, and they bring in this way the qualities and faults that are their own."[71]

What according to Tocqueville is this American manner? Practical, freewheeling, and, paradoxically, somewhat abstract. What are the qualities and faults of America's pursuit of the arts? In accordance with their national character, Americans have "a taste for the tangible and real and a contempt for traditions and forms."[72] Its arts therefore have "a freer and surer but less lofty style."[73] He avers that Americans "prefer the useful to the beautiful and they will want the beautiful to be useful."[74] Tocqueville acknowledges that the commercialization of literature manufactured for the masses lowers its quality, and his concerns about this anticipate those of the Frankfurt School.[75] Yet he is at pains to say that Americans are not indifferent to the arts – Tocqueville notes that there is hardly a log cabin without some odd volume of Shakespeare.[76] America has not yet needed its own literature, because Tocqueville sees it as a kind of provincial England with all of British literature at its disposal. While America has not yet produced a national literature of its own, however, Tocqueville states that "I am sure that in the end they will have one";[77] and he speculates on the nature of an American democratic literature. American artists will not idolize or seek subject matter in the past as aristocracies do, "but they will dream of what will be, and in this direction their imagination has no limits."[78] Tocqueville predicts that democratic literature will focus "only on man" and will be attracted to their collective experiment in democracy: "Democratic nations perceive more clearly than all others their own shape, and that great shape lends itself marvelously to the depiction of the ideal."[79] Tocqueville argues that democratic poets will naturally be tempted to expand from this to try to describe "the shape of the human race" and "a much vaster idea of divinity itself," and that it "will depict passions and ideas rather than persons and deeds."[80] Moreover, Tocqueville's faith in the "natural inequality" of man[81] – an indirect philosophical rebuke of democracy – assures him that some genius who loves truth will always be born. Such people will arise in the United States and other democratic nations, too. In a democracy, there is no need to aid such a one: "it is enough not to stop him."[82] This supposition strengthens Tocqueville's certainty that America will have meritorious arts and sciences of its own, something that anti-Americans seem unable to conceive. Rather than only dismissing American intellectual life for what it lacks, Tocqueville also pays attention to its dynamics and therefore its possibilities.

CONCLUSION

This chapter analyzes Tocqueville's views of America in the context of the assertions of anti-American European thinkers and finds Tocqueville's views subtler, deeper, less shrill, and, I here add, truer. In this conclusion, I meditate on a further question: Why? Why is Tocqueville such a better analyst than the others? This is a question impossible to answer adequately, but we make some progress in doing so by breaking it into its two component parts: Is there something particularly special about Tocqueville or something particularly defective in the anti-American critics? The answer is: both.

As I suggest at the beginning of this chapter, the anti-American critics tend to share an ideological quality that leads them to oversimplify. These generalizations lend a certain kind of power to their analyses, but they also create blind spots. For example, Heidegger and the Frankfurt School may be deep and insightful thinkers about the problems of modernity, but they fall short when placing or characterizing the United States in the context of their general theories. The rupture between their general theory and their claims about America reveals at least three kinds of problems for the latter. First, their theory allegedly tells them everything they need to know so they lack motivation to study the reality of America. Second, lacking the motivation, they do not study it. Judging from their references, bibliographies, and footnotes, few of the theorists even pretend to do so. The works of many of the most vociferous anti-American critics demonstrate little primary or secondary research about America, which in light of their overarching theory they deem unnecessary or unimportant. Instead, they tend to attach "America" or "Americanization" as a label to the universal phenomena that they discuss, as if it lends concreteness to their abstractions. Third, this lack of attention to America of course prevents them from seeing the living, breathing complexity of America as a multifaceted, complicated, contradictory polity with genuine accomplishments as well as defects. In short, while these critics condemn America for lacking "high" theory, it is their very own such theories that prevent them from understanding America's reality.

Tocqueville does not share these ideological blind spots. He too has a theory of modernity, but his work is empirical and well rooted in the realities of America. It would be a mistake, however, to think that *Democracy in America* is the great book it is simply because Tocqueville is empirical. The empirical bent is important and helps Tocqueville appreciate the complex reality that is America, including its modern, premodern, and illiberal features. Yet, while Tocqueville's empiricism is certainly important, it begs a deeper question, namely why did Tocqueville take the time and effort to study America empirically in the first place?

Tocqueville's concern to understand America properly is motivated both by his theory of modernity and by his political judgment. Tocqueville identifies equality with the essence of the modern age. By contrast, the anti-American critics tend to identify more specific phenomena with it. For example, Heidegger equates modernity with technology and the Frankfurt School equates it with capitalism. Along the way, both blame modern science for reducing the cosmos to a crude homogeneity and both lament the resulting sameness of technological culture, but they do not see equality itself as the driving force. By focusing on equality, Tocqueville is equipped with a theory that arguably penetrates deeper into the heart of modernity. However that may be, his theory is fundamentally invested in liberal democracy per se, and thus in its fullest embodiment in the United States. Since America embodies modernity for him much more concretely than for the others, he is motivated to study it more deeply. Because of this theory of modernity, the nature of America is not an abstract theoretical question but revelatory of the *future incarnate*. He really wants to know what is coming, so his theory of modernity motivates Tocqueville to study America unlike anyone else.

Moreover, Tocqueville's political judgment that the liberal democratic version of modernity is more or less as good as human societies can be – and in any case seems to be where the world is headed – further reinforces his deep care to study America. Tocqueville is no utopian. This chapter demonstrates many of the problems and deficiencies that he sees with both America and the liberal democratic modernity that it represents. Yet this motivates him. His political judgment both about the inevitable coming of democracy and the relative goodness of American-style democracy vis-à-vis other likely political systems makes him care deeply about the reality of its greatest existing instantiation. As he writes, "I confess that in America I saw more than America; I sought there an image of democracy itself, its penchants, its character, its prejudices, its passions; I wanted to become acquainted with it if only to know at least what we ought to hope or fear from it."[83] By contrast, for the anti-Americans, liberal democratic modernity is defective and to be discarded. As a result, they do not trouble over inconvenient facts, let alone merits in the soon-to-be-abandoned system or the countries in which it is embodied. They simply cannot be troubled to waste their time studying the ashbin of history. To combat the problems of liberal democratic modernity, Tocqueville does not hearken for a revolution or wait for a god, as the more utopian anti-American critics do. Rather, he looks for resources within democracy to combat the problems he sees within it. It is thus the combination of Tocqueville's theory of modernity and his judgment of liberal democracy's relative goodness that creates in him the incentive for the serious study of America. Unlike other analysts, Tocqueville's theoretical and political judgment create a supreme incentive to dig deep in his study of democracy in America; and Tocqueville does so in such a brilliant way because, what can we say: he is a genius.

As a concluding thought, I reiterate that this chapter examines anti-Americanism in European elites because that is where anti-Americanism began. The reader must be aware, however, that anti-Americanism is not solely a European phenomenon. It has spread around the world in at least three main ways. First, with the rise of the Soviet Union and the movement of world communism, anti-Americanism became deeply ingrained in communist-inspired thinkers and the vanguard Left across the globe. As the horrors of the Soviet Union were exposed, many Leftists abandoned the USSR but, oddly, clung even more tightly and shrilly to anti-Americanism.[84] Second, as Europe's imperial projects sent select subjects to the metropole to be educated to form a collaborative ruling class back in the colonies, they absorbed the anti-Americanism prevalent in European universities and elite intellectual circles and brought it home with them. Third, as US power and the other forces of modernity spread around the world, anti-Americanism also emerged among traditionalist thinkers of the anti-modern Right, such as Ayatollah Khomeini, the Muslim Brotherhood, and al-Qaeda, who saw – in a way parallel to the reactions of earlier European elites – modern forces undercutting their traditional beliefs and power structures. Many of these leaders also spent time in exile in Europe, and so their reactions were cultivated by European discourses. *Democracy in America* thus has much to teach not only to Americans and Europeans but to the world.

NOTES

1. There is a large literature on anti-Americanism. For the best of it, see Russell Berman, *Anti-Americanism in Europe: A Cultural Problem* (Stanford: Hoover Institution Press, 2004); James Ceaser, *Reconstructing*

America: The Symbol of America in Modern Thought (New Haven, CT: Yale University Press, 2000); Aurelian Craiutu and Jeffrey Isaacs, eds., *America through European Eyes: British and French Reflections on the New World from the Eighteenth Century to the Present* (University Park, PA: Penn State University Press, 2009); Max Paul Friedman, *Rethinking Anti-Americanism: The History of an Exceptional Concept in American Foreign Relations* (Cambridge: Cambridge University Press, 2012); Paul Hollander, *Anti-Americanism: Critiques at Home and Abroad, 1965–1990* (New York: Oxford University Press, 1992); Peter Katzenstein and Robert Keohane, eds., *Anti-Americanisms in World Politics* (Ithaca, NY: Cornell University Press, 2006); Andrei Markovitz, *Uncouth Nation: Why Europe Dislikes America* (Princeton: Princeton University Press, 2007); Brendon O'Connor, *Anti-Americanism and American Exceptionalism: Prejudice and Pride about the USA* (New York: Routledge, 2020); and Philippe Roger, *The American Enemy: A Story of French Anti-Americanism*, trans. Sharon Bowman (Chicago: University of Chicago Press, 2005).

2. Tony Judt, *Past Imperfect: French Intellectuals, 1944–1956* (Berkeley: University of California Press, 1992), 201–204.

3. Raymond Aron, *Main Currents in Sociological Thought, Vol 1: Montesquieu, Auguste Comte, Karl Marx, Alexis de Tocqueville, The Sociologists and the Revolution of 1848* (New York: Basic Books, 1965).

4. Max Horkheimer and T. W. Adorno, "The Culture Industry: Enlightenment As Mass Deception," in Horkheimer and Adorno, *The Dialectic of Enlightenment*, trans. John Cumming (New York: Continuum, 1972), 120, 122, 124, 133, 134, 141, 163, 167.

5. Horkheimer and Adorno, "The Culture Industry," 120, 142, 155, and Herbert Marcuse, "Some Social Implications of Modern Technology," in Andrew Arato and Eike Gebhardt, eds., *The Essential Frankfurt School Reader* (New York: Continuum, 1982), 139.

6. Horkheimer and Adorno, "The Culture Industry," 154.

7. Martin Heidegger, "The Fundamental Question of Metaphysics," in Heidegger, *An Introduction to Metaphysics*, trans. Ralph Manheim (New Haven, CT: Yale University Press, 1959), 37 and 46.

8. Stefan Zweig, "The Monotonization of the World" [1925], in Anton Kaes, Martin Jay, and Edward Dimendberg, eds., *The Weimar Republic Sourcebook* (Berkeley: University of California Press, 1994), 398, 399.

9. Cited in Markovits, *Uncouth Nation*, 57.

10. DIA (MW) I. "Author's Introduction," 12. The equality of conditions about which Tocqueville writes applied only to citizens.

11. DIA (MW) I. "Author's Introduction," 7–8.

12. DIA (MW) II.2.i, 480–482.

13. DIA (MW) I.1.iii, 52.

14. DIA (MW) I.2.vii, 236.

15. DIA (MW) I.2.vii, 236, 237, 241.

16. DIA (MW) I.2.vii, 244.

17. DIA (MW) I.2.vi, 234.

18. Cited in Markovits, *Uncouth Nation*, 79.

19. Pierre-Joseph Proudhon, "Letter to Dulieu" (December 30, 1860) and *War and Peace* [1861] in *Selected Writings of Pierre-Joseph Proudhon*, ed. Stewart Edwards (Garden City, NY: Anchor Books, 1969), 184, 183.

20. On Trollope, see Richard Boyd, "From Aristocratic Politesse to Democratic Civility, or What Mrs. Frances Trollope Didn't See in America," in Craiutu and Isaac, *America through Foreign Eyes*, 187–211.

21. Stendhal, *The Charterhouse of Parma*, trans. Lady Mary Loyd (London: Heinemann, 1902), 463.

22. Constantin François Chasseboeuf Volney (Comte de), "Tableau du Climat et des Sol des États-Unis" [1803], in *Oeuvres complètes de Volney* (Paris: Firmin-Didot Frères, 1838), 630.

23. DIA (MW) II.2.xv, 519.

24. DIA (MW) II.2.x, 507. Many of the anti-American critics agree with this point. While venting their spleen at America, they are intending to attack the bourgeois middle class everywhere.

25. DIA (MW) II.2.xi, 508.

26. DIA (MW) II.2.xi, 509.

27. DIA (MW) II.2.xi, 509.

28. DIA (MW) II.2.xi, 509.

29. DIA (MW) II.2.xiii, 512, 514.

30. DIA (MW) II. 3, xvii, 587.

31. DIA (MW) II. 3, xvii, 587.

32. DIA (MW) II. 3, xvii, 588.

33. DIA (MW) II. 3, xvii, 588.

34. DIA (MW) II.3.xvii, 588.

35. DIA (MW) II.3.xviii, 593.

36. DIA (MW) II.3.xviii, 594.

37. DIA (MW) II.3.xviii, 594–595.

38. DIA (MW) II.3.xviii, 595.

39. DIA (MW) II.3.xviii, 595.

40. DIA (MW) II.3.xviii, 591.

41. DIA (MW) II.3.xviii, 596.

42. DIA (MW) I.2.x, 387.

43. Thomas Carlyle, "Latter-Day Pamphlets" [1850], in *The Works of Thomas Carlyle*, Vol. 20, ed. Henry Duff Traill (Cambridge: Cambridge University Press, 2010), 21.

44. Proudhon, *War and Peace* and "Letter to Dulieu," in Edwards, *Selected Writings of Pierre-Joseph Proudhon*, 183–185.

45. Horkheimer and Adorno, "The Culture Industry," 123, 128, 141.

46. Heidegger, "Fundamental Question of Metaphysics," 46.

47. Oswald Spengler, "Letter to Klöres" [October 25, 1914], in *Letters of Oswald Spengler: 1913–1936*, ed. and trans. Arthur Helps (New York: Knopf, 1966), 28.

48. Montherlant, *Le Chaos et la Nuit* (1963), 265. Cited in Ceaser, *Reconstructing America*, 2.

49. DIA (MW) II.1.vii, 426.

50. DIA (MW) I.1.viii, 106.

51. DIA (MW) I.1.viii, 107; I.2.v, 217, 220; I.2.ii, 168; I.1.viii, 149, 143.

52. DIA (MW) I.1.viii, 149; "Author's Introduction," 7.

53. DIA (MW) I.1.viii, 147.

54. DIA (MW) I.1.viii, 160.

55. DIA (MW) I.1.viii, 152. Edmund Burke, *Reflections on the Revolution in France*, ed. Frank M. Turner (New Haven, CT: Yale University Press, 2003), 40.

56. DIA (MW) I.1.viii, 154.

57. DIA (MW) I.1.viii, 156.

58. DIA (MW) I.2.v, 219.

59. DIA (MW) I.1.viii, 156.

60. DIA (MW) I.2.x, 390, 395–396.

61. DIA (MW) I.2.vii, 241.

62. Sartre describes the Soviet Union's special status: "Russia is not comparable to other countries. It is only permissible to judge it when one has accepted its undertaking, and then only in the name of that

undertaking." Jean Paul Sartre, *Situations IV*, trans. Benita Eisler (New York: George Braziller, 1965), 266.

63. DIA (MW) II.1.xx, 472.

64. DIA (MW) I.2.vi, 234.

65. DIA (MW) I.2.vi, 235.

66. DIA (MW) II.1.i, 403.

67. DIA (MW) II.1.i, 403.

68. DIA (MW) II.1.i, 403.

69. DIA (MW) I.1.viii, 147.

70. DIA (MW) II.1.x, 434.

71. DIA (MW) II.1.ix, 429, 432–433.

72. DIA (MW) II.1.x, 433.

73. DIA (MW) II.1.x, 433.

74. DIA (MW) II.1.xi, 439.

75. DIA (MW) II.1.xi, 441–442.

76. DIA (MW) II.1.xiii, 445.

77. DIA (MW) II.1.xiii, 446.

78. DIA (MW) II.1.xvii, 460.

79. DIA (MW) II.1.xvii, 461.

80. DIA (MW) II.1.xvii, 461–462.

81. DIA (MW) II.1.ix, 431.

82. DIA (MW) II.1.x, 437.

83. DIA (MW) "Author's Introduction," 13.

84. Sidney Hook observes the same phenomenon among American thinkers: "the disillusioned fellow-traveling American intellectuals have bequeathed anti-Americanism rather than pro-communism to the contemporary generation of disaffected intellectuals." Sidney Hook, "Communism and the American Intellectuals: From the Thirties to the Eighties," *Free Inquiry* (Fall 1981), 15 as quoted in Arnold Beichman, *Anti-American Myths: Their Causes and Consequences* (New York: Routledge, 1992), xi.

7 Democracy in the (Other) America

José Antonio Aguilar Rivera

In one scene from Jorge Isaacs' canonical 1867 novel *María*, Efraín, a young Colombian *hacendado*, goes over the books in his personal library with a friend. Along with the works of Shakespeare, Calderón de la Barca, and Cervantes, there is a copy of Alexis de Tocqueville's *Democracy in America*.[1] This literary vignette shows that the book was very much a part of the cultural baggage of Spanish American elites in the second part of the nineteenth century. There is no question that *Democracy in America* made a lasting impression in that part of the world, but what was the contemporary reception of Tocqueville's book in Latin America? While the presence of *Democracy in America* was ubiquitous, to what extent did Tocqueville's ideas and analysis of democracy inform political thinking or practice in Spanish America? What is the significance of his all-too-brief treatment of the failed Latin American experiments in self-government? This chapter discusses the contemporary reception of *Democracy in America* in Mexico, Argentina, Colombia, and Chile in the nineteenth century.

A DEMOCRATIC CONUNDRUM

At the heart of the reception of Tocqueville in Spanish America lies a peculiar dilemma. *Democracy in America* offers an account of the success of representative government in the United States. For nation-builders around the world, it conveyed a message of hope. Yet it provided little comfort to Spanish Americans. Things looked very different in the *other* America. Tocqueville was hardly alone here. Skepticism had an early onset. For instance, on December 6,

1813, Thomas Jefferson wrote to Alexander von Humboldt regarding Humboldt's journey to New Spain:

> I think it most fortunate that your travels in those countries were so timed as to make them known to the world in the moment they were about to become actors on its stage. That they will throw off their European dependence I have no doubt; but in what kind of government their revolution will end I am not so certain. History, I believe, furnishes no example of a priest-ridden people maintaining a free civil government.[2]

For his part, Tocqueville echoed the pessimism prevailing in the United States regarding Spanish America after three decades of independent government. Nature had been generous with Spanish Americans, and yet "South America cannot maintain a democracy." In spite of their fertile wilderness, great rivers, and untouched and inexhaustible riches, there were, he claimed, "no nations on earth more miserable than those of South America."[3] In *Democracy in America*, he wrote:

> We are astonished to see the new nations of South America stir, for a quarter century, amid constantly recurring revolutions; and each day we expect to see them recover what is called their natural state. But who can assert that today revolutions are not the most natural state of the Spanish of South America? In this country, society struggles at the bottom of an abyss from which it cannot escape by its own efforts ... When I consider them in this alternating state of miseries and crimes, I am tempted to believe that for them despotism would be a benefit. But these two words will never be found united in my thought.[4]

Copying the institutions of the United States had not produced the desired effects in Spanish America. Thus, in discussing American federalism, Tocqueville noted regarding Mexico:

> The Constitution of the United States resembles those beautiful creations of human industry that shower glory and wealth on those

who invent them, but that remain sterile in other hands. This is what
Mexico has demonstrated in our times. The inhabitants of Mexico,
wanting to establish the federal system, took as a model and almost
completely copied the federal constitution of the Anglo-Americans,
their neighbors. But while importing the letter of the law, they could
not at the same time import *the spirit that gives it life*. So they are
seen constantly encumbered by the mechanism of their double
government. The sovereignty of the states and that of the Union,
leaving the circle that the constitution had drawn, penetrate each
other daily. Still today, Mexico is constantly dragged from anarchy
to military despotism, and from military despotism to anarchy.[5]

What were Tocqueville's Spanish American readers to make of these
discouraging remarks? The obvious lesson was that Spanish America
lacked the distinct civic spirit that animated Anglo-American political institutions. The necessary "mores" – habits, opinions, usages,
and beliefs – were just not there. The causes of this absence – history,
culture, and sheer luck – were clearly beyond the power of political
actors.[6] Equality of conditions was not, however, the key factor:
"almost all the colonies in America were founded by men who either
started as equals among themselves or became so by living there.
There is no single place in the New World where the Europeans
were able to create an aristocracy. Nevertheless, democratic institutions prosper in the United States alone."[7] Other nations in America
had "the same opportunities for prosperity as the Anglo-Americans,
but not their laws or mores, and these nations are wretched. So the
laws and mores of the Anglo-Americans are the particular and predominant causes, which I have been seeking, of their greatness."[8] The
failure to establish viable representative governments, however, was
hardly a feature unique to Spanish America. Tocqueville harbored
little optimism regarding his own country. The nations of South
America were an extreme case of dynamics at work in France.

In short, *Democracy in America* offered neither consolation nor
hope to the new Spanish American nations. The factors that explained

the success of the United States lay beyond the power of political elites. One might be tempted to despair that, no matter how hard they tried, they would never obtain the results of the Anglo Americans. Yet many nineteenth-century Spanish American readers of Tocqueville stubbornly avoided these conclusions. The reception of *Democracy in America* in Spanish America is decisively marked by this conundrum: How can hope and guidance be obtained from a work that explicitly asserted that democracy, as it was known in the United States, was out of reach? Some Spanish Americans simply ignored Tocqueville's pessimistic reflections, while others showed considerable ingenuity in dealing with the challenges posed by Tocqueville's analysis.

MEXICO

Tocqueville's disparaging observations did not prevent him from enjoying considerable popularity in nineteenth-century Mexico, where his ideas had a significant impact on constitutional thinking. Yet what captured the imagination of Mexican readers was *not* Tocqueville's sociological insights on democracy but his *depiction* of American institutions.[9] As Rafael Rojas argues, Tocqueville was read in Mexico as an admiring observer, rather than as a critic, of American democracy.[10] However, it was Tocqueville's analysis of political associations and the risks of the tyranny of the majority, not his assessment of American institutions, that launched him to fame.

Mexicans sought in *Democracy in America* descriptions of particular American institutions and blatantly ignored Tocqueville's subtle criticism and analysis of democratic society more generally. It is not difficult to ascertain why. As Charles A. Hale argues: "for Mexican liberals America was the dream world of utilitarianism ... Mexicans found there, as Alexis de Tocqueville did, the realization of enlightened self-interest. Americans seemed able to combine their own self-interest with the interest of their fellow citizens."[11]

Tocqueville was read in Mexico early on. The first volume of *Democracy in America* was published in 1835. A French-printed Spanish translation appeared two years later.[12] It circulated widely in Mexico and other Spanish American nations.[13] Twenty years later, in 1855, the same edition was reprinted by the daily *El Republicano*.[14] In accounting for the reception of Tocqueville, it is striking that *Democracy in America* was not read as a whole. This was due to the way in which it was received and employed. By and large, Mexican readers would have been acquainted with only the first half of Tocqueville's work. *Democracy in America*, as we know it, was comprised of two volumes. As mentioned, the first was published in 1835 while the second appeared five years later.[15] The first volume was largely devoted to the description and analysis of the institutions of the United States. Here, Tocqueville was more sanguine about democracy in the United States. While it is true that the idea of the tyranny of the majority was already present there as a problem of democratic societies, it was only later, in the second volume published in 1840, that Tocqueville's account of the effects of equality became more critical. This is significant, since Mexicans avoided these warnings. Alas, by the time Sánchez de Bustamante's translation of the first volume of *Democracy in America* was reprinted in 1855, the completed work (volumes 1 and 2) had been available for more than fifteen years. Therefore, it seems fair to say that Mexicans *chose* to read only Tocqueville's first impressions of American institutions.[16]

Between 1837 and 1857, the impact of Tocqueville's ideas in Mexico was particularly significant on two issues: the judiciary and federalism. Substantive debates on the proper interpretation of the ideas of *Democracy in America* and their implications for the political circumstances at the time took place both in the daily press and in the midst of constituent congresses as in no other Spanish American nation.[17] Mexicans read Tocqueville as an interpreter of the political institutions of the United States and highlighted a particular aspect: his description of American judicial power. According to legal historians, the book "enlightened Mexican lawyers on the workings of American judicial review."[18] Tocqueville devoted a whole chapter of the book to judicial power.

Mexicans read this chapter on the power of the judiciary through a peculiar lens.[19] In it, they found a source of inspiration for the protection of rights by means of judicial review. Tocqueville was astounded by the litigious nature of American society and by the prominent role played by judges in it.[20] However, political intervention by judges took place only indirectly. As in other places, in the United States judges could only rule on particular cases and they always had to wait until a lawsuit was brought before them to act. Nonetheless, Americans had vested in their judges the right to use the US Constitution, and not just specific laws, when they made their rulings. "In other words," Tocqueville notes, "they have allowed them not to apply laws that would appear unconstitutional to them."[21] It was this very idea, posed by Tocqueville, that Mexicans found to be of great consequence. It was a solution to several of the problems that the fledging republic faced. They had a glimpse of how they could protect individual rights from encroachments by the state. They also found a way to deal with the constant clashes between powers, particularly between the federation and the states. Finally, they believed that Tocqueville provided them with a road map to establish judicial review.

Tocqueville was also used by federalists and centralists in constitutional debates in the 1840s. The central issue was whether a central or a federal republic was best for the fledging republic. Tocqueville was considered a defender of North American federalism. Indeed, some federalists supported their proposals using Tocqueville's analysis. Yet, in *Democracy in America*, both sides found grist for their mill. They opportunistically borrowed ideas and arguments from Tocqueville to battle each other in the political arena. As we will see, this was hardly unique to Mexico. For instance, in 1842 Mariano Otero, a federalist, defended the federal system with Tocquevillean tropes.[22] He believed that Tocqueville provided him with the institutional key to a successful federation. He defined national power as an *exception* and the local and state powers as normal. In the United States, the federal government had the power not only of passing national laws but of executing them. Likewise,

Tocqueville put forth the idea that the federal government ruled over individuals, and not the states.[23] Yet, as Tocqueville noted, the key to the success of federalism were the mores, not the institutions, of America. Otero and the federalists simply ignored this argument. In a strict sense, Tocqueville was of little use to federalists or centralists. After all, Tocqueville's critical lines on federalism in Mexico are found in the chapter titled "Why the Federal System Is Not Within the Reach of All Nations and Why the Anglo-Americans Have Been Able to Adopt it."[24] The argument is devastating. The problem was not a misunderstanding of the types of centralization and their proper spheres of competence (the subject matter of the debates among Mexicans); it was something more structural and definitive: the absence of a distinctive spirit, able to animate the gears of the system. Contrary to what Otero believed, or wanted to believe, the obstacle was *not* institutional in nature. Mexicans could not afford to acknowledge Tocqueville's thesis because they had no reply to it.

ARGENTINA

In 1835, the year *Democracy in America* was published in France, the strongman Juan Manuel de Rosas attained power in the Argentinian confederation. The Rosas dictatorship (1835–1852) posed a challenge to the New Generation.[25] The men who came of age in 1837 (the New Generation, as they called themselves) rejected the political tradition in which they had been reared.[26] As Domingo Faustino Sarmiento wrote in his *Facundo* (1845):

> What else could have happened when the fundamentals of government and the political beliefs that Europe had given us were riddled with errors and full of absurd, misleading theories and evil principles? Why should our politicians have been under the obligation to know more than the great men of Europe, who up to that time had achieved no definitive knowledge of political organization?[27]

The founders had been under the spell of the political thought of the eighteenth century, which blinded them to the country's economic and social realities. By attending primarily to social conditions, Tocqueville became highly relevant to political elites in search of new political theories. If Mexicans were blind to Tocqueville's social theory, Argentinians could not take their eyes off of it, partly because many of them believed that, in Argentina, as in North America, equality prevailed. In order to understand their present situation, these men argued, observers must begin by analyzing customs and social conditions. As Esteban Echeverría contended, it was necessary "to determine what we are and then by the application of principles to seek what we ought to be and towards what point we must gradually direct ourselves."[28] For these men, one of the most remarkable lessons of Tocqueville's book was that democracy meant equality of conditions. Indeed, Echeverría asserted in 1838 that "Democracy is not a form of government, but the very essence of all republican governments, or instituted by all for the good of the community or the society." Modern political associations sought to establish the equality of classes. Such was the progressive movement taking place in America at the time. Echeverría quoted Tocqueville's introduction to the first volume of *Democracy in America* to argue that the "gradual development of equality of conditions is a providential fact."[29] New definitions of democracy sprung from this sociological insight. For Echeverría, democracy was "the government of the majorities or the uniform *consent* of the reason of all men."[30]

Tocqueville aided the members of the New Generation (Esteban Echeverría, Juan Bautista Alberdi, Juan María Gutiérrez, Vicente Fidel López, and Miguel Cané, among others) to shift attention away from Rosas and toward society as a whole. As Juan Bautista Alberdi argued, "governments are nothing more than the work and the fruit of societies: they reflect the character of the people who create them."[31]

Sarmiento wrote *Facundo* while in exile in Chile during the Rosas regime.[32] In the text, Tocqueville is quoted two times.[33] In the "Introduction," Sarmiento wrote:

> South America in general and, above all the Argentine Republic, have been in need of a Tocqueville. Of someone provided with the

knowledge of social theories, as the travelling scientist is equipped with barometers, octants and compasses, to look into the entrails of our political life, (as if they were a vast and uncharted field not depicted by science) to reveal to Europe, to France ... this new mode of being that is without clear and known precedents ...

Such a traveler might have accounted for the mystery of the protracted fight that tears apart the Republic. The opposing, invincible, elements that inevitably clash with each other would have been classified. Responsibility [for that clash] would have been adjudicated to: geography and to the habits that it engenders; to Spanish traditions, and to the wicked and plebeian national conscience that the Inquisition and Spanish absolutism bequeathed on us; to the influence of opposing ideas that have shaken the political world; to Indian barbarism; to European civilization; to, in the end, democracy enthroned by the 1810 Revolution; to equality, whose dogma has permeated to the lowest strata of society.[34]

Sarmiento recognized himself unfit to tackle such an explanatory endeavor. He acknowledged his own lack of the requisite philosophical and historical instruction. Yet such a study made by competent observers would have revealed to amazed European eyes "a new world in the realm of politics, a simple, frank and primitive struggle among the latest advances of human progress and the vestiges of primitive life; between populated cities and dark forests."[35] Thus, Sarmiento explicitly constructed his dialectical opposition between civilization (cities) and barbarism (the pampa) on the analytical blueprint provided by Tocqueville in *Democracy in America*.[36] The struggle between a dying aristocratic world and a nascent democracy was mirrored in Sarmiento's epic of struggling civilization.[37]

While Sarmiento registered *Democracy in America*'s insights on the impact of equality in society, he blatantly ignored, as the Mexicans did, Tocqueville's pessimistic opinions regarding the political prospects of the Spanish American nations. In the years 1845–1848, Sarmiento journeyed to the United States following the path of

Tocqueville. He wrote a book recounting his impressions of North America. In this work, Tocqueville is cited just once, to the effect that railroads had decreased transportation costs in the United States.[38] It is evident that Sarmiento did not share Tocqueville's critiques of the democratic society he found in America. Not only that; he was certain that one day the bright light shone by the North American Republic would reach its southern brethren.[39] Both Tocqueville and Sarmiento acknowledged the presence of associations in the United States. Sarmiento asserted: "So it follows that wherever ten Yankees meet, poor, ragged, stupid, before striking an ax at the foot of the trees to build a dwelling, they gather to set the bases of the association."[40] Yet, for his part, Tocqueville believed that associations were a remedy to the ills of individualism that Sarmiento ignored: "in our own day freedom of association has become a necessary guarantee against the tyranny of the majority."[41]

As Roldán argues, Sarmiento shared none of the critical socio-logical insights (nor the aristocratic outlook) of Tocqueville regarding a democratic society, such as the corrosive effects of individualism. To the contrary, Sarmiento was extremely sanguine about North Americans: he found them truly civilized. For him, the township was a locus of civilization, not of civic engagement. Thus, the Argentinian replaced Tocqueville's "somber but lucid doubts with willful enthusiasm."[42] He found in the United States, as Roldán points out, a highly civilized people with no "history." In a clear misreading of Tocqueville, Sarmiento posited that a long democratic past was not the sole path to civilization. He ignored Tocqueville's insight that mores were the result not only of social conditions but of the long passage of time. Therefore, for the Argentinian, it appeared quite possible to export the institutions of the United States (markets, publicity, a free press, and associations) to the South.[43] Just as did the Mexicans, Sarmiento found in the United States both inspiration and instruction. In his *Comentarios a la Constitución de la Confederación Argentina* (1853), he asserted: "*La Démocratie en Amérique par* Alexis de Tocqueville. This work, as a thorough and impartial study of the practice, the effects, advantages and vices of North American *institutions*, enjoys a great reputation in the United States and has run nine editions in France. It must be consulted for the study of American *institutions*."[44]

The author of *Facundo* was not the only Argentinian paying close attention to Tocqueville. Alberdi, a member of the New Generation, was also deeply touched by *Democracy in America*.[45] In Montevideo, Alberdi translated a fragment of the first volume and published it in 1840. He adopted Tocqueville's cultural explanation based on mores as well as his skepticism regarding the possibility of combining liberty and equality.[46] Unlike Sarmiento, Alberdi took very seriously the idea that inherited mores were critical to the survival of democratic rule. In North America, democracy inhered in its customs, that is, in the long-standing ideas, beliefs, habits, and usages of the North Americans. "It [custom] was not invented yesterday," he remarks.[47] Alberdi was, perhaps, the only Spanish American reader of Tocqueville who did not look away from the democratic conundrum. Mexico had failed because it had not adopted the "live" constitution of the United States, he conceded. What to do? The true way of changing the constitution of a people was to change their customs.[48] Oddly enough, Alberdi thought that mores could be the result of deliberate acts. In order to create a unified custom, it was necessary to "designate the principle and the political end of the association ... The principle and the end of our society is democracy, equality among the classes."[49] Alberdi fashioned himself, as Botana argues, as an "inventor of customs."[50] One particular mode of "invention" was immigration. Immigrants might carry with them the mores that would enable them to set up a successful democracy. After all, that was how the Anglo-Americans had done it in the first place. Thus, Alberdi concocted a theory of "vital transplantation." According to this "graft theory," an extended period of time for a democratic civilization to become established would not be necessary. The Alberdian dream consisted in European immigration.[51] As Botana argues, the graft theory provided Alberdi with a new starting point for South

America. His response to the democratic conundrum was a new people with a new history.

Alberdi also employed Tocqueville's notion of democracy to argue that democracy and monarchy were compatible. He quoted from *Democracy in America*: "I am very far from believing that they [the Americans] have found the only form possible of democratic government." Alberdi noted that Tocqueville, in referring to America, had asserted the need for a new political science for a new world; but the republican form of government was itself an artifact of the past – indeed, a sad past in the case of Spanish America.[52] Democracy might very well lead to a monarchy, "a form perhaps more compatible with it than a republic."[53] If a monarchy exists in society, "how can a republic exist in the political realm? In America, as Tocqueville notes, the republic is in the Government because it is in society."[54] Tocqueville was assimilated in Argentina and elsewhere into a strain of conservative liberalism that Merquior terms "nation-building" liberalism.[55] This reading was in synchrony with the predominance of doctrinal liberalism in Europe at the time. It is thus not strange that there were few "radical" interpreters of Tocqueville in Spanish America. Even so, Tocqueville's politics were not those of Guizot, a more severe critic of "democracy."[56]

COLOMBIA

Tocqueville was widely read in Colombia in the mid-nineteenth century. As the fleeting appearance of *Democracy in America* in the above-cited novel *María* shows, the Colombian elites were well acquainted with the book.[57] Indeed, Colombia was the only Spanish American country to produce a native translation of *Democracy in America*. Prominent members of the intellectual and political elite read the book: the brothers José María and Miguel Samper, Miguel Antonio Caro, Sergio Arboleda, Salvador Camacho Roldán, Aquileo Parra, Julio Arosamena, and Rafael Núñez. Several members of a younger generation, contemporaries of Tocqueville, were also influenced by *Democracy in America*: Mariano Ospina, José Eusebio Caro,

Joaquín Acosta (who seemed to have met Tocqueville in Paris between 1845 and 1849), and Florentino González.[58]

For the most part, the Colombians, like the Mexicans, found in *Democracy in America* a model to emulate. The United States, as depicted by Tocqueville, was an egalitarian and progressive society where work, wealth, and entrepreneurship were highly valued. America was a nation of small property holders free of aristocratic traditions and bound to a decentralized state that favored progress, democracy, and religious tolerance. Tocqueville was agreeable to some Colombians because in him they found a temperate and restrained liberal, free of revolutionary zeal, a friend of laws and customs and sensitive to the role of "religion as a cohesive agent."[59]

As in Mexico, Tocqueville was instrumental in debates over federalism in Colombia. The book ushered in a rediscovery of the North American federal system. The Colombian radicals, influenced by *Democracy in America*, linked centralism to despotism. Fragmentation of power, they thought, would prevent the government from acting arbitrarily.[60] Centralism favored unrealistic decision-making by distant politicians.[61] The ideas of Anglo-American federalism, as expounded by Tocqueville, were taught at the Colegio del Rosario to future radical leaders.[62] The lawyer Florentino González was a key figure in this transmission of ideas. In the prologue of his influential treatise on public administration, *Elementos de ciencia administrativa* (1840), he claimed that "the precious work of Mr. Tocqueville arrived in this country three years ago. I read it, meditated on it, and it was a torch which led me to an unknown research field."[63] In *Democracy in America*, Gonzalez found arguments to oppose both political and administrative centralization. After reading Tocqueville, he was convinced that "the ill resides in the spirit of centralization of our laws." In the more advanced nations, the national government only intervenes in great affairs, while everything else is left to the localities and to the inhabitants affected by them. Likewise, González believed that federalism was a bulwark against personalistic politics.[64] As happened in Mexico at around the same time, it is very significant that González and his disciples blatantly ignored Tocqueville's argument regarding the impossibility of transplanting North American federalism to the Spanish American nations. They offered no rejoinder to his pessimism.

Leopoldo Borda, another Colombian lawyer, translated the second volume of *Democracy in America* in 1842.[65] His interest in the second volume, ignored for the most part in Spanish America, is in itself remarkable.[66] The preface he wrote is perhaps one of the most interesting contemporary engagements with Tocqueville's ideas at the time. In many ways, Borda was not a follower but a critic of Tocqueville. The preface served the purpose of warning readers against a naïve interpretation of the ideas presented in the book. In light of the favorable reception of the first volume of *Democracy in America*, Borda asserted, it was important to be cautious about the possible effects of democracy in the republics of South America. Readers should not expect to see the same results that Tocqueville documented in North America. Such countries did not enjoy the exceptional position of the United States. Had Tocqueville considered the Spanish American republics, Borda alleged, he would not have concluded that equality of conditions – that is, democracy – made great revolutions rare. Those countries proved that other factors could neutralize the positive effect of equality. Tocqueville was right, Borda argued, in identifying the army as a constant source of turmoil in democratic societies. Yet it was necessary to factor in other elements, such as enlightenment and experience.[67]

Borda seriously doubted that democracy could have the same salutary effects on the intellectual movement, feelings, and mores of the peoples of South America. Institutions lacked stability there. "I am not well persuaded," Borda complained, "that equality produces all the effects that Mr. Tocqueville attributes to it and in spite of the respect that I keep for his opinions, I feel that my reason is not completely in accordance with some of them." The political instability that prevailed in the nations of South America posed a challenge to Tocqueville's preference for decentralization: "When civil strife threatens everything, then you should increase the attributes of power to the maximum, in spite of the fact that Tocqueville, in referring to democracies of a different species, regrets centralization."[68] The lesson offered by the Spanish American republics was that only those governments that, without straying completely from the laws, were able to prevent or suppress disorders managed to survive. Even the best Tocquevillean theory must yield to empirical reality. Borda likewise cautioned against the adoption of North American federalism. He believed that democratic reforms, toleration, and decentralization might endanger the precarious stability of new governments.

The translator also thought that Tocqueville's safeguards against individualism – or an excessive love for material well-being – were irrelevant in Spanish America. Here, he sided with Sarmiento. Democratic despotism was simply not on the horizon of the young republics. Borda wondered, "Why should a people that has not felt the effects of democracy yet share in such distrust? The first thing is to become established, to found democracy, a government, in order that a nation can exist, instead of conceiving misgivings about things that may not come to pass."[69] He further argued that Tocqueville's cultural determinism was misplaced. Men, he charged, perhaps following Rousseau, were *perfectible*. Neither the age nor particular situations could in and of themselves determine the fate of a people. In spite of years of political turmoil in Spanish America, the means to achieve happiness did in fact exist, and men should not despair of finding them. Misfortune entailed valuable experience and, with it, acquired political knowledge. Borda believed that most revolutions in Spanish America had been the doings of a few ambitious men and the army.[70] The key thing was to keep these forces in check.

CHILE

As in so many other countries, the Chileans read *Democracy in America* in the 1840s seeking to find some illumination regarding their own political situation. Some aspects of the book were particularly relevant for them. Such was the case of the treatment accorded to religion in a democratic society. Conservatives quickly seized Tocqueville's assertion that it was a mistake to regard the Catholic religion as a natural enemy of democracy.[71] Liberals retorted that, in the United States, religion could not undermine the "republican system" because toleration existed there.[72]

Oddly enough, some contemporaries in Chile read *Democracy in America* as a defense of direct democracy. A polemic took place between *El Mercurio* and the *Elector Chileno* in 1841. A writer from the latter paper chided those who misinterpreted Tocqueville's work as an apology for that "vicious democracy," combated by "historians and by politicians as one of the most pernicious systems." Whatever Tocqueville and his imitators may say, "the representative system had very different principles, means and ends from democracy."[73]

Regarding the most important intellectual figure of Chile at the time, the Venezuelan Andrés Bello, oddly enough he did not engage with Tocqueville.[74] In his writings, Bello mentions him just once, before the publication of the first volume of *Democracy in America*. He discussed Tocqueville and Beaumont's report on American prisons (1833) that both friends published upon their return to Europe.[75] Even so, Bello indirectly wrestled with Tocqueville's ideas in the course of his famous 1842 polemic regarding the use of the Spanish language in Chile.[76] Sarmiento quarreled with Bello regarding the proper use of Spanish. In languages, as in politics, Bello argued, "a body of wise men is needed to dictate the laws that are convenient to its needs."[77] Sarmiento retorted by quoting Tocqueville on literature in a democratic society.[78] Bello's ideas did not correspond to a republic where "the dogma of the sovereignty of the people was at the base of all institutions and from which all laws and the government emanated."[79] Languages, Sarmiento contended, are not formed by the Academies but by the people in mass. Since democracy – that is to say, an equality of conditions – prevailed in South America, it was only natural, he argued, citing *Democracy in America*, that "the literature of a democracy will never exhibit the order, regularity, skill, and art

characteristic of aristocratic literature; formal qualities will be neg-
lected or actually despised. The style will often be strange, incor-
rect, overburdened, and loose, and almost always strong and bold."[80]
The strictures of grammar were the legacy of political and religious
despotism. Grammarians, a kind of "conservative senate," strangled
the imagination of Chileans. In place of spontaneity, they instituted
a prison, zealously guarded by inflexible *culteranismo*.[81]

Two decades later, *Democracy in America* once again became
relevant in Chile. In the context of the Second Empire in France, the
American Civil War, and European intervention in Mexico, José
Victorino Lastarria used Tocqueville to prop up the republican form
of government. In *La América* (1867), Lastarria charged that the fundamental principle of the European monarchies was "absolute unity
of power that kills the individual and vanquishes its rights."[82] Such
a principle was pagan in inspiration, while "Christian civilization has
found its strength and its form in American democracy." In this saga,
ideas provided customs with their "essence and shape," not the other
way around. Therefore history, philosophy, morality, and the law
must be taught with the perspective of the "new dogma of democracy." A heightened individualism informed Lastarria's vision. The
"great principle" that completely dominated Anglo-American life,
and that made democracy a reality, was a natural mode of being:
*"that Providence has given to each individual, whatever he might
be, enough rationality to take care of himself in the things that
exclusively pertain to him.* This is the maxim – Tocqueville says –
on which civil and political society rests in the United States."[83]

However, since his appraisal of Tocqueville was mediated by an
engagement with the subsequent nineteenth-century French thinker
Édouard Laboulaye, Lastarria was also critical of the author of
Democracy in America.[84] While acknowledging the "potent voice
of the immortal Tocqueville," Lastarria ultimately believed that the
author of *Democracy in America* "did not understand the causes of
progress in the democratic republic of the United States."[85] Following
Laboulaye, he argued that Tocqueville could not break away from the

aristocratic feeling that dominated him. According to Laboulaye, Tocqueville had overlooked the significance of radical individualism, the working principle of American democracy. In America "everything originates in the individual."[86] This was an anti-egalitarian interpretation of *Democracy in America*. In the 1860s what registered with readers were the critical arguments about equality in volume 2. Tocqueville, Lastarria argued, had been the first to bring to Europe:

> among many new and holy ideas, the idea that liberty is not equality, as it was and still is believed in France. Equality adapts to many systems and can coexist with the most absolutist of regimes. He revealed the existence of a mighty republic where democracy was a reality ... He protested against the pagan idea of absolute sovereignty, against a sole, simple, providential and generative power and against the omnipotence of social power and uniformity of rules.[87]

Yet Tocqueville was no republican in France. He "limited himself to serving liberty, justice, and administrative decentralization. He wanted the emancipation of the municipality, complete freedom of the press and to accord the judiciary its proper place in a free country, that is, to make it sovereign." Indeed, Tocqueville was so far ahead of his time that he was hardly understood in France. His "propaganda" had no followers.[88] The voice "of the few that understood it was not even heard during the Revolution of 1848."[89] Tocqueville was praying in the desert. Only after the downfall of the Second Empire did Europe turn once more to America's customs and institutions in search of inspiration. Tocqueville, filtered through the sieve of Laboulaye and Courcell-Seneuille, once more became relevant.[90]

CONCLUSION

As we have seen, Tocqueville's reception in Spanish America was an act of selective appropriation. Some, such as the Mexicans and the Colombians, read *Democracy in America* as a precise and useful description of the political institutions of the United States. There readers could find clues, if not the nuts and bolts, for how to design their own constitutions. Most of them were blind to Tocqueville's argument that the key to the success of the United States relied on mores, not institutions. A deliberate decision was made to ignore cultural determinism. Willful readers, such as Otero, Sarmiento, and the Colombian radicals, thought that Tocqueville had unveiled the inner workings of the judiciary and federalism in the republic of the North. The rest could simply be ignored. This explains the Spanish Americans' general lack of interest in the second volume of *Democracy in America*. As Tocqueville's Colombian translator complained, what was the point of worrying about the hypothetical ills of a society that did not yet exist in the Spanish American nations? If Tocqueville himself was ambivalent about the democratic society he found in North America, that was not the case for readers such as Sarmiento, who was unambiguous in his praise of North American individualism and yeomanship. For these readers, Tocqueville's sociological critical insights were lost.

A different kind of reader, such as Alberdi, took seriously the implications of cultural determinism. Mores could not be decreed. Customs do not exist by fiat. Consequently, they devised social solutions such as the graft theory to provide for a cultural basis of democracy in the new nations. Mores could be imported. Finally, in the wars between the republic and constitutional monarchy, Tocqueville was used by Alberdi and Lastarria to bolster their respective positions. Yet few readers were able to provide a clear reply to Tocqueville's dismay regarding the future of Spanish America. Hence, at the core of the reception of *Democracy in America* lay an omission. This was an omission of the heart.

NOTES

1. Jorge Isaacs, *María* (Madrid: Cátedra, 2007), 130. Isaacs had a copy of the first volume (1835) of *Democracy in America* in his personal library. Jacob Warshaw, "Jorge Isaacs' Library: Light on Two *María* Problems," *Romanic Review* 32 (1941), 397.

2. Thomas Jefferson to Alexander von Humboldt, December 6, 1813, in Thomas Jefferson, *Writings*, ed. Merrill D. Peterson (New York: The Library of America, 1984), 1311.

3. DIA (L) I.2.ix, 306.

4. DIA (N), 226.

5. DIA (N), 266. My emphasis.

6. Inevitably mores were related to time: "It is in the East that the Anglo-Americans have had the longest experience of democratic government and have formed the habits and conceived the ideas most favorable to its maintenance." DIA (L) I.2.ix, 308.

7. DIA (L) I.2.ix, 306. I have examined elsewhere the accuracy of Tocqueville's claim regarding the 1824 Mexican Constitution as a copy of the American Constitution. See José Antonio Aguilar Rivera, *En pos de la quimera: Reflexiones sobre el experimento constitucional atlántico* (Mexico City: FCE/CIDE, 2000), 24–25.

8. DIA (L) I.2.ix, 307.

9. Charles A. Hale, *El liberalismo mexicano en la era de Mora* (Mexico City: Siglo XXI, 1994), 204.

10. Rafael Rojas, "Tocqueville: lecturas mexicanas," *Nexos* 22, no. 262 (1999), 81.

11. Hale, *El liberalismo mexicano en la era de Mora*, 204.

12. Alexis de Tocqueville, *De la democracia en la América del Norte*, Vol. 1, trans. D. A. de Bustamante (Paris: Imprenta de A. Everat y Ca, 1837). This was a translation from the fourth edition of the first volume.

13. Carlos A. Echánove Trujillo, "El juicio de amparo mexicano," *Revista de la Facultad de Derecho* 1–2 (1951), 95.

14. Alexis de Tocqueville, *De la democracia en América*, trans. D. A. Sánchez de Bustamante, 2 vols. (Mexico City: Publicación del Republicano, Imprenta de Ignacio Cumplido, 1855); Héctor Fix-Zamudio, *Ensayos sobre el derecho de amparo* (Mexico City: Porrúa, 1999), 494; Jesús Reyes Heroles, *El liberalismo mexicano*, Vol. 2 (Mexico City: FCE, 1982), 259.

15. Alexis de Tocqueville, *De la démocratie en Amérique*, 2 vols. (Paris: Librairie de Charles Gosselin, 1840).

16. It is likely that French and English editions of the second volume (i.e., the complete work) circulated in Mexico. However, what was widely read – and cited – by political actors and commentators was the

translated first volume. I have not located references to the second volume in the public debates of the time.

17. Tocqueville was also used, less prominently, in discussions about municipal liberty. For a more detailed analysis, see José Antonio Aguilar Rivera, "Omisiones del corazón: La recepción de Tocqueville en México," in *Ausentes del Universo: Reflexiones sobre el pensamiento político hispanoméricano en la era de la construcción nacional, 1821–1850* (Mexico: Fondo de Cultura Económica, 2012).

18. Echánove Trujillo, "El juicio de amparo mexicano," 95.

19. "Of the Judicial Power in the United States and Its Action on Political Society." DIA (N), 167–176.

20. "What a foreigner understands only with the greatest difficulty in the United States is the judicial organization. There is, so to speak, no political event in which he does not hear the authority of the judge invoked." DIA (N), 168. Indeed, Tocqueville was more concerned with the political role played by the judges than with judicial review.

21. DIA (N), 170.

22. Heroles, *El liberalismo mexicano*, 2: 372–394.

23. Mariano Otero, "Examen analítico. El sistema constitucional," *El Siglo Diez y Nueve* (October 3, 1842), 2–3.

24. DIA (N), 266.

25. Jorge Myers, "Ideas moduladas: Lecturas argentinas del pensamiento político europeo," *Estudios Sociales* 26, no. 1 (2004), 171. According to Myers it is impossible to overestimate the impact of Tocqueville on the New Generation in Argentina.

26. José Luis Romero, *A History of Argentine Political Thought* (Palo Alto, CA: Stanford University Press, 1968), 128.

27. Sarmiento quoted in Romero, *A History of Argentine Political Thought*, 128.

28. Echeverrría quoted in Romero, *A History of Argentine Political Thought*, 129.

29. It is possible to see here the influence not only of Tocqueville but also of Guizot. See Darío Roldán, "Liberales y doctrinarios en el Río de la Plata: Echeverría 'traductor' de Guizot," in Noemí Goldman and Georges Lomné, eds., *Los lenguajes de la República: historia conceptual y traducción en Iberoamérica (siglos XVIII y XIX)* (Madrid: Casa de Velázquez, forthcoming).

30. Esteban Echeverría, "Palabras simbólicas," in *Obras completas de d. Esteban Echeverría*, Vol. 4 (Buenos Aires: C. Casaralle, impr. y Librería de Mayo, 1870–1874), reproduced in Echeverría, "Symbolic Words," in Natalio Botana and Ezequiel Gallo, eds., *Liberal Thought in Argentina, 1837–1940* (Indianapolis: Liberty Fund, 2013), 40.

31. Juan Bautista Alberdi quoted in Romero, *A History of Argentine Political Thought*, 131. Tocqueville was by no means the sole or only intellectual influence on this generation of thinkers. As Romero asserts: "influenced by French thought (Saint-Simon, Fourier, Leroux, Lamennais, Lermenier) and in part, by German thought (Hegel and Savigny) ... the Men of 1837 observed that political solutions lacked foundation if social reality was not intensively analyzed." Romero, *A History of Argentine Political Thought*, 133. Also, the impact of the French Doctrinaires on these men has been ignored for the most part.

32. Domingo Faustino Sarmiento, *Facundo o civilización o barbarie en las pampas argentinas* (Paris: Hachette, 1874). This is the fourth edition of the book.

33. Oddly enough, Sarmiento claimed in 1849 that *Democracy in America* had not been translated: "Thirty editions have been made in Spanish of *Mysteries of Paris* while not a single one has been made of Tocqueville's *Democracy in America* ... Thus, Spanish thought is chained to its own poverty" (Sarmiento refers to Eugene Sue's popular book). Sarmiento, *Obras de D.F. Sarmiento, Vol. 2: Artículos críticos y literarios* (Buenos Aires: Felix Lajouane, 1895), 336. By 1850, Bustamante's and Borda's translations had circulated for many years in Latin America. Tocqueville is presented by Sarmiento as a modern social scientist. Along with others, he is credited with debunking the older, idealistic, theories of Rousseau, Montesquieu and Voltaire. Only after the 1830 Revolution in France, he contended, did notions of "race, national habits and historical backgrounds" begin to be discussed. It was then that Guizot revealed the "spirit of history" and Tocqueville unveiled the "secret of North America." Sarmiento, *Obras de D.F. Sarmiento*, Tomo II, 79.

34. Sarmiento, *Obras de D.F. Sarmiento*, 14.

35. Sarmiento, *Obras de D.F. Sarmiento*, 14.

36. Myers, "Ideas moduladas," 171.

37. Along with Tocqueville, Guizot and the Romantics also influenced Sarmiento. I thank Darío Roldán and Eduardo Zimmermann for

pointing this out to me. As Zimmermann notes, Sarmiento's perspective of civilization might also be heavily indebted to Guizot's *The History of Civilization in Europe*. There, Guizot discussed the progress of civilization as a transition from the countryside to cities. See François Guizot, *The History of Civilization in Europe*, trans. William Hazlitt (Indianapolis: Liberty Fund, 2013).

38. Domingo Faustino Sarmiento, *Viajes en Europa, África y América* (Santiago: Imprenta de Julio Belin y Ca, 1851), 44.

39. Sarmiento, *Viajes en Europa, África y América* (1851), 38.

40. Domingo Faustino Sarmiento, *Viajes en Europa, África y América* (Madrid: ALCA XX, 1997), 333.

41. DIA (L) I.2.iv, 192.

42. Darío Roldán, "Sarmiento, Tocqueville, los viajes y la democracia en América." *Revista de Occidente* 289 (2005), 55. On the effects of equality in Argentina according to Sarmiento, see Susana Villavicencio, "Sarmiento lector de Tocqueville," in Marisa Muñoz and Patrice Vermeren, eds., *Repensando el siglo XIX desde América Latina y Francia* (Buenos Aires: Colihue, 2009), 315–323.

43. Roldán, "Sarmiento, Tocqueville, los viajes y la democracia en América," 55.

44. Domingo Faustino Sarmiento, *Obras de D.F. Sarmiento*. Vol. 8 (Buenos Aires: Imprenta y Litografía de Mariano Moreno, 1995), 81. My emphasis. I owe this reference to Eduardo Zimmermann.

45. Natalio Botana has traced the intellectual journey of both Sarmiento and Alberdi. See Natalio Botana, *La tradición republicana: Alberdi Sarmiento y las ideas políticas de su tiempo* (Buenos Aires: Sudamericana, 1997), 263–337.

46. Myers, "Ideas moduladas," 171.

47. Alberdi cited by Botana, *La tradición republicana*, 299.

48. Botana, *La tradición republicana*, 299.

49. Botana, *La tradición republicana*, 299.

50. Botana, *La tradición republicana*, 299–300.

51. Botana, *La tradición republicana*, 303.

52. Juan Bautista Alberdi, *Obras sélectas*, Vol. 13 (Buenos Aires: La Facultad, 1920), 345.

53. "La monarquía en Europa conciliable con la democracia en América." Alberdi, *Obras sélectas*, 182–185.

54. Alberdi, *Obras sélectas*, 346.

55. J. G. Merquior, *Liberalism Old and New* (New York: Twayne Publishers, 1991).

56. On the Doctrinaires in France, see Pierre Rosanvallon, *Le moment Guizot* (Paris: Gallimard, 1985). On Tocqueville's dislike for Guizot, see André Jardin, *Tocqueville: A Biography*, trans. Lydia Davis and Robert Hemenway (New York: Farrar, Straus and Giroux, 1988), 313.

57. Gonzalo Cataño, "Tocqueville y su amigo Mill," in *Historia, sociología y política: ensayos de sociología e historia de las ideas* (Bogotá: Plaza y Janés, 1999), 221–239.

58. Cataño, "Tocqueville y su amigo Mill," 229. On Acosta's personal acquaintance with Tocqueville, see José María Samper, *Selección de Estudios* (Bogotá: Librería Colombiana, 1901), 290.

59. Cataño, "Tocqueville y su amigo Mill," 230.

60. Lázaro Mejía, *Los radicales: Historia política del radicalismo del siglo XIX* (Bogotá: Universidad Externado de Colombia, 2007), 234–235.

61. Edwin Cruz Rodríguez, "El federalismo en la historiografía política colombiana (1853–1886)," *Historia Crítica* 44 (2011), 118.

62. Víctor Alberto Quinche Ramírez, *Preparando a los burócratas en el Rosario. Algunos aspectos de la formación de abogados en el periodo radical*. Report no. 56 (Bogotá: Universidad del Rosario-Escuela de Ciencias Humanas, 2004), 9–13.

63. Florentino González, *Elementos de ciencia administrativa* (Bogotá: Escuela Superior de Administración Pública, 1994), 68.

64. Patricia Cardona Zuluaga, "Florentino González y la defensa de la república," *Araucaria* 16, no. 32 (2014), 435–458.

65. Alexis de Tocqueville, *De la democracia en América, traducida al español por Leopoldo Borda, abogado de la república de Nueva Granada*, 2 vols (Paris: Librería de D. Vicente Salvá, 1842). This is the only contemporary Spanish translation of volume 2 of *Democracy in America* that I am aware of.

66. It is possible that Borda, in translating volume 2, sought to curb the naïve enthusiasm of Colombian radicals, such as Florentino González, eager to imitate the institutions of the United States, in particular the federal structure.

67. Borda, "El traductor," in DEA (B), ix–x.

68. Borda, "El traductor," xii.

69. Borda, "El traductor," xiii.
70. Borda, "El traductor," xiv–xv.
71. "Religion Considered as a Political Institution and How it Powerfully Contributes to the Maintenance of a Democratic Republic Among the Americans." DIA (L) I.2.ix, 287.
72. "Restablecimiento de Jesuitas," *El Valdiviano Federal* (August 15, 1840).
73. "La polémica," *El Elector Chileno* (May 28, 1841).
74. On Bello see Ivan Jaksic, *Andrés Bello: Scholarship and Nation-Building in Nineteenth-Century Latin America* (Cambridge: Cambridge University Press, 2001).
75. The formal mission of the young French magistrates in America was to investigate the prison system of the United States. Gustave de Beaumont and Alexis de Tocqueville, *System Pénitentiarie aux États-unis et de son application en France* (Paris: H. Fournier, 1833). See "Establecimientos de confinación para los delincuentes," *El Auracano* (April 11, 1834), reproduced in Andrés Bello, *Obras completas de don Andrés Bello*, vol. 9 (Santiago: Pedro G. Ramírez, 1885), 48.
76. Fernando Alfón, *La querella de la lengua en Argentina. Antología* (Buenos Aires: Museo del Libro, 2013).
77. Un Quidam, "Ejercicios populares de la lengua castellana," in Alfón, *La querella de la lengua en Argentina*, 104–107.
78. DIA (L) II.1.xiii, 473–474.
79. Domingo Faustino Sarmiento, "Segunda contestación a un Quidan," in *Obras de Domingo Faustino Sarmiento*, Vol. 1 (Santiago: Imprenta Gutenberg, 1887), 218–219.
80. DIA (L) II.1.xiii, 474.
81. Sarmiento, "Segunda contestación a un Quidan," 223.
82. José Victorino Lastarria, *La América* (Gante: E. Vanderhaeghen, 1867). On the ideological milieu in Latin America at the time, see Eduardo Zimmermann, "Domingo Sarmiento, Édouard Laboulaye, y el 'momento Lincoln' en el republicanismo atlántico del siglo XIX," Universidad de San Andrés, unpublished manuscript, 2018.
83. José Victorino Lastarria, *La América: Fragmentos* (Mexico: UNAM, 1977), 14, emphasis in original.
84. Laboulaye was a French liberal and supporter of the Orleans Monarchy until 1848. He was a leader of the liberal opposition to Napoleon III and later a strong supporter of Thiers and the conservative republic. On the

influence of Laboulaye in Spanish America, particularly in Mexico, see Charles A. Hale, *The Transformation of Liberalism in Nineteenth-Century Mexico* (Princeton: Princeton University Press, 1989), 81–82. Laboulaye stated in a conference at the College de France that "the United States, where 'customs uphold the laws' had been a kind of revelation to him 'in a moment of crisis and danger.' Its experience might demonstrate 'what the lasting conditions of liberty were and how a country [like France] that suffers from anarchy can reform its institutions'." Hale, *The Transformation of Liberalism in Nineteenth-Century Mexico*, 81. In a way, Laboulaye rivaled Tocqueville as an expounder of American political institutions in the second part of the nineteenth century. Sarmiento, unlike Lastarria, saw Laboulaye simply as "the follower of Tocqueville's work, that was intended to show France, misguided in its conception of the republican form of government, what were the principles, practice and jurisprudence of the United States, the sole authority in matters of liberty and republicanism." Domingo Faustino Sarmiento, *Obras completes de Sarmiento, Vol. 39: Las doctrinas revolucionarias* (Buenos Aires: Luz del Día, 1953), 68.

85. Lastarria, *La América* (1977), 83.
86. Édouard Laboulaye, *L' etat et ses limites: Suivi d'essais politiques sur Alexis de Tocqueville, l'instruction publique, les finances, le droit de pétition, etc.* (Paris: Imprimerie de P.A. Bourdier et Cie, 1863).
87. Lastarria, *La América* (1977), 84.
88. Lastarria, *La América* (1977), 85.
89. Lastarria, *La América* (1977), 87.
90. On the influence of Courcelle-Seneuil in Chile, see Cristina Hurtado, "La recepción de Courcelle-Seneuil, seguidor de Tocqueville, en Chile," *Polis* 17 (2007), 1–10.

8 Tocqueville in Japan and China
Readings and Questions
James T. Schleifer

INTRODUCTION

This chapter focuses on the reception, reputation, and uses of
Tocqueville in Japan and China, with particular attention to Japanese
and Chinese interest in Tocqueville's *Democracy in America*.[1] As we
will see, Japanese political theorists discovered *Democracy in America*
in the 1870s, almost 150 years ago. In contrast, Chinese interest in
Tocqueville's first masterpiece emerged only in the 1980s, far more
recently; and during the past few years, for reasons discussed in what
follows, Tocqueville's second famous book, *The Old Regime and the
Revolution*, became the center of Chinese attention.

Tocqueville's two great works, despite differences of theme and
emphasis, should not be artificially separated. In both, Tocqueville
addressed the same fundamental questions, examined the meanings
and future of democracy, and sought the best means to establish and
sustain stable, free, and prosperous democratic societies. *Democracy
in America*, like the *Old Regime*, explores the concepts of revolution
and *period of transition*, which anticipates as well as follows any
major social and political upheaval. For Tocqueville, the French revolutionary heritage explained many of the differences between the
healthy democracy in America and the unhealthy one in France during the early nineteenth century; and the *Old Regime*, like his
Democracy, argues for basic civil and political rights, local liberties,
decentralization, and public participation as essential to democratic
freedom. In the 1835 and 1840 portions of *Democracy in America*, as
well as in the *Old Regime*, published in 1856, Tocqueville presented

a complex and nuanced but (mostly) consistent and unified social and political theory.[2] Briefly turning our attention to the recent Chinese fascination with the *Old Regime* is not, therefore, an inappropriate diversion from consideration of Tocqueville's first classic text, *Democracy in America*.

The story of how Tocqueville has been read and understood in Japan and China is part of the larger phenomenon of growing international interest in Tocqueville as a social and political theorist.[3] Perhaps the core issue in the widening contemporary consideration of Tocqueville's message concerns the future of democracy. According to Tocqueville, democracy, as equality of conditions, offered two possible results. It could, with careful efforts, lead to democratic liberty or, more easily, slide toward democratic despotism. In today's world, Tocqueville's dilemma persists. Where is democracy headed, and what can responsible human beings do to encourage democratic freedom and avoid democratic tyranny?

JAPAN

In 1868, the Meiji Restoration ended the Tokugawa Shogunate and reasserted the traditional role and authority of the emperor. This Restoration, more properly called the Meiji Revolution, abolished the rigidly hierarchical social structure of the Shogunate, encouraged existing trends toward greater equality (especially economic and cultural), and launched the history of Japan as a modern nation. After 1868, Japan changed from a predominantly aristocratic to an increasingly democratic society, a pattern of growing equality of conditions that characterized Japanese society throughout much of the twentieth century and into the twenty-first. The Japanese example seems to confirm Tocqueville's most fundamental thesis about the direction of the modern world – the irresistible advance of democracy understood as equality.[4]

In 1873, only a few years after the Meiji Revolution, Obata Tokujiro translated an initial segment on freedom of the press from the 1835 portion of *Democracy in America*. A few other subchapters on public spirit, the idea of rights, and administrative decentralization soon followed. Not long after, in 1881–1882, a full translation of the 1835 *Democracy* into Japanese by Koizuka Ryu appeared.[5] Tocqueville's writings became important to the Movement for Freedom and People's Rights, or Popular Rights Movement, which championed liberal democratic principles, especially during the 1870s and 1880s.

The primary figure among Japanese theorists interested in Tocqueville at this time was Fukuzawa Yukichi (1835–1901), who had traveled to Europe and the United States and knew English and Dutch.[6] Influenced as well by François Guizot and John Stuart Mill, Fukuzawa wrote especially about essential rights, the need for individual and national independence, the importance of administrative decentralization, and the sources of civic spirit or true citizenship. At the end of the nineteenth and into the early decades of the twentieth century, Tocqueville was read in Japan mostly as a guide to the requirements for liberty.

In these early years, Japanese understanding of Tocqueville's *Democracy* was also shaped in part by the effort to build a modern nation-state, capable of maintaining national independence in the face of Western imperialism. For example, Fukuzawa, although a proponent of administrative decentralization, noted Tocqueville's admiration for *governmental* centralization as essential for a strong nation. Individual rights, the freedoms of speech, expression, and association, as well as local liberties, were seen not only as laws essential to liberty but also, following Tocqueville's argument, as ways to develop the habits of public engagement, to support civic spirit, and to produce a thoughtful or reasoned patriotism.

By the 1950s, after the disastrous period of militarism and war, Maruyama Masao (1914–1996) became the leading Japanese student of Tocqueville. In particular, Maruyama highlighted some of Tocqueville's cautions about democracy, including the dangers of mass society, subservience to the crowd, intellectual conformity, and the possible tyranny of an intolerant and hypernationalistic public opinion. These broader cultural and sociological warnings emerged especially from the 1840 *Democracy*, which had attracted little attention in Japan until after World War II, when segments were finally translated.[7] In the past few decades, Japanese commentators have continued to focus on Tocqueville's examination of how democracy transforms *mores* – attitudes, beliefs, ideas, and behaviors. Changes in family values, in particular, have been studied; and, even more recently, Tocqueville's warnings about increasing democratic apathy and detachment from public life have attracted attention.[8]

Japanese scholars have also addressed the theme of revolution in Tocqueville's works. The causes and consequences of both the Meiji Revolution and the Chinese Revolution of 1911 have been studied from the perspective of Tocqueville's writings on revolution in *Democracy in America*, as well as in the *Old Regime*. How does increasing equality, of various sorts, undermine an old aristocratic order and lead to the sudden collapse of a long-standing regime? After revolutionary upheavals, how can social and political stability be reestablished? Further, how does the experience of revolution subsequently color (or discolor) democracy? The Meiji Revolution has been interpreted as a social and political transformation even more radical than the French Revolution because of the acute sense of external threat from imperialist Western nations and the resulting necessity for immediate modernization and nation-building.[9]

So Tocqueville has been understood in Japan as a proponent of necessary rights, an advocate of decentralization, a mentor for public spirit and thoughtful patriotism, an analyst of democracy, and a theorist of revolution. Although the attention given to Tocqueville pales beside that lavished on Weber or Marx throughout much of the twentieth century, the long tradition of Japanese interest in Tocqueville endures. Since the mid-twentieth century, a continuous succession of Japanese scholars has studied and written about Tocqueville's ideas; unfortunately, much of their work remains available only in Japanese. In 2008, Matsumoto Reiji, the outstanding

Japanese Tocqueville scholar of his generation, completed the first full translation into Japanese of the entire *Democracy in America*.

Tocqueville, of course, said nothing about Japan in his work. Nonetheless, his analysis fits Japan in a variety of ways and has served as a useful perspective on Japanese society. Perhaps, as noted, the most striking feature is the unfolding of equality of conditions, which has made Japan today – by many economic, social, and cultural measures – one of the most egalitarian societies in the modern world.[10] Japan also illustrates Tocqueville's understanding of the meanings of democracy. For him, democracy had both social and political dimensions. *Social* democracy, or democracy as social state, meant equality of conditions; *political* democracy evoked particular laws and institutions and could bend toward either liberty or despotism. For the island nation, the advance of democracy has meant not only a long trajectory of increasing equality or social democracy but also the development since 1945 of a vigorous and free political democracy.

Certain elements of Tocqueville's social and political theory shed light on Japanese society since the nineteenth century and, in this way, reaffirm the value of his ideas; but this perspective can be reversed. The example of Japan also forces some reconsideration of a few of Tocqueville's basic arguments. During the last few decades, Japan, like other developed nations, has witnessed a marked increase in inequality, especially growing disparities of wealth and income. The significance of this trend is unclear and hotly debated, but such growing inequality certainly runs contrary to Tocqueville's most fundamental thesis.[11]

The case of Japan presents other dilemmas as well for students of Tocqueville. As he argues, especially in *Democracy in America*, a democracy, to remain free, requires both administrative decentralization and religious faith, among other features. The accumulation of excessive power in the hands of government, according to Tocqueville, threatens to suffocate civic life, discourage public participation, and lead to the death of citizenship; such centralization opens the door to the new democratic despotism, so chillingly described by Tocqueville. Religion – Christianity in particular for Tocqueville – serves as an anchor for healthy mores and as a necessary check on possible social and political excesses.

Japan, however, remains a relatively centralized nation. Reforms after the Meiji Revolution instituted the French administrative organization, with local prefects appointed by the central government. After World War II, during the American occupation, an attempt was made to ensure greater local autonomy, and the system was changed to allow the election of local governors. Older traditions prevailed, however, and localities have continued to be largely financially dependent on and subservient to the national government. Reform attempts continue, but the administrative structure remains quite centralized.[12]

Japan also exemplifies a mostly secularized society where religious or quasi-religious rituals and symbols seem to relate primarily to national commemorations or to major moments in personal life, such as marriage and burial. In Japan, religion is traditionally seen very differently than in the West; believers and religious groups not directly tied to respect for the nation have often come under suspicion for undermining political and social authority.[13] Yet the nation undeniably offers the example of a stable, vigorous, and free democracy. Is administrative centralization so deadly, or religious faith so imperative?

Japan, like some other modern nations in Western Europe, raises these issues. Perhaps a high degree of social and cultural homogeneity can serve in the place of religion to shape and sustain the common values and shared mores so prized by Tocqueville as essential to healthy, free democracies. These speculations lead us to no definitive answers. Such puzzles remain for the ongoing consideration of thoughtful readers.

CHINA

As noted, Chinese interest in Tocqueville is much more recent. The first translation into Chinese of the entire *Democracy in America*, by

Dong Guo-Liang, appeared only in 1988. A Chinese translation, by Feng Tang, of the *Old Regime* dates from 1991, roughly thirty years ago. Since the 1980s, however, Chinese consideration of Tocqueville's work has flourished.

China, unlike Japan, is mentioned in Tocqueville's books – four times in his *Democracy* and once in the *Old Regime*.[14] In the 1835 *Democracy*, he portrayed China as "the most beautiful model of administrative centralization that exists in the universe," with all of the negative consequences predicted by Tocqueville: "tranquility without happiness, industry without progress, stability without strength, physical order without public morality."[15] Although he described China as enlightened, he declared the nation frozen into a "singular type of immobility."[16] Because the Chinese were attached to application more than theory, they could not change or improve once they had reached a certain level of invention and development. "The source of human knowledge had nearly dried up."[17]

So China, for Tocqueville, served as the image of a democratic society, but one without liberty. In the Middle Kingdom, "equality of conditions is very great and very ancient."[18] Public office was attained not by birth or class standing but by competitive examination; and the Chinese enjoyed "a sort of material well-being."[19] The nation had, however, succumbed to some of the grave dangers of democracy: administrative centralization; application over theory; and intellectual, cultural, and even economic stagnation.

Tocqueville's most negative and even insulting comments about China appear in the *Old Regime*. In his text, he condemned the physiocrats, French reformers of the eighteenth century, for their readiness to use the absolute power of the state to reform French society and government. Their attitude, for Tocqueville, foreshadowed the new democratic despotism, and he denounced their "emphatic eulogy of China" as a model, ridiculing their ignorance of the "imbecile and barbarous government that a handful of Europeans [had] mastered at will."[20] Here, his fury at the physiocrats erased the more positive image of Chinese enlightenment he had presented in his *Democracy*.

Much of Tocqueville's depiction of China repeats Western stereotypes prevalent in the eighteenth and early nineteenth centuries. As Françoise Mélonio has pointed out, however, Tocqueville was aware of at least some of the most recent French academic studies of China and East Asia carried out during his lifetime.[21] He was not simply repeating Montesquieu's image of China as an absolute despotism. For him, China served as a troubling example of the possible failings of democracy. This perspective was unusual and makes any consideration of Tocqueville and China especially intriguing.

What explains the growing Chinese interest in Tocqueville's thinking and writing during the past few decades? Tocqueville's assertion about the providential and inevitable advance of democracy in the modern world raises the question of whether this thesis also applies to China. A number of scholars argue that China can be seen as a *social* democracy, a society where equality has deep roots and is increasing, at least since the late nineteenth century.[22] Given that assumption, two major issues seem to dominate: the effort to achieve democratic liberty and escape democratic despotism and the search for ways to avoid some of the dangerous social, psychological, and moral consequences of democracy. Tocqueville's *Democracy* offers a political program for reaching both of these goals.

Many in China praise Tocqueville as a champion of freedom and read his book as an eloquent argument for fundamental civil and political rights (including a free press and freedoms of speech, assembly, association, and religion) and for greater local liberties and decentralization. His proposals are applauded as measures to encourage a vigorous civil society and to broaden genuine political participation; and his masterpiece serves not only as a treatise on liberal democracy but also as a convenient instrument for condemning an overly centralized and authoritarian state.

Despite efforts during the past three decades to strengthen local self-government, China continues to be highly centralized. Robert

T. Gannett, Jr., writing with Tocqueville's praise for local liberties and decentralization in mind, has described recent village reforms in China, asking whether changes meant to strengthen village autonomy are effective or not. In 1987, a reform project mandated local elections in more than 900,000 villages in China, and new laws in 1998 strengthened village self-governance even further. Yet have such measures led to real freedom? Gannett does not come to any conclusions. He merely points out that such reforms in village self-government will bring genuine local liberties only if local citizens and local elected officials learn how to be truly independent from central control and resist efforts by officials at the national level to co-opt local elections, governance, and decision-making.[23]

Wang Jianxun, one of the important Tocqueville specialists in China, has also examined reforms in Chinese villages. After recalling China's long tradition of tension between the center and the localities and provinces, he presents his study of a small group of rural communities operating under the 1987 reforms to demonstrate that Tocqueville's interpretation of the beneficial results of local liberties is correct. In the particular villages he uses as examples, greater peasant participation in decision-making has led, he asserts, to better local services and improved roads, schools, land policies, and fiscal management. In short, public affairs are better run. Administrative efficiency was not, of course, a presumed benefit of decentralization as described by Tocqueville. Yet local improvements, Wang argues, indicate the kind of grassroots political and social involvement and civic responsibility that Tocqueville counted among the fruits of decentralization. Even urban communities in China, Wang points out, are moving toward greater self-government since the 1990s. For him, these developments are hopeful steps toward a freer society, one characterized by less centralization and greater genuine participation by ordinary citizens in public life.[24]

In an important recent essay, titled "Democracy in China: Tocquevillian Reflections," another key Chinese Tocqueville scholar, Chong Ming, has addressed this issue as well. Changes in laws concerning villages and towns have resulted, he agrees, in some increase in self-government and the practice of liberty on the local level. His conclusion, though, is more pessimistic. These beginnings of grassroots democracy, which Tocqueville saw as essential training for effective political participation on the national level, remain, Chong believes, weak and insufficient.[25]

In his article, he also looks at associations, another invaluable school for liberty according to Tocqueville. Associations have multiplied in China and are a hopeful sign of increased public participation and civic responsibility. Nongovernmental political associations are not allowed, however, and civil associations remain closely monitored and restrained. Truly independent associational activity continues to be scarce.[26]

For Tocqueville, religion serves as yet another support for freedom in democratic societies. "Despotism," he declared, "can do without faith, but not liberty."[27] Religion, as mentioned, encourages healthy habits, attitudes, and behavior and stands as a restraint against social and political excesses. In his *Democracy*, he describes Christianity as the source of equality and as the religion most appropriate to democracy. This message has produced considerable discussion of the future in China of religion, in general, and of Christianity, in particular.[28] One topic of research and writing has been the rapid growth in China of Christianity, especially Protestantism, during recent decades. Some commentators see this religious development as a pathway to grassroots activism and democratic liberty.

Another approach to the subject of religion looks instead to Confucianism as a Chinese philosophical substitute for Christianity. Confucianism serves to provide a non-Western framework for overcoming the excessive materialism, individualism, and other ills of the modern democratic world. Confucianism, with its stress on duty, social harmony, family and community solidarity, and respect for legitimate authorities and elites, offers a different understanding of the link between private and public life and of the moral responsibility of the individual for what happens in the wider society.

It also suggests a counterbalance to extreme equality by stressing the importance of hierarchy.

Yet, as Duan Demin asks in a 2014 article, is Confucianism compatible with democracy? For some Chinese scholars, this query remains the central issue.[29] The answer turns, in part, on whether Confucianism will act to stimulate engagement in civic life and encourage an attachment to liberty or simply reinforce deferential attitudes toward authority. As various writers have noted, the matter remains unresolved. Measured against some of the essential requirements recommended by Tocqueville for assuring democratic freedom – local liberties, associations, and religion – the future of liberty in China continues to be questionable.

A second major interpretation of Tocqueville in China involves his role as critic of democracy and his catalogue of the possible dangerous consequences of democratic equality. The remarkable economic developments and growing prosperity since the 1980s have brought a downside. China now suffers from many of the features Tocqueville cautioned against in modern democratic societies. Materialism, the single-minded pursuit of comfort and well-being, has flourished and led to worsening individualism, concentration on private success, a willingness to trade freedom for order, withdrawal from public affairs, and growing political apathy. As Chong has pointed out, generational isolation has even undermined traditional family life.[30] Many of Tocqueville's warnings hit home for Chinese readers.

Even more broadly, Tocqueville's vivid descriptions of the potential (or even likely) pitfalls of democracy are understood by some in China as a powerful general critique of Western liberal democracy.[31] Democracy, Tocqueville argues, transforms mores and reshapes human psychology. What would his new "democratic man" be like? Would frustration, anxiety, and restlessness be the chief characteristics of democratic societies? Would people in democratic nations resent and reject even legitimate elites, undermining standards of excellence and preventing effective political and social leadership? Is cultural and intellectual mediocrity the likely consequence of democracy?

From this perspective, Tocqueville's book relentlessly exposes the failings and dangers of democracy, including corrosive individualism; excessive materialism; social, political, and legal instability; the decay of values; the rejection of legitimate elites; the rise of the least common denominator; and low cultural and intellectual standards. So, instead of exalting the example of liberal democracy, a deeply flawed model, the correct reading of Tocqueville's work, according to this view, urges China to find a different path. Interpreted as a profound and perceptive criticism of Western liberal democracy, Tocqueville's book stands as a caveat to China.

Such a critical understanding also colors the evaluation of Tocqueville's portrait of America. Some Chinese readers wonder whether his portrayal of the American republic is too idealized. He highlights equality of conditions in the United States, but what about the striking racial and economic inequalities that existed (and still exist)? Further, does he misrepresent America? Tocqueville paints the United States as a democracy, but isn't it really a republic? Weren't the American founders afraid of democracy? Doesn't the American Constitution set up a framework with strong checks on the power of the people, including such mechanisms as indirect elections, the Senate, the Electoral College, and even the federal principle itself?[32]

Even granting the accuracy of Tocqueville's description of the American republic at the time of his visit in 1831 and 1832, does it still apply? How can the power of money in politics and the growing gap between rich and poor in contemporary America be reconciled with the image of equality? What can be said about the role of religion in today's America? Tocqueville stressed a careful separation of church and state in the United States, but isn't religion now mixing directly into public life and policy, and isn't religious fervor encouraging a troubling level of political extremism? These questions concerning American society arise not only as resistance to the American example but also as part of a broader skepticism about democracy and its likely consequences.

Such readings are, of course, serious oversimplifications, even distortions of Tocqueville's message, which is nuanced, complex, and carefully balanced. His *Democracy* aims both to temper the excessive enthusiasm of the advocates of democracy and to calm the exaggerated fears of the enemies of democracy. He was neither condemning democracy nor, as he repeatedly assured his French audience, blindly endorsing America as a perfect exemplar.

A third appreciation of Tocqueville in China does not so much emphasize his specific recommendations or his warnings but instead views him as a theorist whose primary effort was to find and examine a model appropriate for understanding tomorrow's world. Unlike most of his French contemporaries, Tocqueville believed that the American republic happened to reveal the democratic future. Yet various nations in vastly different periods of history have been perceived as models, and still other possibilities will emerge in the future. The American republic, so eloquently presented in Tocqueville's *Democracy*, may no longer fit the role. These readers regard Tocqueville as a fellow explorer who was seeking the most effective example for his time. For them, the task is to honor his approach, to trace his path, and, with his subtlety and sensibility, to look for the most appropriate new standard for societies in the twenty-first century to emulate.

A fourth and more strictly scholarly approach in China to Tocqueville centers on the originality and power of his social and political theories. His ideas provide a novel and alternative analysis for understanding the course of modern history. Tocqueville is appreciated as a brilliant political philosopher who tried to understand and explain to his readers the social, political, and cultural tendencies of his contemporary world; he is valued as a fresh voice among major theorists. According to Li Qiang, a leading Chinese expert on the history of Western political ideas, many past interpretations have fallen into disfavor among Chinese political scientists who study

Western political thought.[33] Classical Western European liberalism, Marxism, and Straussian neoconservatism, for example, no longer seem persuasive for a variety of reasons. Where to find another perspective? Two possible alternatives have emerged more recently in China: the Cambridge School and Alexis de Tocqueville. Li describes the growing appeal, since the beginning of the twenty-first century, of the Cambridge School, which proposes a different approach to modern democratic theory. He identifies flaws in the Straussian approach: an overly rigid orthodoxy (what he calls "academic mysticism"); a rejection of pluralism within societies and among nations; a failure adequately to appreciate historical context; and too close an association with an extremely conservative political ideology. According to Li, the theories of the Cambridge School avoid these weaknesses and are, therefore, increasingly attractive to Chinese scholars and students of political science. Tocqueville serves, at least for some Chinese specialists of political philosophy, as a second alternative, a theorist who escapes doctrinaire, absolutist ideas, who appreciates historical and cultural context, and who offers a more moderate and pluralistic view.

So Tocqueville has been seen in China through very different lenses, as advocate of rights and freedom, critic of liberal democracy, seeker after the best model, or political philosopher offering a novel and profound understanding of modern democratic theory. During the last few years, he is also understood as an important theorist of the causes and consequences of revolution. Great interest in Tocqueville's *Old Regime* has recently emerged among Chinese intellectuals and political leaders. Why such an intense and remarkable attention for a work published more than 160 years ago? In 2012, Wang Qishan, trained as a historian and a high-ranking government official, recommended Tocqueville's book as a study of the risks of rapid economic and social change to an established regime, and his endorsement turned a previously overlooked text into a must-read.

As we know, Tocqueville's *Old Regime* is far more about pre-revolutionary and postrevolutionary France than about the French

Revolution itself. In his book, Tocqueville demonstrates how the seeds of revolution were sown during the old regime; and, by implication, he explores the consequences of that historical legacy and resulting revolution for France in the nineteenth century and perhaps beyond. A major part of the originality of the book is his argument that his contemporary France reflected the old regime much more than usually imagined. The Revolution was not so revolutionary.

For prerevolutionary France, Tocqueville describes a society with growing equality but with widening gaps between social classes; a kind of social as well as individual isolation (collective individualism); a relentless preference for centralization; the absence or decay of civil society; a crisis of authority and widespread disillusionment with the ruling elite; and intellectuals who were, despite bold theories, largely outside of decision-making and were, therefore, almost totally lacking in practical political experience. Perhaps more significantly, he argues that revolution is ignited not by abject poverty and frozen institutions but by economic improvements and modest reform. The greatest danger for the old regime in France arose from rapidly rising material and political expectations that remained unmet. Tocqueville's *Old Regime*, from this perspective, is a warning about the true time of crisis and a powerful plea for more thorough and genuine reform. His book suggests how to avoid cataclysmic change.

This understanding of Tocqueville's second major publication suggests two pertinent readings for today's China, both of which are instructive. Understood from the first perspective, Tocqueville's book explores the difficult historical legacy facing postrevolutionary France. Having witnessed a great upheaval, France suffered from a period of uncertainty and found itself in a painful time of transition. Tocqueville wondered whether his country would ever become stable, prosperous, and free. Think of China, facing the successive regime changes and revolutionary movements of the twentieth century, including the Revolution of 1911, Mao's triumph in 1949, the great Cultural Revolution, and the equally profound economic transformation initiated in the 1980s by Deng Xiaoping. With such a legacy of radical change, China's current situation parallels the story of postrevolutionary France.[34] What can be done to find social and political equilibrium and to meet the challenges posed by such a turbulent heritage? This is precisely the question that Tocqueville posed for France.

Yet this possible reading, though pertinent, remains secondary. The primary interpretation among Chinese readers of Tocqueville's *Old Regime* focuses on his history of pre-1789 France as a society headed unknowingly toward revolution.[35] His depiction of the old regime seems, in many ways, suggestive of contemporary China. Tocqueville's book warns of an approaching moment of crisis, when rapid economic progress and limited reforms only heighten the risk of upheaval. Given this sense of urgency, can the recent rise of Xi Jinping be understood as an effort to reassert control and preempt the possibility of revolution?

So, whether China is understood as coping with a legacy of revolution or as facing imminent revolution, Tocqueville's *Old Regime* has something significant to say. His book provides advice about how to avoid the mistakes of the French old regime and, at the same time, suggests how to build a stable, prosperous, and free postrevolutionary regime.

CONCLUSION

We have looked at Japan and China through the lens of Tocqueville's works. How does his analysis clarify past and current challenges and illuminate future possibilities in both countries? This effort, focused on two countries, raises even broader questions. What does Tocqueville's democratic thesis, with its nuanced and shifting definitions, complex analysis, and blend of praise and warning about advancing democracy, have to say to other nations, especially those undergoing rapid development? What can other nations learn from Tocqueville about promoting the benefits and avoiding the pitfalls of democracy? What does the rise of democracy mean in places with histories and cultures very different from the United States and Western Europe? What travels best or worst from *Democracy in America* and the *Old Regime*? Is Tocqueville's work still relevant for the contemporary world?

Social democracy, as equality of conditions, led, Tocqueville believed, to political democracy:

> It is impossible to think, that, in the end, equality would not penetrate the political world as it does elsewhere ... Now I know of only two ways to have equality rule in the political world: rights must either be given to each citizen or given to no one ... It is therefore very difficult to see a middle course between the sovereignty of all and the absolute power of one man ... Peoples can therefore draw two great political consequences from the same social state ... The first to be subjected to this fearful alternative that I have just described, the Anglo-Americans have been fortunate enough to escape absolute power. Circumstances, origin, enlightenment, and above all, mores have allowed them to establish and to maintain the sovereignty of the people.[36]

We might be so bold as to add to Tocqueville's words that Japan, too, has been fortunate enough since the mid-twentieth century to take the path of political rights, sovereignty of the people, and democratic liberty instead of democratic despotism. China still faces Tocqueville's "fearful alternative."

NOTES

1. I extend my thanks for the advice, suggestions for reading, and encouragement that I received concerning this chapter from Professors Matsumoto Reiji and Watanabe Hiroshi in Tokyo; Chong Ming and Liu Qing in Shanghai; and Li Qiang, Duan Demin, and Wang Jianxun in Beijing.
2. For elaboration, see James T. Schleifer, *Tocqueville* (Cambridge: Polity Press, 2018), especially chaps. 3 and 5.

3. See Aurelian Craiutu and Sheldon Gellar, eds. *Conversations with Tocqueville: The Global Democratic Revolution in the Twenty-first Century* (Lanham, MD: Lexington Books, 2009) and Christine Dunn Henderson, ed., *Tocqueville's Voyages: The Evolution of His Ideas and Their Journey Beyond His Time* (Indianapolis: Liberty Fund, 2014). Also consult the special issue on China, Japan, and Tocqueville: Françoise Mélonio, ed., "Tocqueville, la Chine et le Japon," Special Issue, *The Tocqueville Review/La revue Tocqueville* 38, no. 1 (2017); Ewa Atanassow and Richard Boyd, eds., *Tocqueville and the Frontiers of Democracy* (Cambridge: Cambridge University Press, 2013); and Joshua Mitchell, *Tocqueville in Arabia: Dilemmas in a Democratic Age* (Chicago: University of Chicago Press, 2013).

4. See Matsumoto Reiji, "Tocqueville and Japan," in Craiutu and Gellar, *Conversations with Tocqueville*, 295–317.

5. See Matsumoto Reiji, "Tocqueville and 'Democracy in Japan'," in Henderson, *Tocqueville's Voyages*, 425–455, especially 427–429.

6. See Watanabe Hiroshi, *A History of Japanese Political Thought, 1600–1901*, trans. David Noble (Tokyo: International House of Japan, 2012); the chapter on Fukuzawa may be found at 391–416. See also Miyashiro Yasutake, "La philosophie libérale de Yukichi Fukuzawa," *The Tocqueville Review/La revue Tocqueville* 38, no. 1 (2017), 41–61 and Matsumoto Reiji, "Fukuzawa Yukichi and Maruyama Masao: Two 'Liberal' Readings of Tocqueville in Japan," *The Tocqueville Review/La revue Tocqueville* 3, no. 1 (2017), 19–39. More generally, see Matsuda Koichiro, "Public Spirit and Tradition: Tocqueville in the Discourse of Meiji Japanese Intellectuals" and Higuchi Yoichi, "Tocqueville et le constitutionnalisme," papers presented at the international conference commemorating the 200th anniversary of Tocqueville's birth, "France and the United States, Two Models of Democracy," University of Tokyo, June 10–12, 2005.

7. See, for example, Furuya Jun, "Tocqueville and the Origins of American Studies in Postwar Japan," paper presented at the "France and the United States, Two Models of Democracy" international conference, University of Tokyo, June 10–12, 2005. See also Matsumoto Reiji, "Maruyama Masao and Liberalism in Japan," in Ewa Atanassow and Alan S. Kahan, eds., *Liberal Moments: Reading Liberal Texts* (London: Bloomsbury Academic, 2017), 166–173; and Matsumoto "Fukuzawa Yukichi and Maruyama Masao."

8. See Matsumoto Reiji, "Tocqueville on the Family," *The Tocqueville Review/La revue Tocqueville* 8, no. 1 (1986), 127–152; and Matsumoto, "Tocqueville and Japan," 302–304.

9. Consult Watanabe Hiroshi, "The French, Meiji and Chinese Revolutions in the Conceptual Framework of Tocqueville," *The Tocqueville Review/La revue Tocqueville* 38, no. 1 (2017), 63–79, especially 76–79, and Matsumoto, "Tocqueville and Japan," 308–310.

10. Matsumoto, "Tocqueville and Japan," 297–300.

11. See Thomas Piketty, *Capital in the Twenty-First Century*, trans. Arthur Goldhammer (Cambridge, MA: Harvard University Press, 2014) and Matsumoto, "Tocqueville and 'Democracy in Japan'," 438–441.

12. Matsumoto, "Tocqueville and Japan," 300–302.

13. See, for example, the discussions in Watanabe, *Political Thought*, 43–46 and 383–87.

14. See DIA (N) 154, 535, 786, and 1123; also see OR 213 and 370–372, where China is cited in Tocqueville's research notes.

15. DIA (N) 154, Tocqueville's own note 50.

16. DIA (N) 786.

17. Ibid. Also see Tocqueville's chapter, "Why Great Revolutions Will Become Rare," DIA (N) 1144–1151.

18. DIA (N) 1123.

19. DIA (N) 786.

20. OR 213; see also 370–372. Tocqueville's disparaging remarks were written after the first Opium War 1839–1842, a disaster for China and a key event in the long period of Chinese national humiliation.

21. Françoise Mélonio, "Tocqueville, la Chine et le Japon: Introduction," *The Tocqueville Review/La revue Tocqueville* 38, no. 1 (2017), 8–10.

22. See Watanabe, "The French, Meiji and Chinese Revolutions" and Chong Ming, "Democracy in China: Tocquevillean Reflections," *The Tocqueville Review/La revue Tocqueville* 38, no. 1 (2017), 82–85. Also see James Ceaser, "Why Tocqueville on China: An Introductory Essay," Tocqueville on China Project, The American Enterprise Institute, January 2010, 4–5.

23. Robert T. Gannett, Jr. "Village-By-Village Democracy in China: What Seeds for Freedom?," Tocqueville on China Project, American Enterprise Institute, April 2009.

24. Wang Jianxun, "The Road to Democracy in China: A Tocquevillian Analysis," in Craiutu and Gellar, *Conversations with Tocqueville*, 271–294.

25. Chong, "Democracy in China," 90–94.

26. Chong, "Democracy in China," 94–95.

27. DIA (N) 478; and see 467–478.

28. See Richard Madsen, "The Upsurge of Religion in China," *Journal of Democracy* 21, no. 4 (2010), 58–71; Carol Lee Hamrin, "China's Protestants: A Mustard Seed for Moral Renewal?," Tocqueville on China Project, American Enterprise Institute, May 2008; and Chong, "Democracy in China," 96–103.

29. Consult Duan Demin, "Reviving the Past for the Future? The (In) compatibility between Confucianism and Democracy in Contemporary China," *Asian Philosophy: An International Journal of the Philosophical Traditions of the East* 24, no. 2 (2014), 147–157. Also see the pertinent discussion of Confucianism in Cheryl Welch, "Deliberating Democracy with Tocqueville: The Case of East Asia," in Atanassow and Boyd, eds., *Tocqueville and the Frontiers of Democracy*, 111–132.

30. Chong, "Democracy in China," 85–89.

31. In addition to articles and other writings cited, sources for this chapter and for my discussion of various Chinese readings of Tocqueville include conversations with faculty and students, graduate and undergraduate, when I lectured on Tocqueville in Beijing, at Peking University and China University of Political Science and Law, and in Shanghai, at East China Normal University, in 2010. On the point of Tocqueville seen as a critic of liberal democracy, also see Tomoaki Ishii, "Comments," for a day-long conference on Tocqueville, organized by the School of Political Science at Waseda University, Tokyo, March 2, 2013.

32. Li Qiang, "Tocqueville and Reform in China," abstract prepared for a conference on Tocqueville, Waseda University School of Political Science, Tokyo, March 2, 2013.

33. Li Qiang, "History and Ideology: Teaching and Research on the History of Western Political Thought in China since the 1980s," *International Journal of Public Affairs* 3 (2007), 67–79.

34. For further discussion of parallels between the Chinese Revolution of 1911 and France in 1789, see William T. Rowe, *China's Last Empire:*

The Great Qing (Cambridge, MA: Harvard University Press, 2009), 253–283, especially 263 and 280.

35. Consult Li Hongtu, "Transformation des sociétés et naissance des révolutions: La mode de Tocqueville dans la Chine actuelle," *The Tocqueville Review/La revue Tocqueville* 36, no. 1 (2015), 215–233; Watanabe, "The French, Meiji and Chinese Revolutions"; and Chong, "Democracy in China," 81–82 and 103–107. Also see Li, "Tocqueville and Reform in China."

36. DIA (N) 89–90.

PART III **Genres and Themes**

9 "Ideas for the Intellect and Emotions for the Heart"

The Literary Dimensions of *Democracy in America*

Christine Dunn Henderson

That *Democracy in America* was originally intended as a joint work, to be coauthored by Alexis de Tocqueville and Gustave de Beaumont, is general knowledge among Tocqueville scholars, but the story – as well as how that original plan was abandoned and the two came to pen separate works – bears repeating. When the Frenchmen left for the United States in 1831, their official purpose was to study American prisons and penitentiary systems, in order to write a report for the French government. That coauthored report was produced and published, but before they had even boarded the ship in Le Havre that was bound for the United States, they had already begun to discuss another, grander project: a thorough examination of all aspects of American society, including its history, institutions, customs, and character. Letters home refer to this larger project as "a great work," a jointly written product of shared research and reflection "which should secure our reputation some day."[1] At some point during the eight months in America, however, the idea of a coauthored project was abandoned,[2] and in 1835 works by each of the two men were published: volume 1 of *Democracy in America* by Tocqueville and the novel *Marie, ou L'Esclavage aux Etats-Unis* by Beaumont. Both works explored American life in the Jacksonian era, but Tocqueville focused more on institutions in the 1835 *Democracy* whereas Beaumont's novel carried the subtitle *"tableau de moeurs américaines."*

Although published separately, their authors viewed the two projects as connected. Tocqueville's introduction to the 1835 *Democracy* sketches a broad plan for a second part (volume 2, published in 1840) to focus "on civil society, on habits, ideas and mores," but Tocqueville cautioned his reader that "my work will have become nearly useless" because "Someone else will soon show readers the principal features of the American character and, hiding the seriousness of the descriptions behind a light veil, will lend truth charms with which I would not be able to adorn it."[3] Beaumont's introduction also refers to the works as connected, noting "M. de Tocqueville has described the institutions; I myself have tried to sketch the customs."[4]

Built on shared research and reflection, and treating overlapping themes, the most striking difference between the two works was form, with Tocqueville writing a standard discourse and Beaumont penning a romantic novel. In Beaumont's words, although America is depicted by both, "We have not been constrained to use the same colors to depict it."[5] While Beaumont's comment is accurate in general terms, the idea of a categorical distinction of genres between the two works is misleading. Most obviously, it is misleading in the case of Beaumont's *Marie*, for the novel is accompanied by lengthy analytic appendices – exploring familiar Tocquevillian territory such as slavery, American women, and blue laws – that add another 25 percent to the text. This fictive-theoretical combination has led *Marie* to be described as a "mongrel production" or "half-breed."[6]

The idea of a sharp genre-based distinction is also problematic when thinking about *Democracy in America*. Certainly, most of *Democracy* feels like a standard "academic" discourse, but there are moments in which Tocqueville assumes a more expansive and even literary tone. This tonal shift is especially striking in the various mini-portraits, such as the risk-taking merchant of I.2.10 or the sad pioneer wife of II.3.10, with which Tocqueville's treatise is peppered. These sketches are distinct from the merely descriptive passages with which *Democracy in America* is also sprinkled, in that they have a theatrical or impressionistic quality, focusing momentarily on a scene or an individual in order to create a certain effect. This chapter will explore Tocqueville's usage of literary portraiture in *Democracy in America*, with an eye to discovering his purposes in deploying these images at strategic moments in his argument. After first making the case for at least a soft intentionality to Tocqueville's periodic shifts of literary tone, I will more closely examine the various vignettes, focusing both on content and on thematic connections between them. Next, I will discuss these portraits as a literary technique, particularly in terms of spectatorship and sympathetic engagement. Finally, I will offer some speculations about Tocqueville's purpose, in the context of both *Democracy in America* and the democratic age itself, for utilizing this technique.

Of all the plausible explanations that could be offered for the rarity with which Tocqueville utilizes vignettes, the notion that he was literarily disinclined is not one. Tocqueville had literary predispositions, and his American journey provided him with ample material. Tocqueville's best-known literary efforts both stem from the American journey: "A Fortnight in the Wilderness" and "A Journey to Lake Oneida," two extended pieces that chronicle the duo's travels beyond America's cities and towns and whose romantic descriptions of the American landscape and of native inhabitants reveal Chateaubriand's influence upon Tocqueville.

Olivier Zunz notes that at one point Tocqueville intended to publish "A Fortnight in the Wilderness" as an appendix to the 1840 volume of *Democracy in America*. Zunz astutely comments that, by reading these two pieces, "one discovers in these two texts that the austere classicism of much of *Democracy in America* was far from Tocqueville's only stylistic register."[7] In addition to the texts on Lake Oneida and the sojourn in the wilderness, Tocqueville's travel notebooks and correspondence with family and friends in France contain numerous sketches of the people and places he encountered. A letter to his mother, for example, offers a lengthy description of their visit to a Shaker community outside of Albany, while a letter to his sister-in-law contains an extended comparison between Native American women and Chateaubriand's tragic heroine, Atala.[8] To the Abbé Lesueur, Tocqueville details the tedium of a formal dinner the mayor of New York hosted for Tocqueville and Beaumont after they had toured the city's prisons. "They were all excruciatingly solemn," Tocqueville lamented, describing lackluster conversation, plates of cigars, and a dreaded custom of toasting honored guests with small glasses of wine, while also bemoaning to his tutor that dinner itself "was the art of cooking in its infancy: vegetables and fish before meat, and oysters for dessert – as much as to say complete barbarism."[9] Other writings, such as the long set piece on political activity in the United States,[10] dramatically depict a series of themes to which Tocqueville devoted both his analytic and his descriptive powers in *Democracy in America*, including the active interest in politics taken by all manner of citizens, the "irritating" American patriotism, and the constant activity within American life. Still other sketches offer more personalized versions of themes the published text of *Democracy in America* would discuss only theoretically: Tocqueville's notebooks, for example, recount specific examples of polling place harassment deterring free African Americans from voting in order to illustrate his point in volume 1 that majority opinion can oppress minorities even when the law appears to be neutral.[11]

While Tocqueville's general mode in composing *Democracy in America* was to distill the descriptions of his journals, notebooks, and letters into more analytic passages, there are occasional moments, such as his depiction of the pioneer cabin in I.3.9, in which the main text is more expansive and literary than its journal or notebook source material. Comments Tocqueville wrote to himself while drafting *Democracy in America* also reveal internal debates about whether to complement analytic remarks with examples to illustrate them more concretely.[12] Usually, the descriptive additions contemplated were derived from Tocqueville's experiences or from experiences related to him, but notes to himself such as "It would be good to insert here a small portrait in the manner of *Lettres persanes* or of *Les Caractères* of La Bruyère. But I lack the facts ... Perhaps the notes of Beaumont will provide them" indicate Tocqueville's self-consciousness about the rhetorical effect of such "small portraits" and his intentionality in utilizing them.[13]

A deeper exploration of *Democracy in America*'s literary portraits reveals that they form several thematic clusters that are related in both straightforward and complex ways. The first theme around which literary portraits cluster is migration and the settling of America. Surprisingly, Tocqueville offers no imaginative sketches of the Puritan settlement,[14] but the movement of peoples into the wilderness and the juxtaposition of civilized man with untamed surroundings repeatedly capture his imagination. Variant descriptions of the man "who plunges into the wilderness of the New World with the Bible, an ax and some newspapers," and who "fearlessly defies the Indian's arrow," crossing dangerous territory and (temporarily) subduing the wilderness by constructing an isolated cabin, figure several times in *Democracy in America*, evincing Tocqueville's fascination with the opposition between the untamed wilderness and its pioneer inhabitant, a man who "wears city clothing, speaks the language of the city, knows the past, is curious about the future, argues about the present" yet "who, for a time, submits to living in the woods."[15] In these descriptions of the physical transformation of the American frontier, Tocqueville casts the conversion of physical wilderness into farmland as a positive change. The spectacle of a people taming a wilderness, and through a tremendous exertion of will and effort, writing its own future on nature's raw material was something Tocqueville found both inspiring and moving enough that he cast it as one potential source of democratic poetry. Yet this vision of westward expansion was not an uncomplicated one, and as we will see in his depictions of Native Americans, his portraits of the costs of this expansion are more ambivalent.

The constant movement of westward migration is but one manifestation of the deep restlessness Tocqueville believed to be characteristic of democratic peoples. In its more positive aspect, this agitation fueled not simply the territorial expansion and settlement that Tocqueville sketched in several mini-portraits of pioneers. It also inspired the commercial risk-taking that impressed Tocqueville as a "kind of heroism" and that he personified by imagining the sea merchant who "leaves while the storm is still raging; night and day he spreads all of his sails to the wind," who chooses to drink brackish water and eat salted meat rather than lose time stopping for provisions, and who "has fought constantly against the sea, against disease, and against boredom" in order to arrive early in port and sell his goods at a higher price than his more cautious competitors.[16] Tocqueville believed that this same restlessness accounted for the noncommissioned officer's desire for war – foreign or revolutionary – as an outlet for his impatient ambitions.[17] In its more troubling aspect, however, democratic restlessness produces a "feverish ardor" for material goods and individuals who are "tormented constantly" with the fear of missing something, devoting themselves to the "useless pursuit of a complete felicity that always escapes" their grasp. Tocqueville describes the constant activity of such an individual, who painstakingly builds a house but sells it before completion, settles somewhere only to leave, attains peace in private life only to disrupt it by entering the whirl of politics, and finally, travels extensively "in order to distract himself better from his happiness."[18] While this dynamism was a feature of American democracy that Tocqueville clearly admired, he also thought it was one manifestation of the dangerous materialism and obsession with wealth that threatened to become the dominant passion in the democratic soul.[19] Tocqueville feared that a life of constant motion and the endless pursuit of material pleasures would fuel democratic man's psychic restlessness and that he would be consumed by "uneasiness, fears, and regrets," which would fill his soul with "a kind of constant trepidation that leads him to change plans and places at every moment."[20] If unchecked, this restless torment would produce the "singular melancholy" and "disgust for life" that he saw so often seizing Americans; in its darkest manifestation, this restlessness would result in insanity.[21]

In addition to the spectacle of frontier expansion and democratic movement more generally, Tocqueville was struck by the fact that the westward-pushing and wilderness-subduing pioneer was typically accompanied by a wife. Perhaps it is not surprising, then, that women are another frequent subject of Tocqueville's literary portraits.[22] The freedom of the young women who know "how to direct their thoughts and their words amid the pitfalls of a lively conversation" without comprising propriety is described as an example of a successful education, one that inculcates individual self-governance in an era when parental authority has weakened. In his several sketches of the American girl, Tocqueville also recognizes the costs to such an education, noting that it makes "honest and cold women rather than tender wives and amiable companions." Yet his portraits reveal his awareness that her "manly" judgment and strength are the sources of both the marital fidelity and the perseverance in the face of frontier-life trials that he found so impressive. As we might expect, then, American women also are sketched several times in their capacities as pioneer wives. His longest portrait of a frontier home again reveals his fascination with the juxtaposition between civilization and nature in the "barely extinguished taste for finery" still discernible in the Eastern-born wife's appearance, even amidst her rough surroundings, and Tocqueville's descriptions liken her moral strength to spiritual fortitude, an analogy heightened by the monastic combination of wasted body and nourished soul highlighted in his sketch. He writes, "but her delicate limbs seem weakened; her features are tired ... You see spread over her whole physiognomy a religious resignation, a profound peace of the passions." Tocqueville casts the pioneer wife as a sacrificial offering, who has willingly spent her own vigor in order to produce the energetic brood of children surrounding her.[23]

Tocqueville's preoccupation with American women may be partly because they embody a willing renunciation of freedom and partly because they are the sole spots of stillness in democracy's constant agitation, but his interest surely also reflects their role as

guardian of mores and the importance of mores in preserving democratic freedom. The draft opening to his discussion of the education of
young girls makes the political importance of female character clear:
"There have never been free societies without morals, and . . . it is the
woman who molds the morals. So everything that influences the
condition of women, their habits and their opinions, has great political interest in my view."[24] Given that religion is the other main
preserver of mores – as well as the force that "rules with sovereign
power over the soul of the woman"[25] – it is not surprising that religion
is the third major theme of Tocqueville's literary portraiture.

The aspects of religion that captured Tocqueville's literary
imagination mirror those that drew his philosophic attention: its
variety, piety, civic functions, and compatibility with liberty. One
of the longest vignettes from his journey notebooks, not published or
translated until 1975, focuses on American religiosity and the variety
of sects in the United States, vividly recreating Tocqueville's visits to
a Quaker meeting, a Methodist revivalist service, and a Shaker settlement. In a stirring passage, Tocqueville describes the congregation's
reactions to the preacher's revivalist evocations of the torments
awaiting sinners in the afterlife:

> Terror was painted in a thousand manners on all faces and
> repentance continually took the form of despair and furor. Some
> women were raising their children in their arms and letting out
> lamentable cries; others were beating their brows on the ground;
> some men were twisting themselves in their pews while accusing
> themselves of their sins in a loud voice or were rolling themselves
> in the dust. In proportion as the movements of the preacher became
> more rapid and his descriptions more vivid, the passions of the
> assembly seemed to grow and often, it was difficult not to believe
> oneself in one of the infernal habitations which the preacher was
> describing.[26]

These descriptions are not, however, incorporated into the relevant
chapters of the final text; in the published treatment of religion,

Tocqueville merely discusses the variety of sects analytically, and while his draft title for the chapter on American spiritualism included the phrase "bizarre sects," he shifted to a more neutral – and drier – tone during his revision process.[27]

Beyond religious diversity and general piety, however, Tocqueville was impressed by the success with which Americans combined religion and political liberty. Brief sketches offer American missionary zeal and the insistence upon sworn court testimony as examples of religion's peaceful and healthy coexistence with democratic politics.[28] While Tocqueville thought the key to maintaining religion's strength in a democratic age was the separation of religion from politics, he did not favor a diminished religion; the fact that he also saw religious belief as a crucial protection against the materialism that might endanger liberty further explains why he found so striking religion's robust role in American life. In a note appended to the analysis of the Anglo-American point of departure that details the Puritan-rooted blue laws still in existence, Tocqueville includes a two-paragraph portrait describing the piety with which Americans continue to observe the Sabbath, contrasting the "lethargic drowsiness" that begins on Saturday evening with the "feverish activity" that resumes on Monday.[29] This is echoed in published text with a more condensed portrait of Sabbath observance in II.2.15, offered as an illustration of how religious belief can counter democratic materialism. On the Sabbath, writes Tocqueville, "the places consecrated to commerce and industry are deserted; each citizen, surrounded by his children, goes to church" and returning home after having listened to exhortations to virtues seemingly opposed to the ones dominating his daily life, he turns to the Bible, where he finds escape and inspiration in the "sublime or touching portrayals of the grandeur and the goodness of the Creator, of the infinite magnificence of the works of God, of the elevated destiny reserved for men, of their duties and their rights to immortality."[30] Looking up to something greater than the soul was one method of combating the materialism and narrowing individualism to which Tocqueville believed democracy was only too prone.

If the westward expansion of America, its freedom guarded by female-instilled and religiously-inspired mores, captured some of Tocqueville's hopes for democratic society, the final theme of his literary portraiture – race – attests to his misgivings and fears. A striking tableau of a Negro woman, a Creek woman, and a pioneer child Tocqueville encountered encapsulates the key elements of the race situation he found in America, something he viewed as the greatest affront to the principles of liberty and to the mores of a democratic people. Tocqueville's portrait of the trio touches on the "barbaric luxury" and proud independence of the Creek woman, the servility and emulation of the Negro, and the "sentiment of superiority" and "condescension" discernible in the child's responses. For Tocqueville, the scene captured "a bond of affection uniting the oppressed to the oppressors here," as well as "the immense space put between them by prejudice and law."[31]

While Tocqueville's description of the effects of slavery contrasts the enterprising inhabitant of the right bank of the Ohio with his idle counterpart on the slaveholding left bank, and it is clear with which side of the river his sympathies lie, his tone remains that of a detached observer and analyst. His moral indignation is, however, unleashed in his portrait of the elderly white man who had fathered several children by one of his female slaves. Although the father had sought to emancipate his mulatto children for many years, he had been unsuccessful. Tocqueville movingly depicts the father, at the brink of death:

> He then imagined his sons led from market to market and passing from paternal authority to the rod of a stranger. These horrible images threw his dying imagination into delirium. I saw him prey to the agonies of despair, and I then understood how nature knew how to avenge the wounds done to it by laws.[32]

Here, Tocqueville acts as a moralist, clearly seeking to align his reader's sympathies against the slaveholder's various violations of justice and nature.

Several sketches of the Native Americans' plight are also featured in *Democracy in America*. Tocqueville describes Native Americans "prowling about like famished wolves" in former hunting grounds rendered barren by the westward expansion of whites. Hunger, he notes, is the formal cause that eventually chases them from their homeland, but he lays the true blame at the feet of the whites, who alternately employ deceit and veiled threats to persuade the Indians to "voluntarily" relocate. His most extended portrait of the Native Americans' situation depicts the forced relocation of the Choctaws that he observed from Memphis. Tocqueville sets the scene in the middle of an unusually harsh winter in which "the river swept along enormous chunks of ice." He describes a "solemn spectacle that will never leave my memory" of families silently walking, "dragging along behind them the wounded, the sick, the newborn children, the elderly about to die," carrying meager possessions and only a few weapons. As the families stoically boarded the ferry to cross the Mississippi, "their dogs still remained on the bank; when these animals saw finally that their masters were going away forever, they let out dreadful howls, and throwing themselves at the same time into the icy waters of the Mississippi, they swam after their masters."[33]

Tocqueville tells his reader that this moving scene – with its echoes of the story of Xanthippus' dog, from Plutarch's *Life of Themistocles*[34] – would remain etched in his memory forever. As he narrates the episode, he also confesses a surprising worry: a concern that his reader might think "that I am exaggerating" (or "inventing [v: creating]" in the manuscript notes) "descriptions at will here."[35] The very possibility that Tocqueville could embellish or perhaps even invent descriptions rather than merely report facts highlights the intentionality of *Democracy in America*'s literary touches, while also raising the question of Tocqueville's purposes in deploying this technique, which is the next question we will consider. Our inquiry into Tocqueville's purposes divides into the question of why these themes particularly moved him to literary flourish, and the question of what rhetorical purpose is served by his use of the portraiture technique. That latter query will be explored in the more general sense, by inquiring why any given author might supplement a treatise with literary elements, and also in the narrower sense, by asking how this technique fits into *Democracy in America* and Tocqueville's larger project.

In thinking about why Tocqueville chooses to insert literary portraits into his discussions of movement, women, religion, and race, it is tempting to say that he was surprised by the things he discovered about these themes and that the novelty of what he found inspired the vignettes. Yet that is an unsatisfactory response, for *Democracy in America* is full of things that surprised Tocqueville, and not all of those new discoveries were conveyed to the reader with literary touches. Contra suggestions by scholars such as François Furet that Tocqueville arrived in North America with the key elements of his book already in place and therefore found in American only evidence confirming his preexisting theses, both Tocqueville's journey notebooks and the published text itself bear witness to the fact that many things about America surprised the two Frenchmen.[36] Via attention to Tocqueville's language, James T. Schleifer has convincingly demonstrated that, although Tocqueville "reached the shores of America carrying much of the historical and intellectual baggage of 19th century France," the journey yielded new experiences that "provided him with unexpected lessons that deflected his thinking in significant ways."[37] Some of the things that struck Tocqueville – such as the constant agitation of society; the place and role of women; the fusion of liberty and religion; and the dismal situations of Native Americans and slaves – do figure among his vignettes; but the analyses of other things that particularly struck him, such as the role of the judiciary, the absence of political centralization, and the centrality of self-interest to American thinking, are not accompanied by literary sketches of those philosophic notions brought to life.[38]

That the literary portraits reflect things Tocqueville found "striking" is, in the end, unsatisfactory, and we must search for other explanations. One possibility is that these portraits reflect emotional peaks in Tocqueville's thought and that they are therefore expressions of things and ideas about which he was especially impassioned. Certainly, Tocqueville was impassioned about the injustices of slavery and of the tragic fate befalling Native Americans. Similarly, he hoped that religion, via female-instilled mores, could help preserve liberty in the democratic age. It is tempting to think that the literary portraits simply reflect Tocqueville's hopes and fears for American democracy, and while we have just seen that there is truth to this hypothesis, it is also an incomplete explanation. Were this the case, the chapters devoted to Tocqueville's other main hopes and fears would also contain literary portraits; yet the chapters on the omnipotence of the majority and the tyranny of the majority contain no literary sketches. Similarly, although the chapter on soft despotism has many rhetorical touches, it is devoid of literary portraits. Rather than sketching the eternal childhood of soft despotism's citizen, both the published text and the draft notes suggest that Tocqueville was content with standard prose to describe his great fears for the future of democracy.

Thus, although the idea that Tocqueville waxes literary when discussing his hopes and fears for American democracy certainly has some truth, it is also insufficient as an explanation. Another clue to Tocqueville's purposes in creating literary portraits, perhaps, lies in the portraits' placement within *Democracy*. Descriptive interludes are sprinkled throughout the work, but those in the first volume are primarily descriptions of the physical territory though which Tocqueville and Beaumont passed. Only in the final two chapters of the 1835 volume does Tocqueville begin to turn his descriptive powers toward individuals and to sketch vignettes. Worth keeping in mind is the fact that volume 1's final two chapters are in some sense a bridge to volume 2, for the final chapter of the 1835 book – "Some Considerations on the Present State and Probable Future of the Three Races that Inhabit the Territory of the United States" (I.2.10) – was not part of Tocqueville's original plan for the volume dedicated to institutions and was added at the last moment, after the rest of the

1835 *Democracy* had been drafted and reviewed by friends and family. "Of the Principal Causes That Tend to Maintain the Democratic Republic in the United States" (I.2.9) was originally supposed to be the volume's conclusion, and thus the fact that both chapter 9 and chapter 10 anticipate the focus on mores to come in the 1840 *Democracy* might be one explanation for Tocqueville's choice to deploy literary vignettes in these chapters, despite their absence in the rest of the 1835 volume.

Tocqueville himself was aware of a tonal difference between *Democracy in America*'s two volumes, worrying in an 1836 letter to a friend about the shift to a more abstract character in the 1840 volume: "In the first part of my work I confined myself to the laws, which were fixed and visible points. Here, it seems at times that I am up in the air, and that I am certainly going to tumble down."[39] Perhaps the different themes of the two volumes had stylistic implications, as Tocqueville's letter suggests, and the institutional focus lent itself to a more formal tone, while the interpersonal focus (mores) facilitated a more expansive and even literary style. Perhaps the shift in tone resulted from the greater distance between the voyage to America and the writing of *Democracy in America*'s second volume, so that factual reportage had given way to more general impressions, and the literary tableaux were an attempt to anchor a text he felt was slipping away.[40] Or, perhaps by the time Tocqueville was composing *Democracy in America*'s second volume, the publication of *Marie* had influenced his decisions about how to express himself when it came to discussing American mores.[41]

Attributing with certainty Tocqueville's reasons for employing this technique is virtually impossible – and, indeed, it seems entirely plausible that his motivations were a mixture of these speculations – but a long letter to Charles Stöffels opens still further possibilities, by drawing attention to the merits of literary portraiture as a genre and to its utility as a writerly technique. In that letter to Stöffels, Tocqueville focuses on literary style, observing ideas are better understood through examples. "The illustration," he writes, "is the most powerful means to put into relief the matter that you want to make known; but still it is necessary that . . . you understand clearly what type of analogy the author wants to establish."[42] A careful writer such as Tocqueville, then, would surely have been attentive to the harmonies – or disharmonies – between his theoretical statements and the examples he chose to accompany them.

Yet the tableaux Tocqueville uses are not simply examples designed to render concrete a theoretical point. Their quasi-theatrical character adds another dimension, much as the examples utilized by Adam Smith in *The Theory of Moral Sentiments* add a layer to the arguments he there crafts. Like Smith, for whom vignettes such as the poor man's son are interwoven with the main text and play a crucial part in the work's overall design, Tocqueville deploys dramatized examples to engage the reader as spectator, to activate imagination and sympathy, and to direct those imaginative-sympathetic energies in specific directions. In adopting this technique, Tocqueville asks the reader to participate in the scenes he sets, to move beyond the self, and to enter fully into the emotions experienced by the sketched characters. Henry Home, Lord Kames, describes the experience of readers of these types of fictions as being "transported," akin to "a kind of reveries," and "transformed" via what he calls "ideal presence" both into participants in the scenes before them and through a strong imaginative identification with the characters.[43] At a minimum, however, imaginative and sympathetic engagement requires a kind of psycho-emotional identification and connection with the subject of the vignette or example. As David Marshall observes, "This moment of simultaneous imagination, comparison, recognition, transport, and identification does not so much allow sympathy as constitute it."[44]

Tocqueville clearly possesses a similar awareness of the ability of literature and theater to transport his audience, and he shares with both Smith and Kames an interest in using sympathetic identification and imaginative transport to expand the observing spectator's horizons and to displace his or her prejudices. Writing about the theater of democratic peoples, Tocqueville echoes Kames in acknowledging that the immediacy of the spectator's sympathetic engagement with the drama masks the simultaneous transformation of judgment and taste. "The spectator of a dramatic work is in a way taken unprepared by the impression that is suggested to him. He ... does not think about fighting the new literary instincts that are beginning to emerge in him; he yields to them before knowing them."[45] Sympathy transports; judgment can temporally precede or follow sympathy's movement, and sympathy and judgment can be but are not necessarily congruent or in harmony.

Interestingly, science seems to confirm the idea that the engagement of our sympathetic capacities via reading narrative fiction is of the same strength and degree as that produced via interaction with real agents. It is argued that narrative fiction essentially "tricks" the mind's cognitive mechanisms into "'believing' that they are in the presence of agents endowed with a potential for a rich array of intentional stances," thus causing the cognitive mechanisms to respond as if they were experiencing real people.[46] Cognitive psychology and neuroscience further corroborate that imaginative engagement effectively develops empathy. Psychological studies have repeatedly attested to the fact that reading (or hearing) of suffering can provoke the same empathetic responses as actually witnessing it, though this ability, like our ability to attribute states of mind to others, "is intensely context dependent."[47] Neuroscience appears to confirm psychology's findings by showing that brain images reveal heightened activity of the subcortex's mirror neurons, both when the suffering is witnessed by the subject and when it is merely conveyed to the subject by words. Interestingly, there are some suggestions that it might be possible to further classify mirror neuron activity into that representing immediate responses (or a kind of spontaneous sympathy) and that resulting from considered reflection (or a judgment-grounded sympathy).[48]

This combination of spontaneous and considered sympathy is suggestive of the interplay between sympathy and judgment resulting from the combination of theory and theater in texts such as *Democracy in America* and *The Theory of Moral Sentiments*. Writing about Smith's vignettes, Charles Griswold describes them as exercises in the formation of moral judgment: "attempts to get us to 'see' things in a certain light rather than simply to argue us into accepting a philosophical position."[49] Via his own theatrical or literary examples, Tocqueville, too, is attempting to develop a certain type of moral judgment or to – as he characterizes his activity in *Democracy in America*'s introduction – "instruct democracy."[50] For writers working in this vein, the success of the example lies in the reader perceiving what the author intended and judging "rightly," or via a properly cultivated imaginative engagement with the subject of the example. To judge rightly, the mind must be tutored, but so must the moral imagination; and while theory has its own strengths for the honing of the mind, different tools might be required for the shaping of the moral imagination. The interplay of philosophic and theatrical voices provided by dotting the main text with dramatized examples serves this very purpose, with literary episodes developing imaginative capacity by allowing us to "try on" different situations and mental states, which are then responded to as if they were real situations. Joseph Addison calls this combination of imaginative and intellectual engagement a double gratification for the reader and cites it as the pinnacle of literary achievement.[51]

Musing to himself as he drafted the 1840 volume, Tocqueville suggests precisely this type of link between his examples and the cultivation of judgment. He writes, "If I do not make the reader see America clearly, he will perhaps be invincibly opposed to my ideas, because seen in a haze and considered roughly, America seems in fact to provide an opposite view."[52] Via his examples, Tocqueville seeks to shape his readers' judgment and to make them see America correctly: to understand that the kinds of mores instilled by religion and protected by women are the source – more than institutions or laws – of democratic freedom; that the spectacle of democracy's incessant movement is both heroic and imperiling; and that the treatment of

Native Americans and the existence of slavery are America's two greatest offenses against the principles of equality and, thus, two threats unique to the country's future. His intention is not simply to make his readers understand and thus to judge these matters; he seeks also to reinforce their understanding and judgment with an emotional endorsement.

This alignment of sympathy and judgment is key to what Tocqueville is attempting to create or develop via *Democracy in America*'s literary tableaux. As we have seen, these vignette interludes reflect something about Tocqueville's hopes and fears for democratic freedom both in America and beyond. Tocqueville uses them as a supplement to the arguments of the nonliterary main text, looking to the combination of philosophic and theatrical elements as a way to change thinking and, by bringing emotional responses into alignment with that new thinking, to deepen his readers' commitment to the ideas of which *Democracy in America* attempts to persuade them. In the end, Tocqueville wants to win hearts and minds. He wants to convince French skeptics that it is possible to have democracy and liberty, while also making his readers fear democracy's dangers and love both the safeguards of democratic freedom and potential seeds of greatness existing within democracy. The main text of *Democracy in America* is primarily directed to minds, advancing the theoretical case Tocqueville wishes to prove, while the literary tableaux take aim at the heart, orienting the reader's hopes, fears, and passions within the democratic context. In this context, Sheldon Wolin's description of Tocqueville as a "visual theorist" is apt; he deploys images "like the painter who, to attract the attention of the viewer and to entice him into the painter's way of seeing things, tries to establish his canvas as a field or setting against which selected objects are to be placed in a certain 'light'."[53]

This dual strategy of rational and emotional appeal is not an uncommon persuasion tactic, but it might be one that is particularly appropriate within the landscape *Democracy in America* describes. Tocqueville readily concedes that the daily life of the democratic man does not provide ideal material for poetry. "You cannot imagine anything so small, so colorless, so full of miserable interests, so anti-poetical, in a word, as the life of a man in the United States," he asserts.[54] In sketching his tableaux, however, Tocqueville is not exactly creating poetry. His technique of highlighting philosophical teaching with vivid examples is certainly an effective counter to what he sees as Enlightenment philosophy's unfortunate tendency to over-generalization, but as we have seen, the tableaux are also modes of persuading the reader in extra-rational ways via sympathetic engagement and imaginative identification. As such, they reveal something about Tocqueville's audience. Various statements such as "[w]hile I had my eyes fixed on America, I thought about Europe ... about this immense social revolution that is coming to completion among us" and "I did not write a page [of *Democracy in America*] without thinking of her [France] and without always having her, so to speak, before my eyes" attest to the fact that *Democracy in America* was primarily composed for a French audience.[55] From Tocqueville's intellectual content, we can learn what Tocqueville wanted to teach that French audience. Among the lessons he wished to impart was his conviction that the democratic society he believed to be an inevitable future could also remain a free one. The American case study was not a blueprint, but it offered an example that could be adapted and modified, according to the specific needs of the French context. This is not a new or controversial interpretation.

What is new, however, is something we discover by thinking about this technique of supplementing *Democracy in America*'s analytic arguments with literary vignettes. As we have just seen, these vignettes are Tocqueville's efforts to enlist emotional alliance by engaging his readers' sympathies, and sympathetic engagement requires identification between subject and object. Although Tocqueville is writing for a France that is not yet entirely demo-cratic, he is also writing to one that is in the process of transitioning to democracy and, thus, is able to identify and sympathize with the democratic tableaux he paints. To borrow a phrase, the France for which Tocqueville writes is a France situated between two worlds, and *Democracy in America*'s tactic of mobilizing sympathy via its vignettes allows us to glimpse France's movement along that democratic path. In describing the gentling of mores that accompanies the spread of equality, Tocqueville also addresses the expansion of sympathy that occurs in democratic society. He explains, "each one of them can judge in a moment the sensations of all the others ... So there is no misery he cannot easily imagine and whose extent is not revealed to him by a secret instinct. Whether it concerns strangers or enemies, imagination immediately puts him in their place."[56] That Tocqueville is so effectively able to use sketched figures – pioneers, Native Americans, frontier families – foreign to the experiences of his French readers in order to move the sympathies of those readers is itself an indication of how expanded those sympathies had become, how able his readers had become to see shared humanity in distant peoples, and how far along the democratic spectrum France had moved. In developing his French readers' sympathetic skills via engagement with distant figures, Tocqueville's vignettes also encourage equality's further expansion, insofar as the internalization of equality is a precondition for moral autonomy and self-government.[57]

Moreover, Tocqueville's deployment of these literary tableaux enables us to see that his style is not, as some critics have argued, entirely aristocratic. Nor, however, is his style simply democratic.[58] Rather, the vignettes are evidence that Tocqueville employed a mixed technique. On the one hand, his approach is democratic in its creation and alignment of sympathies with certain general ideas. This is consistent with his understandings of democratic philosophy as based on general ideas and democratic history as the story of abstract forces at work. On the other hand, Tocqueville's vignette technique brings him closer to aristocratic history and to nondemocratic philosophy in its focus on particular individuals, with the vignettes also working to attach his readers to particulars, and thus to counter the democratic tendency to generalize.[59] In the end, then,

THE LITERARY DIMENSIONS OF DEMOCRACY IN AMERICA 273

Tocqueville's own mixed style expresses his uneasy relationship to the democracy he sees as inevitable and more just but also as a possible threat to human individuality and greatness.

NOTES

1. Beaumont to his brother, Jules, New York, May 26, 1831. Quoted in James T. Schleifer, *The Making of Tocqueville's "Democracy in America,"* 2nd ed. (Indianapolis: Liberty Fund, 2000), 4.

2. By November of 1832, letters home had begun to refer to "our works." Schleifer, *Making*, 4n6.

3. DIA (N), 29. A similar claim is made in a note Tocqueville included with the final chapter of the 1835 volume: "In a book that I spoke about already at the beginning of this work, and that is now on the verge of appearing, M. Gustave de Beaumont, my traveling companion, has as his principal object to make the position of Negroes among the white population of the United States known in France. M. de Beaumont has thoroughly treated a question that my subject has only allowed me to touch upon ... The work of M. de Beaumont should be read by those who want to understand to what excesses of tyranny men are pushed little by little once they have begun to go beyond nature and humanity." DIA (N), 548n30.

4. Gustave de Beaumont, *Marie*, trans. Barbara Chapman (Baltimore, MD: Johns Hopkins University Press, 1999), 7.

5. Beaumont, *Marie*.

6. Diana J. Schaub, "Perspectives on Slavery: Beaumont's *Marie* and Tocqueville's *Democracy in America*," *Legal Studies Forum* 22, no. 4 (1998), 608–609.

7. Alexis de Tocqueville and Gustave de Beaumont, *Alexis de Tocqueville and Gustave de Beaumont in America: Their Friendship and Their Travels*, ed. Olivier Zunz (Charlottesville: University of Virginia Press, 2010), 395.

8. Tocqueville to his mother, July 17, 1831, in Alexis de Tocqueville, *Letters from America*, ed. and trans. Frederick Brown (New Haven, CT: Yale University Press, 2010), 123–124. Letter of Tocqueville to his sister-in-law Émilie, September 7, 1831, in Tocqueville and Beaumont, *Alexis de Tocqueville and Gustave de Beaumont in America*, 125.

9. Tocqueville to the Abbé Lesueur, May 28, 1831, in Tocqueville, *Letters*, 45.

10. DIA (N), 1365–1372. Entitled "Political Activity in America," this piece appears as appendix 4 of the Nolla edition of *Democracy in America*, but it was not published with earlier editions (French or translated) of *Democracy in America*. Moreover, it was not translated into English until James T. Schleifer published it in "Alexis de Tocqueville Describes the American Character: Two Previously Unpublished Portraits," *South Atlantic Quarterly* 74, no. 2 (1975), 244–258.

11. See, for example, the account of Tocqueville's notebook entries pertaining to the subtleties of the tyranny of the majority in Schleifer, *Making*, 243–245. Compare with I.2.7–8 in *DIA*.

12. For example, Tocqueville's notes to himself while composing *Democracy in America*, DIA (N), 1007–1008.

13. DIA (N), 1072–1073, note c. Schleifer also comments upon this note, but he associates it with a different passage of the published text; see Schleifer, *Making*, 41.

14. While his treatment of Puritan laws is lengthy, it is also – perhaps fittingly – sparse in ornamentation.

15. DIA (N), 461, 492. See also 460, 462, 464, 491, 1050, as well as Tocqueville's extended description in his published note to that final passage; DIA (N), 1287–1290.

16. DIA (N), 641.

17. DIA (N), 1168; see both the main text and note j, citing the manuscript draft, in which Tocqueville draws the connection that "The Americans apply to commerce the same principles and the same manner that Bonaparte applied to war."

18. DIA (N), 943–944. See, for example, Peter Augustine Lawler 's *The Restless Mind: Alexis de Tocqueville on the Origin and Perpetuation of Human Liberty* (Lanham, MD: Rowman & Littlefield, 1993), or Pierre Manent 's *Tocqueville and the Nature of Democracy* (Lanham, MD: Rowman & Littlefield, 1996).

19. In II.2.10, Tocqueville expresses his concern that the desire for material gain will "come to stand between the soul and God"; DIA (N), 937.

20. DIA (N), 944–945.

21. DIA (N), 947.

22. Tocqueville's general interest in American women is, of course, another explanation.

23. DIA (N), 1043, 1045, 1289, 1290.

24. DIA (N), 1041, note c.

25. DIA (N), 473.

26. DIA (N), 1360. Entitled "Sects in America," this piece appears as appendix 3 of the Nolla edition of *Democracy in America*, but it was not published with earlier editions (French or translated) of *Democracy in America*. Like "Political Activity in America," this fragment was first published by James T. Schleifer in 1975 (see Note 10, in this chapter). In the article containing the original translations, Schleifer also suggests that Tocqueville probably did not actually witness a Methodist service and that the passage just quoted might have been based on a secondhand description.

27. Perhaps because of his uncertainty about including the chapter at all; DIA (N), 939, note c.

28. DIA (N), 476. Although Tocqueville does not seem to have picked up on it, the insistence upon sworn testimony could also be read as an example of the tyranny of the majority.

29. DIA (N), 665.

30. DIA (N), 955. Cf. DIA (N), 518–520.

31. DIA (N), 521.

32. DIA (N), 580. Interestingly, there is no clear source for this vignette in Tocqueville's notes.

33. DIA (N), 527.

34. Plutarch say that, "it is reported that Xanthippus, the father of Pericles, had a dog that would not endure to stay behind, but leaped into the sea, and swam along by the galley's side till he came to the island of Salamis, where he fainted away and died." Plutarch, "Life of Themistocles," in *Plutarch's Lives, The Translation Called Dryden's*, vol. 1, ed. and rev. A. H. Clough (Boston: Little, Brown and Company, 1906), 243. I am grateful to Eleanor Schneider for drawing my attention to the allusion.

35. DIA (N), 526.

36. François Furet, "Naissance d'un paradigme: Tocqueville et le voyage en Amérique (1825–1831)," *Annales. Économies, Sociétés, Civilisations* 39, no. 2 (1984), 225–239. Others, such as Jaume and Craiutu, have emphasized Tocqueville's indebtedness to French thinkers of his own or previous generations, downplaying *Democracy in America*'s originality. See Lucien Jaume *Tocqueville: The Aristocratic Sources of Liberty*, trans. Arthur Goldhammer (Princeton: Princeton University Press, 2013);

Aurelian Craiutu, "Tocqueville and the Political Thought of the French Doctrinaires: Guizot, Royer-Collard, Rémusat," *History of Political Thought* 20, no. 3 (1999), 456–493.

37. James T. Schleifer, "Tocqueville's Journey Revisited: What Was Striking and New in America," *The Tocqueville Review/La revue Tocqueville* 37, no. 2 (2006), 404.

38. While it is tempting to say that topics such as the judiciary simply do not lend themselves to these types of literary sketches, Tocqueville's own *Memoir on Pauperism* features a lengthy and moving account of testimony before the bench. See Alexis de Tocqueville, *Memoirs on Pauperism and Other Writings*, ed. and trans. Christine Dunn Henderson (Notre Dame: University of Notre Dame Press, 2021), 22–24.

39. Tocqueville to Louis Bouchitté, May 26, 1836; quoted in Schleifer, *Making*, 30.

40. See Schleifer, *Making*, 345 for a variant of this hypothesis.

41. For an overview of the debate about whether *Democracy in America* is "one part or two," see Seymour Drescher, "More than America: Comparison and Synthesis in *Democracy in America*," in *Reconsidering Tocqueville's "Democracy in America*," ed. Abraham S. Eisenstadt (New Brunswick, NJ: Rutgers University Press, 1988), 77–93, though this major issue of scholarly debate is one of whether

the two halves of *Democracy in America* are philosophically – as opposed to stylistically – consistent. On the question of stylistic unity, Schleifer suggests that the 1840 text is *less* literary out of

deference to Beaumont (see Schleifer, "Character," 247), but as we have seen this is clearly not the case, and literary elements are as – if not more – conspicuous in the 1840 volume.

42. Letter of July 31, 1834, in DIA (N), 810–811, note r.

43. Henry Home, Lord Kames, *Elements of Criticism*, vol. 1, ed. Peter Jones (Indianapolis: Liberty Fund, 2005), 66–77.

44. David Marshall, *The Surprising Effects of Sympathy: Marivaux, Diderot, Rousseau, and Mary Shelley* (Chicago: University of Chicago Press, 1988), 149. Marshall is speaking of Rousseau.

45. DIA (N), 846.

46. Lisa Zunshine, *Why We Read Fiction: Theory of Mind and the Novel* (Columbus: Ohio State University Press, 2006), 9. Zunshine also notes

that cognitive psychology findings suggest that imaginative play causes children's cognitive mechanisms to respond in the same way.

47. Zunshine, *Fiction*, 8.

48. Suzanne Keen, *Empathy and the Novel* (Oxford: Oxford University Press, 2007), especially chap. 2.

49. Charles L. Griswold, Jr., *Adam Smith and the Virtues of Enlightenment* (Cambridge: Cambridge University Press, 1999), 61.

50. DIA (N), 16.

51. Joseph Addison, "Essay No. 421," in Donald F. Bond, ed., *The Spectator* (Oxford: Clarendon Press, 1987).

52. DIA (N), 1207n2.

53. Sheldon S. Wolin, *Tocqueville between Two Worlds: The Making of a Political and Theoretical Life* (Princeton: Princeton University Press, 2001), 140. Gérard Gengembre, however, takes the opposite stance, arguing that Tocqueville describes "sans jugement de valeur." See Gengembre, "De la littérature en Amérique, ou De Mme de Staël à Tocqueville," in Françoise Mélonio and José-Luis Diaz, eds., *Tocqueville et la littérature* (Paris: Presses de l'Universite Paris-Sorbonne, 2005), 73.

54. DIA (N), 837.

55. DIA (N), 28 note o, and letter to Louis de Kergorlay of October 18, 1847, in Alexis de Tocqueville, *Tocqueville on America after 1840: Letters and Other Writings*, ed. and trans. Aurelian Craiutu and Jeremy Jennings (Cambridge: Cambridge University Press, 2009), 321.

56. DIA (N), 853–855, 993.

57. Lynn Hunt, *Inventing Human Rights: A History* (New York: W.W. Norton & Company, 2007).

58. For an interpretation of Tocqueville's writing – and audience – as primarily aristocratic, see M. Pierre Campion, "Tocqueville écrivain: Le style dans *De la Démocratie en Amérique*," *Littérature* no. 136 (2004), 3–21. On democratic elements to Tocqueville's style, see also Claude Millet's "Le Détail et le Général dans la *Démocratie en Amérique*," in Mélonio and Diaz *Tocqueville et la littérature*, 147–165.

59. DIA (N), 853–858, 1272.

10 Tocquevillean Association and the Market

Rachael K. Behr and Virgil Henry Storr

INTRODUCTION

In *Democracy in America*, Alexis de Tocqueville highlighted the facility that Americans have with the art of association as well as how important associational life is within American communities. Tocqueville confessed to admiring "the infinite art with which the inhabitants of the United States succeeded in setting a common goal for the efforts of a great number of men, and in making them march freely toward it."[1] It is through associations that Americans, according to Tocqueville, undertook both small and grand projects. It is through associations that Americans did everything from celebrating a holiday to building a church or prison. Tocqueville also acknowledged the industriousness of Americans. As Tocqueville remarked, "no people on earth ... has made as rapid progress as the Americans in commerce and industry. They form today the second maritime nation of the world; and, although their manufacturing has to struggle against almost insurmountable natural obstacles, it does not fail to make new gains every day."[2] There is a sense in which, however, this observation by Tocqueville presents us with a puzzle: How has America developed both a robust civil society and a vibrant commercial society when markets and community are supposedly at odds with one another?

Currently, a large debate exists about the market and whether it undermines or promotes community.[3] Stephen Gudeman, for instance, has posited that society consists of two separate spheres – the market and the community – that operate on two different logics – anonymous exchange in the market and mutuality in community – and that are more likely to be substitutes for one another than complements.[4] As the market expands and people begin to focus more and more on profits, the space of community shrinks and is eventually overrun by the space of the market. Elizabeth Anderson argues in much the same vein. While she concedes that markets have liberated many societies subject to tyrannical regimes and rigid class structures, she nonetheless alleges that markets should be limited lest they spread beyond the job of liberating the poor and instead lead to the commodification of higher goods (such as relationships and communities). This commodification of higher goods is, she claims, inevitable in a commercialized society.[5] John Gray echoes these concerns. Adopting free market institutions, Gray argues, led to "a fracturing of communities, and a depletion of ethos and trust within institutions, which muted or thwarted the economic renewal which free markets were supposed to generate."[6] Likewise, Jonathan Sacks writes that "the market . . . has subverted other institutions – families, communities, [and] the bonds that link members of a society to a common fate."[7] The growth of markets, according to these scholars, has meant a decline in community.

Robert Putman's celebrated work *Bowling Alone: The Collapse and Revival of American Community* is probably the most popular criticism of how the growth of markets undermines community. Putnam argues that commercial society – with its overworked populace and suburban sprawl – has corroded social bonds and trust. Specifically, Putnam emphasizes that the rise of technology that results from growing markets leads to a decline of social capital. This manifests itself in a precipitous decline in participation in social gatherings, as evidenced by his poignant example of waning participation in bowling leagues. Putnam suggests that larger markets – particularly the technological innovations they bring with them – dehumanize and individualize communities, corroding the Tocquevillean idea that civic engagement is indispensable for a healthy democracy.[8]

This raises an important empirical question, however – namely, do markets really undermine communities, as these and other critics have alleged? After all, there have been several scholars who have argued the opposite view, that is, that markets promote rather than undermine community. These range from the classic works of Adam Smith and Montesquieu to more recent efforts by Deirdre McCloskey.[9] While it seems clear that Tocqueville regarded commercial and civil society, and thus markets and community, as being at least potentially compatible with one another in America – given his acknowledgment of the American penchants for both industry and association – he is mostly silent on the precise relationship between markets and community. Although Tocqueville did spend some time describing how Americans become adept at the art and science of association, and thereby cultivate a habit of association, only once in those discussions did he mention associational life as being strengthened by commercial enterprises, and there only in passing, when he indicates that "commercial and industrial associations" are associations to which almost everyone belongs.[10]

This chapter argues that commercial life is an important space for developing and cultivating the Tocquevillean habits of association; indeed, it may be necessary for such development. Specifically, this chapter adds to the discussion by exploring how markets, especially within advanced commercial societies, facilitate and support associational life as a consequence of the division of labor, incentives to be moral in market settings, and ease of communication and heightened access to information. These aspects of markets offer market participants greater opportunities to nurture and grow Tocquevillean habits of association. We begin with a discussion of Tocquevillean association in the section "The Importance of Association in Civil Life." In the section "Political Association, Civil Association, and the Doctrine of Self-Interest Rightly Understood," we then describe how Tocqueville believes the habit of association is cultivated and the art of association is developed. In the section "Commercial Life As Supportive of Association," we argue that markets promote and strengthen the Tocquevillean art of association through the division of labor, through the values promoted in the market, and through the heightened ease of communication and access to information that markets bring about. The final section serves as a concluding reflection.

THE IMPORTANCE OF ASSOCIATION IN CIVIL LIFE

Tocqueville began his discussion of association by first addressing equality. Generally speaking, Tocqueville explained, equality "provides a multitude of small enjoyments to each man every day" thus causing strong attachments of the people to the value of equality.[11] However, with equality comes "isolat[ion] . . . from the mass of his fellows" and the tendency "to withdraw to the side with his family and his friends, so that . . . he willingly abandons the larger society to itself."[12] Democracy allows for greater equality, but with this democratic equality comes what Tocqueville calls "individualism," where people begin to turn inward and away from their fellow citizens: "Individualism is of democratic origin, and it threatens to develop as conditions become equal."[13] This phenomenon is rooted in democracy specifically because, as Tocqueville noted, democracy lacks the aristocratic institutions that bind "each man tightly to several of his fellow citizens."[14] Consequently, in democracy, "devotion toward one man becomes more rare."[15] Tocqueville went on to describe how such individualism dries up the wellsprings of virtue, because each man has the tendency to withdraw into himself rather than to participate in community. This of course can have disastrous consequences, which Tocqueville goes on to discuss at length.

While democracy allows for an extension of our relationships beyond close familial ties, it also requires less of each individual citizen, putting the impetus for association on the individual, rather than aristocratic conventions bonding people together. Association, then, is critically important as a bulwark against the negative consequences of individualism. "It is clear," Tocqueville explained, "that if each citizen, as he becomes individually weaker and consequently more incapable in isolation of preserving his freedom, does not learn the art of uniting with those like him to defend it, tyranny will necessarily grow with equality."[16] That is, tyranny encroaches and begins to reign wherever civil associations fade or become altogether absent.

America, for Tocqueville then, is something of a wonder. Typically, democratic government leads to a rise of individualism with very little counterbalance from the spirit of association. Yet America in Tocqueville's eyes was an exception. For the people had somehow, almost miraculously, been able to develop bonds with each other so as to deter individualism, thus preventing an ensuing encroachment of tyranny. "Everywhere that ... you see in France the government, and in England, a great lord," Tocqueville observed, "count on seeing in the United States, an association."[17] These associations are nearly infinite because, as Tocqueville noted, "Americans of all ages, all conditions, all minds *constantly unite.*"[18] These associations range anywhere from "religious, moral, serious ones, useless ones, very general and very particular ones, immense and very small ones ... to celebrate holidays, establish seminaries, build inns, erect churches, distribute books, send missionaries ... create hospitals, prisons, schools."[19]

Tocqueville noticed such strong and ever-present associations in America more so than in aristocratic countries, particularly his native France. Tocqueville also noted that the penchant for association that he found in America was much greater than he observed in England.[20] Although many American customs and much of their laws are inherited from England, the English do not make "such constant and skillful use of association" as Americans.[21] Also, "it is clear that the [English] consider association as a powerful means of action, but the [Americans] seem to see it as the only means they have to act."[22] That said, the American penchant for association was at least partially inherited from the English, with English emigrants to America bringing with them township government and the practice with association that occurs within that political form.[23]

Paradoxically, Tocqueville believed that this very same democratic equality, which might otherwise lead to great disaster, nonetheless gives rise to the spirit of association. The American people recognized their own frailty after the Revolution, before and during which they witnessed great tyranny. In democratic nations where "all citizens are *independent and weak*; they can hardly do anything by themselves, and no one among them can compel his fellows to lend him their help."[24] Consequently, Tocqueville detailed that they will "all fall into impotence if they do not learn to help each other freely."[25] Without associating, "man will be less and less able to produce by himself alone the things most common and most necessary to his life."[26] As Americans were acutely aware of what inequality could lead to, they preferred weakly associating out of choice rather than strongly associating out of force. They recognized that their associations must "be very numerous" in order that they have "some power" or ability to bind citizens together.[27] In other words, it is the culmination of many weak and equal actors that brings forth a forceful and capable association. Rather than rule by aristocracy, there can be rule through many, equal citizens uniting.

In aristocracies, one member can "adopt a new idea or conceive of a new sentiment" and he can "introduce [it] easily into the mind or heart of those who surround" him, since he holds some power.[28] This develops naturally because "[s]entiments and ideas are renewed, the heart grows larger and the human mind develops only by the reciprocal action of men on each other."[29] Yet "this action is almost nil in democratic countries," where there exists a loose connection rather than tight bonds between people. Instead, associations "must be created there artificially ... And this is what associations alone are able to do."[30] Through democratic associations, not only can citizens secure themselves from the tyranny with which they are all too familiar but they can also provide for their own well-being.

To summarize, Tocqueville argues that democracy brings with it equality and, with that, individualism; but the very source of individualism, this equality, also potentially opens the door to its solution. If the people use their freedom to gather in civil associations rather than pulling away from each other, they can combat individualism and the tyranny that might follow.

POLITICAL ASSOCIATION, CIVIL ASSOCIATION, AND THE DOCTRINE OF SELF-INTEREST RIGHTLY UNDERSTOOD

Although much of Tocqueville's discussion of associations focuses on the uses that Americans make of associations, he does spend some time describing how it is that Americans become adept at the art of association and how they cultivate this habit of association in the first place. One space where the art of association is cultivated is within political association. According to Tocqueville, while civil associations are where the heart of association beats, "political association develops and singularly perfects civil association."[31] Indeed, Tocqueville explained that there is a "natural and perhaps necessary relationship between the two types of association."[32] This necessary link between the two is the fact that one cannot exist without the other. In other words, while it is not political association that does the heavy lifting in terms of actually practicing the art of association, it begins the teaching of it or, in Tocqueville's words, gives "the taste for the habit of association."[33] The political realm is where each citizen learns *how* to associate, even though it is not where most of the important association takes place. Tocqueville thus believes that it would be harmful to destroy political association, for it would leave civil association all but absent. According to Tocqueville, "where political association is forbidden, civil association is rare."[34] In fact,

> [w]hen citizens have the ability and the habit of associating for all things, they will associate as readily for small ones as for great ones. But if they can associate only for small ones, they will not even find the desire and the capacity to do so. In vain will you allow them complete liberty to take charge of their business together; they will

only nonchalantly use the rights that you grant them; and after you have exhausted yourself with efforts to turn them away from the forbidden associations, you will be surprised at your inability to persuade them to form the permitted ones.[35]

Consequently, doing away with political associations leaves civil associations all but absent because citizens have not formed the initial taste for and practice of association.

Moreover, civil associations require an individual to bear full risk for his actions, whereas political associations do not. Citizens, Tocqueville claims, "hesitate less to take part in political associations ... because in them they are not risking their money."[36] In civil associations, however, one must risk "a portion of [his] patrimony; it is so for all industrial and commercial companies."[37] So, when people are "still little versed in the art of associating and they are ignorant of the principal rules, they fear, while associating for the first time in [a civil] way, paying dearly for their experience."[38] In other words, political associations provide risk-free training grounds for the art of association, while civil associations are where the continual practice and perfection of such associations occur over time, with individuals bearing the majority of the risk.

In Tocqueville's rendering, then, political associations are as important as civil ones because they allow each individual to have a taste of such association. Without them, individuals would not have the taste that motivates them to practice and perfect civil association; it is indeed "a chimera to believe that the spirit of association, repressed at one point, will allow itself to develop with the same vigor at all others."[39]

To be sure, association must be exercised regularly, like a muscle, in order for citizens to "combat individualism,"[40] which is the main problem facing democratic countries. To make his point, Tocqueville employed the doctrine of self-interest, which broadly assumes that each individual acts out of what is best for himself, which also happens to accord with other's actions, making not only himself but also others around him better-off. Adam Smith used this same argument in his famous explanation of the invisible hand. "It is not from the benevolence of the butcher, the brewer, or the baker that we expect our dinner," argued Smith, "but from their regard to their own interest."[41] In other words, Tocqueville, Smith, and of course many others such as Montaigne, whom Tocqueville referenced, all argued that there is some process by which individuals act out of their own best interests which in turn benefits the community at large.[42]

Like Smith's variant of self-interest, the Tocquevillean notion of self-interest focuses on the necessity of feedback from others within the community. Tocqueville began his discussion of self-interest and the art of association with a discussion of virtue. Virtue in the United States, he argued, is very different from virtue in Europe. For example, Tocqueville observed that "[i]n the United States it is almost never said that virtue is beautiful. They maintain that it is *useful* and they prove it every day."[43] Indeed, practicing virtue because it is beautiful may not be the point at all. Instead, "one must say boldly that such sacrifices are as necessary to the one who imposes them on himself as to the one who profits from them."[44]

Self-interest, properly conceived, can thus serve as a key driver toward associational life. Tocqueville observed that Americans "do not deny that each man may follow his interest," but instead Americans must "do their best to prove that the interest of each is to be *honest*."[45] Tocqueville saw in the Americans "how enlightened love of themselves leads them constantly to help each other."[46] Admittedly, pursuing self-interest rightly understood "does not produce great devotions" and "it cannot make a man virtuous."[47] Instead, the doctrine of self-interest rightly understood "suggests small sacrifices every day ... but it forms a multitude of steady, temperate, moderate, farsighted citizens who have self-control; and, if it does not lead directly to virtue by will, it imperceptibly draws closer to virtue by habits."[48] Indeed, self-interest rightly understood means that "[e]ach American knows how to sacrifice a portion of his particular interests in order to save the rest."[49] What Tocqueville meant was that everyone pursuing self-interest, properly understood, does not lead to utter selfishness where each man simply rises or falls on his own, as it were. Instead, it brings everyone together in some sort of spontaneous association that provides a flourishing community.

COMMERCIAL LIFE AS SUPPORTIVE OF ASSOCIATION

As noted, Tocqueville's discussion of how Americans cultivate the habit of association focused on political association as an arena where individuals develop a taste for association; civil society as a space where they cultivate the more general habit of association; and self-interest rightly understood as what teaches them the value of association. He was, however, mostly silent on how commercial life might support or undermine associational life.

We argue that markets, and commercial life in general, can provide training grounds for learning and practicing the art of association. We do so on three fronts that are broadly consistent with at least some of Tocqueville's arguments in *Democracy*. First, markets allow for a more extensive division of labor, meaning more people cooperate on any given day to produce goods and services in commercial societies than noncommercial societies. Second, the values that are rewarded in markets are typically those useful for association, such as hard work, honesty, and cosmopolitanism. Third, markets bring about ease of communication and access to information through technological advances. While Tocqueville discusses the need for political and civil engagement and association, arguably these can and do take place within markets and with the aid of markets. Indeed, the market is not just a place of exchange; it is also a space where people interact, meet, form relationships, and form associations.[50] Moreover, markets do not encourage individualism of the kind Tocqueville warned about, as critics have alleged, but instead they foster self-interest rightly understood of the sort he celebrated. By showing that such conditions hold within markets, we make a case that markets can promote the art of association.

The Division of Labor

Markets make the division of labor possible. Rather than having to be self-sufficient, as is the case where no markets exist, people in societies where markets exist can specialize in one or a few occupations and trade their labor for the goods they need and want or the money to purchase those goods. Markets thus allow for individuals and societies to prosper because market society allows workers to be more productive (i.e., through the development of greater adroitness as workers focus on a limited set of tasks, time savings as workers do not lose time moving between tasks, and the introduction of labor-saving devices). Markets also offer individuals multiple opportunities to work together. The broader and deeper the extent of the market, the greater the range of opportunities. Smith's famous example of the woolen coat detailed the multitude of people who must work together in production to eventually produce this final output good:

> The shepherd, the sorter of the wool, the wool-comber or carder, the dyer, the scribbler, the spinner, the weaver, the fuller, the dresser, with many others, must all join their different arts in order to complete even this homely production. How many merchants and carriers, besides, must have been employed in transporting the materials from some of those workmen to others who often live in a very distant part of the country! How much commerce and navigation in particular, how many ship-builders, sailors, sail-makers, rope-makers, must have been employed in order to bring together the different drugs made use of by the dyer, which often come from the remotest corners of the world! What a variety of labor too is necessary in order to produce the tools of the meanest of those workmen! To say nothing of such complicated machines as the ship of the sailor, the mill of the fuller, or even the loom of the weaver, let us consider only what a variety of labor is requisite in order to form that very simple machine, the shears with which the shepherd clips the wool. The miner, the builder of the furnace for smelting the ore, the feller of the timber, the burner of the charcoal

to be made use of in the smelting-house, the brick-maker, the brick-layer, the workmen who attend the furnace, the mill-wright, the forger, the smith, must all of them join their different arts in order to produce them.[51]

Not only is it nearly impossible to recount every single person who takes part in the production process but it is difficult to discern how all of these people work together, seemingly flawlessly, to turn wool on the back of a sheep into a coat on the back of a person.

Interestingly, Tocqueville railed against the moral consequences brought about by the division of labor: "there is nothing that tends more to materialize man and remove from his work even the trace of soul than the great division of labor."[52] Tocqueville, however, did acknowledge several of the monetary benefits of division of labor:

> It has been recognized that when a worker is occupied every day only with the same detail, the general production of the work is achieved more easily, more rapidly and more economically. It has been recognized as well that the more an industry was undertaken on a large scale, with great capital and large credit, the less expensive its products were.[53]

Indeed, he sees both the greater ease of production and the decreased cost of production as "truths" that have also "been demonstrated" in the real world. Besides the general material benefits that Tocqueville acknowledged, he also sees another area of benefit: the wealthy class, or "the class of masters":[54]

> as it becomes clearer that the larger the scale of manufacturing and the greater the capital, the more perfect and the less expensive the products of an industry are, very rich and very enlightened men arise to exploit industries that, until then, have been left to ignorant and poor artisans. The greatness of the necessary efforts and the immensity of the results to achieve attract them.[55]

However, these material benefits are not enough in Tocqueville's mind to make up for the moral destruction the division of labor has on these "ignorant and poor artisans":

> When an artisan devotes himself constantly and solely to the fabrication of a single object, he ends by acquitting himself of this work with a singular dexterity. But he loses, at the same time, the general ability to apply his mind to directing the work. Each day he becomes more skillful and less industrious, and you can say that in him the man becomes degraded as the worker improves.[56]

As the division of labor becomes more extended, "the worker becomes weaker, more limited, and more dependent. The art makes progress, the artisan goes backward."[57] We should note that Smith expressed similar concerns about the division of labor. According to Smith, the repetition of simple tasks that occurs under the division of labor risks making workers "as stupid and as ignorant as it is possible for a human creature to become."[58] The skills that the worker acquires in his particular trade, Smith lamented, are "acquired at the expense of his own intellectual, social, and martial virtues."[59]

Tocqueville's view of the division of labor was, therefore, a complicated one. On the one hand, Tocqueville acknowledged benefits from the division of labor. On the other hand, he viewed the division of labor as antithetical to the humane element within markets. He saw this as destructive to the working class specifically because investors and businessmen ride on the backs of the workers who allow for cheaper and easier production methods.

Tocqueville's discussion of the division of labor is striking, especially insofar as the division of labor is widely recognized as bringing about associational benefits.[60] Of course, Tocqueville himself argued for association being a main, if not sole, combatant against individualism and ultimately tyranny. So, there appears to be a tension here: Tocqueville argued for association due to its considerable benefits, but he also worried about the moral degradation of the division of labor, which we will argue happens to be a source of association. How can this apparent tension be reconciled?

Despite Tocqueville's concern (and Smith's), the division of labor does not seem to promote individualism of the sort that Tocqueville warned about, as it fosters self-interest rightly understood of the sort that Tocqueville celebrated. Markets appear to be spaces that promote the habit of association. Of course, in discussing association through its effect on individualism and self-interest, we overlook Tocqueville's concerns about the individual moral degradation supposedly brought about by division of labor.[61] For several reasons, though, we believe that the division of labor allows for heightened association, which, by extension, could very well reverse the effects of such degradation if indeed it really were occurring.

First, the division of labor does not increase individualism. Instead, it does just the opposite by increasing the need for people to work together. Again, recall Smith's woolen coat example. For the woolen coat to end up on the back of the day laborer many individuals must practice working together in a multitude of ways. Now envision the even more complex technologies existing today. These arguably need many more stages and steps of production, with many more input goods that must be coordinated between buyers and sellers. This expanded division of labor allows for heightened association due to the even greater need to work together in order to produce more advanced goods. These are not isolated figures who have turned inward away from their fellow citizens. Instead, these are connected creatures who must constantly concern themselves with the wishes and satisfaction of their employers, their suppliers, their coworkers, and their customers. Under the division of labor, the kind of isolated inward-looking individualism that might have been possible where individuals were more self-sufficient is simply not possible. To be sure, the aristocratic institutions that bound individuals together in previous epochs no longer exist, but the market and the division of labor it facilitates bind individuals together, albeit in a different sort of way. These bonds formed within markets need not be inferior to the kinds of bonds formed within political or civic associations.[62]

Second, with a higher division of labor, there exists a lower opportunity cost of association. In other words, if we lived in complete autarky, we would spend most of our days growing, harvesting, and producing all of the goods we needed to survive for ourselves. This means that associating, whether in political or civil settings, would have a very high opportunity cost. A hand-to-mouth society has little room for the development of associations when most time must be spent on finding the next meal or shelter. However, if each individual worked where he or she was most effective, and traded for whatever else he or she needed, there would be a lower opportunity cost of association. In practice, this looks like individuals working a daily job, likely producing some sort of specialized good or service, then shopping for goods and services to sustain life, and also attending civil or political association meetings due to the lower opportunity cost of the time saved from what would have been under autarky. The division of labor, as such, not only brings about advanced production and output but also allows for such heightened association.

Third, while Tocqueville may be correct about the demoralizing aspects brought about by the division of labor, particularly in jobs that require man to "unceasingly and exclusively engage ... in the fabrication of one thing," this emphasis overlooks the possibility that there might be compensating differentials that prevent the kind of moral degradation that leads workers under the division of labor to become less industrious.[63] Particularly unpleasant jobs are typically paid a higher wage because there is a lower supply of workers available to do such jobs. This is more likely to be true the more advanced the market society. If we allow for freedom of association and freedom of labor movement, meaning people can choose when and where to work, a higher wage will naturally arise in unpleasant jobs, all else equal. Admittedly, compensating differentials only pay a higher wage rate or offer some other benefit; they do not "fix" any moral problems ensuing from degrading or monotonous jobs. They do, however, mean that compensation is higher for those willing to do such jobs.

So, the division of labor inhibits individualism if we believe that it brings people together more than it drives them apart. In part, it does this because it brings about greater ease of association, and in part it does so because it lowers the opportunity cost of associating. Moreover, unpleasant jobs brought about through an extended division of labor can be mediated by compensating differentials. In the following section, we will discuss how markets foster Tocquevillean self-interest rightly understood among other values.

Values in the Marketplace

Commercial settings reward values that are critical to the practice of association, including self-interest, rightly understood. Within markets, people have to work together to, say, create a woolen coat. If one trader cheats another, or simply associates in unfriendly ways, he will be "punished" by the market process as his trading partners and customers choose to supply their needs elsewhere. The market process rewards certain values, such as hard work, teamwork, cooperation, and leadership that may not be rewarded in other settings. As Richard Wagner puts it:

> a market order tends to reward practice that conforms to ... morality ... [C]ommercial activity that is consistent with the moral order that, in turn, is complementary with the legal order will yield higher commercial returns than will conduct that runs contrary to that moral order. Such traits as being reliable, energetic, and trustworthy will tend to bring larger commercial return than such traits as being unreliable, lazy and dishonest.[64]

Obviously, these skills could also be learned in a society with no division of labor, such as autarky. That is, if a person is not able to or does not need to trade with others, they have no incentive to be friendly, even though they may very well be anyway. Yet the market aligns the incentives of producers and consumers alike to foster these values, whereas individuals in autarkic regimes have relatively little incentive to be kind to others. The market process rewards "practice that conforms to ... morality" and incentivizes both producers and consumers alike to act virtuously.

Dierdre McCloskey, across her three volumes in the Bourgeois Era series, argues that markets not only make us wealthier but also are compatible with and even depend on certain virtues.[65] As McCloskey maintains, markets foster the bourgeois virtues, which she considers to be the four classical virtues of courage, justice, temperance, and prudence, and the three Christian virtues of hope, faith, and love. As she explains, people in capitalist societies

> have more, not fewer real friends than their great-great-great-great grandparents in "closed-corporate" villages. They have broader, not narrower choices of identity than the one imposed on them by the country, custom, language, and religion of their birth. They have deeper, not shallower contacts with the transcendent of art or science or God, and sometimes even of nature, than the superstitious peasants and haunted hunter-gatherers from whom we all descend. They are better humans – because they in their billions have acquired the scope to become so and because market societies encourage art and science and religion to flourish.[66]

Because markets promote and reward the bourgeois virtues, these virtues tend to exist in communities with vibrant markets; and each of these virtues would seem to promote association.

Similarly, Storr and Choi argue that people in market societies are better connected than people in nonmarket societies.[67] As they suggest, empirical measures that get at Tocquevillean association (e.g., social capital, social cohesion, and civic engagement) are higher in market societies than nonmarket societies. Storr and Choi also find evidence that markets tend to foster several other traits that undoubtedly aid Tocquevillean association. For instance, they find that those in markets tend to be more trusting and trustworthy, more altruistic, less materialistic, less corrupt, and more cosmopolitan than people living in nonmarket societies. Arguably, all five of these traits can increase Tocquevillean association, as they allow for a greater ability to interact, associate, and gather with others.

Taken together, these studies suggest that Tocqueville's concern about the moral degradation that supposedly occurs in markets and, specifically, with the materialism that he observed in the United States was either unwarranted or not properly attributed to the marketplace. Recall, Tocqueville claimed that "it is a strange thing to see with what kind of feverish ardor the Americans pursue well-being, and how they appear tormented constantly by a vague fear of not having chosen the shortest road that can lead to it. The inhabitant of the United States is attached to the goods of this world."[68] This materialism, Tocqueville believed, was behind the restlessness that seemed to plague Americans. There is evidence, however, that suggests that materialism is not a uniquely market phenomenon. Countries that embrace markets to a greater extent, that is, countries with more economic freedom, for instance, are less materialistic on certain empirical measures.[69] Additionally, Tocqueville has also acknowledged that property ownership and access to the market can have a positive effect on the ideas and habits of the poor, encouraging them to plan and to work hard.[70]

Tocqueville also discussed the need for self-interest rightly understood, meaning that some underlying set of values must encourage individuals to work in the interest of not only themselves but of those in their community. In Tocqueville's understanding, businessmen and generally all citizens should attempt to further their self-interest. Yet he went further in suggesting that the self-interest of each individual must be aligned somehow with the interests of others; and the way to do so was by aligning interests so that the work most preferred by each was *honest* work, as Tocqueville suggested. The market does precisely this, as Storr and Choi have suggested: it creates more altruistic people, it makes people less materialistic, it decreases corruption, it weeds out unfriendly views, and it punishes cheaters.

To be sure, not every cheater or corrupt official in a market society will be punished, and some may be allowed to continue their misbehavior. The pure market, however, allows for feedback signals to be sent to producers and consumers alike, so that, throughout the market, incentives are aligned that normally reinforce, rather than undermine, morality, thus allowing for self-interest to work as Tocqueville envisioned.

Communication and Information

Markets have heightened the production and use of technology because of their innovative nature.[71] Technology has greatly aided communication and access to information; there are countless ways in which technology, telephones, email, websites, message boards, social media, and other connection platforms all allow for greater ease of communication. Of course, greater ability to communicate and greater access to information both allow for easier association.

Tocqueville also discussed the greater ease of association brought about by communication and information. He described a "necessary relation between associations and newspapers; newspapers make associations, and associations make newspapers."[72] His point was that newspapers spread the word about a common thought or idea and that, as people begin to unite and associate upon learning or reading of the idea, more associations come into being, bringing with them more newspapers. This self-feeding cycle allows for heightened association.

Further, he claimed this is essential in democracy for several of the reasons discussed, most prominently that democracy promotes equality and individualism. With equality, uniting becomes harder because "a large number of men who have the desire or the need to associate cannot do so; since all are very small and lost in the crowd, they do not see each other and do not know where to find each other."[73] Through newspapers, they can lower the costs of finding other like-minded people and thereby lower the costs of association.

Individualism, too, is feared in democracies for its natural progression into tyranny. To keep men from becoming self-focused and withdrawn, newspapers facilitate the ability of individuals to read current news and associate over such topics. "Newspapers therefore become more necessary," claimed Tocqueville, "as men are more equal and individualism more to be feared."[74] Thus, newspapers do not just "guarantee liberty" through aiding the art of association, they also "maintain civilization" by decreasing the threats stemming from democracy and individualism.[75] Or, in another way, newspapers work not just by drawing people "closer together" but also by continuing to "hold them together."[76] Tocqueville, then, makes the strong case that newspapers are necessary for association, and so too is association necessary for newspapers. With the ability to freely associate and discuss ideas in the general, public sphere, association and newspapers reinforce themselves.

This Tocquevillean idea of association through heightened communication and information plays out in a modern context quite frequently. Storr and Choi discuss how better connection allows for "stronger communities than people living in nonmarket communities."[77] They go on to specifically address technology's role in this heightened communication brought about through markets, similar to Tocqueville's discussion of newspapers:

> [B]logs and online message boards devoted to particular topics or that express particular perspectives have arguably become a new public sphere, promoting the discussion of topics in a forum where all who have access to the Internet can potentially enter. The communication and transportation services available *because of markets* (e.g. telephones, email, automobiles, and airplanes) are likewise important tools for building communities and maintaining desirable relationships across sometimes great distances. Relationships that would have had to rely on infrequent contact in the past (i.e. through traditional mail and infrequent visits) now benefit from the possibility of everyday contact.[78]

Tocqueville argued that newspapers enable communication, which allow for association to follow. Storr and Choi add that markets bring about heightened communication; while newspapers allow for maybe daily or weekly contact that leads to associations, the digital age allows for nearly constant communication, thus leading to a heightened ease of association. Hans Klein also details how online forums bypass many of the large barriers to entry of communication and Tocquevillean association. Participation costs fall drastically with the use of the Internet, as the cost of online engagement is significantly lower.[79]

An example of Tocqueville's, Storr and Choi's, and Klein's ideas might be the Arab Spring. Many of the protests and government upheavals in the Middle East during this time were aided by the use of information and communication technologies (ICTs) and social media websites, particularly Twitter and Facebook.[80] Analyzing Egypt during the Arab Spring in January 2011, Zeynep Tufekci and Christopher Wilson found that Twitter users were more likely to attend the first day of mass protests than nonusers.[81] Moreover, Ekaterina Stepanova suggests that Egyptian protests happened when they did, and not later, due to information on social media: "the fact that the crisis [in Egypt] occurred sooner rather than later, in direct follow-up to protests in Tunisia, was largely due to the initial mobilizing effects of ICT and social media networks."[82] Her conclusion is twofold: "[o]verall, the input of the social media networks was critical in performing two overlapping functions: (a) *organizing the protests* and (b) *disseminating information about them*, including publicizing protesters' demands internationally."[83] Similar to Tocqueville's rendering of the importance of newspapers for association, the Arab Spring largely occurred through the help of ICTs and social media sites. News sources, other media outlets, and ICTs can help disseminate knowledge, which not only allows for individuals to find others with similar interests but also helps them organize effectively. This process leads to a further dissemination of knowledge and information. It seems clear that markets bring about the heightened technology (like cellphones and computers) and media sites (like Twitter and Facebook) that allow for the harnessing and spreading of information in order to improve the art of association.

CONCLUSION

Quite a bit has been written about Tocqueville's notion of association.[84] Most notably, Vincent and Elinor Ostrom have extensively researched the "art and science of association," examining how it is that people tend to cooperate when economic theory predicts they would do otherwise. Elinor Ostrom, for instance, focused on understanding how people band together to overcome collective action problems.[85] Closely related, Vincent Ostrom explored democracy and its crucial components: he saw Tocquevillean association and, in general, individual relationships as the bonds that hold democracy in place.[86] Mark Warren extended Vincent Ostrom's work by exploring not only what associations provide for democracies but why we place the heavy lifting on associations rather than some other entity or designated group.[87] While the existing scholarship has said a lot about the importance of association, less attention has been paid to how Americans become skilled at the art of association, and almost no attention has been paid to how markets, especially within advanced commercial societies, cultivate a habit of association. In fact, Tocqueville himself left us with something of a puzzle. The America that he observed both was a vibrant market economy and had a robust civil society, but markets and community are claimed to be at odds. Tocqueville's own discussion of the division of labor suggests that he is worried about how markets might undermine associational life.

Our chapter has set out to explain how the market is useful for advancing the Tocquevillean notion of association. We proposed that Tocqueville's thoughts on the division of labor may have been misguided, or at least prematurely considered, as he does not mention its potential associational benefits. Primarily, we argued that the division of labor helps inhibit the kind of individualism that emerges in a democracy, which happened to be one of Tocqueville's main concerns for democratic countries. Because it brings together many different people to provide plentiful goods much more efficiently, a highly advanced division of labor also decreases the opportunity cost of association. We do recognize, however, that these arguments may not address the moral concerns of alienation and degradation brought about by an advanced division of labor. Yet we offer the economic rationale that compensating differentials may help alleviate some of the burdens or stresses of a monotonous or degrading job.

We also argued, however, that markets naturally reward moral values. Markets, besides depending on virtues like courage, justice, temperance, prudence, hope, faith, and love,[88] make people more altruistic, less materialistic, less corrupt, more cosmopolitan, and more trusting.[89] We argued that, through the moral guidelines reinforced through the market process, markets help promote self-interest rightly understood – that is, markets can align incentives to allow for individuals to do the best not only for themselves but for those around them.

Last, we maintained that markets aid association by facilitating ease of communication and access to information. Tocqueville described this phenomenon through newspapers, and he discussed the necessity of newspapers for association and vice versa. We applied his thoughts to the notion that markets bring with them greater technology, such as social media sites and other information technologies. Through the use of the example of the Arab Spring, we detailed how social media sites and ICTs aided communication and access to information and generally heightened association that eventually led to organic upheavals in many Arab countries (for better or for worse).

On the whole, we attempted to show that markets "combat" two of the greatest threats that Tocqueville saw to democracy because markets inhibit individualism and they align self-interest. Moreover, contrary to a major line of "neo-Tocquevillean" criticism that regards them with ambivalence, markets are important and indeed might be necessary for Tocquevillean associations to flourish. This is not so much to suggest that the "neo-Tocquevilleans" have misread Tocqueville as that Tocqueville himself may have failed to appreciate fully the associational virtues of markets.

NOTES

1. DIA (N) 897.
2. DIA (N) 976.
3. See Stephen Gudeman, "Remodeling the House of Economics: Culture and Innovation," *American Ethnologist* 1, no. 1 (1992), 141–154 and *The Anthropology of Economy: Community, Market, and Culture* (Malden, MA: Blackwell, 2001); Murray Rothbard, *Man, Economy and State: A Treatise on Economic Principles* (Auburn, AL: Ludwig von Mises Institute, 1993); Elizabeth Anderson, *Value in Ethics and Economics* (Cambridge, MA: Harvard University Press, 1995); John Gray, *Endgames: Questions in Late Modern Political Thought* (Chichester: Polity Press, 1997); Robert Putnam, *Bowling Alone: The Collapse and Revival of American Community* (New York: Simon & Schuster, 2000); Jonathan Sacks, *The Dignity of Difference: How to Avoid the Clash of Civilizations* (London: Bloomsbury Publishing, 2002); Neera Badhwar, "Friendship and Commercial Societies," *Politics, Philosophy & Economics* 7, no. 3 (2008), 301–326; Virgil H. Storr, "The Market As a Social Space: On the Meaningful Extraeconomic Conversations That Can Occur in Markets," *The Review of Austrian Economics* 21, no. 2–3 (2008), 135–150.
4. See Gudeman, "Remodeling the House of Economics" and *The Anthropology of Economy*.
5. See Anderson, *Value in Ethics and Economics*.
6. Gray, *Endgame*, 36.
7. Sacks, *The Dignity of Difference*, 89.
8. See Putnam, *Bowling Alone*.
9. See Adam Smith, *The Theory of Moral Sentiments* (Indianapolis, IN: Liberty Fund, 2007); Montesquieu, *The Spirit of the Laws*, ed. Anne M. Cohler, Basia C. Miller, and Harold S. Stone (Cambridge: Cambridge University Press, 1989); and Deirdre McCloskey, *The Bourgeois Virtues: Ethics for an Age of Commerce* (Chicago: University of Chicago Press, 2006).

10. DIA (N) 896.
11. DIA (N) 876.
12. DIA (N) 882.
13. DIA (N) 883.
14. DIA (N) 883.
15. DIA (N) 884.
16. DIA (N) 895–896.
17. DIA (N) 896.
18. DIA (N) 896, emphasis added.
19. DIA (N) 896.
20. DIA (N) 897.
21. DIA (N) 897.
22. DIA (N) 897.
23. See Robert T. Gannett, Jr., "Bowling Ninepins in Tocqueville's Township," *American Political Science Review* 97, no. 1 (2003), 1–16.
24. DIA (N) 898, emphasis added.
25. DIA (N) 898.
26. DIA (N) 900.
27. DIA (N) 907.
28. DIA (N) 900–901.
29. DIA (N) 900.
30. DIA (N) 900.
31. DIA (N) 912.
32. DIA (N) 912.
33. DIA (N) 912.
34. DIA (N) 912.
35. DIA (N) 915.
36. DIA (N) 913.
37. DIA (N) 913.
38. DIA (N) 913.
39. DIA (N) 915.
40. DIA (N) 918.
41. Adam Smith, *An Inquiry into the Nature and Causes of the Wealth of Nations* (Indianapolis: Liberty Fund, 2005), 13.
42. DIA (N) 920.
43. DIA (N) 920.
44. DIA (N) 920.

45. DIA (N) 920, emphasis added.

46. DIA (N) 921.

47. DIA (N) 921–922.

48. DIA (N) 922.

49. DIA (N) 922.

50. See Storr, "The Market As a Social Space."

51. Smith, *The Wealth of Nations*, 11–12.

52. DIA (N) 642.

53. DIA (N) 981.

54. DIA (N) 982.

55. DIA (N) 982.

56. DIA (N) 982.

57. DIA (N) 982.

58. Smith, *The Wealth of Nations*, 782.

59. Smith, *The Wealth of Nations*, 782.

60. See, for instance, David Ricardo, *On the Principles of Political Economy and Taxation* (Cambridge: Cambridge University Press, 2015) and Ludwig von Mises, *Human Action: A Treatise on Economics*, ed. Bettina Bien Greaves (Indianapolis: Liberty Fund, 2014). In chap. 8, Mises makes the case that cooperation due to division of labor is *the* reason we associate. Without Ricardo's comparative advantage, which induces cooperation, Mises makes the case that association would be absent and society would cease to exist.

61. Though see Virgil Storr and Ginny Choi, *Do Markets Corrupt Our Morals?* (Basingstoke: Palgrave Macmillan, 2019) for a possible response.

62. See Storr, "The Market As a Social Space."

63. DIA (N) 982.

64. Richard E. Wagner, *Politics As a Peculiar Business: Insights from a Theory of Entangled Political Economy* (Cheltenham: Edward Elgar Publishing, 2016), 197.

65. Deirdre N. McCloskey, *Bourgeois Dignity: Why Economics Can't Explain the Modern World* (Chicago: University of Chicago Press, 2010); *Bourgeois Equality: How Ideas, Not Capital or Institutions, Enriched the World* (Chicago: University of Chicago Press, 2016); *The Bourgeois Virtues: Ethics for an Age of Commerce* (Chicago: University of Chicago Press, 2006).

66. McCloskey, *The Bourgeois Virtues*, 28–29.

67. See Storr and Choi, *Do Markets Corrupt Our Morals?*.

68. DIA (N) 943.

69. Megan Teague, Virgil Storr, and Rosemarie Fike, "Economic Freedom and Materialism: An Empirical Analysis," *Constitutional Political Economy* 31, no. 1 (2020), 1–44.

70. Richard Swedberg, *Tocqueville's Political Economy* (Princeton: Princeton University Press, 2018), 141.

71. See Joseph A. Schumpeter, *Capitalism, Socialism, and Democracy* (New York: Harper Perennial, 2008); W. Michael Cox and Richard Alm, "The Churn: The Paradox of Progress," in Federal Reserve Bank of Dallas, *Annual Report* (1992), 5–11; and Peter Leeson, "Two Cheers for Capitalism?" *Society* 47, no. 3 (2010), 227–233.

72. DIA (N) 908.

73. DIA (N) 907.

74. DIA (N) 906.

75. DIA (N) 906.

76. DIA (N) 907.

77. Storr and Choi, *Do Markets Corrupt Our Morals?*, 106.

78. Storr and Choi, *Do Markets Corrupt Our Morals?*, 110, emphasis added.

79. Hans Klein, "Tocqueville in Cyberspace: Using the Internet for Citizen Associations," *The Information Society* 15, no. 4 (1999), 213–220.

80. See Nahed Eltantawy and Julie Wiest, "Social Media in the Egyptian Revolution: Reconsidering Resource Mobilization Theory," *International Journal of Communication* 5 (2011), 1207–1224; Philip N. Howard, Aiden Duffey, Deen Freelon et al., "Opening Closed Regimes: What Was the Role of Social Media During the Arab Spring?" Working Paper No. 2011.1, Project on Information Technology & Political Islam, 2011; Habibul Haque Khondker, "Role of the New Media in the Arab Spring," *Globalizations* 8, no. 5 (2011), 675–679; Ekaterina Stepanova, "The Role of Information Communication Technologies in the 'Arab Spring': Implications Beyond the Region," PONARS Eurasia Policy Memo No. 159, George Washington University, May 2011; Francesca Comunello and Giuseppe Anzera, "Will the Revolution Be Tweeted? A Conceptual Framework for Understanding the Social Media and the Arab Spring," *Islam and Christian–Muslim Relations* 23, no. 4 (2012), 453–470; and Zeynep Tufekci and Christopher Wilson, "Social Media and the Decision

to Participate in Political Protest: Observations from Tahrir Square," *Journal of Communication* 62, no. 2 (2012), 363–379.

81. See Tufekci and Wilson, "Social Media and the Decision to Participate."

82. Stepanova, "The Role of Information Communication Technologies," 1.

83. Stepanova, "The Role of Information Communication Technologies," 2, emphasis added.

84. Vincent Ostrom, *The Meaning of Democracy and the Vulnerability of Democracies: A Response to Tocqueville's Challenge* (Ann Arbor: University of Michigan Press, 1997); Elinor Ostrom, "A Behavioral Approach to the Rational Choice Theory of Collective Action: Presidential Address, American Political Science Association, 1997," *The American Political Science Review* 92, no. 1 (1998), 1–22; William Galston, "Civil Society and the 'Art of Association'," *Journal of Democracy* 11, no. 1 (2000), 64–70; Mark E. Warren, *Democracy and Association* (Princeton: Princeton University Press, 2001); Andrew Sabl, "Community Organizing As Tocquevillean Politics: The Art, Practices, and Ethos of Association," *American Journal of Political Science* 46, no. 1 (2002), 1–19; Gannett, "Bowling Ninepins in Tocqueville's Township"; Aurelian Craiutu, "From the Social Contract to the Art of Association: A Tocquevillian Perspective," *Social Philosophy and Policy* 25, no. 2 (2008), 263–287; Elinor Ostrom and Vincent Ostrom, *Choice, Rules and Collective Action: The Ostroms on the Study of Institutions and Governance*, ed. Paul Dragos Aligica and Filippo Sabetti (Colchester: ECPR Press, 2014).

85. See Ostrom, "A Behavioral Approach to the Rational Choice Theory."

86. See Ostrom, *The Meaning of Democracy and the Vulnerability of Democracies*.

87. See Warren, *Democracy and Association*.

88. See McCloskey, *The Bourgeois Virtues*.

89. See Storr and Choi, *Do Markets Corrupt Our Morals?*

11 Tocqueville on the Federal Constitution

Jeremy D. Bailey

Writing to the German-born jurist Francis Lieber, Supreme Court Justice Joseph Story pointed to Alexis de Tocqueville's *Democracy in America* as evidence that "Europeans know little" about "constitutional law," especially when applied to "forms of government like ours."[1] Story went on to credit the book's "great reputation abroad" to insights that were mostly "borrowed" from his own three-volume *Commentaries on the Constitution* and from *The Federalist*.[2] Even if modern scholars do not go as far as Joseph Story, it is true that most scholars have paid little attention to Tocqueville's constitutional analysis.[3] Judging by the secondary literature, the important part of *Democracy in America* has to do with things that involve political culture or the virtue and habits of the citizenry – religion, local government, and voluntary associations – not the Constitution of 1787.

It is possible that Justice Story did not notice Tocqueville's most revealing comment about the Constitution. That passage comes not in his chapter on the Federal Constitution but rather in the chapter almost immediately following that one, the chapter "On Parties in the United States." The chapter is mostly known for its distinction between "great" and "small" parties. Whereas great parties are revolutionary and motivated by principle, small parties are less principled and agitate society instead of overturning it. Tocqueville uses this distinction to compare the parties he observed in the United States to those of the Founding generation: "America has had great parties; today they no longer exist; it has gained much in happiness, but not in morality."[4] More than using the distinction to merely disparage the parties of the 1830s, however, Tocqueville adds a historical analysis. By his estimation, Jefferson and his Democratic-Republican Party were on the right side of history; or, rather, they were the natural majority in a nation where everyone was born equal. Because "America is the land of democracy," the Federalists "were therefore always in the minority."[5] Yet because they had "almost all the great men the War of Independence had given birth to," and because of the "anarchy" that was imminent after the Revolution, the Federalists enjoyed a temporary opportunity to rule. Consequently, the rule of Washington, Hamilton, and Adams was artificial when viewed from the natural inclinations of the country, for "their theories were wrong in being inapplicable in their entirety to the society they wanted to rule."[6] Even though "what happened under Jefferson" would have come "sooner or later," the Federalists were able to get the country going under the Federal Constitution. That Constitution, with all its anti-democratic features, "is a lasting monument to their patriotism and their wisdom."[7]

The implication of Tocqueville's history of the parties, then, is that the Constitution is a product of a minority party and not of the American people themselves. Americans are naturally inclined to the party of Jefferson and therefore to democracy. Indeed, in the chapter "On the Omnipotence of the Majority in the United States," Tocqueville labels Jefferson as "the most powerful apostle that democracy ever had."[8] Because the American people side naturally with Jefferson, they would never remain Federalist, and, by extension, nor would they live forever under the Federalist Constitution. Tocqueville sees in American democracy, as Robert Kraynak puts it, a distinction "between the sovereign people and their political constitution."[9]

This distinction between the sovereign and the constitution would help explain why the Constitution does not play a leading role in the book. As mentioned, *Democracy in America* is famous for its treatment of American society, not its constitutional analysis. Tocqueville suggests that a constitution is not where power ultimately lies, so the true political analysis must emphasize a people's character and habits rather than their legal arrangements. It is for this reason, no doubt, that Tocqueville devotes so much effort to explaining the United States by way of its "point of departure." In this famous discussion, Tocqueville explains that the "social state of the Americans" was created by the Puritans in the early 1600s, and, by extension, not by the revolutionaries of 1776 or by the Framers of 1787. In this, Tocqueville describes a founding before *the* Founding, thus relegating the latter to be the mere inheritor of the former.[10]

It is nevertheless true that Tocqueville does spend considerable time trying to understand the American Constitution. It is probably no accident that Tocqueville uses the same French word – *monument* – to describe the achievement of the Federalists in creating the Constitution and in a key passage in his chapter "On the Point of Departure." There, Tocqueville analogized a nation to a man: just as the "prejudices, habits, and passions" of a young boy will define the man, the "circumstances" of a nation's origin will determine its development. Yet Tocqueville means more than random events of chance. Rather, he explains that the "first monuments of their history" will reveal the "first cause of prejudices, habits, dominant passions, of all that finally composes what is called national character."[11] Could it be, then, that the Federal Constitution – the monument to the patriotism and wisdom of the Federalists – was a second point of departure for the United States? More generally, Tocqueville devoted an entire chapter, comprising a dense fifty-six pages, to analysis of the Constitution. His preparation included not only Joseph Story's three-volume *Commentaries on the Constitution of the United States* but also *The Federalist* and James Kent's four-volume *Commentaries on American Law*. Tocqueville also consulted a two-volume French edition of Jefferson's writings, edited by L. P. Conseil, and, as we will see, this likely affected his reading of the Constitution.[12]

CONGRESS AND THE PRESIDENCY

Tocqueville's analysis of the Federal Constitution is sharpest in its discussion of the presidency and its powers. Importantly, Tocqueville's discussion of executive power comes about as part of a discussion about presidential selection. In four sections spanning nearly twenty percent of the chapter, Tocqueville reveals the connection between power and the mode of election. In this, Tocqueville departs from the account in *The Federalist* while simultaneously extending its analysis. Before we turn to the presidency, we should first examine Tocqueville's treatment of Congress.

One obvious difference with *The Federalist* is how little attention Tocqueville gives to the legislative power. In *Federalist* No. 48, Madison wrote that the legislative department was the most dangerous department in republican governments, and he spent the next several essays considering ways to maintain separation of powers against legislative power.[13] It is not an accident, then, that *Federalist* No. 51 begins a series of essays on Congress that extends through *Federalist* No. 67. These seventeen essays are on top of what Publius has already written, in Nos. 23 through 36, about the necessity of a government with more energy, that is, with more power held by Congress, than it had under the Articles of Confederation. Tocqueville, by contrast, gives Congress slightly more than three of the fifty-six pages he devotes to the Federal Constitution. By contrast, the executive receives almost seventeen and the courts almost fourteen.

What is also striking about Tocqueville's treatment of Congress is that he devotes almost the entirety of the small section on Congress to the compromise between the small and large states. Tocqueville's analysis on that compromise is straightforward: the Americans were torn between interest and reason, and so "they bent the rules of logic" to accommodate both the "principle of the independence of the states" and the "dogma of national sovereignty."[14] Tocqueville does not explain why the one is a principle and the other a dogma, but he does concede that the difference between the large and small states never really materialized into different coalitions after ratification. If anything, the "irresistible force of the whole people" made the House more powerful than the Senate.[15] Later in the chapter, Tocqueville returns to Congress to show the superiority of the Federal Constitution to the state constitutions. Most of the state constitutions provide for a short tenure of office for members of the upper and lower chambers, but the Framers of the Federal Constitution "lengthened the time of the electoral mandate to allow the deputy a greater use of his free will."[16] Further, under the state constitutions, the members of the two chambers are elected by "the same mode of election," coming from the people, and thus the state legislatures were too connected to "the will of the majority."[17] The Federal Constitution, by contrast, "varied the eligibility and the mode of election," in order to represent different interests and ensure a "superior wisdom" in the upper chamber.[18] Whereas bicameralism does not really exist in the states, it is alive and well under the Federal Constitution.

Strangely, Tocqueville does not write about the powers of Congress. This is all the more surprising given the political controversies of Jacksonian America. First among these controversies was the recharter of the Second Bank of the United States. Andrew Jackson vetoed the bill in 1832, focusing attention on the question of the Bank as well as on executive power. Indeed, Jackson's veto and use of executive power helped form his sometimes disparate opponents into an organized opposition.[19] Tocqueville knew of this controversy and explicitly mentions the Bank twice.[20] Yet he did not seem all that interested in the long-standing controversy, going back four decades, over whether Congress had the power to incorporate the Bank in the first place. Put another way, in the section on legislative power under the Federal Constitution, Tocqueville ignored the single most important question that had divided Americans on policy and constitutional grounds for more than four decades. Instead, Tocqueville seems to have thought about the controversy over the Bank with reference to the executive power and the way the presidency was constructed. It is in this analysis where Tocqueville most explicitly marks his break with Alexander Hamilton's efforts as Publius.

Of particular interest to both Hamilton and Tocqueville was the relationship between the president's mode of election and the president's motivation to defend his office and pursue the public good. Tocqueville had the advantage of time, though, and his analysis goes beyond *The Federalist* by describing how presidential elections happen in fact. Following Hamilton, Tocqueville adds that the Electoral College would have the extra benefit of preventing corruption because its members would be "unknown in the crowd" until they had already pronounced "their decree."[21] As Hamilton predicted, this would make it difficult for European powers to influence the election as they had been able to do in Poland's elective monarchy. Yet Tocqueville departs from Hamilton in discerning that the president had been made a representative under the Constitution or, more precisely, that the Constitution enabled the emergence of presidents who would claim to represent the people. As he understood it, the Electoral College was created primarily to make a "majority more probable." Notably absent from Tocqueville's analysis, then, is any notion that the Electoral College was meant to be a filtering device comprised of, to use Hamilton's language from *Federalist* No. 68, the "men most capable" to decide who should be president. Instead, Tocqueville writes that the Constitution's Framers believed that members of Congress would "insufficiently represent the voice of the people," so some more accurate and recent representative would have to be created.[22] Whereas a common reading of the Constitution is that the Framers of 1787 created a presidency who would filter the popular will, Tocqueville instead sees a constitution that in fact creates a presidency to represent it.[23]

Tocqueville's claim that the creators of presidential selection wanted the president to represent a national majority of the electorate makes more sense if we remember that he likely had in mind the Twelfth Amendment in addition to the Constitution of 1787. That amendment, ratified in 1804, required members of the Electoral College to designate which person would be president and which would be vice president, thus solving the snafu in the election of

1800 that resulted in a tie between the intended president, Thomas Jefferson, and his intended vice president, Aaron Burr. Yet the amendment also lowered the number of available candidates in the contingency election in the House from five to three. This is what Tocqueville means when he writes that the choice in the House "in the case of a split" was restricted to three, suggesting that Tocqueville was well aware of the changes made under the Twelfth Amendment.[24] Given the controversies surrounding the election of 1824 and the corresponding attempts at reform, Tocqueville would have also likely known that the framers of the Twelfth Amendment did in fact understand their efforts as linking the president more clearly to a national majority. By explicitly designating who would be president and who would be vice president, the Jeffersonian framers of the Twelfth Amendment took the mystery out of the process and with it much of the likelihood the Electors would be able to use their own discretion to choose the president. In short, the framers of the Twelfth Amendment made it more likely that an electoral majority declare its preference for some particular candidate.[25]

This point is even clearer in Tocqueville's description of presidential elections. In a chapter he calls the "Crisis of the Election," he explains that the Americans can manage most elections because they are "habituated" to running them, and the size of the country makes "a collision between the different parties less probable and less perilous there than anywhere else."[26] Even though the Americans are rich in practical experience, however, the election of the president is nevertheless a "national crisis." The main reason for this is that the parties use presidential candidates as ways to condense their ideas "around one man in order more easily to reach the intelligence of the crowd."[27] The candidate becomes a "symbol" of the party, and the party's supporters "personify their theories in him." As a result, a presidential election causes a great disturbance, and factious views that normally remain private are offered in "broad daylight." The citizens become "feverish" and more divided than usual until eventually the electoral contest becomes everything, "the goal of all reasoning, the object of all thoughts, the sole interest of the present."[28]

In addition to making the election a dangerous moment of partisan contestation, the election also corrupts the presidency, especially because the Federal Constitution allows the incumbent to run for reelection. In the next section, "On the Reelection of the President," Tocqueville concludes that the Framers of 1787 erred. Tocqueville acknowledges Hamilton's logic in the case for reeligibility: it would be unwise to require a new president in the middle of a crisis, and it would be convenient to return to power a man who has demonstrated that he is good at the job. Tocqueville concedes that these reasons are "powerful," but he concludes that the arguments on the other side are "still stronger." The main problem is that a president is different from a normal politician in that the president is "the head of state." This means he "borrows the force of government for his own use" when he runs for reelection. Treaties and laws are thus reduced to "electoral schemes for him."[29] More generally, "the desire to be reelected dominates the thoughts of the president," and therefore the "whole policy of his administration tends toward that point."[30]

As Tocqueville sees it, the consequence of eligibility for reelection is that the Federal Constitution is less effective than it could be at taming the tyranny of the majority. The Framers of the Constitution wisely "concentrated all of the executive power of the nation in a single hand," giving the president "extensive prerogatives" including a veto power enabling him to "resist the encroachments of the legislature." Yet by allowing the president to serve beyond a single term, the Framers "destroyed their work in part": "They granted a great power to the president and took away from him the will to make use of it."[31] Instead of serving as a check on the majority, the president is "only a docile instrument" in its hands. "He loves what it loves, hates what it hates; he flies to meet its will, anticipates its complaints, bends to its least desires."[32] Instead of guiding the public will, the reelection-minded president follows it.[33] It is worth noting, again, that Tocqueville's criticism here confirmed, at least in part, Jackson's understanding of his own reelection. Tocqueville, no doubt, had in mind Jackson's veto of the bill to recharter the Second Bank of the United States. The controversy of the Bank was the central issue of the election of 1832, and upon reelection Jackson explicitly argued that the election results constituted an approval by the public of his action. Jackson's opponents, eventually calling themselves Whigs, rejected this view, arguing instead that no presidential election could be construed as a mandate for a particular policy, nor could any president claim to represent the people.[34] So even though Tocqueville saw it as a design flaw, it is telling that he sided with Jackson and not the Whigs as to the true design of executive power under the Constitution. Even though he thinks it was a mistake, Tocqueville believes that the Framers of the Constitution created a presidency whose powers would rest not simply on formal legal grants of authority but also on mandates from the people; and even though he criticized the system that allowed Jackson to serve a second term, Tocqueville saw that Jackson was right that the majority had reelected him in order to dismantle the Bank.

THE FEDERAL COMPACT

Cast in the light of Tocqueville's analysis of the two parties, this point about the presidency raises another question. If the Framers of 1787 undermined their work by allowing presidents such as Jackson to seek reelection, what, then, did Tocqueville have in mind when he credited the Federalist Party for establishing the Federal Constitution? The Federalists and their Whig heirs did not embrace the representative presidency, so what was Federalist about the Federalist Constitution? One possible answer to this question is that Tocqueville believed that the Union was both a confederation *and* strong. As he recognized, "the United States of America has not provided the first and only example of a confederation."[35] Moreover, in terms of powers, other confederations "are nearly the same" as the

United States. Where the United States does differ from other confederations, however, is that it "conducts affairs with vigor and ease" while the others throughout history were "feeble and powerless." This is because the Federal Constitution, while resembling prior constitutions at first glance, "in fact rests on an entirely new theory," a theory that "will be marked as a great discovery in the political science of our day."[36] So what is that theory?

One part is that the federal government has the power to execute laws itself. In prior confederacies, the constituent parts "kept the right to ordain and oversee for themselves the execution of the laws of the nation."[37] As a result, if the constituent parts were strong, they felt free to ignore the laws of the federal government. If they were weak, they were instead dominated by it. In the United States, however, the Union is composed of citizens, not states, at least with respect to its powers. "When it wants to levy a tax, it does not address itself to the government of Massachusetts, but to each inhabitant of Massachusetts." Consequently, the Union "does not borrow its force" but rather "draws it from itself."[38]

The other part is that the federal government in the United States operates within a restricted sphere. While it may act "without intermediary on the governed," it may do so only for certain objects.[39] In *Federalist* No. 39, Madison had argued that the Constitution created a government that was "neither wholly federal, nor wholly national." When it acted, it would be national because it would act on people "in their individual capacities" rather than on the states. The extent of its action would be federal, however, "since its jurisdiction extends to certain enumerated objects only."[40] Following Madison, Tocqueville argued that the Federal Constitution defied classification: "the new word that ought to express the new thing still does not exist." Yet Tocqueville also called it "an incomplete national government" and thus went a step further than Madison in giving this new form of government a name.[41] This point brings up the judiciary and suggests another potential difference between Publius and Tocqueville.

In *Federalist* No. 39, Madison acknowledged that "some such tribunal" would have to adjudicate disputes over the extent of the federal authority. Further, this tribunal "ought to be established under the general, rather than under the local governments." Madison went out of his way, though, to argue that the important point is not that the federal judiciary is the decider as to the meaning of the Constitution but rather that the Constitution itself is not national in its extent. This is because the "foundation" of the Constitution is federal, not national. This was itself a big claim, and it has been debated since Madison wrote it. Yet what is also curious about the explanation regarding federal judges is that Madison does not apply the same analysis to the judiciary as he does to Congress and the president. Looking at the electoral constituency of each of the latter departments, he explains that the House is national, the Senate is federal, and the president is a bit of both. However, he never explains whether the judiciary is federal or national. By the logic employed with the other two departments, the judiciary would be "mostly federal" because federal judges are selected by the president (both national and federal) and the Senate (federal). Strangely, though, Madison never makes this argument.[42]

Tocqueville, by contrast, explicitly emphasizes the national constituency of federal judges, especially the Supreme Court. As Tocqueville puts it, it would have been a grave mistake to allow the existing state courts to adjudicate questions of law; or, rather, because each state has its own political constituency, it would "deliver the nation to foreign judges." Thus the designers of the Federal Constitution were wise "to create a federal judicial power to apply the laws of the Union and to decide certain questions of general interest that were carefully defined in advance."[43] So what happens when federal courts and state courts disagree? Normally, some third party would be asked to settle the question, but because the people lack the competence to determine "questions of national sovereignty," one of the two parties had to have the power to settle these controversies. In other words, the Framers of the Federal Constitution "had to give one of the courts the right to judge in its own cause."[44]

They had to do that by the creation of the Union itself, that is, the "very constitution of the state" "necessitates the existence of such a power." As a result, "the Supreme Court of the United States is the sole, unique tribunal of the nation."[45] This means, practically speaking, that the Constitution is a "dead letter" without the Supreme Court, whose members must be "statesmen" who know how "to discern the spirit of the times" while at the same time knowing when "to turn away from the current when the flood threatens to carry away with them the sovereignty of the Union and the obedience due its laws."[46] Even if the country would likely survive "imprudent or corrupt" presidents and members of Congress, it would "perish" if such individuals were on the Court.

Even though he saw the Supreme Court as the glue that bound the Union together, it is true that Tocqueville also doubted that confederacies could be strong enough to manage crisis, especially war. As he puts it in the closing sentences of the chapter on the Federal Constitution, no confederacy could maintain a long war with a nation of equal power but greater centralization.[47] This is because all confederacies rest on the principle of "the fragmentation of sovereignty."[48] The United States goes further than other confederacies in mitigating this principle by acting directly on individuals, but this innovation is in fact a necessary "fiction." The "federal system" presupposes a "complicated theory" that in turn presupposes that the governed will be guided by "a daily use of the enlightenment of their reason." So even though the Federal Constitution is the "most perfect of all known federal constitutions, one is frightened by the quantity and diverse knowledge and by the discernment that it supposes in those whom it must rule."[49]

The problem with this fiction is when it must "make way for reality."[50] If a law "violently collided with the interests and prejudices of a state," would not the individuals in that state find it in their interest to see the law defeated? This is a problem for all governments, but in confederacies the problem is that citizens "find in the share of sovereignty [of] their state" a natural and "wholly prepared organization." So, while the Union has military power, it is none-theless "an abstract being that is attached to only a few external objects."[51] The sovereignty of the states, by contrast, has the natural advantage because the states are more closely intertwined with "the things that render the instinct for one's native country so powerful in the heart of man."[52]

War was not the only problem, and, as Tocqueville explains in a later chapter, the attachments of the people were not the only under-lying cause. Making things worse was the fact that the Union "was formed by the free will of the states."[53] The Union was therefore a "contract" among willing states. If a state wanted "to withdraw its name from the contract, it would be quite difficult to prove to it that it could not do so. To combat it, the federal government would have no evident support in either force or right."[54] This characterization of the Union as a contract was both a historical claim and an explanatory one. As Tocqueville sees it, "People confederate only to derive equal advantages from union," and when those advantages are no longer clear, then people are less likely to honor the "pretended sovereignty" of union.

This historical claim, no doubt, has been the most contested issue over the course of American history, and it is therefore startling that Tocqueville rushes into so clearly embracing one side in that debate. What was his evidence? In his unsurpassed account of *Democracy in America*, James T. Schleifer speculates that Tocqueville had likely been "exposed" to William Rawle's 1825 *A View of the Constitution of the United States* by way of his assistant Francis J. Lippit, one of two Americans living in France whom Tocqueville had hired in 1834 and 1835. Lippitt studied Rawle's book while a student at Brown, and in the context of his recollections of his work with Tocqueville, mentioned that in his senior year "we had Rawle on the Constitution for six months." Schleifer also notes that Tocqueville's French edition of Jefferson's writings included a copy of the Constitution annotated by Rawle. Under Rawle's reading of the Constitution, a state "may wholly withdraw from the Union."[55]

Schleifer rightly focuses on Tocqueville's odd endorsement of secession as possible under the Constitution, but the emphasis on Rawle might distract from a more important question. Was Tocqueville's account of the Union as a "contract" among the states different from that presented in *The Federalist*? It is true that Madison's *Federalist* No. 39, which clearly influenced Tocqueville, included a passage conjuring a similar historical account. Madison wrote that the foundation of the Constitution was federal rather than national because ratification did not come from the nation in the "aggregate." Rather, the Union was achieved by the "unanimous" consent of "the several states that are parties to it." Moreover, each of these parties, the states, was a "sovereign body" at the moment of ratification.[56]

Another source might have been Jefferson. As was mentioned at the beginning of the chapter, Tocqueville owned Conseil's two-volume collection of Jefferson's writings, and he cited Jefferson at least four times in *Democracy*. That collection included Jefferson's 1800 letter to Gideon Granger, his 1811 letter to Destutt de Tracy, and his 1824 letter to Major John Cartwright. In the letter to Granger, Jefferson wrote that the "true theory of our constitution" was that "the states are independent as everything within themselves, & united as to everything respecting foreign nations."[57] In the letter to Tracy, who was a French intellectual, Jefferson praised the state governments as the "true barriers of our liberty" and "the wisest conservative power ever contrived by man." What was so ingenious about the states is that they presented a natural obstacle to usurpation by force. Unlike the "republican government of France," which "was lost without a struggle," the seventeen states in the United States at the time would be able to organize as individual states, each with their own constitutionally prescribed commander in chief and militia trained under officers "legally appointed." As a result, the likely organized resistance of sixteen states against the home state of the usurper would discourage any such attempt at usurpation. Moreover, Jefferson described the federal arrangement in characteristically stark terms: the states were "amalgamated into one as their foreign concerns, but single and independent as to their internal administration."[58] Likewise, in the letter to Cartwright, Jefferson explained that under the Federal Constitution the states, "with one or two exceptions," "reserved all legislation and administration, in affairs which govern their own citizens only," leaving the federal government "whatever concerns foreigners, or the citizens of other States." Viewed this way, the state governments are not "subordinate" to the federal government, as is usually assumed by "foreigners." Rather, the state and federal governments are "co-ordinate departments of one simple and integral whole."[59]

As Tocqueville would have been able to discern from other letters in the Conseil collection, Jefferson's description of the states as "co-ordinate" was significant. In an 1804 letter to Abigail Adams defending his 1801 pardon of James Callender, Jefferson dismissed the idea that the federal judiciary alone could "decide" the constitutionality of the Sedition Act of 1798. Explaining that the three departments of government were "co-ordinate," Jefferson argued that the president also had the power to treat the law as unconstitutional, at least insofar as the president had the power to pardon those convicted under it. Likewise, in his 1819 letter to Virginia judge Spencer Roane, Jefferson rejected the idea that the judiciary is the "last resort" on matters of constitutionality. Instead, he argued, the Constitution established three "co-ordinate and independent" departments.[60] So, for example, in the case of *Marbury v. Madison*, the federal judges may have declared the commission to Marbury valid, but they could not have issued a writ of mandamus ordering the president to deliver it. More broadly, "each of the three departments has equally the right to decide for itself what is its duty under the constitution, without regard to what the others may have decided for themselves under a similar question."[61]

If being a coordinate body requires equality and independence with respect to interpreting the Constitution, and if the states are coordinate partners, then it follows that the states have the power under the Constitution to interpret the Constitution. Although Tocqueville does not mention it, Jefferson made precisely this argument in his draft of the Kentucky Resolutions. Because the Constitution is a "compact," and because the states were the "parties" to the compact, the states and not the federal government were the ultimate judges of "infractions" of the compact, that is, of violations to the Constitution.[62] To be sure, it must be noted that Tocqueville rejected the "doctrine of nullification," as he called it, elaborated by John C. Calhoun of South Carolina.[63] As Tocqueville put it, it would return the United States to the "anarchy" that prevailed under the Articles of Confederation. If, as Calhoun says, the states are "parties that do not acknowledge a common arbiter" and each may "judge for itself the extent of its obligation," then the whole principle of the Federal Constitution would be destroyed. Yet, even as he rejected the principle of nullification, Tocqueville conceded its practical reality. The key example was the nullification crisis of 1832. Even though Andrew Jackson "sustained the rights of the Union with skill and vigor," the crisis was eventually averted when Congress passed a law in 1833 reducing the duties collected under the tariff.[64] While Congress did pass a second law authorizing the president to put down the nullifiers, this was mostly a symbolic measure designed to "conceal" the fact that it had "completely abandoned the principle of the tariff."[65] Tocqueville believed that, even though Jackson made a show of force, the nullifiers actually got what they wanted.

Even as Tocqueville praised the Federal Constitution for creating a Union that went beyond prior confederacies, he also seemed to accept readings of the federal nature of the Union that were closer to the *compact* theories of Jefferson and Madison than they were to Hamilton, John Marshall, and their Whig descendants. Perhaps Tocqueville saw in the compact theory some grounding for his emphasis on local government as a safeguard against the tyranny of the majority. Whatever the case, just as was true of his conclusion that the Constitution unwisely created a president that would be tethered to a national majority, Tocqueville's reading of the Federalist Constitution on the nature of the Union does not seem so Federalist.

RIGHTS

There is one more puzzle about Tocqueville's treatment of the Federal Constitution that is worthy of mention in closing. In the second to last chapter of the book, Tocqueville lists the features of American political and social life that help mitigate the risk of the despotism that democratic nations have to fear. His list includes voluntary associations, a free press, and judicial power. Tocqueville goes on to explain that people in democracies naturally scorn "forms," when instead they more than anyone else need to have "an enlightened and reflective worship of them."[66] A similarly damaging instinct is a disrespect of individual rights. Democratic majorities are naturally impatient with rights, as rights presuppose limits on majoritarian power. As a result, in democracies, rights are generally "unstable" and are given "little importance."[67] Tocqueville therefore recommends that the "true friends of freedom and human greatness" unite to defend rights and cultivate habits of respect for them.

Given the importance of rights, it is striking that Tocqueville does not mention the Bill of Rights in his discussion of the Federal Constitution. In 1833, John Marshall's Supreme Court held in *Barron v. Baltimore* that the Bill of Rights did not apply to the states. It is perhaps unsurprising that Tocqueville does not mention this case, but the bigger point is that Tocqueville does not seem all that interested in asking whether rights are protected by a bill of rights in either the Federal Constitution or the state constitutions. Indeed, in a section of volume 1, Tocqueville calls rights "nothing other than the idea of virtue introduced in the political world."[68] Rights are a form of enlightenment, rather than a product of it, and they teach people the boundaries of freedom and tyranny. It is essential for democracies that people believe in rights, and this belief has something to do with their prior religious belief in rights having a "divine" source.[69] Yet rights also require and come from a culture of rights: rights are strongest in countries that have believed in them the longest.[70]

More fundamentally, Tocqueville does not have all that much to say to democracies about how they might create this culture of rights. It is clear that he thinks it helps if people believe that rights come from God and that their rights are part of their ancient history. He does not say much, though, about whether these rights are fixed or evolving, whether they are particular or universal, or whether they exist by reason or by custom. Nor does he say much about who has the power to determine whether they exist. Given the proximity of these comments to his discussion of judges, it could be that rights and judges are related and that the latter are supposed to be caretakers of the former. Or it could be the case that the state and local governments would protect rights. A lot depends on which solution is best, but Tocqueville's discussion in *Democracy in America* does more to warn about the danger that democracy presents to rights than it does to show how best to protect them against too much democracy. With the centrality of this dilemma in mind, it is even more surprising that his analysis of the Federal Constitution in volume 1 of *Democracy in America* ends up being not so very Federalist in its conclusions.

NOTES

1. The author thanks Douglas S. Van for his research assistance.
2. "Joseph Story to Francis Lieber, 1840," in Joseph Story, *Life and Letters of Joseph Story*, ed. William W. Story, Vol. 2 (Boston: Charles C. Little and James Brown, 1851), 329–330.
3. Notable exceptions include James T. Schleifer, *The Making of Tocqueville's Democracy in America* (Chapel Hill: University of North Carolina Press, 1980), 90–99; Bernard E. Brown, "Tocqueville and Publius," in *Reconsidering Tocqueville's Democracy in America*, ed. Abraham S. Eisenstadt (New Brunswick, NJ: Rutgers University Press, 1988), 43–74; Rebecca McCumbers Flavin, "Tocqueville's Critique of the U. S. Constitution," *The European Legacy: Toward New Paradigms* 24, no. 7–8 (2019), 755–768.

4. DIA (MW) I.2.ii, 167.

5. DIA (MW) I.2.ii, 168.

6. DIA (MW) I.2.ii, 168.

7. DIA (MW) I.2.ii, 169. See also Tocqueville's admiration of Hamilton for his daring to write the passage in *Federalist* No. 71 explaining that the people often need representatives to protect them from themselves; DIA (MW) I.1.viii, 144.

8. DIA (MW) I.2.vii, 249.

9. Robert P. Kraynak, "Tocqueville's Constitutionalism," *American Political Science Review* 81, no. 4 (1987), 1187.

10. James Ceaser, *Designing a Polity: America's Constitution in Theory and Practice* (Lanham, MD: Rowman & Littlefield, 2010), 23–45.

11. DIA (MW) I.1.ii, 28. For the French, see DIA (N) 46 and 284.

12. L. P. Conseil, *Mélanges politiques et philosophiques extraits des mémoirs et de la correspondence de Thomas Jefferson*, 2 vols. (Paris: Paulin, Libraire-Éditeur, 1833); Schleifer, *Making*, 99–100.

13. James Madison, Federalist No. 48, in *James Madison: Writings*, ed. Jack N. Rakove (New York: Library of America, 1999), 282–283.

14. DIA (MW) I.1.viii, 111.

15. DIA (MW) I.1.viii, 112.

16. DIA (MW) I.1.viii, 144.

17. DIA (MW) I.1.viii, 145.

18. DIA (MW) I.1.viii, 145.

19. Michael F. Holt, *The Rise and Fall of the American Whig Party: Jacksonian Politics and the Onset of the Civil War* (New York: Oxford University Press, 1999).

20. In the chapter, "Parties in the United States," he offers it as an example of the majority's inability to judge complicated questions of public policy; DIA (MW) 170. In the chapter "On the Three Races That Inhabit the United States," Tocqueville mentions the Bank as an example of the "great hatred" felt toward the Bank as one "incident in the great combat that the provinces fight against the central power in America"; DIA (MW) I.2.x, 373–374.

21. DIA (MW) I.1.viii, 125.

22. DIA (MW) I.1.viii, 125.

23. James Ceaser, *Presidential Selection: Theory and Development* (Princeton, NJ: Princeton University Press, 1979), 42–51; Jeffrey K. Tulis, *The*

Rhetorical Presidency (Princeton, NJ: Princeton University Press, 1988), 39–40; Jeremy D. Bailey, *The Idea of Presidential Representation: An Intellectual and Political History* (Lawrence: University Press of Kansas, 2019), 64–69.

24. DIA (MW) I.1.viii, 126.
25. For the logic behind the amendment, see Jeremy D. Bailey, *Thomas Jefferson and Executive Power* (New York: Cambridge University Press, 2007), 195–209.
26. DIA (MW) I.1.viii, 126–127.
27. DIA (MW) I.1.viii, 127.
28. DIA (MW) I.1.viii, 127.
29. DIA (MW) I.1.viii, 128.
30. DIA (MW) I.1.viii, 129. See Flavins, "Tocqueville's Critique of the US Constitution," 762–763.
31. DIA (MW) I.1.viii, 129.
32. DIA (MW) I.1.viii, 130.
33. Brown concludes that Tocqueville was simply too much of a monarchist to believe that the electorate could adequately elect the chief executive. See Brown, "Tocqueville and Publius," 60–62.
34. Bailey, *Idea of Presidential Representation*, 64–69.
35. DIA (MW) I.1.viii, 146.
36. DIA (MW) I.1.viii, 147.
37. DIA (MW) I.1.viii, 147.
38. DIA (MW) I.1.viii, 148.
39. DIA (MW) I.1.viii, 149.
40. James Madison, *Federalist* No. 39, in *James Madison: Writings*, 216–217.
41. DIA (MW) I.1.viii, 149.
42. James Madison, *Federalist* No. 39, in *James Madison: Writings*, 214–216.
43. DIA (MW) I.1.viii, 132.
44. DIA (MW) I.1.viii, 134.
45. DIA (MW) I.1.viii, 141.
46. DIA (MW) I.1.viii, 142.
47. DIA (MW) I.1.viii, 161.
48. DIA (MW) I.1.viii, 156.
49. DIA (MW) I.1.viii, 155.
50. DIA (MW) I.1.viii, 157.
51. DIA (MW) I.1.viii, 157.

52. DIA (MW) I.1.viii, 158.

53. DIA (MW) I.2.x, 354.

54. DIA (MW) I.2.x, 354.

55. Schleifer, *Making*, 99–100.

56. James Madison, Federalist No. 39, in *James Madison: Writings*, 214–215.

57. Thomas Jefferson to Gideon Granger, August 13, 1800, in *Thomas Jefferson: Writings*, ed. Merrill D. Peterson (New York: Library of America, 1984), 1079.

58. Thomas Jefferson to A. L. C. Destutt de Tracy, January 26, 1811, in *Thomas Jefferson: Writings*, 1241–1247.

59. Thomas Jefferson to Major John Cartwright, June 5, 1824, in *Thomas Jefferson: Writings*, 1490–1496.

60. Thomas Jefferson to Spencer Roane, September 6, 1819, in *Thomas Jefferson: Writings*, 1426.

61. Thomas Jefferson to Spencer Roane, September 6, 1819, in *Thomas Jefferson: Writings*, 1427–1428.

62. Thomas Jefferson, "Draft of the Kentucky Resolutions," in *Thomas Jefferson: Writings*, 449.

63. DIA (MW) I.2.x, 375.

64. DIA (MW) I.2.x, 377.

65. DIA (MW) I.2.x, 376.

66. DIA (MW) II.4.vii, 669.

67. DIA (MW) II.4.vii, 670.

68. DIA (MW) I.2.vi, 227.

69. DIA (MW) I.2.vi, 228.

70. DIA (MW) I.2.vi, 229.

I2 Religion in *Democracy in America*

Carson Holloway

INTRODUCTION

What is the relationship between religion and modern democracy? Is a religious citizenry necessary for effective and decent self-government? For democracy's ability to sustain itself and to be a just form of rule? Or is religious belief a mere relic of the past, irrelevant and unsuited to, perhaps even hostile to, our modern, democratic, and rationalistic world?

Contemporary debates about these questions tend to be partisan in character. Proponents of religion lament its decline, warning of the social ills that they believe will accompany the waning of its influence. Enemies of religion celebrate its decline, bidding it good riddance as, they think, a source of superstition, rigidity, and intolerance out of place in a modern progressive society. This partisanship in turn leads us to wonder whether there can be an account of these questions that is nonpartisan, an account that achieves the elevation and evenhandedness of philosophy.

Alexis de Tocqueville provides such an account in *Democracy in America* (*DIA*). Religion, Tocqueville contends, is necessary to democracy. Democracy owes its origins to the rise of Christianity, and democracy, once in existence, depends for its continued flourishing on the habits of thought and virtues of character that Christianity fosters. Nevertheless, Tocqueville writes not as an evangelist but as a social philosopher interested in democracy's long-term sustainability. Moreover, although he argues that democracy and religion are inextricably linked, Tocqueville also explains why religion can seem so out of place in a modern democracy. Tocqueville also avoids religious partisanship by teaching proponents of religion that they must conduct themselves with a certain moderation and circumspection. Democracy needs religion, but religious believers cannot simply shape democratic society according to their own beliefs. On the contrary, religion must to some extent accommodate itself to the democratic spirit of the modern age. Finally, Tocqueville acknowledges that Christianity is not the only religion that can provide the moral and spiritual support that a modern democracy needs. By thus rising above intellectual partisanship, by giving due attention to the various sides of the issue, Tocqueville offers an enduring account of the relationship of democracy to religion, an account that is still relevant in our own time.

CHRISTIANITY AND THE ORIGINS OF DEMOCRACY

Tocqueville begins from the European disputes of his own day between the forces of religion and the forces of democracy. In the "Author's Introduction" to *DIA*, he notes that in Europe the proponents of religion and the proponents of democracy tend to view each other as enemies. The most ardent Christians think of democracy as an aggressively anti-religious movement. At the same time, the most zealous advocates of democracy view Christianity as a politically reactionary force, propping up the outmoded and unjust aristocratic order that must be overthrown for democracy to flourish.

According to Tocqueville, this mutual hostility is not the "natural" state of things. It is rather the result of a "strange concatenation of events" whereby "religion" became temporarily "entangled with those institutions" that "democracy overthrows."[1] The state-established churches of the time were necessarily allied with existing aristocratic and monarchical governments. As a result, the defenders of religion and the proponents of democracy had to view each other as enemies in relation to their immediate political interests. Nevertheless, Tocqueville teaches, if both sides would take a longer view of things, they would realize that Christianity and democracy are not mutually exclusive and, indeed, that Christianity planted the seeds of equality that later permitted the growth of the modern democratic movement.

Tocqueville credits Christianity with introducing the idea of human equality into world history, or at least into Western history. As Tocqueville famously teaches, the prevailing social state exercises a prodigious influence on thought. In aristocracies, vast and intractable inequalities are so familiar as to be unquestioned. Accordingly, in ancient Greek and Roman societies established on the basis of slavery, even the most penetrating thinkers assumed slavery to be natural and permanent. "Their minds roamed free in many directions but were blinkered" when it came to the possibility of human equality. Tocqueville thus concludes that "Jesus Christ had to come down to earth to make all members of the human race understand that they were naturally similar and equal."[2]

Tocqueville sees a natural harmony between Christian theology and democratic political ideas: "Christianity, which has declared all men equal in the sight of God, cannot hesitate to acknowledge all citizens equal before the law."[3] Accordingly, the progress of Christianity was accompanied by a gradual amelioration of the inequalities that had so deeply marked the ancient world. At least in premodern times,[4] Christianity "destroyed slavery by insisting on the slave's rights."[5] Later, the political power of the church introduced a democratic element into the otherwise aristocratic order of the Middle Ages. "The ranks of the clergy were open to all, poor or rich, commoner or noble," and so "through the church equality began to insinuate itself into the heart of government, and a man who would have vegetated as a serf in eternal servitude could, as a priest, take his place among the nobles and often take precedence over kings."[6] Tocqueville thus speaks of the modern democratic revolution as a phenomenon taking place in "the Christian world."[7]

More specifically, Tocqueville credits a particular kind of Christianity with the rise of the most successful modern democracy. According to Tocqueville, a nation's "point of departure" – its character at its birth – exercises a tremendous influence on its subsequent development. America's point of departure was provided by the Puritan settlers of New England. They were driven to the New World not by ambition or avarice but by "a purely intellectual craving": the desire to establish societies based on their religious convictions. Those convictions, however, were also very favorable to the development of self-government. "Puritanism," Tocqueville observes, "was not just a religious doctrine; in many respects it shared the most absolute democratic and republican theories."[8] The Puritans had "shaken off the pope's authority" and "acknowledged no other religious supremacy."[9] Their churches were accordingly governed by the members, and they carried this democratic spirit into the administration of their political affairs. Thus, for example, the celebrated pilgrim settlers at Plymouth decided *among themselves* to establish the Mayflower Compact, by which they announced their intention to create a colony for "the glory of God, and the advancement of the Christian faith," but one that would also be governed by "just and equal laws."[10]

Tocqueville (again, avoiding a spirit of narrow partisanship) does not present the Puritans as having created a kind of pious democratic utopia. He acknowledges their errors (such as their neglect of religious liberty) and their follies (such as their modeling of their criminal laws on the prohibitions and punishments of the Old Testament). Nor does he suggest that Puritanism alone, or even Protestantism, is uniquely compatible with democracy. Having left their monarchical homelands, Catholic immigrants to the United States, their minds shaped by the aforementioned generally egalitarian spirit of Christianity, also become sound American democrats. Nevertheless, Tocqueville singles out New England's Puritans for having sown the seeds of democratic republicanism that later came to dominate the whole nation's political life.

Thus, for Tocqueville, once the political alliances and animosities of revolutionary times have been laid to rest, Christianity and democracy, taking the long view and focusing on their deeper relationship, should recognize each other as friends. Christians should view democracy as the political fruit of Christianity, not as some atheistic and hostile movement; and democrats should view Christianity as the seedbed of democracy, not as an inherently reactionary force.

RELIGION AND THE FLOURISHING OF DEMOCRACY

The argument thus far does not fully address the question with which this chapter began, namely what is the relationship between religion and democracy? After all, it is possible that Christianity was a necessary condition for the rise of modern democracy but is no longer necessary to its continuance. Perhaps mature democratic societies, once their cultures are formed and their institutions established, can dispense with religion, just as some individuals benefit from a religious moral formation in their youth but then leave aside religious belief and practice in their adulthood. This is not, however, Tocqueville's view. He contends instead that the spirit of religion is necessary to sustain and elevate democracy, to permit it to be an effective and just form of government, one compatible with the freedom and dignity of human beings. Put another way, Tocqueville regards the spirit of religion as one of the *permanent* requirements of a healthy democracy.

Here, Tocqueville's account of religion points to one of the key aspects of his political teaching. He does not assume that democratic government is necessarily good government or that a democratic society is necessarily a just and decent society. On the contrary, one of the primary aims of his inquiry is to identify the drawbacks and dangers of democracy and to suggest ways to remedy or at least to ameliorate them. *DIA*'s account of religion's important role in this endeavor is complex and subtle, but it is possible to sketch four prominent lines of argument.

Enlightening Democratic Mediocrity

In the first place, Tocqueville contends that democracies are prone to elevate mediocre people to positions of political authority.

Democracy is indirect rule by the people, that is, by the ordinary run of human beings. Those who think that the people are led by some unerring instinct to elect the best leaders to public office are, Tocqueville says, laboring under a delusion. The people ordinarily want what is best for their country, but they are prevented by economic necessity from attending too closely to political affairs. As a result, they lack the information necessary to make sound judgments about the character and abilities of those seeking public office. It is not surprising, then, that the people's confidence is often won (and abused) by political charlatans and quacks who succeed in getting elected. Moreover, the people to some extent do not even want to elect the most fit characters. Democracy, Tocqueville observes, tends to foster a spirit of envy in the people. Democracy opens the way of advancement to all, but the universal competition it unleashes ensures that few are able to rise very far above their origins. As a result, disappointed hopes make many voters reluctant to honor with public office those of superior achievements. Finally, on the other side of the equation, the best citizens tend to hold aloof from seeking office in a democracy. Repelled by the circus-like atmosphere of democratic political campaigns, the most earnest and enlightened members of the community feel they can best maintain their integrity by remaining in private life.

Although no nation can reasonably expect to have excellent political leadership all the time, democracy's tendency toward consistent mediocrity in public office is troubling. After all, democratic nations, like any others, face perplexing problems of foreign and domestic policy that call for foresight and prudence. Accordingly, Tocqueville tries to discover how to counteract this democratic tendency. He notes the importance of unusual circumstances (a genuine crisis can call forth great leaders) and institutions (indirect election can elevate the quality of elected officials). He also, however, points to the kind of moral culture fostered by religion. "In New England," he observes, "where education and liberty spring from morality and religion," the voters "are accustomed to respect intellectual and moral superiority and submit thereto without displeasure; and so we find New England democracy making better choices than those made elsewhere."[11] Christianity famously teaches that envy is a sin, that we should rejoice in the gifts that are given to others and not poison our minds with coveting them for ourselves. To that extent, it counteracts the resentments that lead democratic citizens to withhold public honors from the more virtuous and accomplished.

Opposing the Tyranny of the Majority

In the second place, democracy has a tendency to produce not only mediocre government but also, and much worse, unjust government. Democracy purports to be rule by the people. In truth, however, it is rule by the majority of the people; and, according to Tocqueville, there is nothing in the nature of a political majority to make it immune to unjust impulses. Everyone would admit the danger that a powerful individual might abuse his power over another. A majority "in its collective capacity," however, is nothing more than an "individual with opinions, and usually with interests, contrary to those of another individual, called the minority."[12] Men do not "change their character," do not become more just, simply by "joining together," and do not become "more patient of obstacles" simply by "becoming stronger."[13] For Tocqueville, then, as for the American Founders, one of the great dangers of democracy is majority tyranny.

This problem is compounded, on Tocqueville's account, by the remarkable – and frightening – power that the majority possesses over thought in a democracy. This power arises in part from what Tocqueville calls the "moral authority of the majority."[14] Committed to the belief that all individuals are fundamentally equal, democratic peoples are easily led to the conclusion that truth will be found on the side of the greatest number. As a result, democratic citizens come to view the majority not only as a power to which they must submit but also as an authority with which they must agree. In addition, Tocqueville argues, a democratic majority has a power undreamt of by kings: the power to shame and ostracize. Those who differ from the majority may find themselves treated as social outcasts. Consequently, few citizens have the courage to defy majority opinion.

Tocqueville presents religion – here understood as a generalized Christianity, irrespective of specific denominations – as one of the correctives that can help to hold the tyranny of the majority in check. The Americans, he observes, subscribe to a wide variety of sects, each with its own preferred mode of worship. This diversity of rituals, however, coexists with a fundamental moral consensus. All these sects "agree concerning the duties of men to one another. Each sect worships God in its own fashion, but all preach the same morality in the name of God."[15] Tocqueville does not contend that all Americans are sincere Christians. Some of them, he says, "profess Christian dogmas because they believe in them," while others "do so because they are afraid to look as though they did not believe them."[16] The power of American Christianity arises in part from the genuine faith of its true adherents and in part from its general social respectability. The combination of these two forces, however, is sufficient for Christian ethics to dominate American political life. Even the most politically radical Americans, Tocqueville contends, "are obliged ostensibly to profess a certain respect for Christian morality and equity, and that does not allow them easily to break the laws when those are opposed to the execution of their designs."[17] The result is a public culture in which standards of right and justice are so earnestly affirmed that the possibility of majority tyranny is diminished because no one is willing to endorse it openly. As Tocqueville observes, "[U]p till now no one in the United States has dared to profess the maxim that everything is allowed in the interests of society, an impious maxim apparently invented in an age of freedom in order to legitimize every future tyrant."[18]

Tocqueville does not go so far as to suggest that religion is the only way to combat majority tyranny. He also notes the importance of institutions such as separation of powers and the salutary influence of the legal profession, with its insistence that even the majority must submit to ancient and venerable legal principles. Nevertheless, Tocqueville finds religion so crucial in the fight against majority tyranny that he says that it "should be considered as the first" of the Americans' "political institutions, for although it did not give them the taste for liberty, it singularly facilitates their use thereof."[19]

Discouraging the Pathologies of Individualism

Third, Tocqueville discerns in democracy a dangerous tendency toward excessive individualism. Here, he develops his diagnosis, as he so often does, by comparing the effects of aristocracy and democracy on the minds and souls of human beings. An aristocracy, he observes, fosters strong links among its subjects. The members of an aristocratic society see themselves not primarily as autonomous individuals but instead as parts of a larger whole, or of several larger wholes that are themselves parts of the overarching community. The family, understood as extended through time, looms large in the aristocratic imagination. In an aristocracy, families are linked to a particular plot of land, which the laws and customs of the society do not easily permit them to sell. The family becomes like a little fatherland, with a history and future cherished by its members. Aristocratic peoples accordingly have a very clear conception of their duties to both past and future generations. Moreover, aristocracies are made up of a hierarchy of classes. Because they share so much in common, the members of these classes experience a strong group solidarity. Finally, the social hierarchy of an aristocracy also creates links between the members of different classes. The whole society, Tocqueville suggests, exists as a kind of chain of obligations, in which everyone has duties to those above and below.

Democracy tends to destroy all these links and to leave human beings isolated from each other. The democratic law of inheritance – equal shares for all the children – tends to break up family estates, with the result that the family becomes more of a passing institution, unable to link its members to past and future generations. Although some people are wealthier than others in a democracy, there are no permanent classes such as exist in an aristocracy. Therefore, the members of what are called "classes" in a democracy have little in common and only a weak motive for group solidarity; and since in a democracy one's social status is not secured by law and custom, democrats tend to understand themselves – with some justification – as "self-made." They have achieved their economic and social status through their own efforts, and therefore they have little sense of loyalty to those above them or of *noblesse oblige* to those below them.

The outcome of all these forces, Tocqueville contends, is not total selfishness or "egoism," which he understands to be not a unique characteristic of democracy but a vice incident to human nature under any regime.[20] Democracy does not make citizens completely self-absorbed, but it does tend to focus their minds almost exclusively on their little circles of family and friends, cutting them off from the larger society. This individualism, though not morally depraved, is nevertheless politically dangerous. It does not necessarily destroy all virtue, but it "dams up the springs of public virtue" and thus opens the door to despotism.[21] Democratic citizens tend to be isolated from each other and from the larger society, which is precisely the condition that despots prefer for their subjects. There is then little likelihood of the people cooperating with a view to resisting despotism and taking the affairs of their country into their own hands. Thus Tocqueville warns that democracy is threatened not only by the danger of majority tyranny – abuse of power by a politically active citizenry – but also by the opposite but no less destructive danger of despotism – unchecked rule of the government over a politically passive citizenry.

Aware of this danger, the Americans seek to combat it by a certain kind of public-spirited moral education, an education in what Tocqueville calls "self-interest properly understood."[22] Seeing how powerfully democracy turns the minds of individuals in on themselves and their own immediate circle, American moralists wisely avoid the futile task of trying to interest their fellow citizens in aristocratic conceptions of morality as a beautiful or noble selfless-ness. They instead seek a lower but perhaps more solid moral ground by reminding their countrymen that their own personal interests are often protected by devoting due attention to their social and political duties. One may, for example, have to sacrifice some of one's pursuit of wealth in order to devote time to cooperating with fellow citizens in establishing and administering community schools. The end result of these sacrifices, however, is a convenient institution by which one's own children can be educated, as well as a more educated and therefore more prosperous community. On this view, individuals will be better off in the long run if they overcome their individualism and attend to their civic duties.

Tocqueville adds, however, that the doctrine of self-interest properly understood is not sufficient on its own to combat democratic individualism successfully. It needs to be supplemented by religion. It is not enough to have enlightened attention to one's long-term inter-ests in this world, because "there are a great many" socially necessary "sacrifices which can only be rewarded in the next. However hard one may try to prove that virtue is useful, it will always be difficult to make a man live well if he will not face death."[23] Nations cannot survive unless some of their citizens are willing to confront the dangers of battle, and it would seem impossible to convince soldiers that it is in their personal long-term interest to be killed defending their country. Religion is thus necessary to sustain the virtues on which the community depends for its very existence. Religion also supports the more ordinary social virtues by making all sacrifices of personal interest, even the smallest and most everyday ones, easier than they otherwise would be. After all, the worldly version of self-interest properly understood always involves an element of risk. One might sacrifice one's time and resources in efforts for the public good, and the projects undertaken may end up failing; or, if they succeed, bad fortune may prevent one from sharing in their benefits. These kinds of worries, which undermine commitment to public duty, need not trouble religious believers, who can be secure in the knowledge that their sacrifices and virtues cannot escape finally being rewarded in the next life.

Countering Excessive Materialism

Finally, Tocqueville contends that religion is necessary to combat democracy's inclination to generate in its citizens a dangerously excessive interest in material well-being. Tocqueville does not argue that democracy itself produces the taste for material comforts, which is a trait of human nature and thus can be found in all times and places. Nevertheless, he says, democratic social conditions do tend to inflame this taste beyond measure.

Once more, Tocqueville develops his account by contrasting democracy and aristocracy. The latter tends to quiet the desire for material well-being. Obsession with physical comforts, Tocqueville contends, is fostered most powerfully not by their unimpeded enjoyment nor, on the other hand, by their denial. It is instead stoked by an imperfect experience of them coupled with the fear of losing them. In an aristocracy, the nobles take material comforts for granted because of their easy acquaintance with them. They experience such goods as part of life but not as the aim of life, and their interest turns to politics and the works of the mind. At the other end of the social hierarchy, the poor in an aristocracy have so limited an experience of physical comforts that they take little interest in them. No amount of effort can elevate their economic standing, so they do not long for things they know they will never have. Their minds turn, then, to the consolations of religion, and they tend to "dwell in imagination on the next world."[24]

A democratic nation, however, is predominantly a middle-class nation – exactly the kind of nation in which most citizens win enough of material well-being to take an interest in it but not enough to feel satisfied. Such citizens "never win" physical comforts "without effort or indulge them without anxiety," and they "are therefore continually engaged in pursuing or striving to retain these precious, incomplete, and fugitive delights."[25] Even the poor and the rich in a democracy follow the middle class in its preoccupation with material comforts. Because of democracy's social and economic mobility, the poor hope to raise their condition and already turn their minds to goods they do not yet possess. This same mobility ensures that most of the rich started life on a lower rung of the economic ladder, so that their tastes were formed by the middle-class experience. Thus, in a democracy, the "love of comfort" will be the "dominant national taste."[26]

For Tocqueville, this democratic materialism is pregnant with perils both moral and political. Their taste for physical pleasures does not lead democratic citizens into debauchery. Such extreme hedonism is rather the vice of corrupted aristocrats, who are used to thinking on a grand scale and who have the means to satisfy their vast appetites. The material goods the democratic citizens pursue so earnestly are innocent in themselves – a larger estate, for example, or a more comfortable house. Nevertheless, the quest for such goods is so single-minded that they threaten "to come between the soul and God" and to lead democratic peoples to "lose sight of those more precious goods which constitute the greatness and the glory of mankind."[27] Moreover, the obsessive pursuit of such goods can only lead to melancholy and restlessness. Human beings who treat physical pleasures as the greatest good will be tormented by anxiety, fearing that they may have failed to cram as much pleasure as possible into this short life and knowing that the end of such pleasures is inevitably approaching. Thus, Tocqueville observes, the Americans, though they enjoy immense prosperity, seem "serious and almost sad even in their pleasures."[28]

Politically, democratic materialism, like democratic individualism, threatens a descent into despotism. Citizens whose eyes are fixed exclusively on the pursuit of material pleasures tend to neglect their civic duties. They regard attention to and participation in politics as a waste of time. After all, it does not increase their wealth, which is the means by which they win their physical comforts. With such citizens, if an "able and ambitious man" wins power he will find "the way open for usurpations of every sort."[29] As long as he maintains the public order that allows prosperity to flourish, the citizens will gladly cede their authority to direct public affairs. If the outright despotism of one ruler does not arise, democratic materialism may lead to the despotism of a minority "faction." "When the great mass of citizens does not want to bother about anything but private business, even the smallest party need not give up hope of becoming master of public affairs." Then the "caprice" of a few can rule "everything, changing laws and tyrannizing over moral standards; and one is left in astonishment at the small number of weak and unworthy hands into which a great people can fall."[30]

Once again, religion provides a remedy for this democratic malady. While democracy "lays the soul open to an inordinate love of material pleasure," one of the great benefits of religion is to "inspire diametrically contrary urges" by placing "the object of man's desires outside and beyond worldly goods" and thus "naturally" elevating "the soul into regions far above the senses."[31] Thus Tocqueville finds that, in America, religion alone can free the citizens from "the petty passions" that "trouble" their lives and turn their minds "to an ideal world where all is great, pure, and eternal." For six days of the week, Americans dedicate all their efforts to work and acquisition. On Sunday, however, they go to church and are "reminded of the need to check" their "desires and told of the finer delights that go with virtue alone, and the true happiness they bring."[32] For Tocqueville, the importance of religion's power to counteract popular materialism can hardly be overstated. Thus he remarks that "at all costs Christianity must be maintained among the new democracies."[33]

DEMOCRACY'S NEED FOR RELIGIOUS MODERATION

To recap, Tocqueville contends that Christianity is responsible for the rise of modern democracy, that Puritanism planted the seeds of American self-government, that religion should be considered as the first of America's political institutions, and that in America, and in all the newly democratic countries, Christianity must be maintained at all costs. Such claims might well foster a spirit of triumphalism in America's Christians. After all, their beliefs – and they themselves as the carriers and propagators of those beliefs – are essential to democracy's flourishing. Tocqueville, however, does not encourage American Christians to adopt such an overbearing attitude. On the contrary, he seeks to teach them a certain circumspection and moderation. Religion may be useful and even necessary to democracy, but its proponents should not expect to dominate the society, to shape democracy exclusively according to their own vision of the good.

Although democracy needs religion, it does not tend to foster a deep religiosity in its citizens. Tocqueville famously observes that Americans are natural Cartesians without ever having studied the works of Descartes. Democratic social conditions, he explains, foster a kind of individualistic rationalism in a people. Individuals are free and equal and generally left to manage their own affairs. They succeed reasonably well and are therefore inclined to conclude that "nothing in the world is beyond human intelligence." Thus Americans, and democratic peoples more generally, display a "distaste for the supernatural."[34] Because of their belief in equality, democrats are reluctant to submit to any intellectual authority, even the authority of tradition, which seems to them not the wisdom of venerable ancestors but merely the opinions of their equals who lived long ago. Religion, however, depends on the doctrinal authority of churches in the present and on the authority of traditions that have been handed down from the past. In view of these and similar considerations, Tocqueville concludes that "religions are growing weak" under modern democratic conditions.[35]

For Tocqueville, then, democracy needs religion but tends to undermine religion. Faced with this problem, one might be inclined to use all available tools to promote religious belief. If democratic social conditions threaten religion, why not use the power of the state to safeguard religion and prop it up? After all, according to Tocqueville's account such a project would not be merely partisan or sectarian but would look to ensuring the justice, decency, and stability of democracy.

Nevertheless, Tocqueville warns his readers that this temptation is strictly to be avoided. Religion is powerful in America, he contends, not in spite of but precisely because of the separation of church and state. Efforts to bring political power to bear in support of religion tend to be counterproductive. Any alliance between church and state, Tocqueville observes, exposes religion to all the resentments and animosities that politics necessarily entails. Governments must rule, must decide controversial questions, and therefore must inevitably offend some powerful interests in the community. Thus an official link between government and religion inevitably makes some citizens into the political enemies of religion. Governmental sponsorship of religion is especially to be avoided in a democracy. Democratic governments are necessarily unstable, depending as they do on the constantly turning tides of public opinion. Religions claim to teach eternal truths, and it is therefore not in their interest to be too closely associated with the instability and change characteristic of democratic politics. According to Tocqueville, human beings are naturally inclined to religious belief. Our hearts can never be completely satisfied by this life and we accordingly long for the immortality that religion promises. Religion, therefore, does not need the assistance of the state, and religion is powerful in America precisely because it rejects such artificial aid and relies on its own natural influence over the "human heart."[36]

Tocqueville's lessons in moderation for democracy's religious believers do not end here. Believing that religion is essential to democracy's flourishing, but that one must not rely on political power to support it, the proponents of religion might conclude that they have a duty to preach traditional religion with all the intransigence and zeal they can muster. Tocqueville, however, counsels against such a course. The maintenance of religion under democratic conditions, he suggests, requires a spirit of finesse. Religion can always gain a hearing because of its appeal to human nature. Nevertheless, while human nature is powerful, the social state, and the modes of thought and feeling that it fosters, are powerful as well. The social state conditions the way in which human beings are capable of receiving religion, and accordingly religion – or at least any religion that hopes to have wide appeal and to be socially influential – must accommodate itself to some extent to the prevailing social state.

In democratic times, religion should strive for simplicity of belief and worship and be moderate in its moral demands. The Catholic cult of the saints was so powerful in the Middle Ages, Tocqueville suggests, because the aristocratic mind is so inclined to think in terms of complex hierarchies of rank. It was easy then to dwell on the idea of intermediary spiritual powers between God and man. In ages of equality, however, we are more inclined to think in terms of each person's equally direct relationship to God. Aristocratic peoples love ceremony in social interactions and therefore in their religious rites as well, while democratic peoples are inclined to find too much ceremony tedious and to crave a simple and straightforward mode of worship. The aristocratic mind is inclined to a severe and generous morality, and it is therefore prepared to listen to a religion that tells it to sacrifice all worldly comforts for the heavenly kingdom. The democratic mind, as we have seen, is preoccupied with material comforts; and while it can understand the need to moderate physical desires, it will not listen patiently to any demand to renounce them. Religions in democratic times, Tocqueville suggests, should be prepared to accommodate all of these democratic inclinations. This is not to say, Tocqueville hastens to add, that the teachers of religion should in all things "trim their sails" to the prevailing democratic winds. This they could not do without destroying their credibility as teachers of "general and eternal truths."[37] They must instead carefully safeguard the essentials of the faith while at the same time being prepared to compromise in secondary matters so as to preserve their ability to win a hearing in democratic times.

Finally, Tocqueville's account of the natural weakness of religion in democratic times sheds further light on his aforementioned bold claim that "at all costs Christianity must be maintained among the new democracies."[38] This remark seems to indicate that *only* Christianity can sustain a healthy democracy. Examined more closely, however, Tocqueville's account suggests otherwise. While discussing how to counter the dangers of democratic materialism and individualism, Tocqueville observes that "[e]very religion places the object of man's desires outside and beyond worldly goods and naturally lifts the soul into regions far above the senses," just as "[e]very religion also imposes on each man some obligations toward mankind, to be performed in common with the rest of mankind, and so draws him away, from time to time, from thinking about himself."[39] Tocqueville, then, emphasizes the need to preserve Christianity within existing democracies not because he holds that Christianity is the only religion from which democracy can benefit but because Christianity is America and Europe's ancestral religion, and he fears that under modern democratic conditions religious faith, once lost, will be difficult to revive or replace.

These considerations also point to the continuing relevance of Tocqueville's teaching about democracy and religion. Contemporary America is a much more religiously diverse nation than it was in Tocqueville's day. Christianity, though powerful, no longer holds the dominant position it did in the 1830s. The changes in America's religious landscape, however, do not render Tocqueville's teaching irrelevant. Democracy's dangerous tendencies still exist, and today's Tocquevillean statesman can still find the materials by which to ameliorate them not only in Christianity but also in the other religions that have gained prominence in more recent times.

CONCLUSION

Faced with the contest between the proponents and opponents of religion, Tocqueville defends religion's crucial contribution to the success of democracy. He does so, however, without succumbing to the spirit of partisanship. His teaching is moderate in that it acknowledges both the importance of religion and the limits it must respect. Tocqueville's moderation is made possible by the elevation of his mind. He does not situate himself between the claims of the partisans but seeks to rise above them. He sees beyond the present controversies and bases his judgments on lasting considerations, like the long-term historical development of democracy and the fixed tendencies of the democratic social state, and on permanent ones, like the nature of the human heart. He thus manifests and teaches the lofty virtues of mind necessary to understand, preserve, and improve the democracy we have inherited.

NOTES

1. DIA (L) I. Author's Introduction, 16–17.
2. DIA (L) II.1.iii, 439.
3. DIA (L) I. Author's Introduction, 16.
4. Tocqueville is of course aware of, and devotes considerable attention to, the problem of the establishment of slavery in America by Christians of the modern era.
5. DIA (L) I.2.x, 348.
6. DIA (L) I. Author's Introduction, 10.
7. DIA (L) I. Author's Introduction, 11.
8. DIA (L) I.1.ii, 36.
9. DIA (L) I.2.ix, 288.
10. DIA (L) I.1.2, 39.
11. DIA (L) I.2.v, 200.
12. DIA (L) I.2.vii, 251.
13. DIA (L) I.2.vii, 251.
14. DIA (L) I.2.vii, 247.
15. DIA (L) I.2.ix, 290.
16. DIA (L) I.2.ix, 292.
17. DIA (L) I.2.ix, 292.
18. DIA (L) I.2.ix, 292.
19. DIA (L) I.2.ix, 292.
20. DIA (L) II.2.ii, 506–507.

21. DIA (L) II.2.ii, 507.
22. DIA (L) II.2.viii, 525.
23. DIA (L) II.2.ix, 528.
24. DIA (L) II.2.x, 531.
25. DIA (L) II.2.x, 531.
26. DIA (L) II.2.x, 531.
27. DIA (L) II.2.xi, 533–534.
28. DIA (L) II.2.xiii, 536.
29. DIA (L) II.2.xiv, 540.
30. DIA (L) II.2.xiv, 540.
31. DIA (L) II.1.v, 444.
32. DIA (L) II.2.xv, 542.
33. DIA (L) II.2.xv, 545–546.
34. DIA (L) II.1.i, 430.
35. DIA (L) I.2.vi, 239.
36. DIA (L) I.2.ix, 296.
37. DIA (L) II.1.v, 447.
38. DIA (L) II.1.xv, 545–546.
39. DIA (L) II.1.v, 444–445.

13 Tocqueville's Puritans

Joshua Mitchell

RELIGION PRECEDES POLITICS

Scholars of Tocqueville's *Democracy in America* have long noted Tocqueville's appreciation of Christianity in America and, indeed, the importance of Christianity in the democratic age. They differ about whether Christianity is merely socially useful, as Tocqueville seems to suggest in volume 2,[1] or whether Christianity indeed answers the deepest longings of the human heart, as he seems to suggest in volume 1,[2] but they do not doubt the centrality of Christianity to Tocqueville's analysis of America as a whole. The beginning of *Democracy* sets up all that follows. After the first chapter of volume 1 introduces the reader to geographic distinctions that later shadow Tocqueville's ruminations about slavery,[3] in the first substantive chapter about the American people, he declares that founding events are constitutive events:

> [Go back to] the very first records of [a people's history]; I have no doubt that you should there find the first causes of their prejudices, habits, dominating passions, and all that comes to be called the national character.[4]

Only a few pages later, we are introduced to the Puritans, the true founders of America. Convention in political theory has it that founding events are political events. Should it not then be the case that the American founding be identified with the American Revolutionary period and its constitutional aftermath? Already in the "Author's Introduction," Tocqueville gives some indication that he will not take the conventional course: "one cannot establish the reign of liberty without that of mores, and mores cannot be firmly founded without beliefs,"[5] he writes.

There is a general theory here, lurking under what seems to be an interesting but relatively innocuous passing comment. It is a theory about the relationship between politics, mores, and religion. For political arrangements to work well, austere mores must undergird them. This is in and of itself an uncontroversial claim. Yet Tocqueville goes further: religion is the foundation of mores.[6] Remove religion and mores will erode, after which your once sturdy political arrangements will crack and crumble, or what is perhaps worse, they may perdure without vitality. Religion is the deepest thing; whatever stability you observe in your political arrangements rests on foundations that are pre-political and, finally, religious. Politics is not downstream of culture; it is downstream of religion.

A number of observations in *Democracy* confirm this general theory. In a little-recognized passage about the Islamic world in volume 1, Tocqueville writes:

> The Turkish peoples have never taken any part in the control of society's affairs; nevertheless, they accomplished immense undertakings so long as they saw the triumph of the religion of Muhammad in the conquests of the sultans. Now their religion is departing; despotism alone remains; and they are falling.[7]

This is a prescient remark, which illuminates current circumstances. The problem of "authoritarianism" in the Middle East is a stubborn one, which no contemporary author has been able to understand fully. Tocqueville's general theory suggests that the political form associated with a vibrant and triumphant Islamic world remains, but that the religious substance that must undergird that political form for it to work well has receded. The Middle East is, in effect, *trapped* by the ghost of Islam.[8] Adopting a phrase from an earlier passage in *Democracy*, politics in the Islamic world "hang like the broken chains still occasionally dangling from the ceiling of an old building but carrying nothing."[9]

Tocqueville's insight about the undergirding power of religion is not confined to his observations about the Islamic world. A little further into volume I, he notes that:

> The Constitution of the United States is like one of those beautiful creations of human diligence, which gives their inventors glory and riches but remains sterile in other hands. Contemporary Mexico has shown that. The Mexicans, wishing to establish a federal system, took the federal constitution of their Anglo-American neighbors as a model and copied it almost completely. But when they borrowed the letter of the law, they could not at the same time transfer the spirit that gave it life.[10]

Nations are *not* founded on their political arrangements and the laws that codify them. Those who celebrate political foundings – those who believe their political founding is a *first cause* of their success – have not understood the religious *principle* from which their politics successfully draws sufficient *interest* to have sustained their political success. They see the *interest* – yet they believe it to be the *principle*.

TOCQUEVILLE'S PURITANS

This way of thinking about foundings helps us understand why Tocqueville introduced the Puritans in the first substantive chapter in *Democracy*. We have not gone far enough, however. More needs to be said about the theoretical work that is accomplished by Tocqueville's Puritans. Aside from the claim that religion undergirds politics, there are three additional ideas Tocqueville's discussion of the Puritans allowed him to explore. These I will consider next. After that, I will consider two enigmas associated with Tocqueville's account of the American Puritans.

The first of the three ideas is that the Puritan understanding of liberty provides an antidote to the tyranny that is likely to emerge in the distant democratic future. Readers of volume 2, part 4 of

Democracy will recall that this tyranny is one yet without a name,[11] one that will prevail if citizens of the future are cut off from their neighbors and only look upward, like dependent infants, to the paternal state.

> Over this kind of men stands an immense, protective power which is alone responsible for securing their enjoyment and watching over their fate. That power is absolute, thoughtful of detail, orderly, provident, and gentle. It would resemble parental authority if, father-like, it tried to prepare its charges for a man's life, but on the contrary, it only tries to keep them in perpetual childhood.[12]

Tocqueville defended liberty in everything he wrote. True liberty, he thought, cannot be confused with the truant's freedom to do as one pleases. This, the Puritans understood well.[13] Man discovers his true liberty through being bound by God's ordinances and in reenacting His providential liturgy. Little wonder, then, that Tocqueville was dubious about "individualism,"[14] which he thought to be a corroded version of true liberty. What is the problem with individualism? "A despot will lightly forgive his subjects for not loving him," he wrote, "provided they do not love one another."[15] Encourage citizens to think of themselves as individuals who do not need one another, and you have taken the first sure step toward tyranny. Get them to feel that they are individualists who are self-sufficient and psychologically "on their own," and tyranny will eventually emerge. The Puritans would have found this idea unthinkable. Liberty is covenantal, not individual.

Setting aside the question of Tocqueville's assessment of the *truth* of the Puritan theological claim, about which he said nothing, he seemed keen to point out its psychological and social importance in the democratic age. Attending, for the moment, to its social importance, Tocqueville worried that the *three-tiered* arrangement of society in the aristocratic age – consisting of a king, a landed nobility, and peasants – would be supplanted by a *two-tiered* arrangement in the democratic age – consisting of the state and lonely, isolated citizens, without anything occupying the space between them. All that Tocqueville wrote about civil society and local politics should be understood in the light of this worry. In an earlier age, the landed nobility *mediated* between kings and peasants; in the democratic age, mediating bodies between the state and citizens had to be invented and nourished daily or liberty would be lost. Encouraging their development was one of the most important tasks of our age. "I am firmly convinced that one cannot found an aristocracy anew in this world, but I think that associations of plain citizens can compose very rich, influential, and powerful bodies, in other words, aristocratic bodies," Tocqueville observed.[16]

Without mediating bodies, which gather citizens together, individualism will grow, and so too will the state. The advance of individualism and the growth of the state are coterminous, one with the other. Individualism, Tocqueville wrote, has a proud, public, aspect, giving it the appearance of freedom and independence; yet because each man is weak and on his own, in *secret* each will look to the one visible power that remains – the state – to care for him.[17]

The self-interested individualist, Tocqueville thought, was an untethered man, at one moment proud and independent, at the next moment weak and alone. Self-interest *rightly understood*, on the other hand, tethered man; it is the form of self-interest formed *in and through relations with others*, in the mediational space of voluntary associations, voluntarily chosen marriages, and in the face-to-face relations of everyday life. Social classes of the aristocratic age have been destroyed; democratic man must now voluntarily link himself to others. "Feelings and ideas are renewed, the heart enlarged, and the understanding developed only by the reciprocal actions of men one upon another," Tocqueville wrote.[18] Individualism, far from nourishing liberty, isolated citizens one from another, and prepared the way for the state to grow stronger.

The Puritans were not individualists. Tocqueville found in them the healthy habits needed to nourish liberty and to develop the self-interest rightly understood needed to avert tyranny:

> In most European nations political existence started in the higher ranks of society and has been gradually, but always incompletely, communicated to the various members of the body social ... Contrariwise, in America one may say that the local community was organized before the county, the county before the state, and the state before the Union.[19]

Tocqueville's Puritans organized those local communities. In doing so, they averted the development and emergence of the unbound "individual." Without the antidote that the Puritans provided, the destruction of the social ties of the aristocratic age produces a delinked and isolated individual who looks to the state to provide for his every need.

The second idea Tocqueville explores in his consideration of the Puritans is the *durability* of the habits of true liberty. *That* the Puritans had beneficent habits is important; more important still, because the Puritan founding *was* the American founding, those founding habits would be long-standing. Whatever we find at the beginning endures until the end: "[t]he whole man is there, if one may put it so, in the cradle," Tocqueville wrote.[20] Path-dependency matters.[21]

This second idea in Tocqueville is often overlooked, and it has a number of different implications, which Tocqueville clearly understood. If Puritan habits endure, would this mean that in America there would always be an antidote to the *general tendency* in the democratic age to move toward "social distancing" and the tyranny that attends it?[22] Another question: If the world, so to speak, never really loses its memory of the past, does this mean that all seemingly novel developments are not novel at all? Said otherwise, if the age of aristocracy is the age of *imitation*, and the age of democracy is the age of *innovation*, does this mean that such innovation is a supplement to, rather than a substitute for, imitation? If so, does this mean that all of the mediating institutions that arise in the aristocratic age – family, church, municipal institutions – can be modified but never eradicated in the democratic age? Yet another question: If the Puritans are *originary* in America, and if they thought of themselves as recapitulating the Exodus journey from Egyptian captivity to liberty in the Promised Land, does this mean that, in its foreign policy, America will forever think of itself as the New Israel, shining light out into the darkness, bringing liberty where before there was only servitude?[23] Another question still: If the institution of slavery had become habitual in America, affecting both slave and master, what, then, are the prospects for the eradication not of laws that ensconce slavery but the habits that law can never wholly erase? Yet another question: Will America *always* be Puritan, perhaps in ways we will never quite understand, despite the millions of immigrants who have entered and now call America home?[24] Tocqueville understood that democratic man will always looks toward the future and will do everything he can to unburden himself from the past. Is not John Rawls' *A Theory of Justice*,[25] perhaps the most important work of late twentieth-century American political thought, based on just this idea? What if democratic man cannot actually do this? What if he is compelled, instead, to wander through life without understanding the respect in which he is always bound?

The questions that emerge from Tocqueville's acute understanding that founding habits are durable generally do not occupy political theorists. If they wish to consider habit, they study Aristotle's *Nicomachean Ethics* or Edmund Burke's *Reflections on the Revolution in France*. Tocqueville, they have concluded, wrote about the democratic "philosophical approach" that undermines habit altogether. Indeed, he does.[26] Yet Tocqueville's genius is to have seen that the democratic age will be characterized by a paradox: old habits will perdure *and at the same time old habits will be destroyed*. I do not suggest that all this was well worked out in his writing, rather that the profound tension within *Democracy* revolves around just this paradox and is never resolved.[27] Will the durable *habits* of the Puritans, which nourish liberty in the democratic age, be overcome by a democratic philosophical approach that destroys those (and all) habits that are needed to avert the fall into democratic servitude? *That* is Tocqueville's great question for America.

Although Tocqueville thought the Americans might be saved from democratic servitude if the bounded liberty that the Puritans instantiated endured, his overall assessment of the durable habits of the Americans was painfully mixed. On the one hand, the Puritans bequeathed to America beneficent habits that might yet save liberty. The Puritan founding, however, is not the only founding about which Tocqueville wrote. *Democracy* has, in fact, *two* founding stories: the first one developed at the beginning of volume 1 (part 1, chapter 2), which pertains to the Puritans; and the other at the end of volume 1 (Part 2, chapter 10), which pertains to slavery:

> In one blow oppression has deprived the descendants of the Africans of almost all the privileges of humanity. The United States Negro has lost even the memory of his homeland; he no longer understands the language his fathers spoke; he has abjured their religion and forgotten their mores. Ceasing to belong to Africa, he has acquired no right to the blessings of Europe; he is left in suspense between two societies and isolated between two peoples, sold by one and repudiated by the other; in the whole world there is nothing but his master's hearth to provide him with some semblance of a homeland.[28]

It was this other founding, with its implication that "the race question" in America would never disappear, that haunted Tocqueville and which has been revisited recently in a controversial set of essays published by the *New York Times* in 2019, under the heading of "The 1619 Project."[29] If founding habits are durable, are critics correct to say that "racism" is *systemic* in America – that America is not the *pure* project so many conservatives insist it is but rather *irredeemably stained*? These categories, the reader will note, are *theological* rather than political categories. I will return to them when I consider the second enigma in Tocqueville's treatment of the Puritans. Before turning to both enigmas, let us consider the third idea Tocqueville is able to develop through recourse to the Puritans.

Can civilization be sustained by the nourishment that the Enlightenment provides? In the Puritans, Tocqueville finds an answer to this question. No, it cannot. Human reason is too frail a thing on which to build; its conclusions will always be contested in the democratic age, which is why religion is so important. Religion circumscribes the range of permissible actions, within which freedom can be exercised. This much I have already noted. More than freedom is at stake here, however. Human self-understanding is as well. How deep, really, does man's understanding of himself, of others, and of his world go? Tocqueville's answer is *not very deep*. Reason's light does not go all the way down. In one of the more beautiful passages of *Democracy*, Tocqueville wrote:

> If man were wholly ignorant of himself he would have no poetry in him, for one cannot describe what one does not conceive. If he saw himself clearly, his imagination would remain idle and would have nothing to add to the picture. But the nature of man is sufficiently revealed for him to know something of himself and sufficiently veiled to leave much in impenetrable darkness, a darkness in which he ever gropes, forever in vain, trying to understand himself.[30]

This is not just a claim about the permanent psychological limits of human knowledge, however; it extends to a historical claim as well. The much-vaunted "secularization thesis," which for much of the twentieth century captured the imagination of social scientists, turns out to be false. There is not, in fact, a *development* that begins with *religious* man and ends with *secular* man.

> Eighteenth-century philosophers had a very simple explanation for the gradual weakening of beliefs. Religious zeal, they said, was bound to die down as enlightenment and freedom spread. It is tiresome that the facts do not fit this theory at all.[31]

The European loss of religion is the exception, not the rule.[32] There is no *education of man, the species, unto reason*, as Enlightenment thinkers suppose. Steeped in the Enlightenment belief that there is, Tocqueville's contemporaries looked contemptuously across the Atlantic at the Americans, who were still captivated by the barbarism of Christianity and had somehow been left behind:

> [Our European pedants] constantly ... prove to me that all is fine in America except just that religious spirit which I admire; I am informed that on the other side of the ocean freedom and human happiness lack nothing but Spinoza's belief in the eternity of the world and Cabanis' contention that thought is a [mere] secretion of the brain. To that I have really no answer to give, except that those who talk like that have never been in America and have never seen either religious peoples or free ones.[33]

Tocqueville thought that the Enlightenment could provide no substitute for Christian religion. It offered no moral advance over Christianity; and its authority would always be in doubt. The Puritans of America did not succumb to its temptation and to its false promise.

Let us speculate. What would Tocqueville have thought about the anti-Enlightenment reaction that followed – perhaps inevitably – in the wake of the Enlightenment? Was Kant, who brought us enlightenment reason, *necessarily* followed by Nietzsche, who gave us "the return of the repressed," the return of the *heteronomous*, prerational forces that Kant had banished? Are Kant and Nietzsche *bookends* of a single project – the first of which sought to coronate reason with the crown that God once wore, the second of which dethroned the imposter – reason – that had set itself up to be the sovereign substitute for God Himself, leaving European man with nothing but the prerational upsurges that music elicits and violence celebrates?[34] Were the political developments that mirrored these affirmations – Kant and Hegel's rational state, which succumbed to the enthralling anti-liberal political movements of the twentieth century – the consequence of the first error, namely of the Enlightenment *dethroning of God*? America has certainly had its share of agony, but it never produced either a Kant or a Nietzsche. Its greatest struggle – slavery and its aftermath – has been most profoundly comprehended in theological terms, as a problem *not* of reason or the repressed will, respectively, but of covenants made and broken. America has no Kant or Nietzsche; America has Abraham Lincoln and Reverend Martin Luther King, Jr.[35] The Puritans, who understood their world and their tasks in terms of their covenant with God, never left us. Europe's modern drama, which began with the Enlightenment hope that reason could replace Christianity, ended with a whimper and a solemn promise that the Nietzschean exploration of the subterranean forces of darkness that reason repressed would *never* see the light of day again. On *that* promise hangs the entire project of the European Union – the project of making *nations*, those artifacts of unreason, obsolete. The Americans, Tocqueville might have reminded us, never opened the *first door* to the Enlightenment in the way Kant and other European thinkers did. Not having opened the first door because Christianity reigned supreme, America was not fated to open the *second door* that Nietzsche did.

TWO ENIGMAS

Tocqueville's treatment of the Puritans allows us to grasp a number of his theoretical insights. There are, however, several enigmas that we must consider. The first can be summarized in the brief formulation: *Calvin is not Pascal*. The former is a covenantal thinker; the latter is not. I alluded to the importance of covenantal thinking a moment ago in passing when I mentioned Abraham Lincoln and Reverend Martin

Luther King, Jr. I will return to it in a moment, after we address this first enigma. In the Puritans, as Tocqueville averred, we have a model of the unity of politics and religion. Yet, as I indicated in the previous section,[36] Tocqueville thought that the Europeans railed against Christianity during and after the transition from the aristocratic to the democratic age because the Roman Catholic Church had aligned itself too closely with the existing aristocratic powers:

> When a religion seeks to found its sway only on the longing for immortality equally tormenting every human heart, it can aspire to universality; but when it comes to uniting itself with a government, it must adopt maxims which apply only to certain nations. Therefore, by allying itself with any political power, religion increases its strength over some but forfeits the hope of reigning over all. As long as a religion relies only upon the sentiments which are the consolation of every affliction, it can draw the heart of mankind to itself. When it is mingled with the bitter passions of this world, it is sometimes constrained to defend allies who are such from interest rather than from love; and it has to repulse as adversaries men who still love religion, although they are fighting against religion's allies. Hence, religion cannot share the material strength of the rulers without being burdened with some of the animosity roused against them.[37]

Tocqueville's assertion that the domain of religion must be separated from politics is one a covenantal theologian like John Calvin could not have understood. Tocqueville's account of how religion can thrive in the democratic age rests on a quite different foundation than the one Calvin offered. For Tocqueville, the two domains must be separated rather than unified; and they must be separated because religion and politics pertain to different *modes* of experience.

Here, we discover in Tocqueville's thought the influence of Pascal, for whom "the heart has its reasons that reason does not know."[38] Tocqueville's most impassioned observations about religion in volume 1 – long after he had concluded his sober observations about the Puritans – have overtones careful readers of Pascal will quickly recognize. The most notable is perhaps this:

> The short space of sixty years can never shut in the whole of man's imagination; the incomplete joys of this world will never satisfy his heart. Alone among all created beings, man shows a natural disgust for existence and an immense longing to exist; he scorns life and fears annihilation. These different instincts constantly drive his soul toward contemplation of the next world, and it is religion that leads him thither.[39]

Calvin is not Pascal. Tocqueville accomplishes a great deal through his invocation of the Puritans early in volume 1 of *Democracy in America*, yet his argument about how religion can be saved in the democratic age draws on Pascal rather than Calvin. For Pascal and Tocqueville, there are two kingdoms – not one, as the Puritans would have argued.[40] The "City on the Hill" of the Puritans is *not* a secular city, set apart from the City of God above.[41] It is the New Jerusalem, the Divine light that shines into the darkness in which unredeemed, broken man dwells. The first enigma, then, is that Tocqueville relies on the Puritans to develop a number of important theoretical ideas, and yet, in the end, the covenantal theology the Puritans believed violated Tocqueville's assertion that, if religion is to thrive in the democratic age, it must remain separate from worldly politics.

The second enigma follows from the first. Tocqueville's Puritans are covenantal; there is no mention, however, of original sin in the whole of *Democracy*. In light of the fact that the whole of the Reformation's break with the Roman Catholic Church hangs on a darker view of original sin, for which the covenantal community was Calvin's antidote, this is really quite remarkable. What Tocqueville saw in the Puritans was the bounded, local, covenantal community, which produced healthy mediating institutions that stand between the ever-growing state and the increasingly solitary citizen in the democratic age. This powerful insight fueled several generations of scholarship concerned with the breakdown of those mediating institutions and the emergence of man, the lonely, unhealthy, animal. David Riesman, Robert Nisbet, Robert Bellah, Christopher Lasch, and Robert Putnam, to name only a few of the more prominent figures, all explored the rich psychosocial territory that Tocqueville's theory of mediation revealed, and to great effect.[42]

In America today, however, loneliness and its associated pathologies do not explain the overwhelming, quasi-religious development we call identity politics – though loneliness certainly contributes to the problem.[43] Without developing the idea further, it is worth mentioning that that *other* wager about the modern American predicament set forth in Allan Bloom's *The Closing of the American Mind*,[44] namely that, in abandoning the idea of nature in favor of (German) historicism, Americans had succumbed to relativistic drift, also fails to account for the emergence of identity politics. Identity politics, concerned as it is with *purging stain in order that persons or the covenantal community as a whole be without spot or blemish*,[45] cannot be grasped as a problem of loneliness or as a problem of relativism. It can, however, be grasped as a manifestation of the Puritan fixation on sin and redemption, about which Tocqueville might have said a great deal but in fact says almost nothing. Identity politics has, today, transfigured American politics,[46] and neither those who would follow Tocqueville's lead nor those who would follow Bloom's are able to comprehend it. Identity politics has turned politics into a religious venue of sacrificial offering, conceivable only against the backdrop of Christianity and Protestant Christianity in particular.

Ponder the Christian understanding of sacrificial offering. Without the sacrifice of Christ, the Innocent Lamb of God, there would be no Christianity. Christ, the Scapegoat, renders the impure pure, by taking upon Himself "the sins of the world." In purging the Divine Scapegoat, those for whom He is the sacrificial offering are purified. Identity politics may be seen as a political version of this cleansing, but for groups rather than for individual persons. If purged of the scapegoat, its adherents imagine, the world itself, along with the remaining groups in it, will be cleansed of stain.[47] For now, the scapegoat is the structural racism associated with white, male privilege – but we might worry that the logic of identity politics will require other sacrificial offerings once he is purged and disappears from view. Once he and what he has built have been purged, what sort of political programs will be crafted in order to address the transgressions of the next scapegoated group? The question is chilling.

We *can* understand the origin of the search for a scapegoat that characterizes identity politics if we understand the place of sin and purity in the economy of salvation that the Puritans proposed. If, however, we only find in the Puritans "mediational exemplars," as Tocqueville does, then we will be unable to comprehend the current American predicament, which is to be haunted by Puritan habits of thought, though without the Christian framework of sin and redemption that allows old wounds to be healed. Tocqueville, who towers above so many other social theorists of the nineteenth and twentieth centuries, and whose immense contribution was, among other things, to alert readers to the centrality of Christianity in the democratic age, cannot help us understand the problem of stain and redemption in America, which today, under the guise of identity politics, haunts our every thought and action. This is the second enigma of Tocqueville's consideration of the Puritans. He looked *to* them but not *at* them; he saw *that* they gathered together, but he did not appreciate the problem of stain and redemption that prompted them to gather together.

What are the implications of Tocqueville's silence on the matter of stain and redemptive purity? Tocqueville's overarching theory of health in the democratic age requires, among other things, that Christianity be a vibrant mediating institutional presence and that it bind the moral imagination:

> [Thanks to Christianity] in the moral world everything is classified, coordinated, foreseen, and decided in advance. In the world of politics everything is in turmoil, contested, and uncertain ... Far

from harming each other, these two apparently opposed tendencies work in harmony and seem to lend mutual support.[48]

Conservatives, who have long admired Tocqueville's vision of a modest national government, a prominent role for Christianity, and a competent and commercially vibrant citizenry, have consequently defended federalism, religious liberty, and market commerce. None of these causes, however, has gained a purchase against identity politics. Within the world that identity politics constructs, federalism is a pretext for defending noninclusive laws, churches are heteronormative, and market commerce is an opportunity to practice "woke" capitalism. In short, Tocquevillean conservatives have operated within his framework of *mediation*, while adherents of identity politics have operated within the framework of *stain and purity* – the very categories within Puritan thought that Tocqueville did not, or could not, see in his otherwise capacious account of Puritan habits and ideas.

NOTES

1. DIA (L) II.1.v, 442–449.
2. DIA (L) I.2.ix, 296–297.
3. "[North America] was grave and serious and solemn," Tocqueville wrote. "One might say that it had been created to be the domain of the intelligence, [while southern North America] was that of the senses"; DIA (L) I.1.ii, 26. This north/south distinction reappears in Tocqueville's observations about free and slave labor on the north and south banks of the Ohio River; see DIA (L) I.2.x, 344–347.
4. DIA (L) I.1.ii, 32.
5. DIA (L) "Author's Introduction," 17.
6. Just who Tocqueville had in mind when he wrote this we cannot say; but in light of Tocqueville's mixed admiration of Rousseau, his assertion can be read as a response to one of the seminal ideas of Rousseau's "First Discourse," namely that once austere mores are lost, they cannot be retrieved. "All Demosthenes' eloquences," Rousseau wrote, "could never revive a body that luxury and the arts had innervated"; Jean

Jacques Rousseau, "First Discourse," in *The Major Writings of Jean-Jacques Rousseau*, ed. and trans. John T. Scott (Chicago: University of Chicago Press, 2012), part I, 15. Tocqueville's answer is that mores *can* be revitalized, by "austere talk about religion"; see DIA (L) I.1.ii, 33.

7. DIA (L) I.1.v, 94.

8. In the context of Western Europe, we find the same sort of argument made by Nietzsche a half-century later. "It is the Church and not its poison that offends us," he wrote; see Friedrich Nietzsche, *The Genealogy of Morals*, trans. Walter Kaufmann (New York: Random House, 1967), "First Essay," §9, 36. By this, Nietzsche meant that Europe had lost its Christianity but remained trapped by its artifacts – democracy, equality, rights, and so on. The ghost of Islam in the Middle East has left us with authoritarianism; the ghost of Christianity in the West has left us with democracy. Both civilizations, on Nietzsche's account, are dying; only the political form associated with the ghosts of their religious foundations remain.

9. DIA (L) I.1.ii, 32.

10. DIA (L) I.1.viii, 165.

11. DIA (L) II.4.vi, 691.

12. DIA (L) II.4.vi, 692.

13. DIA (L) I.1.ii, 46.

14. DIA (L) II.2.ii, 506–508.

15. DIA (L) II.2.iv, 509.

16. DIA (L) II.4.vii, 697.

17. DIA (L) II.4.i, 667.

18. DIA (L) II.2.v, 515.

19. DIA (L) I.1.ii, 44.

20. DIA (L) I.1.ii, 31.

21. Robert Putnam wrestles with this problem of path-dependency in his study of northern and southern Italy. His findings prompted one civic leader from the south to proclaim: "This is a counsel of despair. You're telling me that nothing I can do will improve our prospects for success. The fate of the reform was sealed centuries ago." Robert D. Putnam, Robert Leonardi, and Raffaella Nanetti i, *Making Democracy Work: Civic Traditions in Modern Italy* (Princeton: Princeton University Press, 1993), 183.

22. See Joshua Mitchell, "Can Democracy Survive Social Distancing," in *RealClearPolicy*, April 25, 2020, www.realclearpolicy.com/articles/202

0/03/25/the_issue_of_social_distancing_is_bigger_than_corona virus_487447.html (accessed August 18, 2020).

23. The finest account that develops this line of thought is to be found in Sacvan Bercovitch, *The Puritans Origins of the American Self* (New Haven, CT: Yale University Press, 1975).

24. See, for example, Duncan Moesch, "Anti-German Hysteria and the Making of the 'Liberal Society'," *American Political Thought* 7 (Winter 2018), 86–123.

25. See John Rawls, *A Theory of Justice* (Cambridge, MA: Harvard University Press, 1971).

26. DIA (L) II.1.i, 429–433.

27. The best relatively recent work that wrestles with this paradox is Benjamin R. Barber, *Jihad vs. McWorld: Terrorism's Challenge to Democracy* (New York: Ballantine Books, 1996).

28. DIA (L) I.2.x, 317.

29. The "1619 Project" of the *New York Times* (see www.nytimes.com/inter active/2019/08/14/magazine/1619-america-slavery.html) is dedicated to the proposition that this founding is the *real* founding of America and that therefore the American republic is irredeemably stained. Robert Woodson, of The Woodson Center, has pushed back against this account, with an ongoing series of essays in *The Washington Examiner*, begun on February 14, 2020, and written largely by black intellectuals and practitioners (see www.washingtonexaminer.com/1776). See also Joshua Mitchell, "What the New Morality of 'Stain' and 'Purity' Seeks to Accomplish," *The Washington Examiner*, February 14, 2020, www .washingtonexaminer.com/opinion/op-eds/what-the-new-morality-of- stain-and-purity-seeks-to-accomplish (accessed August 19, 2020).

30. DIA (L) II.1.xvii, 487.

31. DIA (L) I.2.ix, 295.

32. See DIA (L) I.1.ix, 300–301: "Therefore with us there must be some accidental and particular cause preventing the human spirit from following its inclination ... I am profoundly convinced that this accidental and particular cause is the close union of politics and religion. Unbelievers in Europe attack Christians more as political than as religious enemies; they hate the faith as the opinion of a party much more than as a mistaken belief, and they reject the clergy less because

they are the representatives of God than because they are the friends of authority."

33. DIA (L) I.2.ix, 294.

34. Here, consider Friedrich Nietzsche, *The Birth of Tragedy*, trans. Walter Kaufmann (New York: Vintage, 1967).

35. When Martin Luther King, Jr. said, on the steps of the Lincoln memorial, "I may not get there with you," he was alerting his listener-parishioners to this biblical account and reminding them that Moses himself did not cross over into the promised land (see Deuteronomy 34:5). King's "I Have a Dream" speech of August 28, 1963, is the high watermark of American covenantal theology in the twentieth century.

36. See Note 32 in this chapter.

37. DIA (L) I.2.ix, 297.

38. See Blaise Pascal, *Pensées*, trans. Roger Ariew (Indianapolis, IN: Hackett Press, 2004), 216.

39. DIA (L) I.2.ix, 296.

40. See, for example, DIA (L) I.1.ii, 41: "The Connecticut lawgivers turned their attention first to the criminal code and, in composing it, conceived the strange idea of borrowing their provisions from the text of Holy Writ."

41. See Augustine, *City of God*, trans. Henry Bettenson (New York: Penguin Books, 1984), preface, 5.

42. David Riesman, Nathan Glazer, and Reuel Denney, *The Lonely Crowd: A Study of the Changing American Character* (New Haven, CT: Yale University Press, 1963); Robert Nisbet, *The Quest for Community: A Study in the Ethics of Order and Freedom* (Wilmington, DE: ISI Books, 2010); Robert Bellah, Richard Madsen, William N. Sullivan, Ann Swindler, and Steven N. Tipton, *Habits of the Heart: Individualism and Commitment in American Life* (Berkeley: University of California Press, 2007); Christopher Lasch, *The Culture of Narcissism: American Life in the Age of Diminishing Expectations* (New York: W.W. Norton & Co., 1991); Robert Putnam, *Bowling Alone: The Collapse and Revival of American Community* (New York: Simon & Schuster, 2000).

43. Loneliness exacerbates identity politics. When citizens are isolated from one another and increasingly look upward to the state for their needs, they may indulge the fantasy that they need not work with their fellow citizens to build a world together. When citizens must work with each other, they are quickly disabused of whatever fantasies they might have

about who they are and about who their fellow citizens are. Identity politics supposes that the *precondition* of working together is respect for each other's "identity." If Tocqueville's doctrine of self-interest rightly understood is to be believed (see DIA (L) II.2.viii, 525–528), we only discover who we are and who our fellow citizens are *as a consequence* of working together.

44. Allan Bloom, *The Closing of the American Mind* (New York, Simon & Schuster, 1987).

45. See 1 Peter 1:18–19: "Forasmuch as ye know that ye were not redeemed with corruptible things, as silver and gold, from your vain conversation received by tradition from your fathers; But with the precious blood of Christ, as of a lamb without blemish and without spot."

46. Joshua Mitchell, *American Awakening: Identity Politics and Other Afflictions in Our Time* (New York: Encounter Books, 2020).

47. The one place in *Democracy* where Tocqueville considers the scapegoat is in I.2.vii, 255–256: "[Public opinion in the democratic age] no longer says, 'Think like me or you will die.' [Instead it says]: 'You are free not to think as I do; you can keep your life and property and all; but from this day you are a *stranger* among us. You can keep your privileges in the township, but they will be useless to you, for if you solicit your fellow citizens' votes, they will not give them to you, and if you only ask for their esteem, they will make excuses for refusing that. You will remain among men, but you will lose your rights to count as one. When you approach your fellows, they will shun you as *an impure being*, and even those who believe in your innocence will abandon you too, lest they in turn be *shunned*. Go in peace. I have given you your life, but it is a life worse than death'" (emphasis added). Here is the "cancel culture" of identity politics.

48. DIA (L) I.1.iii, 47.

PART IV **Democracy's Enduring Challenges**

14 Tocqueville's American Girls

Women, Manners, and the Engendering of Democracy

Eileen Hunt Botting

In the United States, at least since the revolutionary era, it has been an urgent political matter to develop new, democratic forms of manners. In 1776, for example, it was paramount for American patriots to change their ways of relating with those who remained loyal to the British Crown. In his appendix to the third edition of *Common Sense*, Thomas Paine stressed that the fledgling nation's "domestic tranquility" depended upon the "chastity" of its "NATIONAL MANNERS."[1] America, he wrote, was like a woman with a "large and young family" who must protect her own.[2] Her manners of "independence" would allow her to separate from the motherland "uncontaminated by European corruption."[3] Manners of independence, Paine insisted, would make manifest in politics the words of the Declaration of Independence.

Although he did not share Paine's revolutionary enthusiasms, Alexis de Tocqueville agreed with his thesis about the essential role of manners in the preservation of American democratic ways of life. After his 1831 visit to the United States, Tocqueville observed that American manners – despite their variety – were typically as much about equality as they were about independence. By the Jacksonian era, Americans had distinctive "democratic manners": freer and more equal forms of public behavior in dress, speech, body language, and other action relative to European societies of the time.[4] This was a cultural shift, Tocqueville thought, that shaped the political trajectory of the United States as the most significant democracy in the world.

Tocqueville and Paine were not the first European thinkers to underscore the importance of manners in defining the political character of the American people. In his March 1775 "Speech on Conciliation with the Colonies," the Irish statesman Edmund Burke waxed poetic about the American style of rough and risky public behavior. Whether it was in settling the wilderness of North America or whale-fishing in the cold Atlantic, the survivalist ethos and trading culture of the American colonies had made them the most lucrative properties in the British Empire. Reconciliation would be worth it, Burke judged, so he extended a diplomatic handshake across the ocean. The Americans paid back the compliment in the long run. After they left the empire, they included Burke's parliamentary speech in secondary school civics textbooks well into the twentieth century.[5]

What distinguished Tocqueville's analysis of American manners – differentiating it from both Burke and Paine before him – was its strikingly feminine accent. While Burke celebrated the "fierce spirit of liberty" that animated American ways of life, he spoke only of the hardiness, resilience, and daring of "Englishmen" in the colonies – while warning his fellow MPs to be both "safe" and "manly" in their legislative response to the rebels.[6] Although *Common Sense* rhetorically compared revolutionary America to a chaste mother who must insulate her large family from foreign corruption, the author failed to consider the actual condition of American women.[7] Despite his bold claim that America's best line of defense against the British was to stay true to its "NATIONAL MANNERS," Paine did not address the question of how these manners came to predominate in the colonies in the first place.

Tocqueville, by contrast, singled out women's historical role in the inculcation of "democratic manners" in America. In volume 1 of *Democracy in America* (1835), he reflected in a chapter about religion that "it is women who shape mores" in American culture.[8] He fleshed out this argument over the course of the second volume that he published in 1840. "There have never been free societies without mores," he reiterated, "and ... it is woman who shapes these mores. Therefore everything which has a bearing on the status of women, their habits, and their thoughts is, in my view, of great importance."[9]

In volume 1, Tocqueville broadly defined "mores" (*moeurs*), in the spirit of the original Latin term (*mōrēs*, the plural of *mōs*), to mean "ways, character, and morals."[10] Mores encompassed not only its "narrow" contemporary French meaning of "habits of the heart" but also its wider and deeper Latinate meaning of "the whole moral and intellectual state of a people."[11] In volume 2, he specified that mores covered "manners" (*manières*) or "the external formalities of human behavior."[12] "Manners, speaking generally," he wrote, "have their roots in mores."[13] Although he conceded that "nothing, at first sight, seems less important" than the superficialities of manners, Tocqueville wittily observed that "there is nothing to which men attach more importance."[14] People "can get used to anything," he dryly noted, "except living in a society which does not share their manners."[15]

Manners were dear to people, in America and elsewhere, because people associated these ways of life with the example of their mothers. The women whom they loved the most instilled their deepest "habits of the heart" – both the sentimental reciprocation of affection in the family and the outward show of concern for others in public. What Tocqueville initially saw in America, and then fully realized when he returned to France to write his masterpiece on modern democracy, is that women across cultures and political systems did most of the work to inculcate these beloved ways of life in a nation's youth.

Near the end of volume 1, Tocqueville provided his first extended analysis of how the manners of women drive the peculiar democratic culture of America. He signified the complexity of the subject matter by placing it at the beginning of a long chapter titled "The Three Races That Inhabit the United States."[16] In a story drawn from his travels "through the forests that still cover the state of Alabama," Tocqueville recollected the sight of an "Indian woman," a "Negro woman," and the "white" daughter of a "pioneer" sitting together by a spring.[17] The "young savage" gave the child "fond caresses as mothers did," while the "Negro, too, sought by a thousand innocent wiles to attract the little Creole's attention."[18] The girl "showed by her slightest movements a sense of superiority which contrasted strangely with her weakness and her age."[19] In Tocqueville's racialized triangulation of American social behavior, the postures of the "negress" and the "savage" stood in "striking" contrast to each other and the girl.[20] The black woman was "seated on the ground before her mistress," while the Native American stood by looking "almost ferocious" in her protective attitude of "tenderness" toward the settler child.[21]

Tocqueville and his travel companion Gustave de Beaumont encountered this female trio during their rough, stagecoach trek through the Creek Nation wilderness, northeast of the frontier town of Montgomery.[22] Yet Tocqueville reworked the experience, recorded in his travel notebooks, into an allegory for how race shapes the different ways that *women* embody democratic manners in America. The feminist political theorist Jill Locke aptly commented that this and other scenes drawn from his travels read more like dramaturgical set pieces than empirical analyses of the intersection of race and gender roles in Jacksonian America.[23] She wisely advised contemporary readers of Tocqueville to beware of projecting back upon him their own sociological assumptions or political agendas yet endorsed the enduring scholarly value of reading (and critiquing) Tocqueville's artistic vision of American democracy through the lenses of gender, race, class, and nation.

Without saying it, Tocqueville applied these lenses – gender, race, class, and nation – to come to grips with his experience of seeing the native and black women and the white pioneer girl sitting by the spring together. In so doing, he magnified his own racial and class biases as a French aristocrat. At the same time, Tocqueville managed to paint an interesting *feminine* portrait of the manners displayed by three predominant racial groups in the 1830s United States. He reworked the familiar New Testament image of the woman by the well into an image of American democracy, by multiplying and diversifying its female subjects and pushing the male perspective to the side. Tocqueville dramatized the dominance of women over American manners by portraying himself as an awkward interloper into the three females' domestic idyll at the edge of the Alabama woods. "I had come close," he confessed, but "no doubt my curiosity annoyed the Indian woman, for she got up abruptly, pushed the child from her, almost roughly, and giving me an angry look, plunged into the forest."[24]

The Frenchman's gaze is an unwelcome intrusion upon the nonwhite women's kind and playful cultivation of social graces in the imperious white girl. Clearly the pioneer's daughter had not obtained from her father the democratic education in manners she needed, for she "received the attentions of her companions with a sort of condescension."[25] By recalling his disturbance of the white girl's public education in how to relate properly to people of other races, Tocqueville pointed out a profound political irony. Democratization in America was far from complete. The white "oppressors" had not so much abandoned the patrilineal, aristocratic, and imperial culture of Europe but reshaped it to suit their crude economic and political interests.[26]

By capturing the overlay of race and gender at the figurative crossroads of the American frontier, Tocqueville added nuance to his theory that women orchestrate the manners that subsequently define a society's mode of governance. Despite his overt (and inexcusable) perpetuation of racist stereotypes of the period – such as the "barbarous" dress and "savage" demeanor of "the Indian" and the "servile fear" of "the Negro" – Tocqueville acknowledged that women of different ages and races played various roles in shaping the complexity of democratic manners in the United States.[27] The public interactions between the three females represented for Tocqueville the emotionally "touching" – and politically necessary – fostering of a "bond of affection" between "oppressors and oppressed" as the United States strove to become more democratic.[28] Feminine manners had the remarkable power to bring people "close together" who were otherwise made systematically unequal "by prejudices and laws."[29]

The political theorist Laura Janara argued in her book *Democracy Growing Up* (2002) that Tocqueville saw America as a child who was still growing into a freer and more egalitarian form of self-governance.[30] Looking at his picture of the women by the spring, we can see that the young democracy was to Tocqueville like an uppity white frontier girl. She needed to learn better manners from the example of the black and native women who attended to her every need, from land to water to love itself.

Against the background of his own prejudice and condescension, Tocqueville foregrounded how different forms of femininity shaped the "different signs of white predominance" in the United States.[31] According to the political scientist Alvin B. Tillery, Tocqueville critically observed how "whiteness" operated as a form of racial and economic privilege in Jacksonian America.[32] Whiteness was a form of "property" as valuable as the land that the settlers had shamelessly stolen from the Native Americans and forced their African slaves to cultivate.[33] Whiteness was not simply the pallid skin of the European settlers. It was rather, to use Tocqueville's words, an array of "signs of white predominance" – from slaveholding to property ownership to citizenship rights.

It was no accident that Tocqueville set his opening discussion of the "Three Races That Inhabit the United States" in a slave-driven cotton plantation state, near the last remnant of the Creek Nation territory still occupied by its native people.[34] His Alabama pioneer girl exhibits – as Jean Pedersen puts it – "consciousness of the privilege associated with her white race."[35] Like any good writer, Tocqueville chose the characters and setting of his story for effect. Through his narrative, he vividly illustrates how racial inequality compromised women's power to shape the manners suited for a modern democracy. As long as harsh social and political inequalities persisted among blacks, natives, and whites, fully democratic ways of life would be elusive in America.

Having recently survived a rocky coach ride from New Orleans to northeastern Alabama, Tocqueville may have chosen the southern term "créole" to describe the culture of the pioneer girl to underscore how local manners had a mix or "mélange" of sources.[36] If so, Tocqueville converged to some degree with his critic, the political scientist Rogers Smith, that American constitutional culture is a product of "multiple traditions."[37] Among these traditions were not only liberalism of the sort Tocqueville has come to represent but also racism and white supremacy. This was a toxic mix for a nascent democracy. Racism toward blacks and natives eroded the power of women to foster the bonds that could unite Americans in a genuinely democratic mode of government. Tillery has argued that Tocqueville can be read as a "critical race theorist" in his analysis of how white privilege hurt the cause of equality and freedom in the United States.[38] Indeed – as Tillery has also demonstrated – nineteenth-century black Americans looked back to Tocqueville as a resource for their own critical thinking about how to address the injustice of racial hierarchy.[39]

I would only add that Tocqueville can also be read as having some surprisingly "protofeminist" sympathies, too, despite his dislike of revolutionary-era ideas such as the "equality of the sexes" and the "rights of women."[40] At the end of volume 1, Tocqueville gave a prescient look at how race and gender intersected to create conditions of domination that blocked American women, of all racial backgrounds, from fully embodying the freer and more egalitarian manners that would help people to realize the principles of democracy in the United States. That said, Tocqueville failed to push the argument to its logical political conclusion: he never advocated for the full and formal incorporation of women, slaves, and native peoples as citizens with a full slate of rights, whether in the United States or any other nineteenth-century state.[41]

Pedersen highlights that the British utilitarian philosopher John Stuart Mill was the first to show the "considerable limitations" of Tocqueville's critique of race and gender roles in America.[42] In his 1835 review of volume 1, Mill complained that Tocqueville did not query enough the grave problems with the "aristocracy of sex" and "aristocracy of skin" as they persisted and reinforced each other in early nineteenth-century American society.[43] In this critique of Tocqueville, Mill echoed some of the "protofeminist" ideas of Mary Wollstonecraft and her many followers among the British, French, and American women's rights advocates, abolitionists, and socialists before him.[44]

Along with its racial divisions, Tocqueville's account of democracy in America has its share of what the feminist philosopher Judith Butler famously called "gender trouble," in her 1990 book by the same name.[45] As Butler influentially theorized it, *gender* is a cumulative product of people's bodies inhabiting, performing, and modifying – in an iterative fashion – the sex roles prescribed, inflected, and slowly changed over time in their cultures. The *trouble* was that sometimes one's physical and psychological experience of gender stood at the boundaries of broader cultural norms. Butler's famous (though not definitive) example was a drag queen, whose bodily performance of their gender both upended and dramatized prevailing norms – or manners – pertaining to "proper" masculine and feminine behavior.[46]

Butler elaborated her argument about the embodiment of gender in her book *Bodies That Matter* (1993), as did the performance art of transgender theorist Susan Stryker. They reflected on how the conflicts between – and over – a drag queen's and a trans woman's ways of expressing masculine and/or feminine manners could render bodies like these "monstrous" and "abjected."[47] The collective judgment of a gendered body as belonging to "a field of deformation" took place in public and in private.[48] Those who jealously guarded "normal" ways of being men or women looked with disgust upon those who embodied deviations from it in their gestures, movements, and other "modes" and manners.[49] Anybody who wore these deviant manners also bore, physically and psychically, the weight of public revulsion at them, to the point that they could see and feel themselves as "monsters."[50]

In her 1999 introduction to *Gender Trouble*, Butler clarified a number of her more abstract philosophical points, including her distinction between gender and sexuality. There was no simple, one-to-one, correspondence between them, she reiterated. One could have a gender that conformed to norms of femininity, for example, while having a sexual orientation (lesbian, bi) that subverted heterosexual norms. The reverse was also true: one could have a gender that subverted broader norms but a sexual orientation that conformed to them. Despite the discord between gender and sexuality, the hierarchies of gender still "underwrite" the prevailing norms of sexuality in a society, not the other way around.[51] In other words, the historical subordination of women in male-dominated cultural and political systems was the driving force behind the ways that people felt, expressed, and signified their sexualities. One could not come to terms with sexuality without coming to terms with gender first, whether one was analyzing oneself or an entire society.

In this way, Butler and Stryker returned gender theory to some of the philosophical insights of French feminist Simone de Beauvoir. Her groundbreaking treatise *Le deuxième sexe* (1949) argued that women were not born but made by society. Centuries of male-dominant culture had rendered women, in language, literature, and political practice, the subordinates of men. The feminine gender had been forged as the eternal "other" – or "monster" – against which the man, the masculine, and the human were defined.[52]

Without projecting poststructuralism or feminism back upon him, I will make a provocation about Tocqueville. His theory of how women shape the mores and manners that animate, however fraught and imperfectly, the culture of democracy stands in a kind of unexpected philosophical convergence with the main thesis of *Gender Trouble*. Tocqueville was, after all, a French theorist. Twentieth-century French literary and political theory – including one of

Butler's main inspirations, Jacques Derrida – traces some of its roots to Jean-Jacques Rousseau's enormously influential philosophical novel on the formation of gender hierarchies in society, *Emile, or On Education* (1762). This was the most formative book for Tocqueville's understanding of how a binary gender system – with men ideally taking the upper hand in economic and political power but women driving culture from below – was at the very basis of a modernizing society. While he wrote volume 2, Tocqueville told his friend Louis de Kergorlay that Rousseau was one of three French writers that he kept close by.[53]

In volume 2, Tocqueville used a conceptual framework derived from *Emile*, without citing it, to explain at length his view of the complexity of gender relations in 1830s American democracy.[54] Butler one-upped him with a direct reference to Rousseau in *Gender Trouble*.[55] In light of these intellectual overlays, it is not a stretch to say that Butler – akin to Tocqueville before her – theorizes how gender hierarchy shapes modern societies, beginning with mores and manners, and extending to embodied experiences and relationships such as love and sexual attraction.

The gender troubles of Tocqueville's time, quickly followed by signs of his own sexual unrest, bubble to the surface of *Democracy in America* when he turns his "gaze" to girls and women.[56] In an ingenious study, Jean Pedersen has excavated how Tocqueville penned an "arch" letter to his sister-in-law Emilie in November 1831 about the "outrageously flirtatious" girls he'd met in America.[57] He jokingly alludes to his own infidelities, admitting he's "*roamed* this world quite a bit."[58] Yet he rather defensively suggests to his married female confidante that it was the girls who were trying to prey on him during his journey, not the reverse. Tocqueville's obsession with depicting the manners of the American girl – from as early as age five through young womanhood – might lead feminist critics to wonder, were the girls really flirting with him so much as he was leering at them?

Tocqueville's American pioneer girl was only "five or six" in volume 1, but she had grown into a teenager in time to star in volume 2.[59] In his first extended account of the manners of the American girl in the Alabama forest, he recalled looking with unabashed romantic longing upon her older "Indian" companion, "for she still wore that necklace of shells which the bride always deposits on the nuptial couch."[60] In Tocqueville's eyes, the only one with equal "ferocity" to this "savage" was the little Creole girl, who looked down upon the nonwhite women tending to her. He takes some haughty pleasure in looking at the white girl looking down upon the native woman. As he follows his desire to move closer to them, the "Indian" feels revulsion, and by fleeing into the forest, she dissolves Tocqueville's ultra-feminine vision of an American interracial "bon ménage."[61] The native woman's decision to leave can be read as a public rebuke to Tocqueville's possessive and implicitly sexual stare. The fact that Tocqueville wrote this detail into the published story suggests his awareness of his (and other men's) intrusive relations with girls and women.

In volume 2, Tocqueville shifted the direction of his gaze. He was less interested in surveying the manners of American women who were married or on the brink of accepting its "yoke."[62] He devoted a whole chapter, however, to discussing the minutiae of the "audacious" behavior, "bad" thoughts, and "unchaste" spirits of teenage American girls.[63] By way of some underhanded contrasts with the naïvety of Catholic European girls, Tocqueville tartly implied that Protestant American girls were "full of confidence" amid the "burgeoning desires" that defined "the stage between childhood and youth," *precisely because* they lacked the "virgin innocence" of their peers on the Continent.[64] Even as he rather vainly lavished them with praise for displaying conversational skills equal to a "philosopher" like himself, Tocqueville ultimately depicted them – meaning, the series of unnamed white adolescent girls he went out of his way to meet – as trophies he wished he might have taken home, or at least to bed.[65]

When he traveled around the United States, Tocqueville was twenty-five and unmarried but engaged to Mary Mottley. She was an older Englishwoman, from a lower social station, of whom his stuffy aristocratic family did not approve. He married her only after volume 1 was complete.[66] The differences between the two volumes' depictions of the American girl can be explained in light of this fact. In volume 1, the engaged Tocqueville offered a more abstract sociological treatment of girls and women as exemplars or conduits of American manners. In volume 2, the married Tocqueville wistfully shifted his focus to the teenage American girls with whom he once flirted, whereby he identified with the loss of liberty that the young wives faced in marriage.

Over the course of volume 2, Tocqueville reveals some of his sympathies with the gender troubles of the American woman. In a dramatic set piece akin to his story of the female trio by the spring, he paid tribute to the "young wives" whom he had "often met" in his travels throughout the Midwestern United States.[67] Tocqueville identifies with the stoic resolve of these pioneer women, who gave up the comforts of their "parents' prosperous houses" for "leaky cabins in the depths of the forest."[68] While he remarked on how their "features were changed and faded," he admired how "their looks were firm." They exhibited "resilience" and "courage" while they shared the same "dangers and innumerable privations" as their husbands.[69] He suggested that these once audacious American girls were now equals in "virile confidence" to the pioneer men they had married.[70] Tocqueville concluded that, while the "ways" of the American wife were different than her free-wheeling behavior as a girl, her tenacious "spirit is the same."[71]

Tocqueville seems to infuse some of his own spirit into his composite portrait of the American pioneer wife. Creatively revisiting the material from his travel journals, he personifies the moral effects of his own recent marriage (on him) by projecting them onto the transformation of the opposite sex by the bonds of marriage on the

US frontier. Like the American woman, he too is an "audacious" flirt who has matured into a "resolute" acceptance of the confines of marriage for the sake of the virtues of friendship, health, and happiness, in addition to the stability and order of society as a whole.[72] Perhaps due to his more contented married state, Tocqueville also deepened his appreciation for women's role in inculcating mores and manners. In volume 2, women become the crux of the book's defining argument about how mores – and, specifically, manners – propel democratization.

As he contemplated women's dispersion of these habits of the heart, Tocqueville had a change of heart himself. Pedersen illuminates how Tocqueville reverses his view of American women from the time he corresponds with Emilie in November 1831 to the time that he authors volume 2.[73] While he initially wrote home to his sister-in-law that she and other women were better off in France, he went on to conclude near the end of volume 2 that "the chief cause of the extraordinary prosperity and growing power of this nation ... is due to the superiority of their women."[74] American women were superior to their European counterparts, Tocqueville ultimately argued, because they freely spread the mores and manners that were as crucial for the sustenance of American democracy as the laws made by its male legislators. While French women might be better off in terms of their individual freedom, American women were "superior" to them in the sense that they served as foundational moral exemplars for the entire democratic cultural and political system in the United States.

In light of Tocqueville's deeper appreciation of the personal sacrifice of American girls and women, European girls and women looked bad – and the aristocrats among them looked even worse. From girlhood, the latter learned to be "tyrants" who used sexual allure to command a "despotic" sway over their husbands and other lovers.[75] European men saw them as "seductive but incomplete beings," and the women internalized this view, "looking at themselves in the same light."[76] In what may be the most protofeminist moment in

Democracy in America, Tocqueville observes near the end of volume 2 that European women are unfortunately "denied some of the greatest attributes of humanity."[77] While he laments how aristocratic society has made women into monsters – tyrannical, half-formed, subhuman beings – he takes some solace in seeing how democracy in America, by contrast, has made its women into moral leaders. At the same time, he pauses to reflect on the immensity of American women's sacrifice of their personal liberty within marriage and the tragic implications for the individual who bears such a burden.

With the aid of *Emile,* Tocqueville grappled with some of the gender trouble that surfaced in the relations between men and women of his time. He wondered why modern education produced what Rousseau called "monsters," or malformed, unnatural creatures who failed to be fully men or fully women in their ways of being human.[78] Such "feeble men, and unseemly women," Tocqueville wrote in a Rousseauian vein, were seldom seen in the United States as compared to Europe.[79] "American women," he insisted, "are often manly in their intelligence and their energy" but "always have the manners of women."[80] Near the end of volume 2, he concluded that the severity of American *moeurs,* rooted in Puritanical religion, had preserved the democratic country from the sexual corruption and subversion of feminine manners that were prevalent in postrevolutionary Europe. As sincere believers in the Christian faith, American women were willing to sacrifice their youthful sexuality in favor of faithful motherhood. Through their ways of being devoted wives and mothers, they cemented the good moral influence of the feminine gender in society as a whole – albeit perhaps at their own expense.

What made American women's contribution to manners distinctive to Tocqueville was its overtly political impact. Women's leading role in the shaping of *moeurs* was to him "one of the great general causes responsible for the maintenance of a democratic republic in the United States."[81] Although Tocqueville saw in America the evolution of a new form of democracy, he also perceived a deeper level of cultural change, advanced by women.[82] The most surprising and brilliant insight of *Democracy in America* is that women were the true leaders of the United States, for they spread the manners that sustained its democratic ways of life.

Since the Revolution, the hallmark of American democracy has been to strive to uphold equality and freedom for each and every citizen, not only in law but in everyday culture. While Americans have never quite achieved this lofty goal – as Judith Martin, or "Miss Manners," noted with wit – we still have a venerable tradition of *trying* to be better neighbors and citizens by adjusting our manners.[83] While democratic culture was too unruly to ever subject itself to "a precise code of behavior," Tocqueville thought, the Americans were admirable in how seriously they took the practice of good manners.[84] Friendly waves and small talk were then, and are now, historical American signs of solidarity with, and mutual respect for, other citizens – whether they were strangers like Tocqueville, family at home, or neighbors down the street.

Near the outbreak of World War I, the American poet Robert Frost wrote that "Good fences make good neighbors."[85] His 1914 poem "Mending Wall" brings to mind the rock walls that line the fields of New England. Built stone by stone by laborers who turned forests into farms, these short and uneven walls do not force anyone to keep out. They rather stand as symbols of the old ways of life – the quiet stoic manners and small social gestures – that have helped generations of Americans survive the long cold winters of the past.

Tocqueville knew all too well that manners – like Frost's rock walls – are largely symbolic. Manners did not effectively keep imperialism, patriarchy, and racism out of democracy or prevent tyranny and prejudice from crossing their social barriers. Rather than keeping these exclusions out, democratic manners could be the basis of resistance to them. This was a protofeminist idea he shared with Wollstonecraft, who called for a "revolution in female manners" in her internationally renowned *A Vindication of the Rights of Woman* of 1792.[86] Women's manners were, for Tocqueville as for Wollstonecraft, a vital sign of the underlying cultural health of a democratic republic when they stood in critical resistance to centuries of corrupt and hierarchical European culture.

The perennial debate over whether American manners are crass and crude relative to stricter European codes of behavior was not Tocqueville's concern. He rather stressed a moral point. American manners, as engendered by mothers in children, were both good and powerful because they reflected the most precious – or aspirational – values of democracy itself. Freer and more equal manners said something about what America wanted to be when it grew up: a place where women and men, and people of different races, could freely mix in friendly society and concern for the whole community.[87] Whether the United States will ever live up to the democratic promise of its manners, of course, is as much a live question now as it was in Tocqueville's time. Either way, his prediction stands – with Butler and others in the later French style of *féminisme* – that the oppressed gender will be both the monster and the leader behind the outcome.

NOTES

1. Thomas Paine, *Common Sense*, 3rd ed. (Philadelphia: J. Almon, 1776), 41.
2. Paine, *Common Sense*, 42.
3. Paine, *Common Sense*, 42, 47.
4. DIA (L) I.2.x, 314. Tocqueville's term was "moeurs démocratiques." See Alexis de Tocqueville, *De la démocratie en Amérique*, 2 vols. (Paris: Pagnerre, 1850), 1:383. In the first occurrence of the term "democratic manners," near the end of volume 1, Lawrence translated "moeurs" in its wider sense of "mores" but other English translators, such as Henry Reeve, have rendered it in its more specific sense of "manners."
5. Conor Cruise O'Brien, *The Great Melody: A Thematic Biography and Commented Anthology of Edmund Burke* (London: Sinclair-Stevenson, 1992), 150.
6. Edmund Burke, *Speech on Conciliation with America*, ed. Sidney Carleton Newsom (Project Gutenberg, 2013), www.gutenberg.org/5/6/5/5655/ (accessed August 12, 2020).

7. Eileen Hunt Botting, "Thomas Paine amidst the Early Feminists," in *Selected Writings of Thomas Paine*, ed. Ian Shapiro and Jane E. Calvert (New Haven, CT: Yale University Press, 2014), 630–654.

8. DIA (L) I.2.ix, 291.

9. DIA (L) II.3.ix, 590.

10. "Mores," in Félix Gaffiot, *Dictionnaire latin-français* (Paris: Hachette, 1934), 995. See also Jean Elisabeth Pedersen, "'The Whole Moral and Intellectual State of a People': Tocqueville on Men, Women, and Mores in the United States and Europe," in Daniel Gordon, ed., *The Anthem Companion to Alexis de Tocqueville* (New York: Anthem, 2019), 143n1.

11. DIA (L) I.2.ix, 287.

12. DIA (L) II.3.xiv, 605. Tocqueville, *De la démocratie en Amérique*, 2:243.

13. DIA (L) II.3.xiv, 606.

14. DIA I(L) I.3.xiv, 605.

15. DIA I(L) I.3.xiv, 605.

16. DIA (L) I.2.x, 316–320.

17. DIA (L) I.2.x, 320.

18. DIA (L) I.2.x, 320.

19. DIA (L) I.2.x, 320.

20. DIA (L) I.2.x, 320.

21. DIA (L) I.2.x, 320.

22. James L. Noles, Jr., "Democracy in Alabama: Alexis de Tocqueville's Visit to Alabama in 1832," *Alabama Law Review* 64, no. 3 (2013), 706–707. Tocqueville included a shorter version of the story in his original travel notebooks. See Alexis de Tocqueville and Gustave de Beaumont, *Alexis de Tocqueville and Gustave de Beaumont in America: Their Friendship and Their Travels*, ed. Olivier Zunz (Charlottesville: University of Virginia Press, 2010), 312 and Pedersen, "The Whole Moral and Intellectual State of a People," 149.

23. Jill Locke, "Introduction: To Tocqueville and Beyond!" in Jill Locke and Eileen Hunt Botting, eds., *Feminist Interpretations of Alexis de Tocqueville* (University Park: Penn State University Press, 2009), 1–18.

24. DIA (L) I.2.x, 320.

25. DIA (L) I.2.x, 320.

26. DIA (L) I.2.x, 320.

27. DIA (L) I.2.x, 320.

28. DIA (L) I.2.x, 320.

29. DIA (L) I.2.x, 320.

30. Laura Janara, *Democracy Growing Up: Authority, Autonomy, and Passion in Tocqueville's Democracy in America* (Albany: State University of New York Press, 2002).

31. DIA (L) I.2.x, 320.

32. Alvin B. Tillery, "Tocqueville, Black Writers, and American Ethnology: Rethinking the Foundations of Whiteness Studies," in Locke and Botting, *Feminist Interpretations of Alexis de Tocqueville*, 253–280.

33. Alvin B. Tillery, "Tocqueville As Critical Race Theorist: Whiteness As Property, Interest Convergence, and the Limits of Jacksonian Democracy," *Political Research Quarterly* 62, no. 4 (2009), 639–652.

34. See Noles, "Democracy in Alabama."

35. Pedersen, "The Whole Moral and Intellectual State of a People," 150.

36. Tocqueville, *De la démocratie en Amérique*, 1:377, 389.

37. Rogers M. Smith, "Beyond Tocqueville, Myrdal, and Hartz: The Multiple Traditions in America," *The American Political Science Review* 87, no. 3 (1993), 549–566.

38. Tillery, "Tocqueville As Critical Race Theorist."

39. Alvin B. Tillery, "Reading Tocqueville Behind the Veil: African American Receptions of Democracy in America, 1835–1900," *American Political Thought* 7, no. 1 (2018), 1–25.

40. Eileen Hunt Botting, "Tocqueville and Wollstonecraftian Protofeminism," in Locke and Botting, *Feminist Interpretations of Alexis de Tocqueville*, 99–124. DIA (L) II.3.xii, 601–602.

41. Jennifer Pitts, "Introduction," in WES, ix–xxvi; Janara, *Democracy Growing Up*, 74, 158.

42. Pedersen, "The Whole Moral and Intellectual Character of a People," 92.

43. Pedersen, "The Whole Moral and Intellectual Character of a People," 92.

44. Botting, "Tocqueville and Wollstonecraftian Protofeminism."

45. Judith Butler, *Gender Trouble: Feminism and the Subversion of Identity* (New York: Routledge, 2007).

46. Judith Butler, "Preface (1999)," in *Gender Trouble*, xxiii, xxiv.

47. Judith Butler, *Bodies That Matter: On the Discursive Limits of Sex* (New York: Routledge, 2011), xxiv, 66.

48. Butler, *Bodies That Matter*, xxiv.

49. Susan Stryker, "My Words to Victor Frankenstein Above the Village of Chamounix: Performing Transgender Rage," *GLQ* 1, no. 3 (1994), 237–254, at 239.

50. Stryker, "My Words to Victor Frankenstein," 250.

51. Butler, "Preface (1999)," xiii.

52. Simone de Beauvoir, *The Second Sex*, trans. H. M. Parshley (New York: Random House, 1989), 169, 186, 202.

53. Steven B. Smith, *Political Philosophy* (New Haven, CT: Yale University Press, 2012), chap. 10.

54. For an extended reading of Tocqueville's debt to Rousseau, see Botting, "Tocqueville and Wollstonecraftian Protofeminism." Tocqueville's allusions to the narrative tropes of *Emile* are largely found in DIA (L) II.3.ix–xii, 590–603.

55. Butler, *Gender Trouble*, 168, 227n49.

56. Here, I unearth in Tocqueville's writing what the feminist film critic Laura Mulvey called the "male gaze," an implicitly masculine perspective in art and literature that tends to frame women's bodies as objects of sexual desire. See Laura Mulvey, "Visual Pleasure and Narrative Cinema," *Screen* 16, no. 3 (1975), 6–18.

57. Jean Elisabeth Pedersen, "Outrageous Flirtation, Repressed Flirtation, and the Gallic Singularity: Alexis de Tocqueville's Comparative Views on Women and Marriage in France and the United States," *French Politics, Culture and Society* 38, no. 1 (2020), 69, 88n30. Pedersen credits Cheryl Welch for drawing her attention to the "arch" content of Tocqueville's letter to his sister-in-law. See Welch, "Beyond the Bon Ménage: Tocqueville and the Paradox of Liberal Citoyennes," in Locke and Botting, *Feminist Interpretations of Alexis de Tocqueville*, 28.

58. Pedersen, "Outrageous Flirtation, Repressed Flirtation, and the Gallic Singularity," 68.

59. DIA (L) I.2.x, 320.

60. DIA (L) I.2.x, 320.

61. Welch, "Beyond the Bon Ménage," 19–46.

62. DIA (L) II.3.xii, 602.

63. DIA (L) II.3.ix, 590–591.

64. DIA (L) II.3.ix, 590–591.

65. DIA (L) II.3.ix, 590–591. See also Tocqueville's letter to his sister-in-law, Emilie, dated July 25, 1831, in which he comments lasciviously on the

"four blue eyes" of "two charming daughters" of a politician in Canandaigua. "Suffice it to say," he confesses on behalf of himself and his traveling partner Gustave de Beaumont, "we examined them even more enthusiastically than we examined their father's books." See Tocqueville and Beaumont, *America*, 87–88.

66. Ross Carroll, "The Hidden Labors of Mary Mottley," *Hypatia* 33, no. 4 (2018), 643–662.

67. DIA (L) II.3.x, 594.

68. DIA (L) II.3.x, 594.

69. DIA (L) II.3.x, 594.

70. DIA (L) II.3.iii, 568.

71. DIA (L) II.3.iii, 568.

72. DIA (L) II.3.iii, 568; DIA (L) II.3.x, 594. See also Pedersen, "Outrageous Flirtation, Repressed Flirtation, and the Gallic Singularity."

73. Pedersen, "Outrageous Flirtation, Repressed Flirtation, and the Gallic Singularity."

74. DIA (L) II.3.xii, 603.

75. DIA (L) II.3.xii, 602.

76. DIA (L) II.3.xii, 602.

77. DIA (L) II.3.xii, 602.

78. Jean-Jacques Rousseau, *Emile, or On Education (includes Emile and Sophie; or, The Solitaires)*, ed. Alan Bloom and Christopher Kelly (Hanover: University Press of New England, 2010), 161.

79. DIA (L) II.3.xii, 601.

80. DIA (L) II.3.xii, 601.

81. DIA (L) I.2.ix, 287.

82. DIA, "Author's Introduction," 19.

83. Judith Martin, "Republic of Manners," *The Atlantic* (November 2007), www.theatlantic.com/magazine/archive/2007/11/republic-of-manners/306311/ (accessed August 12, 2020).

84. DIA (L)II.3.xiv, 607.

85. Robert Frost, "Mending Wall" (1914), www.poetryfoundation.org/poems/44266/mending-wall (accessed August 12, 2020).

86. Mary Wollstonecraft, *A Vindication of the Rights of Woman*, in *The Works of Mary Wollstonecraft*, Vol. 5, ed. Janet Todd and Marilyn Butler (New York: NYU Press, 1989), 114.

87. Janara, *Democracy Growing Up*.

15 Picturing American Democracy
Tocqueville, Morrison, and the "Three Races"

Lawrie Balfour

THE DEMOCRATIC SCENE

Among the most vivid moments in Alexis de Tocqueville's *Democracy in America* is the account of his encounter with two women and a young girl in the forests of Alabama. After offering a quick sketch of the "Indian" and the "Negro" – two of "the three races in America" – Tocqueville tells the story of how he happened on the group while stopping to rest near a pioneer's cabin. Recalling the women's competition for the girl's attention, Tocqueville presents each figure as a mirror of her race. He identifies one woman as indigenous, probably Creek, by her dress ("barbarous luxury") and her bearing ("free, proud, and almost fierce"). The second woman, who is identified as African American, appears to be torn between "maternal affection and servile fear"; while the white child behaves "with a sense of superiority which contrasted strongly with her weakness and her age."[1] In this tableau of intimacy and difference, Tocqueville is moved to note that "a bond of affection united oppressors and oppressed, and nature bringing them close together made the immense gap formed by prejudices and by laws yet more striking."[2] The scene thus crystallizes Tocqueville's view of three races whose coexistence in North America is incompatible with the long-term flourishing of American democracy.

Today's readers have much to learn from Tocqueville's discernment of the racial injustice that structured life in the nineteenth-century United States, a polity that had been built on and was busily expanding chattel slavery and indigenous dispossession at the time of his travels. *Democracy* is especially prescient in its account of the depth of antiblack racism in the segregationist North during the decades before the Civil War. Indeed, Tocqueville's understanding that the pride so essential to American liberty was rooted in racial hierarchy resonates with Toni Morrison's observation, more than 150 years later, that "nothing highlighted freedom – if it did not in fact create it – like slavery."[3] His scathing account of "the most chaste affection for legal formalities," which legitimized the violent theft of indigenous lands and lives, stands apart from much of the political theory canon in acknowledging the horror of US policies toward the original inhabitants of the land.[4]

Despite the acuity of his critique, Tocqueville's staging of the scene in Alabama suggests why *Democracy* may be equally valuable as a caution about the limits of political theories that aim to educate readers about the nature of and prospects for democracy. His meditation on "The Three Races That Inhabit the United States," which is the longest chapter in either volume of *Democracy*, is set apart from Tocqueville's lessons about democratic life in two ways. Not only does he declare the topic to be substantively tangential, "American but not democratic," but he treats it as temporally distinct.[5] Where *Democracy* is oriented toward the future, the final chapter of volume 1 sees no livable options for Africans or their descendants and mourns the destruction of a world already "gone," in the case of Native Americans.[6] The scene in the woods thus serves as an illustration of timeless racial traits and an anthropological record of a vanishing present rather than a model for new relations in a society whose defining feature is equality.

Many commentators have noted how Tocqueville insulates his account of American democracy from the history and legacies of slavery and settler colonialism, even as he decries their brutality.[7] My aim in this chapter is not to rehearse these failings but to consider what is lost or distorted in the way he distills the varied experiences of white settlers, enslaved and free African Americans, and Native Americans into a theory of democratic freedom.

I suggest why fiction may offer a more illuminating resource for understanding the relationship of race and democracy insofar as its animating impulse is exploratory rather than explanatory. Reading Tocqueville's chapter on the "three races" alongside Toni Morrison's 2008 novel *A Mercy*, I ask how the entanglement of indigenous, black, and white histories are figured by the two authors. Together, the two texts press readers to consider whether a work of fiction discloses truthful alternatives to the writerly elements of Tocqueville's "new political science" and to ask what that means for thinking democratically today.[8]

Set in the late seventeenth century, more than a century before Tocqueville's travels, *A Mercy* conjures a quite different image of the American wilderness. Like Tocqueville, Morrison attends to the *moeurs* or "habits of the heart" that sustain democratic life in the face of tyranny. Like Tocqueville, furthermore, Morrison could be said to recreate the interactions of European, African, and indigenous women in the North American wilderness; and she likewise captures a tension between intimate connections forged in the "new" world and the destructive ordering of humanity by law and custom. In her telling, however, the "three races" appear in the form of "three unmastered women and an infant" (who are indigenous, black, and racially ambiguous). Their situation is laid out by Lina, a native woman whose village has been destroyed by "the deathfeet of the Europes,"[9] and who understands the peril they will face if their white mistress dies: "None of them could inherit; none was attached to a church or recorded in its books. Female and illegal, they would be interlopers, squatters, if they stayed on after Mistress died, subject to purchase, hire, assault, abduction, exile."[10] Morrison's staging of the scene decenters the settler's perspective. Although the future she limns is grim, the novel discredits the idea that destruction is inevitable. Instead, it asks readers to consider what Tocqueville calls "the shape of democracy" through the eyes of women and men who not only observed the interactions among the "three races" but lived them.[11]

Juxtaposing the two scenes suggests why *pictures* of democracy matter. Approaching theory as a practice of vision and of making visible, the next section, "Images of America," considers the role of images in expressing the connections between the constellation of features that are combined to produce the concept of "race" and those that are associated with "American democracy." Although he admits that some of his preconceptions of life in North America were confounded by the reality he encountered,[12] Tocqueville presents himself as a careful observer who records a wide range of information about the conditions, customs, and institutions of Jacksonian America and assembles an argument, punctuated by vivid images, in the service of educating the reader. Morrison's writing proceeds from a different direction and moves toward different ends. Her aim, she insists, is not to explain or to vindicate but to reinhabit the lives of "the people no one inquired of."[13] Moving from image to narrative, rather than argument to image, Morrison probes the complex experiences of women like those who furnish Tocqueville's portrait of racial difference.

The section "Fables of Three Races" looks closer at the stories that *Democracy* and *A Mercy* tell about the different peoples who inhabited North America in the years preceding and after the founding. By separating his reflections on racial difference from the account of America political development, Tocqueville creates a space in which to probe the past and present of white violence against indigenous and black people without envisioning alternative futures. Morrison, by contrast, crafts fiction distinctively fitted for the challenges of interpreting the ways of life that are possible "in a nation of people who *decided* that their world view would combine agendas for individual freedom *and* mechanisms for devastating racial oppression."[14] The final section, "Democracy Out of Wilderness," considers the two texts as different kinds of touchstones for our own times. Where Tocqueville writes with a sense of urgency, hoping to offer lessons about how to preserve liberty in the face of modern democracy's unstoppable rise, Morrison focuses on women and men for whom Tocqueville sees no future. She thereby writes another "new world" into being, one in which the women and men who provoke Tocqueville's pity and despair point the reader toward alternative ways of conceiving freedom.

IMAGES OF AMERICA

What is the difference between approaching images as instruments of instruction and images as spurs to the imagination? Part of the lasting power of *Democracy* is the degree to which readers are able to visualize the world as Tocqueville saw it. Although he presents the book as a product of observation, conversation, and research, not a fiction, Tocqueville's success at producing a relationship between images and ideas requires creative acts that can be compared to those of other kinds of writers.[15] The juxtaposition of *Democracy*'s approach with Morrison's reconstruction of the prehistory of "democracy in America" accentuates the political significance of Tocqueville's authorial choices. It is unsurprising that Tocqueville and Morrison picture the "races" differently, but I hope to show how their divergent understandings of the role of images in the writing process may be as significant as the images themselves. Where Tocqueville uses images to crystallize a concept or reinforce an idea, Morrison identifies them as starting points for a creative process that defies political science's predictive and explanatory pretensions.

In the "Author's Introduction," Tocqueville's bold pronouncement that "a new political science is needed for a totally new world" alerts readers toward the unprecedented character of the phenomena he studies and the importance of the method by which he studies them.[16] His mode of analysis not only depends on the powers of observation to reveal the contours of the democratic revolution that Tocqueville foresees as the future for European nations; it also relies on figurative language and imagery to impress his claims upon the reader. As Sheldon Wolin notes, there is a "strategic element" to Tocqueville's writerly choices: "the deploying of certain theoretical notions as images to produce a desired political effect."[17] Tocqueville acknowledges as much when he concludes the first volume of *Democracy* with a memorable image of his own method:

> I shall be like a traveler who has gone out beyond the walls of some vast city and gone up a neighboring hill; as he goes farther off, he loses sight of the men he has just left behind; the houses merge and the public square cannot be seen; the roads are hard to distinguish; but the outline is easier to see, and for the first he grasps its shape. Like that, I fancy I can see the whole future of the English race in the New World spread before me. The details of this huge picture are in shadow, but I can see the whole and form a clear idea of it.[18]

Calling his conclusion "less detailed but more certain" than the chapters that precede it, Tocqueville is quite conscious of the degree to which his argument relies on pictures.[19]

The lasting power and dangerous limitations of this approach are on full display in the longest chapter of *Democracy*'s two volumes: the analysis of the "three races." *Democracy* stands apart from most canonical treatments of European modernity for its probing assessment of the ways in which racial hierarchy and indigenous dispossession were enacted through the tyranny of law and, insidiously, through custom where the law's command did not reach.[20] If Tocqueville's skillful deployment of scenes from his travels impresses the depth of black and indigenous suffering on his readers, the same images that alert us to injustice also sort the people he studies into fixed categories. They are rendered as permanently recognizable members of natural groups, whose victimhood is legible in their skin color and temperament. The processes through which indigenous nations became "Indian" or African peoples were made "black" and the settler-master classes emerged as "white" go unremarked. As Jennifer Pitts comments, Tocqueville's treatment of the fate of the "three races" is "highly aestheticized," "more tableau than argument."[21] By offering a touchstone for a meditation on the future of the United States, the scene in the Alabama woods tells the reader more about how Tocqueville's conception of racial difference informs his method and his ethical unease with the violent development of democracy in America than it does about the individuals or groups on which he reports.

Consider the intimacy that serves Tocqueville so well as a pictorial device. Rather than opening up inquiry into the points of contact among human beings who were, often violently, brought together through chattel slavery and settler colonial expansion, it forestalls deeper reflection.[22] Although the scene is not motionless, like a conventional tableau, it is silent; any words spoken by the women remain unrecorded. As Roxanne Euben remarks, "*Democracy in America*, while intellectually and stylistically complex, is univocal rather than multivocal."[23] When Tocqueville notes that "no doubt my presence annoyed the Indian woman," for example, her actions remain wordless, available for his interpretation.[24]

Much can be learned by considering details that Tocqueville records but does not remark upon. Most strikingly, the picture of the "three races" is entirely female. That Tocqueville does not comment on this fact might reflect a general inattention to gender in the first volume of *Democracy*. Although he closes this gap in the second volume, his account of the domesticity of Anglo-American women sidesteps the intimate relationship between gender norms and the development of racial categories in the United States. When he remembers the three figures in Alabama, Tocqueville misses an opportunity to consider the *moeurs* that sustained power relations between black and white women and instead conjures a picture of the former's natural servility. Yet, in the world through which Tocqueville traveled, the display of "almost maternal affection" by black women was bound up with their subjection. Nor does he acknowledge the importance of *partus sequitur ventrem* – the legal innovation through which the status of children followed that of their mothers from the colonial era forward – or the role of black maternity as an instrument for the reproduction of slavery. Thus the image that Tocqueville uses to capture ethnographic truths reenacts "the *loss* of gender" and the denial of kinship upon which chattel slavery in the United States depended.[25]

Where Tocqueville's nine months in North America lead him to declare the supremacy of "the great Anglo-American family" as an accomplished or impending fact,[26] Morrison asks whether another kind of journey might yield different results. In *Playing in the Dark*, she explains that her fiction disrupts narratives of American founding that isolate the story of the United States from the other colonial territories in the New World: "I want to draw a map, so to speak, of a critical geography and use that map to open as much space for discovery, intellectual adventure, and close exploration as did the original charting of the New World – without the mandate for conquest."[27] Notwithstanding Tocqueville's pronouncement that "the Americans have no neighbors,"[28] *A Mercy* ties colonial North America to Europe and Africa, on the one hand, and locates it in a hemispheric neighborhood of slave capitalism and settler expansion, on the other. The action unfolds in places as far apart as London, West Africa, the American "wilderness," Barbados, and Maryland; it is both "transatlantic" and "hemispheric."[29] Although the present-tense narration of an enslaved girl named Florens structures the novel, her observations and reflections are interwoven with those of other characters. Morrison conjures a cacophonous, multilingual world in which characters speak with and past each other, not simply about ideas and principles but also about their histories, desires, and dreams. Where Tocqueville looks to the present to foresee the future and deploys images to capture an idea or concept, Morrison's imagination roams over a context when slavery was widely practiced but its relation to racial difference was only beginning to become entrenched. She also traces some of the visible marks of indigenous dispossession before "removal" became national policy.

Images, for Morrison, are not tools of argument but avenues toward the kinds of discovery that she believes are only possible in fiction writing. Creation begins with the visual remnants of memory and shards of history that "serve as my route to a reconstruction of a world, to an exploration of an interior life that was not written and to the revelation of a kind of truth."[30] By taking images as a starting point for an inquiry into lives that have been lost to official history, rather than summations of those lives, Morrison practices something akin to what Tina Campt calls "listening to images": "listening attentively to ... mundane details means not accepting what we see as the truth of the image. Attending to their lower frequencies means being attuned to the connections between what we see and how it resonates."[31] Although Morrison works with scraps of memory, rather than the photographs about which Campt writes, her novels move across the boundaries that conventionally divide the senses, connecting "felt sound"[32] to complex phenomenologies of sight, taste, and smell.

The effect of this process is not simply descriptive. The images provide Morrison's initial access to the past and open up ways of reimaging its relationship to the reader's present. Uninterested in the project of *explaining* African American history, Morrison trains her eyes on the ways that things might have unfolded differently. She counters the inevitability of what came before by exploring "what could have been," bringing to life the contingent events and vexed choices that shaped people's efforts to live free lives.[33] For "only by defamiliarizing both the object of the past and the established methods for apprehending that object," Lisa Lowe argues, "do we make possible alternative forms of knowing, thinking, and being."[34] *A Mercy* looks past the sedimented assumptions of what we think we know about the relationship of race, slavery, colonial settlement, and democracy to open up new avenues for exploration. "Unlike the successful advancement of an argument," Morrison observes, "narration requires the active complicity of a reader willing to step outside established boundaries of the racial imaginary."[35] The role of images, then, is twofold: they activate Morrison's creative process and they attune readers to possibilities not imagined by even the most sensitive theorists.

FABLES OF THREE RACES

One of the most striking features of Tocqueville's meditation on the "three races" is the detail with which he examines the distinct forms of violence through which white communities established and sustained themselves in America. Structurally set apart from the rest of *Democracy*, the chapter is divided into discrete sections about native peoples and African Americans. This approach effectively separates the figures who come together in the Alabama woods and disavows the profound interconnection between settler colonialism and racial slavery.[36] Although both groups might be said to exist "outside of history,"[37] in Tocqueville's view, their relationships to the past and future of the United States appear as independent stories.

Tocqueville's account of "The Present State and the Probable Future of the Indian Tribes Inhabiting the Territory of the Union" registers his horror at the process of forced migration that he witnessed on his journey. Arriving in the United States shortly after the Indian Removal Act of 1830, his travels coincided with the early phase of the Trail of Tears in which 46,000 Native Americans were forcibly dislocated.[38] Tocqueville's rendering of this dispossession mixes commentary with resonant images that continue to affect readers. Chickasaw scholar Jodi Byrd recalls, for example, her father's preoccupation with the fact that Tocqueville was present at one moment of destruction. Warning the reader that he has "witnessed afflictions beyond my powers to portray," Tocqueville recounts how Choctaw families were forced from their land in the middle of winter: "All the Indians had already got into the boat that was to carry them across; their dogs were still on the bank; as soon as the animals finally realized that they were being left behind forever, they all raised a terrible howl and plunged into the icy waters of the Mississippi to swim after their masters."[39] Moved by the injustice of the dispossession, Tocqueville uses his pictorial gifts to heighten the condemnation. His matter-of-fact observation that "nowadays the dispossession of the Indians is accomplished in a regular and, so to say, quite legal manner" is thus contrasted with this scene to powerful effect.[40] Yet neither the image nor the condemnation leaves open a possible future for the Choctaws, from Tocqueville's vantage, or for any of the communities whose lives stood in the way of the continental expansion of people "belonging to the same family, having the same point of departure, the same civilization, language, religion, habits, and mores, and among whom thought will circulate in similar forms and with like nuances."[41] Although *Democracy*'s driving concern is to teach readers how to sustain practices of freedom against the equalizing tide of democracy, Tocqueville assumes that the "obstinate love of freedom [that] lies concealed in the forests of the New World" holds no lesson for the future.[42]

In "Situation of the Black Race in the United States; Dangers Entailed for the Whites by Its Presence," Tocqueville tells a different kind of story about the impasse produced by European enslavement of Africans in North America. Again, he makes it amply clear that what he observes, chattel slavery in this case, is an "evil."[43] At the same time, however, he accepts Thomas Jefferson's view that there is no prospect for black and white Americans to coexist as equals.[44] Cohabitation is a curse for both groups, Tocqueville remarks, because New World slavery has combined the temporary condition of servitude with the permanent mark of "race."[45]

One of the striking features of this telling is how Tocqueville's powers of observation fail him at those points where he so acutely identifies white Americans' investment in constituting a racially homogeneous republic. If indigenous peoples are trapped in their past, in Tocqueville's view, African Americans have no past. Indeed, he mentions the introduction of slavery in a terse footnote to his chapter "Concerning Their Point of Departure and Its Importance for the Future of Anglo-Americans," and treats it as a fait accompli thereafter.[46] Yet, when *Democracy* appeared in 1835, fewer than thirty years had elapsed since the formal end of the transatlantic slave trade; and enslaved Africans would continue to arrive in the United States for nearly another thirty years.[47] On what grounds could Tocqueville plausibly assert that "the United States Negro has lost even the memory of his homeland"?[48] He offers none.

Although Tocqueville separates his treatment of chattel slavery from the account of American democracy, he draws on the condition of black Americans for general lessons about the fate of democracy. When he compares the laws of European aristocracy to American slavery, he denounces both: "What could be more fictitious than a purely legal inferiority!"[49] Tocqueville's purpose is not to suggest that race is simply a legal invention. Instead, he seeks to demonstrate the impossibility of overcoming racial hierarchies through an analogy to European struggles against hierarchies grounded in law, rather than the natural "fact" of race. In this telling, the enslaved become an illustration of a general point about democracy, offering a kind of surrogacy that belies the *tangential* character of the "three races" chapter.[50]

As a novelist, Morrison eschews the scientific tasks that frame Tocqueville's analysis. She has the freedom and, in her view, the responsibility, to create characters who are neither stylized representatives of racial temperament nor symbols of the crimes committed against them. Settler dispossession and the persistence of indigenous life are fundamental to the plot of *A Mercy*, but the narrative pulse comes from the characters' complex efforts to create lives that exceed their conditions. Unfolding at a time when many indigenous communities were already destroyed and the cartographic evidence of their existence roughly overwritten by European names, the novel dwells in the space between what the dispossessors saw and how their coming was experienced by the dispossessed. When Morrison introduces Jacob Vaark, the Anglo-American settler who is master of a multiracial household of women, she recounts his journey through the mid-Atlantic territories "from Algonquin to Sesquehanna via Chesapeake on through Lenape since turtles had a life span longer than towns."[51] Rather than present this movement as evidence of an annihilation already accomplished, however, the narrator calls attention to the tension between the settler's conscious reliance on these trails and his perception that he is traveling through "forests untouched since Noah."[52] Similarly, the novel reveals how Vaark's sensitivity to the contingency of European ownership does nothing to slake his desire to become a landowner or to build a magnificent house as a monument to his enterprise. Neither does it prevent him from purchasing Lina and Florens (or enriching himself through the slave trade in Barbados), while clinging to the belief that "flesh was not his commodity."[53]

Lina is the sole survivor of an indigenous community that has been devastated by disease and then burned by settlers. Living as an "exile" in the land of her birth, she nonetheless builds a new life from that loss. Mixing what she can remember from the language of her childhood and bits of her mother's teachings with elements of an imposed Christianity, "she sorted and stored what she dared to recall and eliminated the rest, an activity which shaped her inside and out."[54] Lina also joins herself to the future by serving as surrogate mother to Florens and organizing Vaark's household after his death. When Morrison writes that Lina "found, in other words, a way to be in the world," she invites readers to grasp the ongoingness of dispossession and the refusal to be done in by it.[55]

Intertwined with these stories are the experiences of African travelers to North America and their descendants. These characters, enslaved and free, move across the land at a time when race and bondage were just beginning to be conjoined. Florens' mother, known only as "a minha mãe," survives theft, the Middle Passage, and the harrowing trip from Barbados to Maryland, learning along the way "that I was not a person from my country, nor from my families. I was negrita."[56] In a stunning rebuttal to Tocqueville's declaration that "the Negro has no family,"[57] the relationship between a minha mãe and Florens, the daughter she gives away, reveals the difference between feelings of kinship that are unrecognized by white authority and those that are destroyed by it. Although the lines of communication between mother and daughter are broken, when the former persuades Vaark to take the child as partial payment of her master's debt, the reader sees what the mother sees at the moment of unspeakable loss: a helpless girl in "the shoes of a loose woman" with a cloth inadequately hiding growing breasts from white eyes.[58] The novelist's art is to inhabit the "interior life" of a minha mãe and so many others who bore similar losses, to counter the effects of what Morrison calls "the discourse that proceeded without us."[59]

DEMOCRACY OUT OF WILDERNESS

As countless commentators have remarked, *Democracy* is a living document. It remains a vital source for political theorists and interested citizens to read and reread. Pairing Tocqueville and Morrison, however, discloses *Democracy*'s double legacy: as an incisive account of the mores that have sustained racial hierarchy long after the abolition of slavery and the original practices of indigenous dispossession into the twenty-first century; and as a model of democratic theorizing that cannot be enlarged or stretched to provide an alternative to white domination. Despite its clarity of vision and critique, Tocqueville's text traffics in images that efface key features of the nineteenth-century world through which he traveled and seal the inevitability of "a settler future."[60] Morrison, like Tocqueville, is particularly attuned to the kinds of tyranny nurtured by democratic societies. Yet, where *Democracy* is "written under the impulse of a kind of religious dread,"[61] and aims to provide readers with the tools to manage an impending future, *A Mercy* travels to the past to explore forgotten possibilities. Morrison's novel re-narrates voyages to and around a "new world" in which Euro-American bondage-to-freedom stories of the American founding are intermixed with the stories of the enslaved, dispossessed, and exploited. Unlike *Democracy*, furthermore, the novel does not aim to impart a lesson or serve as a warning for coming generations. Morrison's novel remains in the seventeenth century; there are no explicit lines drawn from that time to ours.[62] Instead, she asks readers to re-view US history as if members of the "three races" were not symbols or archetypes but characters with complex stories and aspirations of their own.

For Morrison, the task of the writer is not to picture the past in light of the prejudices of the present. Nor is it "to consider the whole future,"[63] as though the features of what came before are settled. She spurs readers to regard those same "terrible afflictions" that haunt Tocqueville and that continue to haunt women and men who inherited the crimes of the American founding. Yet she draws on images and other fragments of memory to reconstruct history from the vantages of people who lived through those crimes. We might say that Morrison attempts to fulfill the promise of Tocqueville's own declaration that "the inhabitants of the New World may be considered from more than one point of view."[64] Crafting stories told in many voices, Morrison invites the reader to step inside the lives she narrates and to move away from settled expectations. Her novels press readers to consider the difference between texts that aim to theorize democratic freedom and writerly practices that essay to enact it on the page.

Tocqueville remains an exceptional reporter of the ways that American freedom was entwined with racial categories, even if he does not integrate those insights into his analysis. Where *Democracy* falls short, however, is precisely where it aims to intervene: in its account of how to sustain freedom in the modern era. *A Mercy* suggests another possibility. The story of Florens' abandonment by her mother is told from a variety of perspectives – including that of the white man who accepts ownership of Florens and the vantage of the girl herself. Only in the final chapter does Morrison give voice to the mother. Addressing a daughter who cannot hear her,[65] a minha mãe retells the horrors of her own odyssey and of her response to the knowledge that her growing daughter would soon be subject to the same kind of sexual violence that she endures ("To be female in this place is to be an open wound that cannot heal").[66] Forestalling the inevitable destruction of her daughter, Florens' mother extracts a kind of freedom from enslavement. She sets the terms for her own loss by encouraging the sale of her daughter to a man who regards her "as a human child, not pieces of eight."[67] Not as prey, in other words. In this way, the novelist accomplishes something the political theorist does not. She gestures toward an orientation toward the past that might enable readers who live in the shadow of the crimes Tocqueville decried to conceive different futures. "There is no protection," the enslaved mother tells her child, "but there is difference."[68]

NOTES

1. DIA (L) I.2.x, 320.

2. DIA (L) I.2.x, 320.

3. Toni Morrison, *Playing in the Dark: Whiteness and the Literary Imagination* (Cambridge, MA: Harvard University Press, 1992), 38.

4. DIA (L) I.2.x, 339.

5. DIA (L) I.2.x, 316.

6. Joanne Barker, "Territory As Analytic: The Dispossession of Lenapehoking and the Subprime Crisis," *Social Text* 36, no. 2 (2018), 19–39.

7. In the field of political theory, these include George Shulman, *American Prophecy: Race and Redemption in American Political Culture* (Minneapolis: University of Minnesota Press, 2008); Jack Turner, "American Individualism and Structural Injustice: Tocqueville, Gender, and Race," *Polity* 40, no. 2 (2008), 197–215; Margaret Kohn, "The Other America: Tocqueville and Beaumont on Race and Slavery," *Polity* 35, no. 2 (Winter 2002), 169–193; Mark Reinhardt, *The Art of Being Free: Taking Liberties with Tocqueville, Marx, and Arendt* (Ithaca, NY: Cornell University Press, 1997); William Connolly, "Tocqueville, Territory, and Violence," *Theory, Culture and Society* 11, no. 1 (1994), 19–41; Rogers M. Smith, "Beyond Tocqueville, Myrdal, and Hartz: The Multiple Traditions in America Author," *American Political Science Review* 87, no. 3 (1993), 549–566; and Michael Rogin, "Liberal Society and the Indian Question," *Politics and Society* 1, no. 3 (1971), 269–312.

8. DIA (L) I, Author's Introduction, 12.

9. Toni Morrison, *A Mercy* (New York: Vintage, 2008), 54.

10. Morrison, *A Mercy*, 58.

11. DIA (L) I, Author's Introduction, 19.

12. See Tocqueville, "Two Weeks in the Wilderness," in DIA (K), 879–880.

13. Toni Morrison, "Unspeakable Things Unspoken: The Afro-American Presence in American Literature," *Michigan Quarterly Review* 28, no. 1 (Winter 1989), 22.

14. Morrison, *Playing in the Dark*, xiii, emphasis in original.

15. For an approach to *Democracy in America* as part of a trilogy, along with Gustave de Beaumont's novel *Marie* (1835) and *On the Penitentiary System in the United States and Its Application in France* (1833) by Tocqueville and Beaumont, see Sarah Benson, "Democracy and Unfreedom: Revisiting Tocqueville and Beaumont in America," *Political Theory* 45, no. 4 (2017), 466–494.

16. DIA (L) I, Author's Introduction, 16.

17. Sheldon S. Wolin, *Tocqueville between Two Worlds: The Making of a Political and Theoretical Life* (Princeton: Princeton University Press, 2001), 100. See also Cheryl Welch, *De Tocqueville* (Oxford: Oxford University Press, 2001).

18. DIA (L) I, Conclusion, 408.

19. DIA (L) I, Conclusion, 408.

20. For example, Laura Janara notes how Tocqueville's use of fraternal imagery in his discussion of Indigenous peoples emphasizes the colonial violence that his contemporaries' references to brotherhood obscured. Janara, *Democracy Growing Up: Authority, Autonomy, and Passion in Tocqueville's Democracy in America* (Albany: State University of New York Press, 2002), 55–56.

21. Jennifer Pitts, *A Turn to Empire: The Rise of Imperial Liberalism in Britain and France* (Princeton: Princeton University Press, 2006), 198. James Schleifer calls this "the technique of the telling snapshot." See James T. Schleifer, "Tocqueville's *Democracy in America* Reconsidered," in Cheryl B. Welch, ed., *The Cambridge Companion to Tocqueville* (Cambridge: Cambridge University Press, 2007), 124.

22. This discussion is inspired by Lisa Lowe, *The Intimacies of Four Continents* (Durham, NC: Duke University Press, 2015).

23. Roxanne L. Euben, *Journeys to the Other Shore: Muslim and Western Travelers in Search of Knowledge* (Princeton: Princeton University Press, 2006), 124.

24. DIA (L) I.2.x, 320. Morrison notes that Tocqueville's contemporaries in the American literary world believed they could "observe [Native and

African Americans], hold them in prolonged gaze, without encountering the risk of being observed, viewed, or judged in return." Morrison, "Unspeakable Things Unspoken," 13.

25. Hortense J. Spillers, "Mama's Baby, Papa's Maybe: An American Grammar Book," *Diacritics* 17, no. 2 (Summer 1987), 77, emphasis in original.

26. DIA (L) I, Conclusion, 412.

27. Morrison, *Playing in the Dark*, 3.

28. DIA (L) I.2.ix, 278.

29. Anna Brickhouse, "Transatlantic vs. Hemispheric: Toni Morrison's Long Nineteenth Century," in Russ Castronovo, ed., *The Oxford Handbook of Nineteenth-Century American Literature* (Oxford: Oxford University Press, 2011), 137–159.

30. Toni Morrison, "The Site of Memory," in William Zinsser, ed., *Inventing the Truth: The Art and Craft of Memoir* (Boston: Houghton Mifflin, 1987), 115.

31. Tina M. Campt, *Listening to Images* (Durham, NC: Duke University Press, 2017), 33.

32. Campt, *Listening to Images*, 7.

33. Lowe, *Intimacies of Four Continents*, 40–41.

34. Lowe describes this as "past conditional temporality." Lowe, *Intimacies of Four Continents*, 137.

35. Toni Morrison, "Home," in Wahneema Lubiano, ed., *The House that Race Built: Black Americans, U.S. Terrain* (New York: Pantheon, 1997), 8–9.

36. Eve Tuck and K. Wayne Wang, "Decolonization Is Not a Metaphor," *Decolonization: Indigeneity, Education and Society* 1, no. 1 (2012), 6. For an account of the "distinct racial logics" in the "three races" chapter, see Adam Dahl, *Empire of the People: Settler Colonialism and the Foundations of Modern Democratic Thought* (Lawrence: University Press of Kansas, 2018).

37. Ralph Ellison, *Invisible Man* (New York: Vintage, 1995).

38. Tuck and Wang, "Decolonization Is Not a Metaphor," 16.

39. DIA (L) I.2.x, 324; Jodi A. Byrd, *The Transit of Empire: Indigenous Critiques of Colonialism* (Minneapolis: University of Minnesota Press, 2011), xi–xii, 32–38.

40. DIA (L) I.2.x, 324.

41. DIA (L) I, Conclusion, 412.

42. DIA (L) I.1.i, 29.

43. DIA (L) I.2.x, 340.

44. DIA (L) I.2.x, 355–356n46.

45. DIA (L) I.2.x, 341.

46. DIA (L) I.1.ii, 35n4.

47. The recently reissued volume of Zora Neale Hurston's interviews with Cudjo Lewis (Kossola), who was born in West Africa around 1841 and was the last survivor of the *Clotilda*, which arrived in Mobile, Alabama, shortly before the beginning of the Civil War, offers just one window into the complex reality that the stylized account of the "three races" elides. Where Tocqueville paints a portrait of black life severed from Africa in fact and memory, Hurston explores the ongoing costs of the Atlantic trade: "How does one sleep with such memories beneath the pillow?" Zora Neale Hurston, *Barracoon: The Story of the Last "Black Cargo,"* ed. Deborah G. Plant (New York: HarperCollins, 2018), 16.

48. DIA (L) I.2.x, 317.

49. DIA (L) I.2.x, 342.

50. Morrison explores "black surrogacy" in white American literature in *Playing in the Dark*.

51. Morrison, *A Mercy*, 13.

52. Morrison, *A Mercy*, 12.

53. Morrison, *A Mercy*, 22.

54. Morrison, *A Mercy*, 50.

55. Morrison, *A Mercy*, 48.

56. Morrison, *A Mercy*, 165.

57. DIA (L) I.2.x, 317.

58. Morrison, *A Mercy*, 166.

59. Morrison, "Site of Memory," 111.

60. Tuck and Wang, "Decolonization Is Not a Metaphor," 3.

61. DIA (L) I, Author's Introduction, 12.

62. In this sense, it contrasts with Michael Rogin's account of the connections between Indian removal and the violence of urban renewal and the war in Vietnam. Rogin, "Liberal Society and the Indian Question," 295.

63. DIA (L) I, Author's Introduction, 20.

64. DIA (L) I.2.x, 316.

65. As Stephen Best remarks, "Failed scenes of address pervade the novel." Best, "On Failing to Make the Past Present," *Modern Language Quarterly* 73, no. 3 (2012), 468.

66. Morrison, *A Mercy*, 163.

67. Morrison, *A Mercy*, 166.

68. Morrison, *A Mercy*, 166.

16 *Democracy in America* in the Twenty-First Century

New Challenges of Diversity and Inequality

Rogers M. Smith

INTRODUCTION

In his early thirties, Alexis de Tocqueville published two volumes analyzing the still-new United States of America that, even in the twenty-first century, constitute a monumental contribution to political and social inquiry. I have nonetheless suggested in the past that there are some disadvantages in relying on Tocqueville to understand America, and here I do so again.[1] I also argue, however, that central elements of Tocqueville's work not only help us see more clearly how our times and our challenges differ from his; *Democracy in America* develops important themes concerning diversity and democracy that can help us think about how we should confront our difficulties constructively today.

To preview the argument: though Tocqueville saw many challenges to American democracy in the 1830s, including issues of racial and economic inequality, he most emphasized dangers of the tyranny of the majority in politics and of an oppressive conformity, a stultifying uniformity, in social and cultural life. Both of these could foster human mediocrity at best and popular willingness to acquiesce in dictatorial governance, political and intellectual, at worst. As partial remedies, he favored extensive governmental decentralization and a robust civil society with many civic associations that, aided by a free press and an independent judiciary, could foster an ethos of political and social participation and concern for the common good – an ethos that might work against political tyranny, mindless social uniformity, and narrowly self-interested forms of individualism.

Today, our leading challenges appear to be not so much majority tyranny and uniform social conformity but instead the ever-growing cultural, demographic, and economic diversity and inequality that sharply divide us, making self-governing majorities of any sort, and any kind of strong sense of shared civic identity, difficult to achieve. Instead of a stultifying tyranny of the majority, we appear threatened by the disorder of multiplicity and fragmentation. Instead of resistance to conformity, we seem to need ties that can rebind us, though they must do so in ways consistent with modern notions of freedom, equality, and morality. Instead of despotic centralized governance, we confront deep divisions, political paralysis, and legislative gridlock.

These challenges are in some respects strikingly different from the ones Tocqueville emphasized. Consequently, I will suggest that we need to guide and govern modern American democracy through some innovations in democratic theory and democratic practice that in certain respects go beyond what he suggested. Nonetheless, Tocqueville's reflections on how many forms of diversity can strengthen the American republic, and on the institutions that can foster and sustain them, are useful in thinking about how best to meet contemporary challenges. Building in part on Tocqueville, I believe we need to develop criteria to judge what forms of cultural and economic diversity serve goals of equal democratic citizenship, and what forms subvert them. We need to develop a civic ethos that encourages all to pursue, among the diverse forms of excellence and happiness they may achieve, those that are most valuable to others as well as to themselves. Further, we need to develop governmental policies, sometimes central governmental policies, that can combat invidious forms of inequality and diversity, while accommodating insofar as possible the wide range of cultural differences America now encompasses. In pursuit of these ends, we are still likely to find many advantages in encouraging the robust civil society, the multiple and diverse civil associations, the ethical critique of narrow individualism, and at least some of the forms of governmental decentralization that Tocqueville favored.

TOCQUEVILLE'S FEARS

This argument starts with Tocqueville's fears for American democracy. It then turns to how Americans have sought to deal with the problems he feared in the more than 180 years since he wrote, before discussing the new challenges that have emerged from our efforts and how we might best respond to them.

Tocqueville ended each of the two volumes of *Democracy in America* with his deepest concerns about the future of democratic societies, using 1830s America as his vanguard example. Toward the end of the first volume, focused on formal political and legal institutions, Tocqueville said his "chief complaint against democratic government as it has been organized in the United States is not that it is weak, as many in Europe maintain, but rather that its strength is irresistible."[2] Tocqueville argued that the fact that Americans believed the nation's democratic majority to be the rightful source of all political authority meant that they set few effective checks against fickle majorities that changed laws too often or against arbitrary, autocratic officials who claimed to act in the name of the majority. Worst of all, Tocqueville contended, was the social fact that the moral prestige of views shared by majorities meant there was less "independence of mind and true freedom of discussion" in America than any country he knew, even though Americans have free speech rights.[3] As a result, there were few truly outstanding leaders, even as American governance still tended, in Tocqueville's view, toward a centralized majoritarian democratic despotism.

Tocqueville believed these tendencies were partly offset by a number of elements, including the fact that the administration of government programs was often decentralized in America, permitting, even fostering, diverse local adaptations that mitigated tendencies to undue uniformity. Tyranny of the majority was also resisted by the work of lawyers, courts, and juries in sometimes protecting minority rights versus majorities; by the many religions flourishing due to the freedom they enjoyed in America, as they mostly supported the same principles of public morality and liberty; and by the healthy civic manners Americans gained through participating in local democratic institutions. At times, Tocqueville appeared to gain confidence from the fact that Americans seemed united by shared beliefs, by common ideas not only of morality but also of the value of universal enlightenment and quests for practical improvements. Nonetheless, he was not sure that any of these features of American life were enough to avoid the ills of tyranny of the majority.

In his second volume, focused on the social and cultural features of American democracy, Tocqueville contended that a democratic attachment to "equality in fact produces two tendencies." The first leads "directly to independence," a sense that there are no superiors entitled to tell people what to do, convictions that can be so fierce as to raise fears of anarchy. However, Tocqueville most feared the second tendency, which he said conducted people "by a longer, more hidden, but also more certain path to servitude."[4] Tocqueville argued that commitments to equality led democratic citizens to favor "uniform legislation" emanating from the concentrated political power of a central government professing to express the will of the sovereign people.[5] Tocqueville believed that democratic peoples feel that the only kinds of laws that are just are those that treat all persons as identical, even if they are not; and because democratic individuals see themselves as essentially the same as their neighbors, while they live in a society of rapidly shifting fortunes with few sources of security, many pay attention only to their own individual and familial economic concerns and to "petty" and "vulgar" private pursuits.[6] They are largely indifferent to how their fellow citizens and country fare.

Because such citizens tend to elect democratic officials who are mediocre and corrupt, and because inattentive, uninformed, and unreflective majorities are not always right, Tocqueville again emphasized the need in America, and in modern democratic societies generally, for significant political decentralization, a strong legal system, and a free press. He also elaborated how, if a democratic central government was not to dictate everything, and if democratic citizens were not to be wholly caught up in their own private concerns, their hearts and minds must be enlarged and developed by participation in civil as well as political associations. Through these, they could do many of the tasks that governments would otherwise assume, and in the process, they might themselves be improved. Tocqueville concluded that if "men are to remain civilized, or to become so, they must develop and perfect the art of associating to the same degree that equality of conditions increases among them."[7]

These, then, were the most stressed fears about democracy in general and about democracy in America, expressed in Tocqueville's two volumes; but he expressed other concerns as well. Tocqueville recognized the institution of human enslavement as an unjust practice even if it did work against centralized governance in the United States, as each region sought to govern its political economy in its own way. He could see that these differences were sowing seeds of the disunion that eventually came to fruition a quarter-century after he wrote. Even more, however, Tocqueville saw the existence of "three races" on American soil, and particularly the presence of African American enslaved people in America, as "the most redoubtable of all the ills that threaten the future of the United States."[8] Even if enslaved labor should one day be ended, Tocqueville feared that white Americans would never accept living "on a footing of equality" with nonwhites.[9] He also warned that, because the uncertain fortunes of America's great mass of equal citizens drove them to pursue trade and industry to gain material security, and some in trade and industry were acquiring great wealth, a new "manufacturing aristocracy" might arise on the backs of "impoverished" and "brutalized" employees.[10]

At the same time, consistent with his concerns about unduly uniform treatment, Tocqueville appeared to applaud Americans for educating women but *not* having them participate equally with men in political and economic life. American men, with support from many women, instead kept women confined to "the quiet circle of domestic occupations," while nonetheless respecting their equal "reasoning abilities."[11] Tocqueville contended that these practices produced women of such "superiority" that they were "primarily responsible for the singular prosperity and growing power" of the United States.[12] This argument fit with his claim that, if democratic equality were held to support imposing uniformity on all persons, the results would hinder the progress of civilization. His argument was not, however, favorable to equal economic, civil, or political rights for women.

THE ARC OF CITIZENSHIP AFTER TOCQUEVILLE

Though many Americans admired Tocqueville's great work upon its initial publication, it did not loom large in American thought and scholarship until after 1945, when Alfred A. Knopf published a new edition. Tocqueville became a favorite inspiration for scholarly studies in the 1950s and has since remained so. We can see some reasons for this renewed interest in Tocqueville in midtwentieth-century America by noting the most prominent features in the development of American citizenship from the 1830s to the 1960s.

First and perhaps most fundamentally, regional tensions centered on enslaved labor did produce disunion and civil war. That war led to the adoption of new constitutional amendments and federal statutes that established on paper something Tocqueville thought Americans could not achieve: equal citizenship rights for Americans of African descent. For a generation, many African Americans even enjoyed meaningful political and economic rights, gaining education and some wealth as well as high political offices.[13] Tocqueville was not wrong, however, to believe that whites would resist these changes. During decades of intense contestation that culminated in the election of Woodrow Wilson, the first southern Democratic president since before the Civil War, the nation built new systems of racial hierarchy in the form of Jim Crow systems of segregation, jury exclusion, and disenfranchisement. These new institutions paid only "separate but equal" lip service to the postwar constitutional guarantees of civic equality.[14]

At the same time, as the industrial revolution spurred on by the US Civil War produced heights of economic inequality in the Gilded Age never before seen in American experience, and never surpassed until our own time, democratizing economic and social movements formed, from Greenbackers, to labor unions, to Populists, to Progressives, and, eventually, after the Depression, to Franklin Roosevelt's New Dealers. These movements sought to combat what they saw as a new industrial aristocracy by strengthening and, increasingly, centralizing the regulatory powers of America's governments, even as they further democratized political institutions through the direct election of senators, primaries, initiatives and referenda, and other innovations. The democratizing changes included the enfranchisement of women in 1920, the culmination of a "century of struggle" that involved complex alliances with white supremacists and anti-immigrant nativists as well as many economic and social reformers.[15]

I have argued that the New Deal brought to dominance in America a civic ideal portraying the nation as a "consumers and workers democracy," one bonded above all by a common concern for material progress.[16] New Dealers sought to achieve that goal through a centrally regulated market economy in which democratic governments attentive to the interests of all consumers and workers as well as businesses provided needed countervailing power to the immense resources that wealthy financial and manufacturing enterprises could wield. Like many others, I have also contended that the post–World War II rise of global competition with communist nations, especially the USSR, led to a domestic discrediting of left-leaning economic views and of labor unions, most significantly embodied in the 1947 Taft–Hartley Act. As these developments occurred, the early New Deal's "consumers and workers democracy" increasingly became simply a "consumers' democracy." From 1932 to 1945, Roosevelt repeatedly argued for a new economic bill of rights that would have guaranteed not just a safety net but public jobs for all. His partisan heir, John F. Kennedy, called in 1963 only for a new "consumers' bill of rights" that might prevent some business abuses but that would not directly assist workers or their unions.

Beginning in the 1950s, many scholars across the political spectrum have criticized this post–World War II American "consumers' democracy" for reasons much like those that concerned Tocqueville – hence the revival of interest in him during these years. For many scholars on the Left, America's postwar consumer society was a crassly commercial and conformist mass of citizens caught up in their self-interested material pursuits.[17] These citizens were all too subject to manipulation in the marketplace and in government by powerful corporate interests, increasingly unopposed by the nations' declining unions. In most of these scholars' eyes, the key problem was that corporations and their allies were shaping government regulations, mass media and advertisements, and cultural institutions to serve their own inegalitarian and exploitative purposes. At the same time, many scholars on the Right saw this mass consumer society as shallow, championing mediocrity in the name of equality and incapable of achieving either the intellectual and cultural heights of older aristocratic societies or the spiritual depth of older religious ones. Most of these more conservative scholars denounced twentieth-century America's trends toward more centralized and regulatory governance as precisely displaying the path toward democratic despotism that Tocqueville so feared.[18]

The rise of consumerist civic ideals was, however, not the only major development in American citizenship during these years. African Americans struggled magnificently against the subordinating and stigmatizing limitations imposed on them by Jim Crow policies and practices. In the 1950s and 1960s, prodded by domestic protests and by the reality that those policies and practices were huge liabilities for the United States in its Cold War competition with international communism, the national government finally formally repudiated racial segregation and disenfranchisement and began to redeem the promise of the post–Civil War amendments. Those successes, though limited, helped inspire the modern women's movement and a host of other civil rights struggles, on behalf of religious, cultural, and linguistic minorities, nonwhite immigrants, disabled persons, LG and then LGBT and then LGBTQ+ individuals, and more. The most important legislative achievements of these struggles were the 1964 Civil Rights Act, the 1965 Voting Rights Act, and the 1965 Immigration Act, along with their later amendments and the 1990 Americans with Disabilities Act, all of which fostered a far more demographically diverse nation.[19] The most important judicial achievements were *Brown v. Board of Education* banning segregation in 1954; *Frontiero v. Richardson* and *Roe v. Wade*, heightening equal protection guarantees for women and permitting abortions in 1973; and *Lawrence v. Texas* in 2003, upholding rights to same-sex intimacy, extended in 2015 to rights to same-sex marriages in *Obergefell v. Hodges*.

THE RISE OF POST-TOCQUEVILLEAN AMERICA

In these latter developments, we can locate the point where Tocqueville's most prominent concerns about democracy in America diverge in part from those raised by our own time. Up through the great laws of the mid-1960s, the most prominent defenders and opponents of equal civil rights – for African Americans, for other racial, ethnic, cultural, and religious minorities, and for women – primarily depicted these contests as struggles to establish the kind of uniformity in citizenship laws that worried Tocqueville. They were efforts to end forms of second-class citizenship by providing for all American citizens identical bundles of rights and duties. They were presented as efforts to end invidious discriminations by making American society color-blind, gender-blind, and difference-blind.

To be sure, to a greater degree than many scholars have recognized, participants in all these struggles often actually had more complex and varied views than this now-standard account indicates.

Nevertheless, equality as uniformity has long been the leading account of what civil rights proponents were seeking, from the time these civic transformations were happening up through today. To their advocates, progress toward more uniform citizenship laws represented proof that Tocqueville had been too pessimistic about the prospects for racial and gender equality in America. To their critics, these developments instead proved that Tocqueville was right to fear that quests for equality-as-uniformity, imposed by a heavy-handed central government, would generate democratic despotism, or perhaps modern liberalism's Leviathan.

In the half-century since the major civil rights laws of the 1960s, however, we have seen the burgeoning of a related range of civic phenomena that Tocqueville did not clearly anticipate. They are efforts to realize civic equality not through uniformity but through appropriately differentiated citizenship, with different bundles of rights and duties assigned, sometimes temporarily, sometimes permanently, to different groups of citizens, based on distinctive features of their personal or group identities. The claimants for differentiated treatment include racial, ethnic, and linguistic minorities, religious bodies, immigrant communities, the disabled, women, nonheterosexuals, the very young, and the very old. Public programs and economic aid and development also continue to be sought to address the distinct needs of different regions and occupations, especially those that are faring badly.

The core argument put forth by advocates for all these groups is that public policies generally reflect the values and interests of economically, culturally, and politically powerful communities – not those of all American communities and individuals. The result is that, if public policies and practices simply impose uniform treatment on all and fail to accommodate a wide range of differences, they will not produce meaningful equality of rights and opportunities. Instead, precisely because of their uniformity, American laws and practices will unjustly privilege some already highly advantaged citizens at the expense of all others.

This debate over whether treating individuals and groups identically, without regard to their differences, is the right way to treat them equally has a long history. It includes in this country the debates among early twentieth-century women's rights advocates about whether protective labor laws aided or hindered the progress of women.[20] It also reflects the long-standing disputes among diverse African American leaders about whether black nationalist initiatives or demands for integration were the best ways to combat the ills of Jim Crow segregation and racial discrimination, along with the debate over whether goals of racial advancement require fundamental restructuring of American economic and political institutions or simply egalitarian inclusion within them.[21] Today, it often builds on claims like those of Jehovah's Witnesses at the mid-century who believed they were being denied equal religious freedom if their children were required, like all others, to salute the American flag at school.[22] Analysts now commonly identify this debate between equality as uniformity and equality as appropriately differentiated treatment with controversies over racial affirmative action programs. Those measures spread in the 1970s, though they have older roots, because many civil rights advocates decided that banning formal racial discrimination was insufficient to move the nation beyond the deeply entrenched patterns of economic, educational, political, residential, and medical inequalities built up by centuries of discriminatory measures and practices that in important respects still continue.

It is, however, a great error to identify calls for "different but equal" bundles of citizenship rights simply with advocacy for racial affirmative action or even with liberal positions more broadly. Americans across the political spectrum regard young children as citizens, and if they have earnings, they often pay taxes, unlike many wealthy adults. Yet few urge that children gain voting rights. Most Americans believe that some kinds of special accommodations for disabled persons in public institutions – such as extra time on standardized tests – are both fair and desirable. Many Americans think it is suitable to allow all persons over the age of sixty-five to ride free on public transit, as we do in Philadelphia, regardless of their income. Many conservatives today argue fiercely that religious believers who direct businesses or nonprofits should generally have their faiths accommodated through granting them special exemptions from requirements to assist employees in obtaining medical coverage that includes contraceptives and exemptions from duties to serve LGBTQ members of the public, duties that are legal obligations for all other citizens. It is, to be sure, mostly liberals who favor race- and gender-based affirmative action and special public school curricula focused on ethnic and racial identities and experiences. Nevertheless, in twenty-first-century America, if we look for beliefs that some individuals and groups need to be treated differently by public policies and social practices from most other citizens in order to treat them truly equally, we find that such beliefs are so widespread as to be nearly universal.

These beliefs are so common in part because the notion that equality means universally uniform treatment, while appealing in the abstract, has *always* had implications that, for greatly varied reasons, many have found unrealistic and undesirable. Advocacy of "equality as appropriate differentiation" has become far more prevalent and visible today, however, due to the partial triumphs of the civil rights movements that generally sought more uniform treatment up through the 1960s. The dissatisfactions with the material achievements of those laws that led to calls for racial affirmative action programs are only part of the story. The major story is the increased ethnic, cultural, and religious diversity in the United States wrought by the 1965 Immigration Act, which ended the race-based National Origins Quota system created in the 1920s, along with the mounting resistance of many white, older-stock Americans to that diversity.

Ronald Reagan spearheaded the "Reagan Revolution" of the 1980s by adding to the economic and military conservatives to whom he had chiefly appealed in the 1960s new advocacy on behalf of racial and religious conservatives. By the 1970s, most racial conservatives had abandoned support for segregation, but they opposed all measures that redistributed resources *toward* racial and ethnic minorities. Moreover, after the failure of the 1986 Immigration Reform and Control Act to stem the migrant tide, racial conservatives also increasingly denounced, especially, Latino immigrants. Simultaneously, religious conservatives were terrified that federal civil rights policies would lead to their losing tax exemptions and other public benefits provided to their organizations, since they were reluctant to embrace gender equality, in some cases to become racially inclusive, and in most cases to recognize LGBTQ rights.[23]

These racial and religious conservative constituencies, added to the more long-standing economic and military conservative base of the Republican Party, made the Grand Old Party predominant in American politics from 1980 through 2008. They also fostered a heightening ideological polarization of the political leadership of the nation's two major parties, with the Republicans, in particular, moving strongly to the right. That polarization only became more severe as traditional Republican leaders like the Bushes failed to resist the demographic and cultural transformations these constituencies abhorred, instead embracing policies of economic globalization that made many feel vulnerable to heightened foreign competition, economic but also cultural. The America Tocqueville perceived, in which most Americans shared ideas of fundamental principles and purposes, has appeared increasingly remote. The results of this heightened polarization have included paralytic governmental gridlock, rather than centralized governmental despotism, on many national issues over the past decade. That paralysis and gridlock have led in turn to popular dissatisfactions with the leadership of both parties, producing strong insurgent campaigns in both parties' presidential primaries in 2016. The Republican insurgent gained the nomination and won the election, placing in the White House a man whose base lay more with racial and religious conservatives than with economic and military conservatives, whose free trade and foreign interventionist positions he challenged, even as he affirmed their stances on many other economic and national security issues.

Widespread demands across the political spectrum for equality as differentiation, not equality as uniformity; mounting trends toward central government incapacity and weakness rather than centralized despotism; a rise of fragmentation rather than mass conformity – these are the twenty-first-century phenomena that go against the grain of Tocqueville's most emphasized worries. Yet precisely because he did fear equality as uniformity and centralized despotism, as well as demagoguery, he is still an invaluable source for considering how to meet today's difficulties.

RESPONDING TO CHALLENGES OF DIVERSITY AND INEQUALITY IN THE TWENTY-FIRST CENTURY

The current severely troubled state of American democracy shows that no one, me included, has found magic answers to these post-Tocquevillean challenges to American democracy. America's political project is, however, far too valuable to abandon. Three related suggestions for strengthening American democratic thought and practice may have promise.

The first is recognition that, both in democratic theory and in constructing democratic public policies, we must heed Tocqueville's call not to conceive of equality as uniformity and embrace explicitly a task that he did not explore but that his work illuminates. We must undertake, as a continuing central endeavor of all democratic theorizing and all public policymaking, explicit consideration of what sorts of differential treatment of varied groups and individuals can work to give all groups and individuals meaningful opportunities to pursue their rights of life, liberty, and happiness, with prospects of success roughly equal to those of their fellow citizens. We must simultaneously decide what sorts of differential treatment instead represent forms of unjust privilege for some groups and individuals, often at the expense of others. These are tough questions. The answers are rarely if ever clear or incontestable, and they will also change as social, economic, and political contexts change. Catholics in the United States were a stigmatized, oppressed minority in the 1840s, when Protestants in Philadelphia demanded that public schools use Protestant bibles and rioted murderously against Catholics who objected. Catholics in the United States have much less claim to be a stigmatized, oppressed minority who deserve special aid and accommodation today, when six of the nine Supreme Court justices are Catholic and the sole Protestant is an Episcopalian raised as a Catholic.

This example suggests, however, that these tough questions are ones to which we *can* find plausible answers, based on good empirical evidence of current social, economic, and political conditions and practices as well as good studies of what the likely consequences of different policies are. If, for example, the accommodation of the religious owners of closely held private corporations in *Burwell v. Hobby Lobby* proves in practice to be a major obstacle to the opportunities for many employees to exercise their constitutionally protected right to obtain contraceptives, then that religious accommodation can rightly be judged to burden constitutional rights of privacy and equal protection excessively. If, however, the number of companies claiming this accommodation proves to be small, and it proves possible to provide coverage for contraceptives to their employees by other means that are not especially costly, then it seems right and just to grant that accommodation, a form of differentiated citizenship rights for these religious believers. Even if this religious exemption proves not burdensome to the rights or pocketbooks of other citizens, however, empirical investigations might show that other religious exemptions are far more damaging and costly. My first suggestion, then, is that both in theory and in public policy practice, we should focus on what the actual impacts of constructing rights and duties in differentiated ways are likely to be. Only then can we judge whether uniform or differentiated policies will result in roughly equal opportunities for all to benefit from their rights.

Pragmatically persuasive as this claim may be, it may well seem unprincipled and unjust to many, urging governments to decide on a shifting and ad hoc basis to treat some people better than others, instead of respecting all as equals. Tocqueville analyzed persuasively how ideals and conditions of relative equality can make "legislative uniformity" seem "the primary perquisite of good government."[24] Despite the heroic efforts of other interpreters, moreover, I believe his discussion of the differentiated citizenship of American women is a poor model for identifying differentiations that are just.[25] Tocqueville is, however, far more persuasive in arguing that, if we wish "to make rules for men instead of subjecting all men indiscriminately to the same rule," we must "examine an endless host of details" about particular circumstance; and he is right to contend that it is just to do so.[26] Yet his analysis leaves us with a great challenge. Given the appeal of uniformity, what might persuade governments and citizens to undertake the hard and unending tasks of determining what differentiations in civic rights and duties make sense in their time?

In response to this question, in recent writings I note that many modern political societies professing liberal democratic principles have defined the justice they seek to establish in terms consistent with the harm principle of John Stuart Mill, who had a kind of mutual admiration society with Tocqueville. Mill's harm principle contended: "the only purpose for which power can be rightfully exercised over any member of a civilized community, against his will, is to prevent harm to others."[27] Modern Millians often fear governments will define these "harms" in terms of the ethnocentric standards that Mill himself sometimes endorsed, especially when he defended British imperialism. Consequently, many adapt Mill's harm principle along lines like those of the nineteenth-century American Romantic thinker Ralph Waldo Emerson. Today, many suggest that each person is entitled to the maximum amount of "self-defined" freedom and self-realization possible, consistent with the self-defined freedom and self-realization of others.

In the more economically, socially, culturally, and politically diverse America of the twenty-first century, however, we have come to recognize ourselves as complex, multiply-constituted beings who might seek satisfying forms of self-realization in a number of different ways – ways that, while they would provide roughly equal satisfaction for us, might have very different consequences for others. I believe it is not only consistent with justice but commendably just and good for us to consider those consequences. I have therefore suggested that it would be right and beneficial for Americans, and members of other societies, to adopt a modified Millian maxim as both a personal and a civic ethos.[28]

That maxim is, "the best uses of their powers by communities and individuals are those that aid others, without doing harm to themselves." Both to meet our own needs and goals and to do what is just and good for our fellow citizens in the twenty-first century, Americans need a new focus not just on preventing harm to others but on exercising our freedoms in ways that benefit others. Doing so means we should recognize that, at times, it is just not to insist that every other person has exactly the same array of rights and duties as we do, and no more. It is instead just to make the effort to determine if giving certain special accommodations and exemptions to others is appropriate. We should do so when it appears very likely that doing so will work no significant material harm to ourselves or others, while it will enable some persons to enjoy the rights of life, liberty, and the pursuit of happiness, as they define happiness, more fully and successfully, and in ways that are more practically equal to our own opportunities. I submit that the pursuit of such opportunities for all is the heart of the justice that American democracy, which originated with the Declaration of Independence, promises for all and conceives to be our duty to advance for all.[29]

My third suggestion concerns how Americans might implement this civic ethos. Rather than placing public policy thumbs on the scales to set them against any differential treatment, as is the case now, governments should instead only deny the claims of groups to special accommodations for their preferred ways of life when those denials are necessary to achieve compelling governmental purposes – purposes that must be more than simple hostility to the groups in question.

This position will surely give pause to conservatives like the late Justice Antonin Scalia, who worried that granting religious free exercise claims, in particular, would make each person's conscience a law unto itself. He also condemned racial affirmative action as unjust. It will understandably worry liberals like the late Justice Ruth Bader Ginsburg, for she feared that undue deference to religious groups, especially, would permit them to engage in unjust discrimination. Similar concerns must shadow accommodations and exemptions for all ethnic and racial, linguistic, and cultural minorities, for immigrant communities, for the disabled, women, LGBTQ+ individuals and communities, children, the elderly, and indeed any and all such claimants.

These worries and fears are sensible. To gain reassurance against them, we must recognize that in order to grant each group and individual public rights that have comparable value to, but not more value than, those granted to other groups and individuals, we must *frequently* find that denials of demands for special rights and accommodations are necessary. Just and equal treatment of all groups requires that, if governments provide special accommodations to some, they must provide them to all who claim them. We must ask, for example, what the consequences will be of granting exemptions from Affordable Care Act requirements not only to religious groups but also to all who make similar demands. If there are many other such groups, then the accommodations in total will be too costly, both in dollars and in terms of the rightful opportunities of others, to approve.

If, however, demands for accommodations really are confined to a small number of groups and individuals, while the interests of those adversely affected by those accommodations can be met through relatively costless alternative policies, then and only then is it wise and just to support those accommodations. So long as accommodations do not substantially endanger what modern America has defined as persons' basic civil rights or the achievement of other compelling public goals, they may well contribute both to civic peace and to better prospects for more people to lead what they regard as truly fulfilling lives. In a twenty-first century that is already extraordinarily diverse in many respects and is becoming more so, it is reasonable to expect that many requests for special privileges will be so limited that they can be granted.

Pursuing these policies is, moreover, conducive to the flourishing of a wide variety of civil associations, of the sort that Tocqueville thought to be America's best schools for citizenship, for developing the habits and practices of working cooperatively with others in the pursuit not just of individual self-interest but also of common goods.[30] He maintained persuasively that, in "democratic nations," the "science of association is the fundamental science" for enabling people to resist tyranny and advance human civilization.[31] A public ethos and politics devoted to identifying appropriate forms of civic differentiation would both foster and benefit from practices of forming diverse associations to pursue different conceptions of personal and group happiness. A conception of national purpose as mandating egalitarian differentiated policies might well mean that a wide range of communities, from fundamentalist Christians to militantly proud deaf culture groups to families with transgender members, would all feel truly part of the larger American political community. Implementation of these policies of accommodation would often involve varying, and therefore effectively decentralizing, administration of many government programs and initiatives, in the ways Tocqueville thought beneficial.[32] So adopting this approach to claims of difference would reinforce many of the features of American life that Tocqueville identified as valuable obstacles to excessive uniformity and centralized democratic despotism.

Even so, I do not believe that these accommodations alone would be enough to combat effectively the huge economic inequalities and the many other forms of unjust discrimination in modern America. Central governmental initiatives must address many of the ills accompanying our economic inequalities and diversity. Yet policies of appropriate accommodations might mean that centralized governmental efforts to meet human needs, like the Affordable Care Act, would be implemented in ways that might gain broader support, precisely because some accommodations would be offered to, for example, religious groups with different beliefs. Adoption of appropriately differentiated citizenship policies would also have beneficial consequences for racial, ethnic, linguistic, religious, and cultural minorities who rightly see uniform policies in public institutions as representing the values and interests of dominant groups at the expense of their own communities. When their distinctive aspirations are instead recognized, respected, and assisted, many of these groups might come to feel that they have valuable opportunities to experience the benefits of being Americans, while pursuing their distinctive identities, on a more truly equal basis with traditionally privileged citizens.

Perhaps that hope is too optimistic. Scholars still debate whether Tocqueville, who said he often saw "decadence" in the rise of equality, really believed this trend was "progress" in "the eye of man's creator," because equality "is less lofty, perhaps, but more just, and its justice is the source of its grandeur and beauty."[33] Some interpreters believe that a bitter Tocqueville secretly felt that the alleged greatness, beauty, and justice offered by equality were not sufficient compensation for the elevated achievements and virtues of aristocratic societies. Others think that Tocqueville trusted what he believed to be God's judgment about the trend toward greater equality more than his own.

In any case, today we may well doubt that America's path is inevitably toward greater equality of conditions, due to divine will or other forces. Instead, it seems vital to give greater priority to confronting unjust inequalities than Tocqueville did. Yet we can share with him the belief that, if equality only means centrally imposed uniformity, we should resist it. We can also share with him the conviction that resistance is not futile. Tocqueville said at the close of *Democracy in America* that Providence traced around each man "a fatal circle beyond which he may not venture, but within the ample limits thus defined man is powerful and free, and so are peoples." He thought it "within their power to decide whether equality will lead them into servitude or liberty, enlightenment or barbarism, prosperity or misery."[34] With Tocqueville, Americans should see that it is within their power to determine if their democracy will succumb to division and fragmentation or new forms of despotism – or whether they will embrace and mobilize the nation's diversity and democratic commitments to achieve more truly free, more truly equal, and more truly fulfilling lives for all.

NOTES

1. See, for example, Rogers M. Smith, "Beyond Tocqueville, Myrdal, and Hartz: The Multiple Traditions in America," *American Political Science Review* 87, no. 3 (1993), 549–566.
2. DIA (G) I.2.vii, 290.
3. DIA (G) I.2.vii, 293.
4. DIA (G) II.4.i, 787; cf. II.1.ii, 492.
5. DIA (G) II.4.ii, 789, 795–796.
6. DIA (G) II.2.ii, 586; II.3.xiv, 711; II.4.i, 789.
7. DIA (G) II.ii.5, 599.
8. DIA (G) I.2.x, 392.
9. DIA (G) I.2.x, 411.
10. DIA (G) II.2.xx, 652.
11. DIA (G) II.3.xii, 706–707.
12. DIA (G) II.3.xii, 708.
13. See, for example, Richard M. Valelly, *The Two Reconstructions: The Struggle for Black Enfranchisement* (Chicago: University of Chicago Press, 2004).
14. Philip A. Klinkner and Rogers M. Smith, *The Unsteady March: The Rise and Decline of Racial Equality in America* (Chicago: University of Chicago Press, 1999), 72–169.

15. An excellent overview is Michael McGerr, *A Fierce Discontent: The Rise and Fall of the Progressive Movement in America, 1870–1920* (New York: Free Press, 2003).

16. Rogers M. Smith, "The Progressive Seedbed: Claims of American Political Community in the Twentieth and Twenty-First Centuries," in Stephen Skowronek, Stephen M. Engel, and Bruce Ackerman, eds., *The Progressives' Century: Political Reform, Constitutional Government, and the Modern American State* (New Haven, CT: Yale University Press, 2016), 264–288. See also Lawrence B. Glickman, *A Living Wage: American Workers and the Making of Consumer Society* (Ithaca, NY: Cornell University Press, 1997).

17. See, generally, Juliet B. Schor and Douglas B. Holt, eds., *The Consumer Society Reader* (New York: The New Press, 2000).

18. For a later statement of this critique that explicitly builds on Tocqueville, see Christopher Wolfe, "The Cultural Preconditions of American Liberty," *National Review*, April 29, 2010. www.nationalreview.com/m agazine/2010/05/17/cultural-preconditions-american-liberty/ (accessed August 7, 2020).

19. A useful overview is John D. Skrentny, *The Minority Rights Revolution* (Cambridge, MA: Harvard University Press, 2002).

20. See, for example, Judith A. Baer, *The Chains of Protection: The Judicial Response to Women's Labor Legislation* (New York: Praeger Publishers, 1978).

21. These debates can be traced in Sherrow O. Pinder, ed., *Black Political Thought: From David Walker to the Present* (New York: Cambridge University Press, 2020).

22. Shawn Francis Peters, *Judging Jehovah's Witnesses: Religious Persecution and the Dawn of the Rights Revolution* (Lawrence: University Press of Kansas, 2000).

23. See, for example, Gil Troy, *Morning in America: How Ronald Reagan Invented the 1980s* (Princeton: Princeton University Press, 2005).

24. DIA (G) II.4.ii, 789.

25. DIA (G) II.3.xii, 705–708. Cf., for example, Delba Winthrop, "Tocqueville's American Woman and 'The True Conception of Democratic Progress'," *Political Theory* 14, no. 2 (1986), 239–261.

26. DIA (G) II.4.iii, 195.

27. John Stuart Mill, *On Liberty*, ed. David Spitz (New York: W.W. Norton, 1975), 10–11.

28. See, for example, Rogers M. Smith, *Political Peoplehood: The Roles of Values, Interests, and Identities* (Chicago: University of Chicago Press, 2015), 198–199.

29. I develop this argument more fully in Rogers M. Smith, *That Is Not Who We Are! Populism and Peoplehood* (New Haven, CT: Yale University Press, 2020).

30. DIA (G) II.2.v, 596.

31. DIA (G) II.2.v, 598–599.

32. See DIA (G) I.1.v, 97–104, among many other discussions.

33. DIA (G) II.4.viii, 833.

34. DIA (G) II.4.viii, 834.

References

Académie française. *Le Dictionnaire de l'Académie française*. Paris: J. B. Coignard, 1694.

Adams, Henry. *The Education of Henry Adams*. Oxford: Oxford University Press, 1999.

Addison, Joseph. "Essay No. 421." In Donald F. Bond, ed., *The Spectator*. Oxford: Clarendon Press, 1987.

Agresto, John. "Was Promoting Democracy a Mistake?" *Commentary* 134, no. 5 (2012), 32–38.

Aguilar Rivera, José Antonio. *En pos de la quimera: Reflexiones sobre el experimento constitucional atlántico*. Mexico City: FCE/CIDE, 2000.

"Omisiones del corazón: La recepción de Tocqueville en México," in *Ausentes del Universo: Reflexiones sobre el pensamiento político hispanomericano en la era de la construcción nacional, 1821–1850*. Mexico: Fondo de Cultura Económica, 2012.

Alberdi, Juan Bautista. *Obras sélectas*, Vol. 13. Buenos Aires: La Facultad, 1920.

Alexander, Jeffrey C. "Tocqueville's Two Forms of Association." *The Tocqueville Review/La revue Tocqueville* 27 no. 2 (2006), 175–190.

Alfón, Fernando. *La querella de la lengua en Argentina: Antología*. Buenos Aires: Museo del Libro, 2013.

Alinsky, Saul D. *Reveille for Radicals*. Chicago: University of Chicago Press, 1946. *Reveille for Radicals*. New York: Vintage Books, 1969.

Allen, Barbara. *Tocqueville, Covenant, and the Democratic Revolution: Harmonizing Earth with Heaven*. Lanham, MD: Lexington Books, 2005.

Alletz, Édouard. *De la démocratie nouvelle*. Paris: Lequien, 1837.

Anderson, Elizabeth. *Value in Ethics and Economics*. Cambridge, MA: Harvard University Press, 1995.

Arendt, Hannah. *Eichmann in Jerusalem: A Report on the Banality of Evil*. New York: Penguin Books, 1977.

On Revolution. New York: Penguin Books, 1990.

Aron, Raymond. *Main Currents in Sociological Thought, Vol. 1: Montesquieu, Auguste Comte, Karl Marx, Alexis de Tocqueville, The Sociologists and the Revolution of 1848*. New York: Basic Books, 1965.

Atanassow, Ewa. "Colonization and Democracy: Tocqueville Reconsidered." *American Political Science Review* 111, no. 1 (2017), 83–96.

Atanassow, Ewa and Richard Boyd, eds. *Tocqueville and the Frontiers of Democracy*. Cambridge: Cambridge University Press, 2013.

Audier, Serge. *Tocqueville retrouvé: Genèse et enjeux du renouveau Tocquevillien français*. Paris: VRIN, 2004.

Augustine, *City of God*, trans. Henry Bettenson. New York: Penguin Books, 1984.

Avramenko, Richard and Noah Stengl. "Looking Down Tocqueville's Nose: On the Problem of Aristocratic Etiquette in Democratic Times." In Richard Avramenko and Ethan Alexander-Davey, eds., *Aristocratic Souls in Democratic Times*. Lanham, MD: Lexington Books, 2018, 275–296.

Avramenko, Richard and Brianne Wolf. "Disciplining the Rich: Tocqueville on Philanthropy and Privilege." *Review of Politics* 83, no. 3 (2021), 351–374.

Babbitt, Irving. *Democracy and Leadership*. Boston: Houghton, Mifflin and Company, 1924.

  Literature and the American College: Essays in Defense of the Humanities. Boston: Houghton, Mifflin and Company, 1908.

Badhwar, Neera K. "Friendship and Commercial Societies." *Politics, Philosophy and Economics* 7, no. 3 (2008), 301–326.

Baer, Judith A. *The Chains of Protection: The Judicial Response to Women's Labor Legislation*. New York: Praeger Publishers, 1978.

Bailey, Jeremy D. *The Idea of Presidential Representation: An Intellectual and Political History*. Lawrence: University Press of Kansas, 2019.

  Thomas Jefferson and Executive Power. New York: Cambridge University Press, 2007.

Barber, Benjamin R. *Jihad vs. McWorld: Terrorism's Challenge to Democracy*. New York: Ballantine Books, 1996.

  Strong Democracy: Participatory Politics for a New Age. Berkeley: University of California Press, 1984.

Barker, Joanne. "Territory As Analytic: The Dispossession of Lenapehoking and the Subprime Crisis." *Social Text* 36, no. 2 (2018), 19–39.

Beaumont, Gustave de. *Marie*, trans. Barbara Chapman. Baltimore, MD: Johns Hopkins University Press, 1999.

Beaumont, Gustave de and Alexis de Tocqueville. *System Pénitentiarie aux États-unis et de son application en France*. Paris: H. Fournier, 1833.

Beauvoir, Simone de. *The Second Sex*, trans. H. M. Parshley. New York: Random House, 1989.

Beichman, Arnold. *Anti-American Myths: Their Causes and Consequences*. New York: Routledge, 1992.

Bellah, Robert, Richard Madsen, William N. Sullivan, Ann Swidler, and Steven N. Tipton. *Habits of the Heart: Individualism and Commitment in American Life*. Berkeley: University of California Press, 2007.

Bello, Andrés. *Obras completas de don Andrés Bello*, vol. 9. Santiago: Pedro G. Ramírez, 1885.

Bénichou, Paul. *The Consecration of the Writer, 1750–1830*, trans. Mark K. Jensen. Lincoln: University of Nebraska Press, 1999.

Benoît, Jean-Louis. *Tocqueville: Un destin paradoxal*. Paris: Perrin, 2013.

"Malesherbes, l'abbé Lesueur et Hervé de Tocqueville, trois clés de la formation d'Alexis de Tocqueville." *Bulletin de la Société des antiquaires de Normandie*, 78 (2019), 71–94

Benson, Sarah. "Democracy and Unfreedom: Revisiting Tocqueville and Beaumont in America." *Political Theory* 45, no. 4 (2017), 466–494.

Bercovitch, Sacvan. *The Puritan Origins of the American Self*. New Haven, CT: Yale University Press, 1975.

Berger, Peter and Richard John Neuhaus. *To Empower People: From State to Civil Society*. Washington, DC: American Enterprise Institute, 1996.

Berman, Russell. *Anti-Americanism in Europe: A Cultural Problem*. Stanford: Hoover Institution Press, 2004.

Best, Stephen. "On Failing to Make the Past Present." *Modern Language Quarterly* 73, no. 3 (2012), 453–474.

Blanc, Louis. "De la Démocratie en Amerique." *Revue républicaine* (May 1835), 129–163.

Bloom, Allan. *The Closing of the American Mind*. New York: Simon & Schuster, 1987.
Giants and Dwarfs. New York: Simon & Schuster, 1990.

Blosseville, Ernest de. "De la démocratie en Amérique," *L'Echo français*, February 11, 1835, 1–3.

Boesche, Roger. *The Strange Liberalism of Alexis de Tocqueville*. Ithaca, NY: Cornell University Press, 1987.

Botana, Natalio. *La tradición republicana: Alberdi Sarmiento y las ideas políticas de su tiempo*. Buenos Aires: Sudamericana, 1997.

Botting, Eileen Hunt. "Thomas Paine amidst the Early Feminists." In *Selected Writings of Thomas Paine*, ed. Ian Shapiro and Jane E. Calvert. New Haven, CT: Yale University Press, 2014, 630–654.

"Tocqueville and Wollstonecraftian Protofeminism." In Jill Locke and Eileen Hunt Botting, eds., *Feminist Interpretations of Alexis de Tocqueville*. University Park: Penn State University Press, 2009, 99–124.

Boyd, Richard. "From Aristocratic Politesse to Democratic Civility, or What Mrs. Frances Trollope Didn't See in America." In Aurelian Craiutu and

Jeffrey Isaac, eds., *America through European Eyes: British and French Reflections on the New World from the Eighteenth Century to the Present*. University Park: Penn State University Press, 2009, 187–211.

"Tocqueville and the Napoleonic Legend." In Ewa Atanassow and Richard Boyd, eds., *Tocqueville and the Frontiers of Democracy*. Cambridge: Cambridge University Press, 2013, 264–288.

Uncivil Society: The Perils of Pluralism and the Making of Modern Liberalism. Lanham, MD: Lexington Books, 2004.

Boyte, Harry and Benjamin Barber. "Civic Declaration: A Call for a New Citizenship," A Project of the American Civic Forum. An Occasional Paper of The Kettering Foundation, December 9, 1994.

Boyte, Harry C. *The Backyard Revolution: Understanding the New Citizen Movement*. Philadelphia: Temple University Press, 1980.

Brickhouse, Anna. "Transatlantic vs. Hemispheric: Toni Morrison's Long Nineteenth Century." In Russ Castronovo, ed., *The Oxford Handbook of Nineteenth-Century American Literature*. Oxford: Oxford University Press, 2011, 137–159.

Brogan, Hugh. *Alexis de Tocqueville: A Life*. New Haven, CT: Yale University Press, 2007.

Brown, Bernard E. "Tocqueville and Publius." In *Reconsidering Tocqueville's Democracy in America*, ed. Abraham S. Eisenstadt. New Brunswick, NJ: Rutgers University Press, 1988, 43–74.

Brown, Robert Warren. "The Generation of 1820 during the Bourbon Restoration in France: A Biographical and Intellectual Portrait of the First Wave, 1814–1824." PhD dissertation, Duke University, 1979.

Bryce, James. *The American Commonwealth*. Indianapolis: Liberty Fund, 1995.

Burke, Edmund. *Reflections on the Revolution in France*, ed. Conor Cruise O'Brien. London: Penguin Books, 1986.

Reflections on the Revolution in France. Indianapolis: Liberty Fund, 1999.

Reflections on the Revolution in France, ed. Frank M. Turner. New Haven, CT: Yale University Press, 2003.

Speech on Conciliation with America, ed. Sidney Carleton Newsom. Project Gutenberg, 2013. www.gutenberg.org/5/6/5/5655/ (accessed August 12, 2020).

Butler, Judith. *Bodies That Matter: On the Discursive Limits of Sex*. New York: Routledge, 2011.

Gender Trouble: Feminism and the Subversion of Identity. New York: Routledge, 2007.

Byrd, Jodi A. *The Transit of Empire: Indigenous Critiques of Colonialism*. Minneapolis: University of Minnesota Press, 2011.

Campion, M. Pierre. "Tocqueville écrivain: Le style dans De la Démocratie en Amérique." Littérature, no. 136 (2004), 3–21.

Campt, Tina M. Listening to Images. Durham, NC: Duke University Press, 2017.

Cardona Zuluaga, Patricia. "Florentino González y la defensa de la república." Araucaria 16, no. 32 (2014), 435–458.

Carlyle, Thomas. "Latter-Day Pamphlets," in The Works of Thomas Carlyle, Vol. 20, ed. Henry Duff Traill. Cambridge: Cambridge University Press, 2010.

Carreira da Silva, Filipe and Monica Brito Vieira. "Books that Matter: The Case of Tocqueville's Democracy in America." The Sociological Quarterly 61, no. 4 (2020), 703–726.

Carroll, Ross. "The Hidden Labors of Mary Mottley." Hypatia 33, no. 4 (2018), 643–662.

Cataño, Gonzalo. "Tocqueville y su amigo Mill," in Historia, sociología y política: ensayos de sociología e historia de las ideas. Bogotá: Plaza y Janés, 1999.

Ceaser, James. "Alexis de Tocqueville on Political Science, Political Culture, and the Role of the Intellectual." American Political Science Review 79, no. 3 (1985), 656–672.

Designing a Polity: America's Constitution in Theory and Practice. Lanham, MD: Rowman & Littlefield, 2010.

Liberal Democracy and Political Science. Baltimore, MD: Johns Hopkins University Press, 1992.

Presidential Selection: Theory and Development. Princeton, NJ: Princeton University Press, 1979.

Reconstructing America: The Symbol of America in Modern Thought. New Haven, CT: Yale University Press, 2000.

"Why Tocqueville on China: An Introductory Essay." Tocqueville on China Project. The American Enterprise Institute. January 2010.

Chambers, Edward T. and Michael A. Cowan. Roots for Radicals: Organizing for Power, Action, and Justice. New York: Continuum, 2003.

Chambers, Simone. "A Critical Theory of Civil Society." In Simone Chambers, ed., Alternative Conceptions of Civil Society. Princeton: Princeton University Press, 2002, 90–110.

Chambers, Simone, and Jeffrey Kopstein. "Bad Civil Society." Political Theory 29, no. 6 (2001), 837–865.

Chasseboeuf Volney (Comte de), Constantin François. "Tableau du Climat et des Sol des États-Unis," [1803] in Oeuvres complètes de Volney. Paris: Firmin-Didot Frères, 1838.

Chateaubriand, François-René de. *Atala, ou Les Amours de deux sauvages dans le désert*. Paris: 1801.

De l'Ancien Régime au Nouveau Monde: Écrits politiques, ed. Jean-Paul Clément. Paris: Hachette, 1987.

Grands écrits politiques, Vol. 2, ed. Jean-Paul Clément. Paris: Imprimerie nationale Éditions, 1993.

Mémoires d'outre tombe, 2 vols, ed. Maurice Levaillant and Georges Moulinier. Paris: Bibliothèque de la Pléiade, 1951.

Voyage en Amérique, Vol. 1, ed. Richard Switzer. Paris: Marcel Didier, 1964.

Chevalier, Michel. *Society, Manners, and Politics in the United States*. Boston: Weeks, Jordan & Co., 1839.

Chong Ming. "Democracy in China: Tocquevillean Reflections." *The Tocqueville Review/La revue Tocqueville* 38, no. 1 (2017), 81–111.

Clark, Thomas. "'The American Democrat' Reads 'Democracy in America': Cooper and Tocqueville in the Transatlantic Hall of Mirrors." *Amerikastudien/American Studies* 52, no. 2 (2007), 187–208.

Coats, Dan and John Kasich. *Project for American Renewal*. Washington, DC: Empower America, 1995.

Cohen, Jean and Andrew Arato. *Civil Society and Political Theory*. Cambridge, MA: MIT Press, 1994.

Cohen, Joshua and Joel Rogers. *Associations and Democracy*. London: Verso, 1995.

Coleman, Charly. *The Virtues of Abandon*. Stanford: Stanford University Press, 2014.

Compagnon, Antoine. "Tocqueville et Chateaubriand: Deux anti-modernes?" In Françoise Mélonio and José-Luis Diaz, eds., *Tocqueville et la littérature*. Paris: Presses de l'Université Paris-Sorbonne, 2005, 37–59.

Comunello, Francesca and Giuseppe Anzera. "Will the Revolution be Tweeted? A Conceptual Framework for Understanding the Social Media and the Arab Spring." *Islam and Christian–Muslim Relations* 23, no. 4 (2012), 453–470.

Connolly, William. "Tocqueville, Territory, and Violence." *Theory, Culture and Society* 11, no. 1 (1994), 19–41.

Conseil, L. P. *Mélanges politiques et philosophiques extraits des mémoirs et de la correspondance de Thomas Jefferson*. 2 vols. Paris: Paulin, Libraire-Éditeur, 1833.

Cooper, James Fenimore. *Notions of the Americans: Picked up by a Travelling Bachelor*. London: Henry Colburn, 1828.

The American Democrat. Washington, DC: Regnery Publishing, 2000.

Corcelle, Francisque de. "De La Démocratie Américaine." *Revue des deux mondes,* June 14, 1835: 739–761.

Corral, Luis Díez del. *El liberalismo doctrinario.* Madrid: Instituto de Estudios Políticos, 1956.

El pensamiento político de Tocqueville. Madrid: Alianza Editorial, 1989.

Cox, W. Michael and Richard Alm. "The Churn: The Paradox of Progress." In Federal Reserve Bank of Dallas *Annual Report* (1992), 5–11.

Craiutu, Aurelian. "From the Social Contract to the Art of Association: A Tocquevillian Perspective." *Social Philosophy and Policy* 25, no. 2 (2008), 263–287.

Liberalism under Siege: The Political Thought of the French Doctrinaires. Lanham, MD: Lexington Books, 2003.

"Tocqueville and the Political Thought of the French Doctrinaires." *History of Political Thought* 20, no. 3 (1999), 456–493.

"Tocqueville and Eastern Europe." In Christine Dunn Henderson, ed., *Tocqueville's Voyages: The Evolution of His Ideas and Their Journey Beyond His Time.* Indianapolis: Liberty Fund, 2014, 390–424.

"Tocqueville's 'Sacred Ark'." *Araucaria* 21, no. 42 (2019), 351–370.

Craiutu, Aurelian and Sheldon Gellar, eds. *Conversations with Tocqueville: The Global Democratic Revolution in the Twenty-first Century.* Lanham, MD: Lexington Books, 2009.

Craiutu, Aurelian and Matthew N. Holbreich. "On Individualism, Authority, and Democracy As a New Form of Religion: A Few Tocquevillian Reflections." In Michael Zuckert, ed., *Combining the Spirit of Religion and the Spirit of Liberty: Tocqueville's Thesis Revisited.* Chicago: University of Chicago Press, 2017, 123–152.

Craiutu, Aurelian and Jeffrey Isaacs, eds., *America through European Eyes: British and French Reflections on the New World from the Eighteenth Century to the Present.* University Park, PA: Penn State University Press, 2009.

Crouzet, Michel. *Stendhal et l'Amérique.* Paris: Éditions de Fallois, 2008.

Cruz Rodríguez, Edwin. "El federalismo en la historiografía política colombiana (1853–1886)." *Historia Crítica* 44 (2011), 104–127.

Dahl, Adam. *Empire of the People: Settler Colonialism and the Foundations of Modern Democratic Thought.* Lawrence: University Press of Kansas, 2018.

Damiron, Jean-Philibert. *Les philosophes français du XIXᵉ siècle.* Paris: CNRS Éditions, 2011.

Damrosch, Leo. *Tocqueville's Discovery of America.* New York: Farrar, Straus and Giroux, 2011.

Demier, Francis. *La France de la Restauration (1814–1830): L'impossible retour du passé*. Paris: Gallimard, 2012.

Demin, Duan. "Reviving the Past for the Future? The (In)compatibility between Confucianism and Democracy in Contemporary China." *Asian Philosophy: An International Journal of the Philosophical Traditions of the East* 24, no. 2 (2014), 147–157.

Derré, Jean-René. *Lamennais, ses amis, et le movement des ideés à l'époque romantique 1824–1834*. Paris: Klincksieck, 1962.

Dobson, William J. *The Dictator's Learning Curve: Inside the Global Battle for Democracy*. New York: Random House Anchor Books, 2012.

Drescher, Seymour. "More than America: Comparison and Synthesis in *Democracy in America*." In *Reconsidering Tocqueville's "Democracy in America,"* ed. Abraham S. Eisenstadt. New Brunswick, NJ: Rutgers University Press, 1988, 77–93.

  Tocqueville and England. Cambridge, MA: Harvard University Press, 1964.

  "Tocqueville's Two Democracies." *Journal of the History of Ideas* 25, no. 2 (1964), 201–216.

  "Who Needs *Ancienneté*: Tocqueville on Aristocracy and Modernity." *History of Political Thought* 24, no. 4 (Winter 2003), 624–646.

Drolet, Michael. *Tocqueville, Democracy, and Social Reform*. New York: Palgrave, 2003.

Dumont, Louis. *Essais sur l'individualisme*. Paris: Seuil, 1983.

Echánove Trujillo, Carlos A. "El juicio de amparo mexicano." *Revista de la Facultad de Derecho* 1–2 (1951), 91–116.

Echeverría, Esteban. "Palabras simbólicas," in *Obras completas de d. Esteban Echeverría*. Vol. 4. Buenos Aires: C. Casaralle, impr. y Librería de Mayo, 1870–1874.

  "Symbolic Words." In Natalio Botana and Ezequiel Gallo, eds., *Liberal Thought in Argentina, 1837–1940*. Indianapolis: Liberty Fund, 2013, 27–47.

Ellison, Ralph. *Invisible Man*. New York: Vintage, 1995.

Elshtain, Jean Bethke. *A Call to Civil Society: Why Democracy Needs Moral Truths*. New York: Institute for American Values, 1998.

  Democracy on Trial. New York: Basic Books, 1995.

Elster, Jon. *Alexis de Tocqueville: The First Social Scientist*. Cambridge: Cambridge University Press, 2009.

Eltantawy, Nahed, and Julie Wiest. "Social Media in the Egyptian Revolution: Reconsidering Resource Mobilization Theory." *International Journal of Communication* 5 (2011), 1207–1224.

Englert, Gianna. "'The Idea of Rights': Tocqueville on the Social Question." *The Review of Politics* 79, no. 4 (2017), 649–674.

Euben, Roxanne L. *Journeys to the Other Shore: Muslim and Western Travelers in Search of Knowledge*. Princeton: Princeton University Press, 2006.

Everett, Edward. "De Tocqueville's Democracy," *North American Review*, July 1836, 179–182.

Faucher, Léon. "De la démocratie aux Etats-Unis." *Le Courrier français*, December 24, 1834.

Fénelon, François. *Fénelon: Moral and Political Writings*, ed. Ryan Patrick Hanley. Oxford: Oxford University Press, 2020.

Ferguson, Robert A. *Law and Letters in American Culture*. Cambridge, MA: Harvard University Press, 1984.

Fix-Zamudio, Héctor. *Ensayos sobre el derecho de amparo*. Mexico City: Porrúa, 1999.

Flavin, Rebecca McCumbers. "Tocqueville's Critique of the U. S. Constitution." *The European Legacy: Toward New Paradigms* 24 no. 7–8 (2019), 755–768.

Foley, Michael and Bob Edwards. "The Paradox of Civil Society." *Journal of Democracy* 7, no. 3 (1996), 38–52.

Friedman, Max Paul. *Rethinking Anti-Americanism: The History of an Exceptional Concept in American Foreign Relations*. Cambridge: Cambridge University Press, 2012.

Frohnen, Bruce. *Virtue and the Promise of Conservatism: The Legacy of Burke and Tocqueville*. Lawrence: University Press of Kansas, 1993.

Frost, Robert. "Mending Wall" (1914). www.poetryfoundation.org/poems/44266/mending-wall (accessed August 12, 2020).

Fukuyama, Francis. "The End of History?" *National Interest* 16 (1989), 3–18.

The End of History and the Last Man. New York: Free Press, 1992.

"The March of Equality." *Journal of Democracy* 11, no. 1 (2000), 11–17.

Fumaroli, Marc. *Chateaubriand: Poésie et Terreur*. Paris: Éditions de Fallois, 2003.

Fung, Archon. "Associations and Democracy: Between Theories, Hopes, and Realities." *Annual Review of Sociology* 29, no. 1 (2003), 515–539.

Furet, François, "The Intellectual Origins of Tocqueville's Thought." *The Tocqueville Review/La revue Tocqueville* 7 (1985), 117–129.

Interpreting the French Revolution. Cambridge: Cambridge University Press, 1981.

"Naissance d'un paradigme: Tocqueville et le voyage en Amérique (1825–1831)." *Annales. Économies, Sociétés, Civilisations* 39, no. 2 (1984), 225–239.

Revolutionary France, 1770–1880, trans. Antonia Nevill. Cambridge, MA: Blackwell, 1992.

Furuya Jun. "Tocqueville and the Origins of American Studies in Postwar Japan." Paper presented at the "France and the United States, Two Models of Democracy" international conference, University of Tokyo. June 10–12, 2005.

Galston, William A. "Civil Society and the 'Art of Association'." *Journal of Democracy* 11, no. 1 (2000), 64–70.

"Tocqueville on Liberalism and Religion." *Social Research* 54, no. 3 (1987), 499–518.

Gannett, Robert T., Jr. "Bowling Ninepins in Tocqueville's Township." *American Political Science Review* 97, no. 1 (2003), 1–16.

"Tocqueville and Local Government: Distinguishing Democracy's Second Track." *Review of Politics* 67, no. 4 (Fall 2005), 721–736.

"Tocqueville and the Politics of Suffrage." *The Tocqueville Review/La revue Tocqueville* 27, no. 2 (2006), 208–226.

Tocqueville Unveiled: The Historian and His Sources for The Old Regime and the Revolution. Chicago: University of Chicago Press, 2003.

"*Village-By-Village Democracy in China: What Seeds for Freedom?*" Tocqueville on China Project. American Enterprise Institute, April 2009.

Gauchet, Marcel. "Tocqueville, America, and Us: On the Genesis of Democratic Societies." *The Tocqueville Review/La revue Tocqueville* 37 (2016), 163–231.

Gellner, Ernest. *Conditions of Liberty: Civil Society and Its Rivals*. London: Penguin, 1994.

Gengembre, Gérard. "De la littérature en Amérique, ou De Mme de Staël à Tocqueville." In Françoise Mélonio and José-Luis Diaz, eds., *Tocqueville et la littérature*. Paris: Presses de l'Universite Paris-Sorbonne, 2005.

Glendon, Mary Ann. "Introduction." In Mary Ann Glendon and David Blankenhorn, eds., *Seedbeds of Virtue: Sources of Competence, Character, and Citizenship in American Society*. Lanham, MD: Madison Books, 1995, 1–4.

Glickman, Lawrence B. *A Living Wage: American Workers and the Making of Consumer Society*. Ithaca, NY: Cornell University Press, 1997.

Goblot, Jean-Jacques. *La Jeune France libérale: Le Globe et son groupe littéraire 1824–1830*. Paris: Plon, 1995.

Golemboski, David. "Federalism and the Catholic Principle of Subsidiarity." *Publius: The Journal of Federalism* 45, no. 4 (2015), 526–551.

González, Florentino. *Elementos de ciencia administrativa*. Bogotá: Escuela Superior de Administración Pública, 1994.

Gottfried, Paul. *Conservatism in America: Making Sense of the American Right*. London: Palgrave Macmillan, 2007.

Gaffiot, Félix. *Dictionnaire latin-français*. Paris: Hachette, 1934.

Gray, John. *Endgames: Questions in Late Modern Political Thought*. Chichester: Polity Press, 1997.

Griswold, Charles L., Jr. *Adam Smith and the Virtues of Enlightenment*. Cambridge: Cambridge University Press, 1999.

Gudeman, Stephen. "Remodeling the House of Economics: Culture and Innovation." *American Ethnologist* 19, no. 1 (1992), 141–154.

  The Anthropology of Economy: Community, Market, and Culture. Malden, MA: Blackwell, 2001.

Guizot, François. *The History of Civilization in Europe*, trans. William Hazlitt. Indianapolis: Liberty Fund, 2013.

Gunn, J. A. W. *When the French Tried to be British: Party, Opposition, and the Quest for Civil Disagreement 1814–1848*. Montreal and Kingston: McGill-Queen's University Press, 2009.

Hale, Charles A. *El liberalismo mexicano en la era de Mora*. Mexico City: Siglo XXI, 1994.

  The Transformation of Liberalism in Nineteenth-Century Mexico. Princeton: Princeton University Press, 1989.

Hall, Basil. *Travels in North America in the Years 1827 and 1828*. Edinburgh: Cadell & Co., 1829.

  "Tocqueville on the State of America." *Quarterly Review* 57 (1836), 133–134.

Hamrin, Carol Lee. "China's Protestants: A Mustard Seed for Moral Renewal?" Tocqueville on China Project. American Enterprise Institute. May 2008.

Hanley, Ryan Patrick. *Love's Enlightenment*. Cambridge: Cambridge University Press, 2017.

  The Political Philosophy of Fénelon. Oxford: Oxford University Press, 2020.

Harpaz, Ephraïm. *L'École libérale sous la Restauration*. Geneva: Droz, 1968.

Harrison, Lawrence. "After the Arab Spring, Culture Still Matters." *The American Interest*, September 1, 2011. www.the-american-interest.com/2011/09/01/after-the-arab-spring-culture-still-matters/ (accessed June 23, 2020).

Hartz, Louis. *The Liberal Tradition in America*. New York: Harcourt, Brace, 1955.

Hawley, George. *Right-Wing Critics of American Conservatism*. Lawrence: University Press of Kansas, 2017.

Hayek, Friedrich. *The Constitution of Liberty*. Chicago: University of Chicago Press, 2011.

  Individualism and Economic Order. Chicago: University of Chicago Press, 2012.

Hebert, L. Joseph. "Individualism and Intellectual Liberty in Tocqueville and Descartes."*Journal of Politics* 69 (2007), 523–537.

Heidegger, Martin. "The Fundamental Question of Metaphysics." In Heidegger, *An Introduction to Metaphysics*, trans. Ralph Manheim. New Haven, CT: Yale University Press, 1959.

Henderson, Christine Dunn, ed. *Tocqueville's Voyages: The Evolution of His Ideas and Their Journey Beyond His Time*. Indianapolis: Liberty Fund, 2014.

Herold, Aaron. "Tocqueville on Religion, the Enlightenment, and the Democratic Soul." *American Political Science Review* 109, no. 3 (2015), 523–524.

Higuchi Yoichi. "Tocqueville et le constitutionnalisme." Paper presented at the "France and the United States, Two Models of Democracy" international conference, University of Tokyo. June 10–12, 2005.

Himmelfarb, Gertrude. "Introduction" in Alexis de Tocqueville, *Memoir on Pauperism*, trans. Seymour Drescher. London: Civitas, 1997.

Hollander, Paul. *Anti-Americanism: Critiques at Home and Abroad, 1965–1990*. New York: Oxford University Press, 1992.

Holt, Michael F. *The Rise and Fall of the American Whig Party: Jacksonian Politics and the Onset of the Civil War*. New York: Oxford University Press, 1999.

Home, Henry, Lord Kames. *Elements of Criticism,* vol. 1, ed. Peter Jones. Indianapolis: Liberty Fund, 2005.

Horkheimer, Max and T. W. Adorno, "The Culture Industry: Enlightenment As Mass Deception," in Horkheimer and Adorno, *The Dialectic of Enlightenment*, trans. John Cumming. New York: Continuum, 1972, 120–167.

Horwitt, Sanford D. *Let Them Call Me Rebel: Saul Alinsky – His Life and Legacy*. New York: Alfred A. Knopf, 1989.

Howard, Marc Morjé. *The Weakness of Civil Society in Post-Communist Europe*. Cambridge: Cambridge University Press, 2003.

Howard, Philip N., Aiden Duffey, Deen Freelon, Muzammil M. Hussain, Will Mari, and Marwa Mazaid. "Opening Closed Regimes: What Was the Role of Social Media During the Arab Spring?" Working Paper No. 2011.1. Project on Information Technology & Political Islam. 2011.

Hunt, Lynn. *Inventing Human Rights: A History*. New York: W.W. Norton & Company, 2007.

Huntington, Samuel. "The Clash of Civilizations?" *Foreign Affairs* 72, no. 3 (Summer 1993), 22–49.

"Cultures Count." In Lawrence Harrison and Samuel Huntington, eds., *Culture Matters: How Values Shape Human Progress*. New York: Basic Books, 2000, xiii–xvi.

Political Order in Changing Societies. New Haven, CT: Yale University Press, 1968.

Who Are We? The Challenges to America's National Identity. New York: Simon & Schuster, 2004.

Hurston, Zora Neale. *Barracoon: The Story of the Last "Black Cargo,* ed. Deborah G. Plant. New York: Harper Collins, 2018.

Hurtado, Cristina. "La recepción de Courcelle-Seneuil, seguidor de Tocqueville, en Chile." *Polis* 17 (2007), 1–10.

Hurtado, Jimena. "Adam Smith and Alexis de Tocqueville on Division of Labour." *European Journal of the History of Economic Thought* 26, no. 6 (2019), 1187–1211.

Ignatius, David. "A War of Choice, and One Who Chose It," *Washington Post,* November 2, 2003, p. B 01. https://www.washingtonpost.com/archive/opin ions/2003/11/02/a-war-of-choice-and-one-who-chose-it/0284d57c-b2b5-44 76-89b3-72cecfa55ee8/ (accessed June 23, 2020).

Ikuta, Jenny and Trevor Latimer. "Aristocracy in America: Tocqueville on White Supremacy." *Journal of Politics* 83, no. 2 (2021), 547–559.

Isaacs, Jorge. *María.* Madrid: Cátedra, 2007.

Jaksic, Ivan. *Andrés Bello: Scholarship and Nation-Building in Nineteenth-Century Latin America.* Cambridge: Cambridge University Press, 2001.

Janara, Laura. *Democracy Growing Up: Authority, Autonomy, and Passion in Tocqueville's Democracy in America.* Albany: State University of New York Press, 2002.

Jardin, André. *Tocqueville: A Biography,* trans. Lydia Davis and Robert Hemenway. New York: Farrar, Straus and Giroux, 1988.

Jaume, Lucien. *L'individu effacé ou le paradoxe du libéralisme français.* Paris: Fayard, 1997.

Tocqueville: Les Sources aristocratiques de la liberté. Paris: Fayard, 2008.

Tocqueville: The Aristocratic Sources of Liberty, trans. Arthur Goldhammer. Princeton: Princeton University Press, 2013.

Jech, Alexander. "Tocqueville, Pascal, and the Transcendent Horizon." *American Political Thought* 5, no. 1 (2016), 109–131.

Jefferson, Thomas. *Writings,* ed. Merrill D. Peterson. New York: Library of America, 1984.

Jouffroy, Théodore. "De la philosophie morale de M. Droz ou de l'Éclectisme moderne." *Le Globe* 92 (April 9, 1825), 457–458.

How Dogmas Come to an End in *Philosophical Miscellanies of Cousin, Jouffroy, and B. Constant,* Vol. 2, ed. and trans. George Ripley. Boston: Hilliard, Gray, and Company, 1838.

Judt, Tony. *Past Imperfect: French Intellectuals, 1944–1956*. Berkeley: University of California Press, 1992.

Kahan, Alan S. *Alexis de Tocqueville*. London: Bloomsbury, 2013.

    Aristocratic Liberalism: The Social and Political Thought of Jacob Burckhardt, John Stuart Mill, and Alexis de Tocqueville. New York: Oxford University Press, 1992.

    Tocqueville, Democracy and Religion: Checks and Balances for Democratic Souls. Oxford: Oxford University Press, 2015.

Kammen, Michael. *Alexis de Tocqueville and Democracy in America*. Washington, DC: Library of Congress, 1998.

Katzenstein, Peter and Robert Keohane, eds., *Anti-Americanisms in World Politics*. Ithaca, NY: Cornell University Press, 2006.

Keen, Suzanne. *Empathy and the Novel*. Oxford: Oxford University Press, 2007.

Kelly, George Armstrong. *The Humane Comedy: Constant, Tocqueville, and French Liberalism*. Cambridge: Cambridge University Press, 1992.

Keslassy, Eric. *Le libéralisme de Tocqueville à l'épreuve du paupérisme*. Paris: L'Harmattan, 2000.

Khondker, Habibul Haque. "Role of the New Media in the Arab Spring." *Globalizations* 8, no. 5 (2011), 675–679.

Kirk, Russell. "Burke and the Philosophy of Prescription." *Journal of the History of Ideas* 14, no. 3 (1953), 365–380.

    The Conservative Mind: From Burke to Santayana. Chicago: Henry Regnery Co., 1953.

Kirkpatrick, Jennet. *Uncivil Disobedience: Studies in Violence and Democratic Politics*. Princeton: Princeton University Press, 2008.

Klein, Hans K. "Tocqueville in Cyberspace: Using the Internet for Citizen Associations." *The Information Society* 15, no. 4 (1999), 213–220.

Klinkner, Philip A. and Rogers M. Smith. *The Unsteady March: The Rise and Decline of Racial Equality in America*. Chicago: University of Chicago Press, 1999.

Kloppenberg, James T. *The Virtues of Liberalism*. Oxford: Oxford University Press, 1998.

Kohn, Margaret. "The Other America: Tocqueville and Beaumont on Race and Slavery." *Polity* 35, no. 2 (Winter 2002), 169–193.

Koritansky, John C. *Alexis de Tocqueville and the New Science of Politics*. Durham, NC: Carolina Academic Publishers, 2009.

Kraynak, Robert P. "Tocqueville's Constitutionalism." *American Political Science Review* 81, no. 4 (1987), 1175–1195.

Kubik, Jan. *Power of Symbols against the Symbols of Power: The Rise of Solidarity and the Fall of State Socialism in Poland*. University Park: Penn State University Press, 1994.

Kumar, Krishan. *1989: Revolutionary Ideas and Ideals*. Minneapolis: University of Minnesota Press, 2001.

Laboulaye, Édouard. *L'etat et ses limites: Suivi d'essais politiques sur Alexis de Tocqueville, l'instruction publique, les finances, le droit de pétition, etc.* Paris: Imprimerie de P.A. Bourdier et Cie, 1863.

Lamberti, Jean-Claude. *Tocqueville and the Two Democracies*. Cambridge, MA: Harvard University Press, 1989.

Lamennais, Félicité Robert de. *Essai sur l'indifférence en matière de religion*, Vol. 2. Paris: Tournachon Molin & Segun, 1830.

Lamennais: A Believer's Revolutionary Politics, ed. Richard A. Lebrun and Sylvain Milbach. Leiden: Brill, 2018.

Lange, Victor. "Visitors to Lake Oneida: An Account of the Background of Sophie von la Roche's Novel Erscheinungen Am See Oneida." *Symposium: A Quarterly Journal in Modern Literatures* 2, no. 1 (1948), 48–78.

Lasch, Christopher. *The Culture of Narcissism: American Life in the Age of Diminishing Expectations*. New York: W.W. Norton, 1991.

Lastarria, José Victorino. *La América*. Gante: E. Vanderhaeghen, 1867.

La América: Fragmentos. Mexico: UNAM, 1977.

Lawler, Peter Augustine. "The Human Condition: Tocqueville's Debt to Rousseau and Pascal." In Eduardo Nolla, ed., *Liberty, Equality, Democracy*. New York: New York University Press, 1992, 1–20.

The Restless Mind: Alexis de Tocqueville on the Origin and Perpetuation of Human Liberty. Lanham, MD: Rowman & Littlefield, 1993.

"Tocqueville on Pantheism, Materialism, and Catholicism." *Perspectives on Political Science* 30, no. 4 (2001), 218–226.

Lear, Jonathan. *Radical Hope: Ethics in the Face of Cultural Devastation*. Cambridge, MA: Harvard University Press, 2006.

Le Brun, Jacques. *Le Pur Amour de Platon à Lacan*. Paris: Éditions du Seuil, 2002.

Leeson, Peter T. "Two Cheers for Capitalism?" *Society* 47, no. 3 (2010), 227–233.

Lefort, Claude. *Democracy and Political Theory*. Minneapolis: University of Minnesota Press, 1988.

Lerner, Ralph. *Revolutions Revisited: Two Faces of the Politics of Enlightenment*. Chapel Hill: University of North Carolina Press, 1994.

Li Hongtu. "Transformation des sociétés et naissance des révolutions: la mode de Tocqueville dans la Chine actuelle." *The Tocqueville Review/La revue Tocqueville* 36, no. 1 (2015), 215–233.

Lilla, Mark, ed. *New French Thought: Political Philosophy*. Princeton: Princeton University Press, 1994.

Lincoln, Abraham. "'A House Divided' Speech" in *Political Writings and Speeches*, ed. Terence Ball. Cambridge: Cambridge University Press, 2013.

Lipset, Seymour Martin. *The First New Nation: The United States in Historical and Comparative Perspective*. New York: Basic Books, 1963.

Li Qiang. "History and Ideology: Teaching and Research on the History of Western Political Thought in China since the 1980s." *International Journal of Public Affairs* 3 (2007), 67–79.

"Tocqueville and Reform in China." Abstract prepared for a conference on Tocqueville. Waseda University School of Political Science, Tokyo. March 2, 2013.

Locke, Jill. "Introduction: To Tocqueville and Beyond!" In Jill Locke and Eileen Hunt Botting, eds., *Feminist Interpretations of Alexis de Tocqueville*. University Park: Penn State University Press, 2009, 1–18.

Locke, Jill and Eileen Hunt Botting, eds. *Feminist Interpretations of Alexis de Tocqueville*. University Park: Penn State University Press, 2009.

Lowe, Lisa. *The Intimacies of Four Continents*. Durham, NC: Duke University Press, 2015.

Madison, James. *James Madison: Writings*, ed. Jack N. Rakove. New York: Library of America, 1999.

Madsen, Richard. "The Upsurge of Religion in China." *Journal of Democracy* 21, no. 4 (2010), 58–71.

Maguire, Mathew. *The Conversion of Imagination: From Pascal through Rousseau to Tocqueville*. Cambridge, MA: Harvard University Press, 2006.

Mahoney, Daniel J. "Wisdom, Human Nature, and Political Science," a response to Aurelian Craiutu, "Tocqueville's New Science of Politics Revisited," posted May 9, 2014, *Liberty Matters: An Online Discussion Forum*. http s://oll.libertyfund.org/pages/tocqueville-s-new-science-of-politics.

Mancini, Matthew. *Alexis de Tocqueville and American Intellectuals: From His Times to Ours*. Lanham, MD: Rowman & Littlefield, 2006.

"Too Many Tocquevilles: The Fable of Tocqueville's American Reception." *Journal of the History of Ideas* 69, no. 2 (2008), 245–268.

Manent, Pierre. "Tocqueville, Political Philosopher." In Cheryl B. Welch, ed., *The Cambridge Companion to Tocqueville*. Cambridge: Cambridge University Press, 2006, 108–120.

Tocqueville and the Nature of Democracy. Lanham, MD: Rowman & Littlefield, 1996.

Tocqueville et la nature de la démocratie. Paris: Fayard, 1993.

Mansfield, Harvey. "Intimations of Philosophy in Tocqueville's *Democracy in America*." In Christine Dunn Henderson, ed., *Tocqueville's Voyages: The Evolution of His Ideas and Their Journey Beyond His Time*. Indianapolis: Liberty Fund, 2014, 202–241.

Tocqueville: A Very Short Introduction. Oxford: Oxford University Press, 2010.

Mansfield, Harvey and Delba Winthrop, "Editors' Introduction." In Alexis de Tocqueville, *Democracy in America*. Chicago: University of Chicago Press, 2002.

Marcuse, Herbert. "Some Social Implications of Modern Technology." In Andrew Arato and Eike Gebhardt, eds., *The Essential Frankfurt School Reader*. New York: Continuum, 1982, 138–162.

Markovitz, Andrei. *Uncouth Nation: Why Europe Dislikes America*. Princeton: Princeton University Press, 2007.

Marshall, David. *The Surprising Effects of Sympathy: Marivaux, Diderot, Rousseau, and Mary Shelley*. Chicago: University of Chicago Press, 1988.

Marshall, Lynn and Seymour Drescher, "American Historians and Tocqueville's Democracy." *The Journal of American History* 55, no. 3 (1968), 512–532.

Martin, Judith. "Republic of Manners." *The Atlantic*. November 2007. www .theatlantic.com/magazine/archive/2007/11/republic-of-manners/306311/ (accessed August 12, 2020).

Matsuda Koichiro. "Public Spirit and Tradition: Tocqueville in the Discourse of Meiji Japanese Intellectuals." Paper presented at the "France and the United States, Two Models of Democracy" international conference, University of Tokyo. June 10–12, 2005.

Matsumoto Reiji. "Fukuzawa Yukichi and Maruyama Masao: Two 'Liberal' Readings of Tocqueville in Japan." *The Tocqueville Review/La revue Tocqueville* 38, no. 1 (2017), 19–39.

"Maruyama Masao and Liberalism in Japan." In Ewa Atanassow and Alan S. Kahan, eds., *Liberal Moments: Reading Liberal Texts*. London: Bloomsbury Academic, 2017, 166–173.

"Tocqueville and 'Democracy in Japan'." In Christine Dunn Henderson, ed., *Tocqueville's Voyages: The Evolution of His Ideas and Their Journey Beyond His Time*. Indianapolis: Liberty Fund, 2014, 425–455.

"Tocqueville and Japan." In Aurelian Craiutu and Sheldon Gellar, eds., *Conversations with Tocqueville: The Global Democratic Revolution in the Twenty-first Century*. Lanham, MD: Lexington Books, 2009, 295–317.

"Tocqueville on the Family." *The Tocqueville Review/La revue Tocqueville* 8, no. 1 (1986), 127–152.

May, Gita. "Tocqueville and the Enlightenment Legacy." In Abraham S. Eisenstadt, ed., *Reconsidering Tocqueville's Democracy in America*. New Brunswick, NJ: Rutgers University Press, 1988, 25–42.

McClay, Wilfred. *The Masterless: Self and Society in Modern America*. Chapel Hill: University of North Carolina Press, 1994.

McCloskey, Deirdre N. *Bourgeois Equality: How Ideas, Not Capital or Institutions, Enriched the World*. Chicago: University of Chicago Press, 2016.

   Bourgeois Dignity: Why Economics Can't Explain the Modern World. Chicago: University of Chicago Press, 2010.

   The Bourgeois Virtues: Ethics for an Age of Commerce. Chicago: University of Chicago Press, 2006.

McGerr, Michael. *A Fierce Discontent: The Rise and Fall of the Progressive Movement in America, 1870–1920*. New York: Free Press, 2003.

McLendon, Michael Locke. *The Psychology of Inequality: Rousseau's "Amour Propre."* Philadelphia: University of Pennsylvania Press, 2019.

Mejía, Lázaro. *Los radicales: Historia política del radicalismo del siglo XIX*. Bogotá: Universidad Externado de Colombia, 2007.

Mélonio, Françoise. *Tocqueville and the French*, trans. Beth G. Raps. Charlottesville: University of Virginia Press, 1998.

   "Tocqueville, la Chine et le Japon: Introduction." *The Tocqueville Review/La revue Tocqueville* 38, no. 1 (2017), 7–17.

   "Tocqueville à l'Est." *The Tocqueville Review/La revue Tocqueville* 15 (1994), 193–205.

   "Tocqueville, la Chine et le Japon," Special Issue, *The Tocqueville Review/La revue Tocqueville* 38, no. 1 (2017).

Mélonio, Françoise and José-Luis Diaz. *Tocqueville et la littérature*. Paris: Presses de l'Université Paris-Sorbonne, 2005.

Mencken, H. L. *Notes on Democracy*. New York: Alfred A. Knopf, 1928.

Merquior, J. G. *Liberalism Old and New*. New York: Twayne Publishers, 1991.

Mill, John Stuart. *Autobiography*. London: Penguin, 1989.

   "Centralization," in *The Collected Works of John Stuart Mill, Vol XIX: Essays on Politics and Society*, ed. John M. Robson. Toronto: University of Toronto Press, 1977, 580–614.

   "Considerations on Representative Government," in *On Liberty and Other Essays*, ed. John Gray. Oxford: Oxford World Classics, 1991.

   On Liberty, ed. David Spitz. New York: W.W. Norton, 1975.

   "On Liberty," in *On Liberty and Other Essays*, ed. John Gray. Oxford: Oxford World Classics, 1991.

Principles of Political Economy. New York: Harper & Brothers, 1885.

"Review of *Democracy in America.*" *Edinburgh Review* 72 (1840).

"Tocqueville on Democracy in America [I] 1835," in *The Collected Works of John Stuart Mill, Vol XVIII: Essays on Politics and Society*, ed. John M. Robson. Toronto: University of Toronto Press, 1977, 49–91.

"Tocqueville on Democracy in America [II] 1840," in *The Collected Works of John Stuart Mill, Vol. XVIII: Essays on Politics and Society*, ed. John M. Robson. Toronto: University of Toronto Press, 1977, 154–204.

Millet, Claude. "Le Détail et le Général dans la *Démocratie en Amérique.*" In Françoise Mélonio and José-Luis Diaz, eds., *Tocqueville et la littérature.* Paris: Presses de l'Université Paris-Sorbonne, 2005, 147–165.

Mises, Ludwig von. *Human Action: A Treatise on Economics*, ed. Bettina Bien Greaves. Indianapolis: Liberty Fund, 2014.

Mitchell, Harvey. "The Changing Conditions of Freedom: Tocqueville in the Light of Rousseau." *History of Political Thought* 9 (Winter 1988), 431–453.

Mitchell, Joshua. *American Awakening: Identity Politics and Other Afflictions in Our Time.* New York: Encounter Books, 2020.

"Can Democracy Survive Social Distancing," *RealClearPolicy*, April 25, 2020. www.realclearpolicy.com/articles/2020/03/25/the_issue_of_social_distan cing_is_bigger_than_coronavirus_487447.html (accessed February 20, 2021).

The Fragility of Freedom: Tocqueville on Religion, Democracy, and the American Future. Chicago: University of Chicago Press, 1999.

Tocqueville in Arabia: Dilemmas in a Democratic Age. Chicago: University of Chicago Press, 2013.

"What the New Morality of 'Stain' and 'Purity' Seeks to Accomplish," *Washington Examiner*, February 14, 2020. www.washingtonexaminer.com/opinion/op-ed s/what-the-new-morality-of-stain-and-purity-seeks-to-accomplish.

Miyashiro Yasutake. "La philosophie libérale de Yukichi Fukuzawa." *The Tocqueville Review/La revue Tocqueville* 38, no. 1 (2017), 41–61.

Moesch, Duncan. "Anti-German Hysteria and the Making of the 'Liberal Society'." *American Political Thought* 7 (Winter 2018), 86–123.

Montesquieu, Charles de Secondat, Baron de. *The Spirit of the Laws*, ed. Anne M. Cohler, Basia C. Miller, and Harold S. Stone. Cambridge: Cambridge University Press, 1989.

Morrison, Toni. "Home." In Wahneema Lubiano, ed., *The House that Race Built: Black Americans, U.S. Terrain.* New York: Pantheon, 1997, 3–12.

A Mercy. New York: Vintage, 2008.

Playing in the Dark: Whiteness and the Literary Imagination. Cambridge, MA: Harvard University Press, 1992.

"The Site of Memory." In William Zinsser, ed., *Inventing the Truth: The Art and Craft of Memoir*. Boston: Houghton Mifflin, 1987, 183–200.

"Unspeakable Things Unspoken: The Afro-American Presence in American Literature." *Michigan Quarterly Review* 28, no. 1 (Winter 1989), 1–34.

Mulvey, Laura. "Visual Pleasure and Narrative Cinema." *Screen* 16, no. 3 (1975), 6–18.

Myers, Jorge. "Ideas moduladas: Lecturas argentinas del pensamiento político europeo." *Estudios Sociales* 26, no. 1 (2004), 161–174.

Nicot, Jean. *Thresor de la langue francoyse*. Paris: David Douceur, 1606.

Nietzsche, Friedrich. *The Birth of Tragedy*, trans. Walter Kaufmann. New York: Vintage, 1967.

The Genealogy of Morals, trans. Walter Kaufmann. New York: Random House, 1967.

Nimtz, August. *Marx, Tocqueville and Race in America: The "Absolute Democracy" or "Defiled Republic."* Lanham, MD: Lexington Books, 2003.

Nisbet, Robert. "Many Tocquevilles." *The American Scholar* 46, no. 1 (1977), 59–75.

The Quest for Community: A Study in the Ethics of Order and Freedom. New York: Oxford University Press, 1953.

The Quest for Community. Wilmington, DE: ISI Books, 2010.

Noles, James L., Jr. "Democracy in Alabama: Alexis de Tocqueville's Visit to Alabama in 1832." *Alabama Law Review* 64, no. 3 (2013), 697–708.

O'Brien, Conor Cruise, *The Great Melody: A Thematic Biography and Commented Anthology of Edmund Burke*. London: Sinclair-Stevenson, 1992.

O'Connor, Brendon. *Anti-Americanism and American Exceptionalism: Prejudice and Pride about the USA*. New York: Routledge, 2020.

Ostrom, Elinor. "A Behavioral Approach to the Rational Choice Theory of Collective Action: Presidential Address, American Political Science Association, 1997." *American Political Science Review* 92, no. 1 (1998), 1–22.

Ostrom, Vincent. *The Meaning of Democracy and the Vulnerability of Democracies: A Response to Tocqueville's Challenge*. Ann Arbor: University of Michigan Press, 1997.

Ostrom, Elinor and Vincent Ostrom. *Choice, Rules and Collective Action: The Ostroms on the Study of Institutions and Governance*, ed. Paul Dragos Aligica and Filippo Sabetti. Colchester: ECPR Press, 2014.

Otero, Mariano. "Examen analítico. El sistema constitucional." *El Siglo Diez y Nueve*. October 3, 1842.

Paine, Thomas. *Common Sense*, 3rd ed. Philadelphia: J. Almon, 1776.

Palmer, R. R. *The Two Tocquevilles, Father and Son: Hervé and Alexis de Tocqueville on the Coming of the French Revolution*. Princeton: Princeton University Press, 1987.

Pappe, H. O. "Mill and Tocqueville." *Journal of the History of Ideas* 25 (1964), 217–234.

Parise, Eugenia. *Pasione e ordine nella trama del moderno tra Tocqueville e Stendhal*. Naples: Edizione Scientifiche italiane, 1989.

Pascal, Blaise. *Pensées*, trans. A. J. Krailsheimer. London: Penguin Books, 1995.

Pensées, trans. Roger Ariew. Indianapolis, IN: Hackett Press, 2004.

Pedersen, Jean Elisabeth. "Outrageous Flirtation, Repressed Flirtation, and the Gallic Singularity: Alexis de Tocqueville's Comparative Views on Women and Marriage in France and the United States." *French Politics, Culture and Society* 38, no. 1 (2020), 67–90.

"'The Whole Moral and Intellectual State of a People': Tocqueville on Men, Women, and Mores in the United States and Europe." In Daniel Gordon, ed., *The Anthem Companion to Alexis de Tocqueville*. New York: Anthem, 2019, 143–166.

Peel, Sir Robert. *A Correct Report of the Speeches Delivered by The Right Honourable Sir Robert Peel, BART., MP., at Glasgow, January 1837*. London: John Murray, 1837.

Peters, Shawn Francis. *Judging Jehovah's Witnesses: Religious Persecution and the Dawn of the Rights Revolution*. Lawrence: University Press of Kansas, 2000.

Pierson, George Wilson. *Tocqueville and Beaumont in America*. New York: Oxford University Press, 1938.

Tocqueville in America. Gloucester, MA: P. Smith, 1969.

Tocqueville in America. Baltimore: Johns Hopkins University Press, 1996.

Piketty, Thomas. *Capital in the Twenty-First Century*, trans. Arthur Goldhammer. Cambridge, MA: Harvard University Press, 2014.

Pinder, Sherrow O. ed., *Black Political Thought: From David Walker to the Present*. New York: Cambridge University Press, 2020.

Pitts, Jennifer. *A Turn to Empire: The Rise of Imperial Liberalism in Britain and France*. Princeton: Princeton University Press, 2005.

Plutarch. "Life of Themistocles." In *Plutarch's Lives, The Translation Called Dryden's*, vol. 1, ed. and rev. A. H. Clough. Boston: Little, Brown and Company, 1906.

Proudhon, Pierre-Joseph. *Selected Writings of Pierre-Joseph Proudhon*, ed. Stewart Edwards. Garden City, NY: Anchor Books, 1969.

Putnam, Robert D. "Bowling Alone." *Journal of Democracy* 6 (1995), 65–78.

Bowling Alone: The Collapse and Revival of American Community. New York: Simon & Schuster, 2000.

Putnam, Robert D., Lewis M. Feldstein, and Don Cohen. *Better Together: Restoring the American Community*. New York: Simon & Schuster, 2003.

Putnam, Robert D., Robert Leonardi, and Raffaella Nanetti. *Making Democracy Work: Civic Traditions in Modern Italy*. Princeton: Princeton University Press, 1993.

Quinche Ramírez, Víctor Alberto. *Preparando a los burócratas en el Rosario. Algunos aspectos de la formación de abogados en el periodo radical*. Report no. 56. Bogotá: Universidad del Rosario-Escuela de Ciencias Humanas, 2004.

Rahe, Paul. *Soft Despotism, Democracy's Drift: Montesquieu, Rousseau, Tocqueville, and the Modern Project*. New Haven, CT: Yale University Press, 2009.

Rawls, John. *A Theory of Justice*. Cambridge, MA: Harvard University Press, 1971.

Reardon, Bernard. *Liberalism and Tradition: Aspects of Catholic Thought in Nineteenth-century France*. Cambridge: Cambridge University Press, 1975.

Reinhardt, Mark. *The Art of Being Free: Taking Liberties with Tocqueville, Marx, and Arendt*. Ithaca, NY: Cornell University Press, 1997.

Rémond, René. *Les Etats-Unis devant l'opinion française, 1815–1852*, 2 vols. Paris: Libraire Colin, 1962.

Rémusat, Charles de. *Critiques & études littéraires ou passé et présent*, Vol. 2. Paris: Didier, 1859.

La Pensée politique doctrinaire sous la Restauration. Textes choisis, ed. Darío Roldán. Paris: L'Harmattan, 2003.

"L'Esprit de réaction: Royer-Collard et Tocqueville." *Revue des deux mondes*, October 15, 1861, 777–813.

Mémoires de ma vie, Vol. 2, ed. C.-H. Pouthas. Paris: Plon, 1959.

Mémoires de ma vie, ed. Jean Lebrun. Paris: Perrin, 2017.

Redier, Antoine. *Comme disait Monsieur de Tocqueville*. Paris: Perrin, 1925.

Reyes Heroles, Jesús. *El liberalismo mexicano*, Vol. 2. Mexico City: FCE, 1982.

Ricardo, David. *On the Principles of Political Economy and Taxation*. Cambridge: Cambridge University Press, 2015.

Richter, Melvin. "Comparative Political Analysis in Montesquieu and Tocqueville." *Comparative Politics* 1 (January, 1969), 129–160.

"The Deposition of Alexis De Tocqueville?" *The Tocqueville Review/La Revue Tocqueville* 23, no. 2 (2002), 173–199.

"Tocqueville on Algeria." *Review of Politics* 25, no. 3 (1963), 362–398.

"The Uses of Theory: Tocqueville's Adaptation of Montesquieu." In Melvin Richter, ed., *Essays in Theory and History: An Approach to the Social Sciences*. Cambridge, MA: Harvard University Press, 1970, 74–102.

Riesman, David, Nathan Glazer, and Reuel Denney. *The Lonely Crowd: A Study of the Changing American Character.* New Haven, CT: Yale University Press, 1950.

The Lonely Crowd: A Study of the Changing American Character. New Haven, CT: Yale University Press, 1963.

Roger, Philippe. *The American Enemy: A Story of French Anti-Americanism,* trans. Sharon Bowman. Chicago: University of Chicago Press, 2005.

Rogin, Michael. "Liberal Society and the Indian Question." *Politics and Society* 1, no. 3 (1971), 269–312.

Rojas, Rafael. "Tocqueville: lecturas mexicanas." *Nexos* 22, no. 262 (1999). www .nexos.com.mx/?p=9428 (accessed August 9, 2020).

Roland-Marcel, Pierre. *Essai politique sur Alexis de Tocqueville.* Paris: Félix Alcan, 1910.

Roldán, Darío. *Charles de Rémusat: Certitudes et impasses du libéralisme doctrinaire.* Paris: L'Harmattan, 1999.

"Liberales y doctrinarios en el Río de la Plata: Echeverría 'traductor' de Guizot." In Noemí Goldman and Georges Lomné, eds., *Los lenguajes de la República: historia conceptual y traducción en Iberoamérica (siglos XVIII y XIX).* Madrid: Casa de Velázquez, forthcoming.

"Sarmiento, Tocqueville, los viajes y la democracia en América." *Revista de Occidente* 289 (2005), 35–60.

Romero, José Luis. *A History of Argentine Political Thought.* Palo Alto, CA: Stanford University Press, 1968.

Rosanvallon, Pierre. *Democracy Past and Future.* New York: Columbia University Press, 2006.

"The History of the Word 'Democracy' in France." *Journal of Democracy* 6, no. 4 (1995), 140–154.

Le Moment Guizot. Paris: Gallimard, 1985.

Rosenblum, Nancy. *Membership and Morals: The Personal Uses of Pluralism in America.* Princeton: Princeton University Press, 1998.

Rothbard, Murray N. *Man, Economy and State: A Treatise on Economic Principles.* Auburn, AL: Ludwig von Mises Institute, 1993.

Rousseau, Jean-Jacques. *The Discourses and Other Early Political Writings,* ed. Victor Gourevitch. Cambridge: Cambridge University Press, 1997.

Emile, or On Education (includes Emile and Sophie; or, The Solitaires), ed. Alan Bloom and Christopher Kelly. Hanover: University Press of New England, 2010.

The Major Political Writings of Jean-Jacques Rousseau, ed. and trans. John T. Scott. Chicago: University of Chicago Press, 2012.

Rowe, William T. *China's Last Empire: The Great Qing*. Cambridge, MA: Harvard University Press, 2009.

Royer-Collard, Pierre. *La Vie politique de M. Royer-Collard: Ses discours et ses écrits*, Vol. 2, ed. Prosper de Barante. Paris: Didier, 1861.

Sabl, Andrew. "Community Organizing As Tocquevillean Politics: The Art, Practices, and Ethos of Association." *American Journal of Political Science* 46, no. 1 (2002), 1–19.

Sacks, Jonathan. *The Dignity of Difference: How to Avoid the Clash of Civilizations*. London. Bloomsbury Publishing, 2002.

Sagar, Paul. *The Opinion of Mankind*. Princeton: Princeton University Press, 2018.

Sainte-Beuve, Charles Augustin. *Portraits littéraires*, ed. Gérald Antoine. Paris: Robert Laffont, 1993.

Samper, José María. *Selección de Estudios*. Bogotá: Librería Colombiana, 1901.

Sanders, Marion K. *The Professional Radical: Conversations with Saul Alinsky*. New York: Harper & Row, 1970.

Sarmiento, Domingo Faustino. *Facundo o civilización o barbarie en las pampas argentinas*. Paris: Hachette, 1874.

Obras de D.F. Sarmiento, Vol. 2: Artículos críticos y literarios. Buenos Aires: Felix Lajouane, 1895.

Obras de D.F. Sarmiento. Vol. 8. Buenos Aires: Imprenta y Litografía de Mariano Moreno, 1995.

Obras completes de Sarmiento, Vol. 39: Las doctrinas revolucionarias. Buenos Aires: Luz del Día, 1953.

"Segunda contestación a un Quidan," in *Obras de Domingo Faustino Sarmiento*, Vol. 1. Santiago: Imprenta Gutenberg, 1887.

Viajes en Europa, África y América. Santiago: Imprenta de Julio Belin y Ca, 1851.

Viajes en Europa, África y América. Madrid: ALCA XX, 1997.

Sartre, Jean Paul. *Situations IV*, trans. Benita Eisler. New York: George Braziller, 1965.

Schaub, Diana J. "Perspectives on Slavery: Beaumont's *Marie* and Tocqueville's *Democracy in America*." *Legal Studies Forum* 22 (1998), 607–626.

Schleifer, James T. "Alexis de Tocqueville Describes the American Character: Two Previously Unpublished Portraits." *South Atlantic Quarterly* 74, no. 2 (1975), 244–258.

"How Many Democracies?" In Eduardo Nolla, ed., *Liberty, Equality, Democracy*. New York: New York University Press, 1992, 193–206.

The Making of Tocqueville's "Democracy in America." Chapel Hill: University of North Carolina Press, 1980.

The Making of Tocqueville's "Democracy in America," 2nd ed. Indianapolis: Liberty Fund, 2000.

Tocqueville. Cambridge: Polity Press, 2018.

"Tocqueville's *Democracy in America* Reconsidered." In Cheryl B. Welch, ed., *The Cambridge Companion to Tocqueville.* Cambridge: Cambridge University Press, 2007, 121–138.

"Tocqueville's Journey Revisited: What Was Striking and New in America." *The Tocqueville Review/La revue Tocqueville* 37, no. 2 (2006), 403–424.

Schnapper, Dominique. *Community of Citizens: On the Modern Idea of Nationality.* New Brunswick, NJ: Transaction Publishers, 1998.

Schor, Juliet B. and Douglas B. Holt, eds. *The Consumer Society Reader.* New York: The New Press, 2000.

Schumpeter, Joseph A. *Capitalism, Socialism, and Democracy.* New York: Harper Perennial, 2008.

Schweber, Howard H. *The Creation of American Common Law, 1850–1880: Technology, Politics, and the Construction of Citizenship.* Cambridge: Cambridge University Press, 2004.

Selby, David. "Tocqueville's Politics of Providence: Pascal, Jansenism, and the Author's Introduction to *Democracy in America.*" *The Tocqueville Review/La revue Tocqueville* 33 (2012), 167–190.

Selinger, William. "*Le grand mal de l'époque:* Tocqueville on French Political Corruption." *History of European Ideas* 42, no. 1 (2016), 73–94.

Sharp, Gene. *From Dictatorship to Democracy: A Conceptual Framework for Liberation.* New York: The New Press, 2012.

The Politics of Nonviolent Action, Part One: Power and Struggle. Boston, MA: Extending Horizon Books, 1984.

Social Power and Political Freedom. Boston, MA: Extending Horizon Books, 1980.

Shulman, George. *American Prophecy: Race and Redemption in American Political Culture.* Minneapolis: University of Minnesota Press, 2008.

Simpson, M. C. M., ed. *Correspondence and Conversations of Alexis de Tocqueville with Nassau William Senior, 1834–1859.* London: Henry King, 1872.

Skocpol, Theda. "The Tocqueville Problem: Civic Engagement in American Democracy." *Social Science History* 21, no. 4 (1997), 455–479.

Skrentny, John D. *The Minority Rights Revolution.* Cambridge, MA: Harvard University Press, 2002.

Smith, Adam. *An Inquiry into the Nature and Causes of the Wealth of Nations.* Indianapolis: Liberty Fund, 2005.

The Theory of Moral Sentiments. Indianapolis: Liberty Fund, 2007.

Smith, Rogers M. "Beyond Tocqueville, Myrdal, and Hartz: The Multiple Traditions in America." *American Political Science Review* 87, no. 3 (1993), 549–566.

Political Peoplehood: The Roles of Values, Interests, and Identities. Chicago: University of Chicago Press, 2015.

"The Progressive Seedbed: Claims of American Political Community in the Twentieth and Twenty-First Centuries." In Stephen Skowronek, Stephen M. Engel, and Bruce Ackerman, eds., *The Progressives' Century: Political Reform, Constitutional Government, and the Modern American State*. New Haven, CT: Yale University Press, 2016, 264–288.

That Is Not Who We Are! Populism and Peoplehood. New Haven, CT: Yale University Press, 2020.

Smith, Steven B. *Political Philosophy*. New Haven: Yale University Press, 2012.

Spandri, Francesco. "La vision de l'histoire chez Stendhal et Tocqueville." *Revue d'Histoire littéraire de la France* 106, no. 1 (2006), 47–66.

Spengler, Oswald. "Letter to Klöres," in *Letters of Oswald Spengler: 1913–1936*, ed. and trans. Arthur Helps. New York: Knopf, 1966.

Spillers, Hortense J. "Mama's Baby, Papa's Maybe: An American Grammar Book." *Diacritics* 17, no. 2 (Summer 1987), 64–81.

Spitzer, Alan B. *The Generation of 1820*. Princeton: Princeton University Press, 1987.

Stendhal. *The Charterhouse of Parma*, trans. Lady Mary Loyd. London: Heinemann, 1902.

Stepanova, Ekaterina. "The Role of Information Communication Technologies in the 'Arab Spring': Implications Beyond the Region." PONARS Eurasia Policy Memo No. 159. George Washington University. May 2011.

Stolberg, Sheryl Gay. "Shy U.S. Intellectual Created Playbook Used in a Revolution," *New York Times*, February 17, 2011.

Storr, Virgil H. "The Market As a Social Space: On the Meaningful Extraeconomic Conversations That Can Occur in Markets." *The Review of Austrian Economics* 21, no. 2–3 (2008), 135–150.

Storr, Virgil H. and Ginny S. Choi. *Do Markets Corrupt Our Morals?* Basingstoke: Palgrave Macmillan, 2019.

Story, Joseph. *Life and Letters of Joseph Story*, ed. William W. Story, Vol. 2. Boston: Charles C. Little and James Brown, 1851.

Stryker, Susan. "My Words to Victor Frankenstein Above the Village of Chamounix: Performing Transgender Rage." *GLQ* 1, no. 3 (1994), 237–254.

Swart, Koenraad W. "'Individualism' in the Mid-Nineteenth Century (1826–1860)." *Journal of the History of Ideas* 23, no. 1 (1962), 77–90.

Swedberg, Richard. *Tocqueville's Political Economy*. Princeton: Princeton University Press, 2009.

Taylor, Charles. *The Ethics of Authenticity*. Cambridge, MA: Harvard University Press, 1991.

Taylor, F. Flagg, IV. "Montesquieu, Tocqueville, and the Politics of Mores." In Brian Danoff and L. Joseph Hebert, eds., *Alexis de Tocqueville and the Art of Democratic Statesmanship*. Lexington: University of Kentucky Press, 2010, 93–116.

Teague, Megan, Virgil Storr, and Rosemarie Fike. "Economic Freedom and Materialism: An Empirical Analysis." *Constitutional Political Economy* 31 (2020), 1–44.

Tillery, Alvin B. "Reading Tocqueville Behind the Veil: African American Receptions of Democracy in America, 1835–1900." *American Political Thought* 7, no. 1 (2018), 1–25.

"Tocqueville As Critical Race Theorist: Whiteness As Property, Interest Convergence, and the Limits of Jacksonian Democracy." *Political Research Quarterly* 62, no. 4 (2009), 639–652.

"Tocqueville, Black Writers, and American Ethnology: Rethinking the Foundations of Whiteness Studies." In Jill Locke and Eileen Hunt Botting, eds., *Feminist Interpretations of Alexis de Tocqueville*. University Park: Penn State University Press, 2009, 253–280.

Tismaneanu, Vladimir. *Reinventing Politics: Eastern Europe from Stalin to Havel*. New York: Free Press, 1992.

Tocqueville, Alexis de. *De la democracia en la América del Norte*, Vol. 1, trans. D. A. de Bustamante. Paris: Imprenta de A. Everat y Ca, 1837.

De la democracia en América, trans. D. A. Sánchez de Bustamante, 2 vols. Mexico City: Publicación del Republicano, Imprenta de Ignacio Cumplido, 1855.

De la democracia en América, traducida al español por Leopoldo Borda, abogado de la república de Nueva Granada, 2 vols. Paris: Librería de D. Vicente Salvá, 1842.

De la démocratie en Amérique, 2 vols. Paris: Librairie de Charles Gosselin, 1840.

De la démocratie en Amérique, 2 vols. Paris: Pagnerre, 1850.

Democracy in America, trans. Henry Reeve. New York: Adlard & Saunders, 1838.

"Journey to Lake Oneida," in *Journey to America*, ed. J. P. Mayer. New Haven, CT: Yale University Press, 1960, 321–327.

Letters from America, ed. and trans. Frederick Brown. New Haven, CT: Yale University Press, 2010.

Memoirs on Pauperism and Other Writings, ed. and trans. Christine Dunn Henderson. Notre Dame, IN: University of Notre Dame Press, 2021.

"Report on Abolition." In Seymour Drescher, ed., *Tocqueville and Beaumont on Social Reform*. New York: Harper & Row, 1968, 98–136.

Tocqueville on America after 1840: Letters and Other Writings, ed. and trans. Aurelian Craiutu and Jeremy Jennings. Cambridge: Cambridge University Press, 2009.

"Tocqueville to *The Liberty Bell*, 1855." In *Tocqueville on America after 1840: Letters and Other Writings*, ed. and trans. Aurelian Craiutu and Jeremy Jennings. Cambridge: Cambridge University Press, 2009.

Tocqueville, Alexis de and Gustave de Beaumont. *On the Penitentiary System in the United States and Its Application in France*, trans. Francis Lieber. New York: Augustus M. Kelley, 1970.

Alexis de Tocqueville and Gustave de Beaumont in America: Their Friendship and Their Travels, ed. Olivier Zunz. Charlottesville: University of Virginia Press, 2010.

Tomoaki Ishii. "Comments." Delivered at a conference on Tocqueville. Waseda University School of Political Science, Tokyo. March 2, 2013.

Trollope, Frances. *Domestic Manners of the Americans*. London: Whittaker, Treacher & Co., 1832.

Troy, Gil. *Morning in America: How Ronald Reagan Invented the 1980s*. Princeton: Princeton University Press, 2005.

Tuck, Eve and K. Wayne Wang. "Decolonization Is Not a Metaphor." *Decolonization: Indigeneity, Education and Society* 1, no. 1 (2012), 1–40.

Tufekci, Zeynep and Christopher Wilson. "Social Media and the Decision to Participate in Political Protest: Observations from Tahrir Square." *Journal of Communication* 62, no. 2 (2012), 363–379.

Tulis, Jeffrey K. *The Rhetorical Presidency*. Princeton, NJ: Princeton University Press, 1988.

Turner, Jack. "American Individualism and Structural Injustice: Tocqueville, Gender, and Race." *Polity* 40, no. 2 (2008), 197–215.

Valelly, Richard M. *The Two Reconstructions: The Struggle for Black Enfranchisement*. Chicago: University of Chicago Press, 2004.

Villa, Dana. "Tocqueville and Civil Society." In Cheryl B. Welch, ed., *The Cambridge Companion to Tocqueville*. Cambridge: Cambridge University Press, 2006, 216-44.

Teachers of the People: Political Education in Rousseau, Hegel, Tocqueville and Mill. Chicago: University of Chicago Press, 2017.

Villavicencio, Susana. "Sarmiento lector de Tocqueville." In Marisa Muñoz and Patrice Vermeren, eds., *Repensando el siglo XIX desde América Latina y Francia*. Buenos Aires: Colihue, 2009, 315–323.

Wade, L. L. "Tocqueville and Public Choice." *Public Choice* 47, no. 3 (1985), 491–508.

Wagner, Richard E. *Politics As a Peculiar Business: Insights from a Theory of Entangled Political Economy*. Cheltenham: Edward Elgar Publishing, 2016.

Walzer, Michael. "The Idea of Civil Society: A Path to Social Reconstruction." *Dissent* 39 (Spring 1991), 292–304.

Wang Jianxun, "The Road to Democracy in China: A Tocquevillian Analysis." In Aurelian Craiutu and Sheldon Gellar, eds., *Conversations with Tocqueville: The Global Democratic Revolution in the Twenty-first Century*. Lanham, MD: Lexington Books, 2009, 271–294.

Warren, Mark E. *Democracy and Association*. Princeton: Princeton University Press, 2001.

Warshaw, Jacob. "Jorge Isaacs' Library: Light on Two *María* Problems." *Romanic Review* 32 (1941), 389–398.

Watanabe Hiroshi. *A History of Japanese Political Thought, 1600–1901*, trans. David Noble. Tokyo: International House of Japan, 2012.

"The French, Meiji and Chinese Revolutions in the Conceptual Framework of Tocqueville." *The Tocqueville Review/La revue Tocqueville* 38, no. 1 (2017), 63–79.

Welch, Cheryl. "Beyond the Bon Ménage: Tocqueville and the Paradox of Liberal Citoyennes." In Jill Locke and Eileen Hunt Botting, eds., *Feminist Interpretations of Alexis de Tocqueville*. University Park: Penn State University Press, 2009, 19–46.

"Colonial Violence and the Rhetoric of Evasion: Tocqueville on Algeria." *Political Theory* 31, no. 2 (2003), 235–264.

De Tocqueville. Oxford: Oxford University Press, 2001.

"Deliberating Democracy with Tocqueville: The Case of East Asia." In Ewa Atanassow and Richard Boyd, eds., *Tocqueville and the Frontiers of Democracy*. Cambridge: Cambridge University Press, 2013, 111–132.

"Tocqueville's *Recollections* in Trump's America." *The Tocqueville Review/La revue Tocqueville* 37, no. 1 (2017), 157–167.

Whittington, Keith. "Revisiting Tocqueville's America: Society, Politics, and Association in the Nineteenth Century." *American Behavioral Scientist* 42, no. 1 (1998), 21–32.

Wiebe, Robert H. *Self-Rule: A Cultural History of American Democracy*. Chicago: University of Chicago Press, 1995.

Wills, Gary. "Did Tocqueville 'Get' America?" *New York Review* 51 (2004), 52–56.

Winthrop, Delba. "Tocqueville's American Woman and 'The True Conception of Democratic Progress'." *Political Theory* 14, no. 2 (1986), 239–261.

Wolfe, Christopher. "The Cultural Preconditions of American Liberty." *National Review*. April 29, 2010. www.nationalreview.com/magazine/2010/05/17/cultural-preconditions-american-liberty/ (accessed August 7, 2020).

Wolin, Sheldon S. *Tocqueville between Two Worlds: The Making of a Political and Theoretical Life*. Princeton: Princeton University Press, 2001.

Wolloch, Nathaniel. "Alexis de Tocqueville, John Stuart Mill, and the Modern Debate on the Enlightenment." *The European Legacy* 23, no. 4 (2018), 349–364.

Wollstonecraft, Mary. *A Vindication of the Rights of Woman*, in *The Works of Mary Wollstonecraft*, Vol. 5, ed. Janet Todd and Marilyn Butler. New York: New York University Press, 1989, 79–267.

Zakaria, Fareed. "The ABCs of Communitarianism: A devil's dictionary," *Slate Magazine*, July 26, 1996. https://slate.com/news-and-politics/1996/07/the-abcs-of-communitarianism.html (accessed February 21, 2021).

Zemach, Ada. "Alexis de Tocqueville on England." *Review of Politics* 13 (1951), 329–343.

Zimmermann, Eduardo. "Domingo Sarmiento, Édouard Laboulaye, y el 'momento Lincoln' en el republicanismo atlántico del siglo XIX." Universidad de San Andrés. Unpublished manuscript, 2018.

Zuckert, Catherine. "Not by Preaching: Tocqueville on the Role of Religion in American Democracy." *Review of Politics* 43, no. 2 (1981), 259–280.

Zunshine, Lisa. *Why We Read Fiction: Theory of Mind and the Novel*. Columbus: Ohio State University Press, 2006.

Zunz, Olivier, ed. *Alexis de Tocqueville and Gustave de Beaumont in America: Their Friendship and Their Travels*. Charlottesville: University of Virginia Press, 2010.

"Tocqueville and the Americans." In Cheryl B. Welch, ed., *The Cambridge Companion to Tocqueville*. Cambridge: Cambridge University Press, 2006, 359–396.

Zweig, Stefan. "The Monotonization of the World." In Anton Kaes, Martin Jay, and Edward Dimendberg, eds., *The Weimar Republic Sourcebook*. Berkeley: University of California Press, 1994, 397–400.

Index

OTHER VOLUMES IN THE SERIES OF CAMBRIDGE
COMPANIONS *(continued from page ii)*

EXISTENTIALISM *Edited by* STEVEN CROWELL

"THE FEDERALIST" *Edited by* JACK N. RAKOVE *and* COLLEEN A. SHEEHAN

FEMINISM IN PHILOSOPHY *Edited by* MIRANDA FRICKER *and* JENNIFER HORNSBY

FICHTE *Edited by* DAVID JAMES *and* GUENTER ZOELLER

FOUCAULT 2nd edition *Edited by* GARY GUTTING

FREGE *Edited by* TOM RICKETTS *and* MICHAEL POTTER

FREUD *Edited by* JEROME NEU

GADAMER 2nd edition *Edited by* ROBERT J. DOSTAL

GALEN *Edited by* R. J. HANKINSON

GALILEO *Edited by* PETER MACHAMER

GERMAN IDEALISM 2nd edition *Edited by* KARL AMERIKS

GREEK AND ROMAN PHILOSOPHY *Edited by* DAVID SEDLEY

HABERMAS *Edited by* STEPHEN K. WHITE

HAYEK *Edited by* EDWARD FESER

HEGEL *Edited by* FREDERICK C. BEISER

HEGEL AND NINETEENTH-CENTURY PHILOSOPHY *Edited by* FREDERICK
    C. BEISER

HEIDEGGER 2nd Edition *Edited by* CHARLES GUIGNON

HERMENEUTICS *Edited by* MICHAEL N. FORSTER *and* KRISTIN GJESDAL

HIPPOCRATES *Edited by* PETER E. PORMANN

HOBBES *Edited by* TOM SORELL

HOBBES'S "LEVIATHAN" *Edited by* PATRICIA SPRINGBORG

HUME 2nd Edition *Edited by* DAVID FATE NORTON *and* JACQUELINE TAYLOR

HUME'S "TREATISE" *Edited by* DONALD C. AINSLIE *and* ANNEMARIE BUTLER

HUSSERL *Edited by* BARRY SMITH *and* DAVID WOODRUFF SMITH

WILLIAM JAMES *Edited by* RUTH ANNA PUTNAM

KANT *Edited by* PAUL GUYER

KANT AND MODERN PHILOSOPHY *Edited by* PAUL GUYER

KANT'S "CRITIQUE OF PURE REASON" *Edited by* PAUL GUYER KEYNES ROGER
    E. BACKHOUSE *and* BRADLEY W. BATEMAN

KIERKEGAARD *Edited by* ALASTAIR HANNAY *and* GORDON DANIEL MARINO

LEIBNIZ *Edited by* NICHOLAS JOLLEY

LEVINAS *Edited by* SIMON CRITCHLEY *and* ROBERT BERNASCONI

LIBERALISM *Edited by* STEVEN WALL

CPSIA information can be obtained
at www.ICGtesting.com
Printed in the USA
LVHW081050040822
725112LV00004B/236

9 781316 639436